SOCIAL WORK FUTURES

Also edited by Robert Adams, Lena Dominelli and Malcolm Payne:

Social Work: Themes, Issues and Critical Debates (2nd Edition)*
Critical Practice in Social Work*

Other titles by Robert Adams:

A Measure of Diversion? Case Studies in IT (co-author)
Prison Riots in Britain and the USA (2nd Edition)*
Problem-solving with Self-help Groups (co-author)
Protests by Pupils: Empowerment, Schooling and the State
Quality Social Work*
Self-help, Social Work and Empowerment
Skilled Work with People
Social Work and Empowerment (3rd Edition)*
The Abuses of Punishment*
The Personal Social Services: Clients, Consumers or Citizens?
Social Policy for Social Work*

Other titles by Lena Dominelli:

Community Action and Organising Marginalised Groups
Women in Focus, Community Service Orders and Female Offenders
Love and Wages: The Impact of Imperialism, State Intervention and Women's
   Domestic Labour on Workers' Control in Algeria
Anti-Racist Social Work (2nd Edition)*
Feminist Social Work (co-author)
Women and Community Action
Women Across Continents: Feminist Comparative Social Policy
Gender, Sex Offenders and Probation Practice
Getting Advice in Urdu
International Directory of Social Work
Anti-Racist Perspectives in Social Work (co-author)
Anti-Racist Probation Practice (co-author)
Sociology for Social Work*
Community Approaches to Child Welfare: International Perspectives
Beyond Racial Divides: Ethnicities in Social Work (co-author)
Anti-Oppressive Social Work: Theory and Practice*
Feminist Social Work Theory and Practice*
Broadening Horizons: International Exchanges in Social Work (co-author)
Social Work: Theory and Practice for a Changing Profession

Other titles by Malcolm Payne:

What is Professional Social Work?
Social Work and Community Care*
Linkages: Effective Networking in Social Care
Modern Social Work Theory (3rd Edition)*
Writing for Publication in Social Services Journals (3rd Edition)
Social Care in the Community
Teamwork in Multiprofessional Care*
Power, Authority and Responsibility in Social Services: Social Work in Area Teams
Anti-bureaucratic Social Work
The Origins of Social Work: Continuity and Change*

*Also published by Palgrave Macmillan

Social Work Futures
Crossing Boundaries, Transforming Practice

Edited by

Robert Adams, Lena Dominelli and Malcolm Payne

Consultant editor: Jo Campling

First published 2005 by
PALGRAVE MACMILLAN
Houndmills, Basingstoke, Hampshire RG21 6XS and
175 Fifth Avenue, New York, N.Y. 10010
Companies and representatives throughout the world

PALGRAVE MACMILLAN is the global academic imprint of the Palgrave Macmillan division of St. Martin's Press, LLC and of Palgrave Macmillan Ltd. Macmillan® is a registered trademark in the United States, United Kingdom and other countries. Palgrave is a registered trademark in the European Union and other countries.

ISBN-13: 978–1–4039–1614–3
ISBN-10: 1–4039–1614–4

This book is printed on paper suitable for recycling and made from fully managed and sustained forest sources.

A catalogue record for this book is available from the British Library.

A catalog record for this book is available from the Library of Congress.

10 9 8 7 6 5 4 3 2 1
14 13 12 11 10 09 08 07 06 05

Printed in Great Britain by
Creative Print & Design (Wales), Ebbw Vale

Contents

v

List of Figures and Tables

List of Abbreviations Used in This Book

A and E	Accident and Emergency (Department of Hospital)
AASW	American Association of Social Workers (now NASW)
AASW	Australian Association of Social Workers
ADSS	Association of Directors of Social Services
ASBO	Antisocial Behaviour Order
AUT	Association of University Teachers
BASW	British Association of Social Workers
CARAT	Counselling, assessment, referral, advice and throughcare
CCETSW	Central Council for Education and Training in Social Work
CDT	Community Drugs Team
CEBSS	Centre for Evidence-based Social Services
CMHT	Community Mental Health Team
CPA	Care Programme Approach
CSA	Care Standards Act 2000
CSO	Child Safety Order
DDA	Disability Discrimination Act 1995
DH	Department of Health
DHSS	Department of Health and Social Security
DRC	Disability Rights Commission
DSS	Department of Social Security
DTO	Detention and Training Order
DTTO	Drug Treatment and Testing Order
EBM	Evidence-based medicine
EBP	Evidence-based practice
ESRC	Economic and Social Research Council
EU	European Union
GCSE	General Certificate of Secondary Education
GIPA	Greater Involvement of People Living with HIV/AIDS
GP	General Practitioner

GSCC	General Social Care Council (England)
HEARD	Health Economics and HIV/AIDS Research Division
HEFCE	Higher Education Funding Council for England
HREOC	Human Rights and Equal Opportunity Commission
HSE	Health and Safety Executive
HV	Health Visitor
IASSW	International Association of Schools of Social Work
IFSW	International Federation of Social Workers (Australia)
IND	Immigration and Nationality Directorate
IO	Information/Orientation sub-test
ISSP	Intensive Supervision and Surveillance Programme
IT	Information technology
LAC	Looking After Children
LSI-R	Level of Service Inventory-Revised
JUC/SWEC	Joint Universities Council for Social and Public Administration, Social Work Education Committee
MMSE	Mini-Mental State Examination
NALGO	National Association of Local Government Officers
NAO	National Audit Office
NAPO	National Association of Probation Officers
NAPWA	National Association for People Living with HIV/AIDS
NASS	National Asylum Support Service
NASW	National Association of Social Workers (USA)
NATFHE	National Association of Teachers in Further and Higher Education
NCH	National Children's Homes
NGO	Non-governmental organisation
NHS	National Health Service
NHSCCA	National Health Service and Community Care Act 1990
NSF	National Service Framework
NSPCC	National Society for the Prevention of Cruelty to Children
NTA	National Treatment Agency
PSR	Pre sentence report
PSS:PAF	Personal Social Services: Performance Assessment Framework
QAA	Quality Assurance Agency for Higher Education
RAE	Research assessment exercise
RCT	Random controlled trial
SCIE	Social Care Institute for Excellence
SCODA	Standing Conference on Drug Abuse – now *Drug Scope*
SMART	(criteria) specific, measurable, achievable, relevant, time-limited
SMART	(principle) strength-focused, meaning reconstruction, affirmative and appreciative, resilience, transformation
SSI	Social Services Inspectorate
SSRG	Social Services Research Group
SSSC	Scottish Social Services Council
SWSG	Social Work Services Group
TAC	Treatment Action Campaign
TOPSS	Training Organisation for the Personal Social Services
TSWR	Theorising Social Work Research seminar series
UN	United Nations
WHO	World Health Organization
YJB	Youth Justice Board
YOT	Youth Offending Team

Notes on the Contributors

Robert Adams is Professor of Social Work (part time) at the University of Teesside. He also works in the voluntary sector in Hull and East Yorkshire, in particular with the local community group concerned with stimulating playwork and training opportunities in social enterprise. He has written more than a dozen books on social work, social policy, empowerment and protest, including *Protests by Pupils*, published by Falmer Press and *Social Work and Empowerment, Social Policy for Social Work, Prison Riots in Britain and the USA* and *The Abuses of Punishment*, published by Palgrave Macmillan.

Norma Baldwin is Professor of Child Care and Protection at the University of Dundee. Her research interests are in the links between disadvantage and harm, neighbourhood approaches to prevention and individual and community-wide assessment of need and risk. She works extensively with central and local government and health authorities and in the voluntary sector on strategic planning and the evaluation of services.

Sarah Banks is Senior Lecturer in Community and Youth Work at the University of Durham. Her research interests centre around professional ethics and community development. Recent publications include *Ethics, Accountability and the Social Professions* (Palgrave Macmillan, 2004), *Ethics and Values in Social Work* (Palgrave Macmillan, 2001) and edited collections on *Ethical Issues in Youth Work* (Routledge, 1999) and *Managing Community Practice* (Policy Press, 2003).

Di Barnes is Research Felow in the Centre for Applied Social and Community Studies at the University of Durham. Her recent research has focused on mental health policy and service evaluation and Di has a particular interest in advocacy.

Lorna Bell is Reader in Social Work at Kingston University/St George's Hospital Medical School, London. She teaches on aspects of child welfare and child protection and critical thinking, evidence-based practice and research methods. Her research interests have focused on interprofessional and inter-agency working and her PhD explored multidisciplinary child protection teams in New Jersey, USA. She has a particular interest in trying to ensure that her research impacts on practice and is currently engaged in an action research project aimed at integrating staff from two units providing care and education to children and their parents.

Linda Briskman is an Associate Professor of Social Work at the Royal Melbourne Institute of Technology in Australia. She has practised, written and researched in the areas of professional ethics, Indigenous child welfare and the social work response to asylum seekers and refugees. She is married to an asylum seeker who was incarcerated in an Australian detention centre for more than three-and-a-half years and has now been released while awaiting his court appeal. His future remains uncertain. The chapter is dedicated to him and all those who aspire to freedom, justice and true open democracy.

Helen Brown is a Principal Lecturer and Curriculum Leader for Social Work at Middlesex University. She worked in an inner London social services department for ten years as a social worker and a manager. She has remained engaged with social work practice in relation to fostering since moving into academia. Her research and practice areas of interest have been focused on fostering and adoption and the development of social work practice with lesbians and gay men. Her publications include *Social Work and Sexuality: Working with Lesbians and Gay Men* (Macmillan – now Palgrave Macmillan, 1998).

Cecilia L.W. Chan is a Professor in the Department of Social Work and Social Administration at the University of Hong Kong. She is a pioneer in applying the conceptual framework of Chinese medicine and traditional holistic health practices to psychosocial intervention, for which she has developed the Eastern body-mind-spirit approach. Her current research area is psychosocial oncology.

Viviene E. Cree is a qualified social worker and practice teacher with 16 years experience working mainly in voluntary and statutory social work agencies with children and families. She is currently Senior Lecturer in Social Work and Associate Dean (Admissions), College of Humanities and Social Science, at the University of Edinburgh.

Lena Dominelli, an experienced researcher and educator, is Director of the Centre for International Social and Community Development at the University of Southampton and President of the International Association of Schools of Social Work, 1996–2004. She has published extensively in the fields of sociology, social policy and social work. Her latest single-authored books are *Feminist Social Work: Theory and Practice* (Palgrave Macmillan, 2002), *Anti-Oppresive Social Work: Theory and Practice* (Palgrave Macmillan, 2002) and *Social Work: Theory and Practice for a Changing Profession* (Polity Press, 2004).

Helen Gorman is a freelance educational consultant, trainer and research supervisor. Her PhD explored care management and practice skills and she has publications on law, community care and professional development.

Angela Grier is a Senior Lecturer in the School of Social Sciences, Leeds Metropolitan University, where she teaches youth and community workers, social workers and students on a joint criminology degree, and is part of the team developing a new BA in criminology. Previously, she was a probation officer for nine years and a worker with Irish travelling families. She has co-authored several journal articles on aspects of criminal justice.

Debra Hayes is a Senior Lecturer in the Department of Applied Community Studies at Manchester Metropolitan University. She has worked for the Greater Manchester Probation Service. Since her time at Manchester Metropolitan University, her research and writing has focused on immigration and asylum issues, and in particular their relationship to the delivery of welfare and the role of social work.

Stephen Hicks works in the School of Community, Health Sciences and Social Care at the University of Salford. He is a founder member of the Northern Support Group for lesbian and gay foster carers and adopters, and is co-editor of *Lesbian and Gay Fostering and Adoption: Extraordinary Yet Ordinary* (Jessica Kingsley, 1999).

Margaret Holloway is Professor of Social Work at the University of Hull. She entered social work education after 10 years experience as a practitioner and has specialised in teaching community care policy and practice. Her research interests are around death, dying and bereavement, with a particular interest in spirituality, and social aspects of Parkinson's disease.

Beth Humphries was born in Belfast, Northern Ireland and worked as a social worker there as well as in Scotland and England. She completed her PhD at Edinburgh University in 1983, and has taught and researched in social work since then. She has written widely on research methodologies. She is currently Reader in Social Work at Lancaster University, and for several years has studied UK immigration and asylum policy and its practical implications for welfare and for the involvement of social workers in implementing internal controls. Her most recent book is the jointly edited volume with Debra Hayes, *Social Work, Immigration and Asylum* (Jessica Kingsley, 2004).

Fiona Measham has conducted research in the field of drugs and alcohol, gender, licensed leisure, historical and cultural criminology for fifteen years and has been a criminology lecturer at Lancaster University since 2000. She is co-author of *Illegal Leisure* (1998) and *Dancing on Drugs* (2001), based on two large-scale studies of young people's alcohol and drug use, for both of which she was lead researcher. Recent research includes a study of 'binge' drinking and bounded consumption, a historical analysis of the attempted criminalisation of English barmaids and ongoing research on the criminology of transgression and the regulation of leisure.

Siu Man Ng is a Lecturer and Clinical Coordinator at the Centre on Behavioural Health at the University of Hong Kong. His research area is the application of Chinese medicine and traditional Chinese philosophies in mental health practice.

Ian Paylor is a Senior Lecturer in Applied Social Science at Lancaster University. His teaching and research interests are in the field of substance use, youth justice and the 'art' of evaluation.

Malcolm Payne is Director, Psycho-social and Spiritual Care, St Christopher's Hospice and Emeritus Professor, Manchester Metropolitan University. He has worked in probation, social services and the local and national voluntary sector. Among his many books and articles are *Modern Social Work Theory* (3rd edn, 2005), *Teamwork in Multiprofessional Care* (2000) and *The Origins of Social Work: Continuity and Change* (2005), all published by Palgrave Macmillan.

Tanusha Raniga is a Lecturer at the School of Social Work and Community Development at the University of KwaZulu Natal. She completed a Master of Social Science (social work) degree at the University of Natal in 2000 and is presently pursuing a PhD. She was a practising social worker for nine years, including work in child welfare, with older people and in community development and project management. Her 'passionate' fields as an academic are policy analysis, HIV/AIDS and community development.

Liz Sayce is Director of Policy and Communications at the Disability Rights Commission. She was previously Policy Director of Mind and has published widely on mental health and disability rights.

Vishanthie Sewpaul is Professor and the Postgraduate Programme Director in the Centre for Social Work, University of KwaZulu Natal, Durban, South Africa.

Terry Thomas is a Reader in the School of Social Sciences, Leeds Metropolitan University, teaching on the old Diploma in Social Work, and the new BA in Social Work and is part of the development team for a new BA in criminology. He was a former social services department social worker and team leader and is the author of *The Police and Social Workers* (Arena, 1994), *Privacy and Social Services* (Arena, 1995) and *Sex Crime: Sex Offending and Society* (Willan Publishing, 2002) and a co-author of *Policing Europe* (Macmillan – now Palgrave Macmillan, 1995).

Susan Wallace is a qualified social worker and practice teacher with fourteen years experience working in statutory criminal justice social work. She is currently Director of the MSc programme in Advanced Social Work Studies in Criminal Justice at the University of Edinburgh.

Linda Walker is a Lecturer in Social Work at the University of Dundee, currently seconded for two years to the Scottish Institute for Excellence in Social Work Education (SIESWE). Her interests include collaborative inquiry and practice, organisational transformation and the development of learning cultures.

Introduction

Robert Adams, Lena Dominelli and Malcolm Payne

This book is written with the aim of enabling social work students and practitioners to tackle the challenges of new basic qualifications and post-qualifying programmes, in the UK and other countries. It provides material to enable us to engage with the concepts, evidence-base and practicalities of the three crucial components of these educational and training programmes: Part I – how we develop our understanding of the social work process, Part II – how we develop our social work practice and Part III – how we develop as researching practitioners.

Social work is changing in many different ways. Social work varies in different countries because it is a product of the welfare regimes in which it exists. Every country has its cultural, political and social history and direction, which constructs social work in a characteristic way, responding to particular needs and preferences. Efforts have been made by social workers and social work educators to strengthen their global links and associations, most recently by re-establishing a new agreed international definition and exploring the possibility for international standards in providing social work education. However, the situation of social work in the different continents remains extremely diverse.

In Western European countries, there has been a trend towards practitioners and academics sharing ideas and information about policies, social work models and approaches. This is supported by the work of the European Union in ensuring that the social elements of the commercial markets that it regulates do not create unfair inequalities in economic markets. The result has been some valuable exchanges of ideas and practices.

In the four countries of the UK, devolution to different parliaments, assemblies and administrations has led to some increased diversification in the organisation of social work. For example, each country now has different organisations for regulating social care, and different legal and administrative systems and political polices and priorities are leading to differences in the role of social work. For example, in Scotland the full cost of long-term residential care is paid by government allowance, while in England and Wales, the provision is more restricted. Consequently, social workers need to learn different things in different countries. The settings in which social work is practised are becoming more diverse and the problems presented by people, more complex.

For the last quarter of the twentieth century, social work was provided through large local government social services social work departments focused on responding to social issues. Increasingly, the priority given to child protection and organising and constraining the cost of long-term care for elderly people has led to a separation of these two strands of work into 'adult' and 'children and families' work. This has led to alliances with government healthcare and education agencies. More recently, it has been possible to set up joint agencies between education and social services departments of local government for providing services to children, and between health and social services departments for various adult services: mental health and learning disabilities have been the strongest area of development. These changes reflect in some degree professional dissatisfaction with the administrative separation of social work and social care from related work by professional colleagues. They also reflect a political priority to education and healthcare, accompanied by a view that social factors should be secondary to that priority. This political preference also reflects a shift from a concern for social issues as a focus of political commitment, together with an assumption that social concern does not engage political support in a more individualised society. Following from this, there is a focus on individual choice by service users as consumers, rather than on collective provision to meet social needs as an aspect of citizens' rights.

There are more situations where collaboration, joint working and team working are required. The consequences include increasing demands made on the entire range of health and social services and on social workers in particular. This is partly because social workers occupy pivotal positions in the assessment, planning, implementation and evaluation of many key services for adults and children, communities and families, disabled people and people with mental health problems and many others. The responsibilities of practitioners are growing and with them the uncertainties and complexities faced by social workers, in settings where work involving geographical, organisational, cultural and professional boundaries is in constant flux.

The challenges this presents can be regarded as problems, or as opportunities to engage in practice development. This book sets out to engage with these challenges and with them the more difficult aspects encountered in practice. It is concerned with practice which involves taking responsibilities, rather than merely using techniques of social work practice to fulfil requirements and carry out procedures. This implies that practitioners will be able to use sufficient space to become creative and develop practice which is genuinely transformational.

Transformational practice uses reflexive and critical practice with individuals, communities, families and groups to achieve social changes that enhance social solidarity and reduce or remove inequalities in societies. Practice is not merely transformational in achieving change that removes inequality, social division or barriers to solidarity between people; it can also involve any social action or community work aimed at widespread change, because each barrier removed is a step forward in improving social relations. It therefore requires a worker to select methods that will contribute to transformation. If there is a choice, an action that transforms is to be preferred to one that merely helps. Moreover, everyday social work actions may be extended with little effort towards transformation. For example, it may help someone to overcome relationship difficulties with their parents, but to emphasise the skills and self-confidence learnt in the process is transformational. It may be satisfactory to the agency to get an elderly woman to agree to go into a nursing home, to help her safety. But it is transformational to help the son and daughter-in-law to understand why this will help, rather than circumventing them, because it increases the stock of knowledge in the family and community about such difficult life decisions, and may make the people involved more resilient when they are faced with other difficulties in the future. However, all this does require of the social worker a consideration of where each piece of practice is going to end up, and so it requires a focus on the future.

It is not possible to have a focus on the future of solidarity among the people with whom social workers work, without having a concern for the connections within social work and between social work and other professions. A piece of work that alienates nursing and teaching colleagues disadvantages other social workers and the people they work with in the future. A piece of work that helps them to value and respect social work enhances services, removes barriers between agencies and will help other people who are served by agencies in the future.

Therefore, we advocate a practical focus on the future, not only an ideological one. Transformational practice attests to the value of our work, even if it is at times devalued and inadequate. In this way all transformations will have positive effects on the worker, the service user, the immediate setting and the wider context, affecting social work and ensuring its future is as unpredictable as its past has been troubled and its present uncertain. This book offers the reader the chance to share our experience with that of the authors, to explore material which engages with the integration of theory and practice in more complex settings, notably where multi-agency and multidisciplinary collaboration takes place.

How this book is structured

The aim of the book is to enable you, the reader, to put practice in context, seek out the tensions arising in the different forms of service delivery and different agencies involved, and seek to develop a more articulate and self-explanatory practice than is expressed simply in the following of conventions, procedures and rules. The book opens up for debate the different futures for social work arising from its extension, as it crosses geographical, organisational, professional, conceptual and cultural boundaries.

The book is structured in three parts. Part I (Chapters 2–6) deals with social work processes and is designed particularly to focus on how life processes move forward all the time. As a consequence, social work processes must move with the developing situation in people's lives and experience. Social work processes are not just a way of understanding how we move from assessment to planning to intervention and onwards to review. To maintain only that focus is to neglect the other processes going on around us. We may start out on an assessment of the troubles of Julie, a single parent whose capacity to care for her child has been questioned. Merely by the questions we ask, we may help Julie to realise some of the things that are missing in her life. As we see how this causes her to rethink her life, we may see her becoming more creative. Reflexivity takes place, because our experience of her change causes us to amend our assessment that there is little hope of change. We can feed back how she has changed and give her confidence to believe that she can change again. At the end of this process, in review, we can explore with her how she changed from disbelieving in herself towards having greater confidence in her abilities. We can show her through this process that in the future she could do this for herself, she could help others, she could participate more with others in social life because she has a higher estimation of herself.

The objective of Part II (Chapters 7–15) is to enable you as a social worker to tackle the complexities of particular areas of practice and develop this beyond the routines and procedures which are required as we move through the stages of assessment, planning, implementation and review. We set out to show how, through reflective and critical practice in social work settings, social workers can enhance their understanding and through that extend their ability to communicate with service users, engage and help them, intervene successfully in a planned way in their lives and develop their practice in a forward-looking way. Part II selects particular areas of social work practice and examines issues which arise from their complexities and create tensions and dilemmas for the practitioner. The chapters cover issues which are relevant to particular settings that many students will encounter.

Each chapter discusses issues, tensions, dilemmas and dichotomies, in the light of illustrations from practice, bringing research evidence to bear on the discussion. These include risk and protection, being troubled and in trouble as it affects young people, truancy and offending, sexuality, care and control, frailty and dignity as they affect older people, risk and rights in work with disabled people and people with mental health problems, policy and practice tensions in work with asylum seekers and refugees, public and private concerns over drug use and abuse and issues of confidentiality and transparency in work with children and families.

Part III considers what is involved in developing an inquiring approach to practice and critically reflective research in and for social work. It focuses on the crucial task of developing our research-mindedness as practitioners. It puts this in critical context and provides a critical overview of evidence-based practice. Chapters 16–21 follow through the key stages of actually doing research as a practitioner: getting started, carrying out, producing results and using and evaluating the research done.

How you can use this book

You may be a student, part way through a qualifying course, or a practitioner involved in continuing professional development. Whatever your circumstances, we anticipate that you will be able to apply the material in chapters you find particularly relevant to examples from your own practice. To help you do this, the authors of the different chapters use examples of relevant research and practice, to enable you, the practitioner, to develop a research-minded approach which empowers service users throughout the entire process of planning and carrying it out. *Throughout the book, all cases are anonymised. Fictitious names are used for all examples.* The structure of the book enables you to dip in and out of it, using the introductory chapters as signposts to the content of other chapters in each part of the book. At the start, we assume that you have some familiarity with what social work is and what social workers do. However, immediately after this Introduction, we offer a brief explanation of some of the terms and ideas that are important to this book. These terms have been highlighted in **bold** in Chapter 1.

Each of the three parts is introduced by one of the editors with a longer chapter anticipating the key aspects of that part, highlighting common themes, making links between chapters and delineating significant areas of contrast and for further debate. Shorter chapters in each part provide more in-depth discussion of selected aspects. Each chapter concludes with a short list of recommended further reading, which we hope you will find useful in extending your reading and developing your thinking on specific issues.

Note on Terminology

We have used a number of terms in the book. Sometimes they have generally recognised meanings. At other times we have used them in a particular way. We set out here our list of the main ones the reader is likely to encounter, with our brief description of what each means to us.

Boundary crossing Circumstances in which people work and/or live across geographical, cultural, organisational or professional divides, between different and often diverse areas.

Complexity thinking The professional thinking process by which multiple and alternative points of view and contextual knowledge of political, social and value issues is incorporated into assessment, planning and action in social work.

Contextualising The process whereby the practitioner sets out to understand the practice against the backcloth of whichever social, legal, policy, organisational, psychological and other factors are relevant.

Critical theory Social theory emphasising agency and the capacity of individuals, particularly through collective interaction, reflection and action, to create for themselves social knowledge identifying possibilities for social change.

Critical practice A social work practice that emphasises developing the capacity of individuals to reflect, interact and act collectively to create social knowledge to identify possibilities for social change. This may enable them to achieve transformation in social relations to enhance social solidarity and reduce or remove barriers to equality in societies.

Critical thinking The capacity to examine knowledge and understanding, to identify how its historical and social origins influence its creation, how its elements are constructed in relation to one another and how possibilities for change may be identified within it.

Dichotomies The division of an issue or area of knowledge and understanding into two opposing or irreconcilable views.

Dilemmas A choice between two alternatives each with unpleasant consequences; more generally a choice between alternatives that is difficult or impossible to resolve.

Discourse A concept referred to particularly in Chapters 2 and 10. Discourse is often used to refer to language, including the range of written and spoken language, which affects, and may regulate or control, how people think. In Chapter 10, Hicks notes that a discourse of sexuality regulates what can and cannot be known, allowing some ways of thinking but attempting to exclude others. More generally, discourses are social interactions, expressed in language, through which social groups and societies reach shared understanding about the meanings of the social behaviour in which they engage. Discourses may include actions, discussion and writing because meaning is demonstrated by what people do as well as what they say and write. All social meaning is expressed in language, and therefore the language used both constructs and reveals discourses.

Evidence-based practice Practice that is informed by knowledge that has been gathered and tested empirically in the most rigorous ways possible to provide evidence of the form of action that is most likely to achieve its objectives for the benefit of and according to the wishes of the people or social groups served (see Chapters 1, 5, 6, 16 and 20 for critical discussion of EBP).

Globalisation The process by which changes in travel and information technologies enhance contact and communication between different cultures, leading to greater economic and social interdependence and cultural homogenisation, which particularly benefit developed Western cultures.

Managerialism The view and policy that management is a practice that controls activity in pursuit of organisational outcomes, often defined quantitatively, using general techniques and disciplines that are separable from the activity managed (such as social work).

Proceduralism A way of managing social work so that it is carried out mainly in compliance with procedures set by agencies, rather than by workers exercising professional discretion in the application of agency procedures to the social situations with which they work.

Problematising The process whereby we identify and highlight those aspects of a concept, approach or issue, which are, or should be, argued about, critically scrutinised and not taken for granted as simple, matter of fact or uncontroversial.

Random controlled trial The research process used in real-world situations where experiments are not desirable, possible or useful, in which an intervention is evaluated by participants being randomly assigned to an experimental group, which follows the intervention, or to a control group, which does not receive the intervention. Statistically significant results in an RCT permit generalisation about the causes and effects of the intervention for the population from which the groups studied are drawn.

Reflection A process of practical experimentation in which professionals such as social workers pay attention to an experience that has occurred in their practice, reflect upon it in an organised way and, as a result of the reflection, confirm or change the actions they take in situations where the experience arises, so developing and strengthening their professional understanding and knowledge.

Reflective practice Practice in which professionals such as social workers consistently reflect on their experiences, sometimes using supervision, consultation or a structured process for identifying incidents that, if subjected to reflection, would contribute to the development of professional knowledge, skill or understanding.

Reflexiveness A cycle in which experiences and actions affect thinking, which changes subsequent experiences and actions, in turn affecting subsequent thinking. Consequently, all social knowledge is subjective because it depends on the history and social context within which it emerges and all social actors are subjects, because by their participation in a social interaction they contribute to the knowledge and understanding that emerges from it.

Transformational practice A form of social work practice that uses reflexive and critical practice with individuals, communities, families and groups, to achieve social changes that enhance social solidarity and reduce or remove inequalities in societies.

Transformational Social Work

Robert Adams, Lena Dominelli and Malcolm Payne

We have chosen *Social Work Futures* as the title of this book to indicate our faith in the future of social work. This belief in the profession is rooted in the knowledge that, paradoxical as it may seem, as social work changes, its past is reinvented in the present and in its futures. Some features of social work – its ambiguous role, the uncertainties of its context, its problematic nature and controversies surrounding its subject matter and the complexity of practice – are enduring features. Yet some aspects of social work, particularly the contexts in which social workers practise, are changing in major ways and a key concern of social work historically has been change. A principal one amongst these has been that of enabling people to change themselves and their lives. So practice is intimately bound up with change. The constant interaction between the enduring aspects of social work and change means that links between the past, present and the future constantly interweave and interlock. These links form a complex entity, like a knot in which many different strings of thinking and practice are tied together.

Social work is about human beings in their social worlds. Human beings are complex in themselves and we live in complicated worlds. Social work practice, therefore, is challenging because it constantly requires dealing with complexity. This book sets out to show that social workers grapple with varying complexities in order to provide relevant services, and at times creative and innovative practice. In this sense, we are looking at futures and asking questions about what lies ahead and what interacts with complexity. We answer this in three ways. First, chapters integrate policy and social and value issues with practice, as social workers do every day, to demonstrate the complex interaction of humanity, society and political values. Second, practice examples throughout, and especially those in Part II, aim to illuminate particularly tough issues that are routinely faced by social workers. Third, each chapter seeks to disentangle the complexity of any human issue by looking at situations in detail and in their historical and social contexts, again as social workers do daily. We are looking at futures: for social work, service users, the societies we serve and ourselves in our careers and practice.

The aim of this book and in its predecessors (Adams et al., 2002a, b) is a transformational social work that explores complexities in the profession and comes up with answers, albeit temporary and unfinished ones. Social work is transformational when it addresses people's lives as they are now and helps them to change in such a way that enhances their social relationships and well-being both now and in the future. Therefore, transformational social work requires that what we do in the present focuses on the changes we want to see in our individual and collective futures. Present acts of social work not only help the particular individuals, families and communities that we work with; they also aim to move them forward in their social relationships in order to transcend the limitations of their current social networks and circumstances. By enabling service users to create different narratives about their situations, practitioners and service users shift their perceptions of social work and what is on offer, and eventually move both service users and the profession into a different future. Additionally, how we as professionals act towards service users alters their perceptions of social work and what it offers. To decide how we work with individuals, families and communities, we also need to think about the social advancement that will result from the work we are undertaking and include it in our plans for moving towards the future.

Moving forward in social relationships implies increased *sociality*, or promoting the bonds that cement social relationships and deepen social interaction. To achieve this end, we seek to remove barriers and divisions between people, because otherwise their social relationships cannot improve. It follows that we must seek greater equality, otherwise inequality will act as a barrier between people to (re)affirm existing social divisions and create new ones. We must also aim for greater mutuality, because for most people social relationships are reciprocated exchanges in which we both give and receive care, support and opportunity (Dominelli, 2002). Transformational social work, then, meets our immediate aims in daily practice and in doing so seeks to improve social relationships and social work in the future.

Being transformational also means paying attention to process, having aims for *how* we do things as well as *what* we want to achieve to ensure that there is a fit between the ends sought and the means used in reaching them. **Transformational practice**, then, meets the objective of promoting well-being by changing current configurations of inequality and diswelfare that prevent people from realising their full potential as self-determining agents. Additionally, securing these improved relationships in practice requires us as social workers to connect our interpersonal interactions with our political objectives and thereby model and demonstrate increased sociality to remove barriers that cause inequalities and promote social change. Thus, how we behave as practitioners is a social and political statement about how we think social relationships should move forward as well as a therapeutic, educational or developmental process that deals with the issues that social work practice presents for our attention.

These understandings inform the structure of this book and have led us to focus on social work processes in Part I (Chapters 2–6). In it, we examine social work processes, how the interactions between workers and service users take place at different stages of social work. These depict social work as a generic activity that explores how ideas about practice can be applied to a wide range of situations.

The practice topics in Part II (Chapters 7–15) are designed to identify areas of challenge and difficulty in current practice, and, in examining various responses to them, consider social work's futures. These areas are challenging and difficult because they involve the affirmation of human rights and a continuing engagement with oppression and discrimination within a society and welfare system that increasingly values individual responsibility and participation in choosing an appropriate service from the array on offer. General prescriptions for service delivery and professional intervention for social groups are no longer satisfactory. The services provided must address the barriers that accompany inequality by offering increased empowerment and participation. Each area demonstrates a growing necessity for social workers to engage with, at and across various geographical, cultural, organisational and professional boundaries and shows how complexity intensifies when organisational and social boundaries are crossed in practice.

Shifting boundaries will present new challenges for the profession to address as part of its future development. Changing family patterns are amongst these. For example, a Guyanan man and woman, who have lived in England for many years and require social care services as elders, come from a black minority ethnic group with complex family relationships that have to be considered sensitively, without preconceptions either about their needs or family relationships. They may have children living throughout the UK, and family members residing in Guyana and elsewhere, for example the USA. If this were to be the case, it would be known as a *transnational family* (Goulbourne, 2002) and have different patterns of communication and ways of responding to calls for assistance from a family with members wholly located in the same neighbourhood. **Globalisation** increasingly affects the welfare of people in different countries. As geographical mobility increases, communities and families are likely to be dispersed throughout the globe. Combined with the ties of diaspora (Brah, 1996), human mobility makes geographical and cultural boundaries a more significant element of practice now than it was twenty years ago. The extended Guyanan family in this instance may experience different kinds of services and responses to need in old age in each country. Advice about the man's Alzheimer's disease given by the woman's sister who is a nurse in the USA may differ from that given by their doctor in the UK. What are they to make of this? A person who is the responsibility of a different agency, profession or administration raises difficulties of coordination and may confuse those involved.

Organisational and professional boundaries are also at stake in settings such as community care, mental health and childcare, where practitioners from various agencies and sectors work together. As social workers engage with people, they move across these boundaries with increasing frequency. They collaborate with other practitioners, in multidisciplinary teams, and work across different employing and providing agencies. We may be aware of these divisions, but the boundaries may act as high walls or fences that become difficult to cross. Other social boundaries that have important meanings for people may be like the white lines on a sports field where it is easy to step across without being aware of their significance. Boundaries move, merge, disappear. They may be crossed and recrossed with impunity (for **boundary crossing** see Glossary). Boundaries are not all 'Berlin walls'; their nature and importance to the people involved must be understood, otherwise the consequences may be serious.

The increasing complexity of people's lives and the need to understand the boundaries that guide our actions, to include or exclude professionals and clients, mean that social workers have to develop new ways of thinking. At the same time, the new challenges of complexity offer new opportunities to transform both the lives of the people we work with and our professional practice.

One of the ways in which we can move towards transformation is through using research to build knowledge effectively. That is the focus of Part III (Chapters 16 onwards) of this book. In it we see that removing the social barriers that create inequalities, while offering choice and empowerment, point to focusing decisions about research on our values and objectives. Research on practice can help us decide how to practise effectively to achieve desired outcomes. Research on society and policy can help us understand how people and social structures may be affected by our aims and values because understanding our values informs our decisions about what our practice and policy set out to achieve.

The practitioner is required increasingly to be research-minded and research-capable, with practice that is **evidence-based practice (EBP)** as though these are magic wands for deciding the direction of work (see Chapters 6, 16 and 18 for further critical discussion of EBP). Some advocates of evidence-based approaches focus on **random controlled trials (RCTs)** as providing the most robust evidence of causation that allows us to have confidence in 'what works', making an analogy with the best evidence in natural sciences. This claim has been strongly challenged (Webb, 2001; Gibbs and Gambrill, 2002; Thyer and Kazi, 2004). Drawing on this debate, we focus on several reasons why this restricted view of the legitimate evidence base for practice is not appropriate to the transformational approach to social work on which this book is based. We argue that research on which transformational practice is based should be broadened to be more inclusive of other kinds of knowledge:

1. Research that does not meet the standards of RCT-based experimental research provides qualitative insights. These focus on experiential knowledge and yield a richness of data that connects the outcomes of practice with the quality of the process of relationships and interaction with service users and workers (including those involved in the research relationship) that, we argued above, is crucial to the impact of social work.

2. Social situations that social workers engage with are complex and open-ended, so using knowledge in practice requires analysis of complex interrelationships in which the participants construct anew knowledge about the situation and respond to the social context. This is intrinsically different from the circumstances of natural science research.

3. Because of this complexity, social actions and interventions are not governed by linear explanations that action 'x' causes event 'y', but require more complex kinds of knowledge, including those provided by those participating in the collection of information.

4. Research outcomes are often inconclusive and conflicting, so that judgements about how they may be implemented in practice require thoughtful critical interaction between values and knowledge, rather than a straight application of research findings.

5. Some messages from research which are clear and important may antagonise powerful others or they may not be specific enough to be put into practice.

A number of approaches (Everitt et al., 1992; Kirk and Reid, 2002) to using research are available including:

- Classifications of types of interventions, so that workers can match interventions to the problems they have identified

- Research-minded practice, so that workers are aware of the research that might influence their work

- Evidence-based practice, so that workers can go through a process of deciding with the people they serve what interventions will be most effective according to any available research

- Service evaluation, so that workers can see what organisation of services is most effective with various social issues

- Practitioner research, so that workers can test their own practice as they go along

- Practice guidelines, so that agreed approaches to particular issues can be built on research and policy and agency requirements.

Each approach contributes to the potential range of research options through which our values and social objectives may be achieved.

Complexity thinking

Our practice develops complexity continually as we revisit and reflect upon basic ideas we encountered earlier in our practice. This is an important and often underestimated process, akin to rereading a beloved book or repeatedly listening to a significant piece of music. Revisiting ideas through reflection and critical thinking and doing enables us to re-evaluate them in the light of our developing

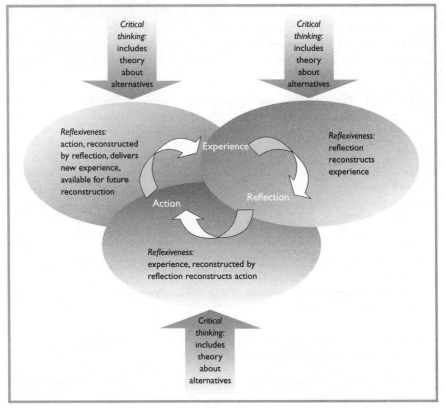

Figure 1.1 The discourse of complexity thinking

practice and reading about practice, as our understanding of those ideas becomes deeper and refined. It also allows us to test and change ideas about the situation that faces us throughout every moment of our practice.

This chapter begins this process by considering these basic ingredients of good social work practice – **reflection**, criticality and transformation. In our first co-edited book (Adams et al., 2002a), we discussed the ingredients of **reflective practice**. In the second book (Adams et al., 2002b), we examined how **critical practice** builds on that reflectiveness. In this third book, we pay particular attention to how criticality and reflectiveness contribute to transforming practice through understanding and incorporating complexity. We call this **complexity thinking**. We explore what we mean in this section, showing how these ideas develop from reflective practice and critical practice and move towards transformational practice. This developmental process also is a complexity, because these ideas not only move on from one another, but they overlap with and return to each other, calling on different aspects of all of them. Finally, we examine the links between these ideas and the social work relationship.

Central to this book is the thought that practice means more than the work we do with service users, more than 'doing'. For a start, theories and values are embedded in all that we do. Practice also entails reflection, reflexivity and being critical in and through action. These elements put what we do in wider context during our education but also continuously as we practise later in our careers. All this involves complex combinations of practical skills, knowledge, values, thoughts, feelings and actions.

Practice as doing

Practice is a word that can mean doing, or rehearsing, as in the practice a musician does. We argue that the social work practitioner engages in practice much as a musician performs. Each performance is unique. Practice, therefore, is a creative act of choosing between myriad possibilities.

Doing is the visible, more obvious part of social work, but it should not be regarded as irrelevant to or separate from the thinking, reflecting and evaluating that accompanies action. Often, practitioners accuse managers and college tutors of taking refuge in planning or theory at one remove from the 'coal face' of interaction with service users and practice situations. Academics equally complain that practitioners and managers follow procedures or assumptions without thinking critically about them. Managers say that practitioners and academics want to criticise everything, when they have a duty to deliver a service according to legislation and public policy. We suggest that social work requires a concern for the complexity of the way all these things interact together: users, their needs and wishes; policy and public objectives; reflecting and evaluating; continuity and critique. The mutual criticisms made by different interest groups within social work imply alternatives. Therefore, to practise, manage or develop ideas and policy, we have to engage with those alternatives and find ways of thinking about our aims and how we can achieve them differently.

One way of thinking about alternatives is in **dichotomies**: either/or decisions. Practitioners are often accused of doing too much or too little, intervening too readily in people's lives, or not intervening enough. They are criticised for making the wrong decision or being indecisive. The difficulties encountered by practitioners in balancing or mediating between these equally undesirable alternatives arise partly from the complexity of the situations with which they work. Practice often feels like choosing between unsatisfactory alternatives – if only there were more resources, or a more imaginative or supportive team. Casting the situation in dichotomous terms means missing the opportunities for helping people to progress their aims for a better quality of life contained within every piece of practice.

Complexity thinking presses us away from dichotomous thinking. It is against the oversimplified way of thinking that says: if we do this, we cannot do that; if we think this, we cannot think that. Instead, complexity thinking is *inclusive* thinking, holding within it both logic that enables us to hold competing claims and contradictions while looking for solutions. We look for alternatives and different sides of the situation and try to grasp them and integrate them into a **discourse**. Because the meanings that a social group gives to events or actions are always constructed in a discourse, social meanings always include complex and competing elements, reflecting competing and shared interests in the situation; they are never one thing or the other. How we react to them and interact with others as they react to them provides opportunities for moving in different directions and opening up new possibilities. The account in this section builds up a picture of complexity thinking, shown in Figure 1.1.

Let us illustrate this with an example. A woman may come to see her male partner as abusive. She may then experience a **dilemma**: should she stay for the financial security that his household affords, or leave for her own safety? But she has children that she is concerned about and so it is not just a matter of the violence affecting her, awful though that is. Thus, there is a possible risk of violence to the children of the relationship. If we include the children in the picture, other scenarios open up and these are likely to guide our reactions. The dominant discourse presents this as a choice between going or staying. But complexity thinking suggests that there are other alternatives and assists in thinking about more nuanced responses. These might include: going now, with the intention of negotiating a return on better conditions; staying now, but setting up arrangements to go to a safe place if violence returns; and going now with the aim of starting a new life elsewhere. The 'going/staying' discourse is limiting. Complexity thinking extends the gaze of both woman and practitioner to highlight other opportunities for resolving the dilemma.

Thoughtfulness in practice

Let us move on to consider the centrality in practice of critical reflection. We argue that it is indivisible from doing. One of the more obvious aspects of practice apart from the doing is the quality of thoughtfulness that should be the foundation for all our actions, including decisions. Thoughtfulness is, or should be, the six-sevenths of the iceberg of practice lying below the surface of visible actions.

Thoughtfulness is a quality inherent in all good practice. It invariably accompanies action, reflection, decision-making and evaluation. Thoughtfulness lies behind much care work, close to sensitivity and self-awareness. Is this quality of thoughtfulness inherent in us, or a skill we can acquire? It can be both. Some of us may be naturally more thoughtful, but we can all learn thoughtfulness. The everydayness of the word 'thoughtfulness' is not very helpful. Unfortunately, much of social work is like that. The basic ingredients of social work are described by words like 'caring', 'thoughtful', 'reflective', 'critical', 'decisive' – words used in everyday speech. In social work, they have an additional meaning – combining doing with thinking in complex ways.

For example, an elderly person in a hospital bed is ready, according to the doctor, for discharge. She cannot go home: the social worker must find a bed in a nursing home quickly or the social services department may be charged the cost of her remaining in the hospital bed under the Community Care (Delayed Discharges) Act 2003. The social worker can explain this to her, discuss her preferences and the views of her family, and set about finding a bed that meets her wishes. This is 'doing'. But to be seen as 'thoughtful' involves talking through the strong feelings of loss and change that will be taking place for the woman and her family, including the possibility of never seeing a loved family home again, or having to sell it to pay nursing home costs. This is 'thoughtful', because people involved will see it as sensitive. Although this does not deal with the structural constraints that other professional and policy objectives place before the practitioner, we argue that it is transformational because it allows the woman and her family the best possible chance of making the transfer with a sense of satisfaction and forward movement. So being thoughtful is also doing, and a more complex doing than the actions required by social and agency policy. It is also transferable to other families who may come to appreciate the skill of social workers, and value the public services provided. This is transformational in that it increases the social valuation placed on effective services and effective 'thoughtful' help.

Thoughtfulness contributes to reflection

We have argued so far that thoughtfulness in relation to the people we serve is essential to transformational practice. How does that connect with reflection, which involves thought? Reflection is a three-phase sequence, shown in Figure 1.1, which Jasper (2003) summarises as 'ERA', experience–reflection–action:

- Examining or revisiting our experiences in our thoughts; this means paying attention to an experience, either now as we are involved, or afterwards, looking back

- Reflecting on the experience, by paying attention to the feelings associated with our experiences and re-evaluating these to become more aware of their implications, significance and outcomes

- Deciding on action that we can take, either immediately as we are involved, or, looking back, to alter the action we took, or to change our approach when we encounter similar experiences in the future.

This account of reflection again raises alternatives: the possibility of reflecting in the present as we act, or in the future, as we review our experience. Schön (1983, 1987; Argyris and Schön, 1974), who more than anyone else codified the idea of reflective practice, distinguishes *reflection-in-action*, meaning reflection as we go along, from *reflection-on-action*, meaning reflection afterwards. However, this presents a dichotomy, which complexity thinking questions as a way of working on ideas. Complexity thinking develops these ideas as a discourse which would include a range of different issues rather than a simple choice, suggesting that reflection should look at how an experience has affected our thinking and our thinking affects our action, and the action is changed by the interaction of experience and thinking.

Reflection contributes to reflexiveness

Reflection becomes reflexive. **Reflexiveness** is a cycle in which experiences and actions affect thinking, which changes subsequent experiences and actions, in turn affecting subsequent thinking. So it goes on. Reflexiveness, shown in Figure 1.1 as extensions of the reflection process that connect elements within the process, emphasises that we cannot stand outside something that we are involved with; instead our involvement changes that something. We start from an experience and reflect on it. Our reflection examines not only the experience, but the connection of the experience and our reflection. Our reflection incorporates the experience, how it has affected us and how we think about it. How we are affected by our thought on the experience then influences our action, as well as how we think in the future.

All this sounds complicated as we set it out because complexity thinking includes different aspects of the situation, and by doing so it means that we interact with complex realities instead of an oversimplified model of the situation. Perhaps an example will explain what is happening in reflexive reflection.

CASE EXAMPLE

Ed, a young man being looked after by the local authority, is fascinated by fast cars and commits several offences of taking cars without the consent of the owners. His residential social worker spends time with him talking over the situations in which he steals cars: usually when he is with a group of friends, has been drinking and needs the car to get home. They discuss ways in which some of the factors can be removed: arranging transport in advance, drinking locally, drinking less, finding a different group of friends. Then, Ed takes a car and crashes it, under the influence of alcohol. The social worker meets him after he returns from the accident and emergency unit, and at the beginning of the interview feels himself getting angry. Ed is sullen and unresponsive, until the worker explodes when expressing concern about the risk that Ed might have been killed, and will now get into trouble. Ed shouts back that the worker is only concerned that there will trouble for him because he did not keep Ed under control.

There are many things to reflect on in this situation. This incident has a history: both Ed and the worker are revisiting the past in the present angry incident, and changing the meaning of the past by what they are doing now. The worker finds he is emphasising their rational attempts at behavioural planning. Reflecting on his anger, he realises that it is not only about the failure of his attempt at treatment, but fear of Ed being injured or dying. At first the worker experiences shame at being angry, but reflection tells him that demonstrating his fear may get a more positive reaction from Ed. So when Ed emphasises the treatment aspect of the past, the worker's response is not first to reinforce the treatment (this is what behavioural models of practice would propose), but to emphasise his fear for Ed's safety. But reflection tells him that mixed in with his emotional reaction, the incident might reinforce the treatment, by emphasising to Ed the relationship between them. Therapy relies on relationships to work, as well as well-worked-out, rational treatment plans.

In the reflexiveness of this incident, complexity thinking identifies the discourse that is going on in the reflection. Discourses are one step away from the immediate thinking and reacting: they express the overall pattern of what is going on. It is about the personal interacting with the rational and professional. We see the worker first reacting with anger (the experience) reflecting on the experience and working out some complexities within it. He is standing outside the experience to reflect upon it while it is going on ('in-action', as Schön would say). But as soon as he does this, he gains understanding about the connection of the experience with the reflection: reflexively, one way of thinking changes the interpretation of the experience so that it is not only about treatment but about personal concern. The reflection on the experience changes the action. Instead of hiding his anger, the worker sees it as not only a reaction to the failure of the treatment but also as a demonstration of concern. This then allows him to reinterpret his action to incorporate both of his insights: he sees how it can enhance his relationship and how this will enhance the treatment. By experiencing inside himself and reflecting also outside himself, he brings together many different aspects of the incident. In the future, this may cause him to reflect ('on-action', as Schön would say) that he needs to judge personal reactions not only in terms of being non-professional, but also in terms of the value of demonstrating personal involvement.

Criticality contributes alternatives to the discourse

Where does **critical thinking** come in? In a chapter on critical thinking in our previous book (Payne et al., 2002), we focused on critical thinking as a way of looking at the agenda, language, context and content of our experiences. Five ways of thinking add a critical element:

- *Being reflexive:* standing to observe and act from both inside and outside the situation allows us to identify the 'taken-for-granted'

- **Contextualising**: the wider context of social relations and policy in which practice in this situation takes place

- **Problematising**: debates about policy and law inform us where the present agendas, language and situations should not be assumed

- *Being self-critical:* we do not take for granted that our actions and those of our agencies are unproblematic

- *Engaging with transformation:* identifying barriers and divisions in social relations that lead to oppression helps to move beyond the status quo of this person's situation and wider circumstances.

Each of these ways of thinking raises the possibility of questioning the 'taken-for-granted'. The first and last connect with other aspects of complexity thinking. Reflexiveness is a form of critical thinking as well as an extension of being reflective, as discussed above and in Payne (2002). This is because being reflexive emphasises both standing inside our experience and actions to reflect and bring in outside ideas to question ourselves; the latter being the critical element.

Turning again to the example of Ed, reflexiveness as part of criticality questions the relevance of the assumption that we are helping and disciplining this individual. The idea of discourse tells us that this is only part of the story. Helping and disciplining will both be present, alongside other social, political and organisational factors that influence the discourse, among other social elements in the situation. What happens to him is only part of the experience of the life of the residential establishment where he is looked after. His actions and the worker's responses will have consequences for other residents. They also have consequences for the victims: the owner of the car, for example, and people who were put at risk by the car crash. The worker's treatment of him is contextualised, perhaps to refer to the estate and binge-drinking culture of young people in the area. Perhaps the worker's attempt to change him was unrealistic or unhelpful in this context, without a response to the local culture. We may also problematise the policy, which focuses on being punitive or controlling about Ed's behaviour, rather than on the poverty of opportunity, support, services and hope for many working-class young men. Being self-critical also points to the inadequacy of the agency's programme for Ed in the social and policy context. Each of these areas of criticality may have an impact on reflexive responses at every stage of the reflective cycle, as shown in Figure 1.1.

From critical reflexiveness to transformation

The fifth element of critical thinking leads to **critical theory** and transformation. Critical theory identifies divisions and oppression as the source of individual problems in social relations, and connects them with political issues. Individual behaviour, such as Ed's, expresses social divisions and oppressions. Through critical reflexiveness in the reflective cycle, complexity thinking has identified the complexity of the reactions and interactions in Ed's situation. Transformational social work suggests that when the worker intervenes to express his anxiety about the risks to Ed, and the treatment attempts to change his behaviour, the cycle of actions and reactions draws attention to the weaknesses we have identified in the personal interaction between worker and service user and the social work service, resource and policy contexts and social relations that have put Ed where he is. We do not suggest that all these things may be tackled at once, but being alive to these complexities means that our reactions can be informed about them. The worker will probably not be successful in putting pressure on Ed to comply with the treatment programme without both his personal reaction that expresses his relationship and valuation of Ed as a human being and the social fabric that must be mended, remade and extended if general progress with people in Ed's situation is to be achieved. The consequences of oppression and disadvantage for Ed may have to be tackled in a practical, immediate and individualised way. However, accepting the impact of the oppression and disadvantage and interacting with these also validates the social work response with Ed. It values the worker's political and value base and the agency's overall social purposes and policy, even though it suffers from contradictions that the individualised response of much social work will not resolve the oppressions that underpin the problems that social workers try to tackle.

Transforming practice

The word 'critical' may have the negative connotations of criticism. It is possible to be critical in a thoroughly negative way. However, we argue that critical practice is positive and capable of transforming the situation through reflexiveness in practice. It other words, it can be transformational, not only for the lives of the people with whom we work, but also the profession, social work practice and policy and oppressive social relations. Transformation involves not just moving beyond the situation as it is now, expressing the oppressive social relations of the past, but achieving change in social relations so that they are less oppressive in the future. As critical practitioners, we engage with a range of transforming possibilities and alternatives. These offer the prospect of transcending the status quo. Rather than engaging with now, we move towards engaging with future choices and options.

In referring to 'transformation', we are not implying it is synonymous with 'radicalism'. Transformation in social work does not mean revolution. It is a mainstream idea. It is about continuity as well as change. Continuity involves preserving and retaining. For instance, pessimists assert that changes in social work will cause it to disappear. However, it is more likely to change its form as it continues to change. We should not turn away from change. Just as we face people receiving services with the need to change, so we should face up to it ourselves.

Transformational practice is creative and moves beyond **proceduralism**. Although it takes account of the law and procedures, and is bound by them, it also transcends them, that is, operates beyond them. Procedurally dominated practice is accountable to the rule book rather than the service user. It is content to fill in the form, complete the schedule. It is full of ritualistic behaviour. In some situations, **managerialism** imposes priority accountability to the manager and the organisation. Transformational practice also moves beyond managerialism and accountability primarily to the organisation and asserts accountability to professional values, principles and approaches as well.

Some idea of the richness of practice can be gained by considering the related idea of transformational grammar. This is a grammar that explains equivalences and relations between sentences by using transformations to generate an infinite number of actual sentences from an infinite set of supposed underlying structures. Similarly, transformational practice in social work is about engaging with the future possibilities of a potentially infinite variety of circumstances, generated from current situations.

Earlier, we used the analogy of the social work practitioner being like the musician who practises and performs; let us pursue this further. How can the musical performer transform the music?

- *Transposition:* changing the key, into a higher or lower intensity, major or minor mood
- *Changing* the setting, players or parts
- *Variations:* developing and changing the situation to identify many different possibilities
- *Extemporisation:* enhancing unpredictability and using creativity.

We can see how regarding practice as a creative performance rather than merely the application of techniques bound by procedures enables us to view it as potentially transformational. Let us return to our criticism above of the more restricted approaches to evidence-based practice. If each performance is unique, the narrower view of evidence-based practice is unrealistic. It assumes that if we can identify the research which best fits the situation, we can arrive at a formula that highlights the practice with the best outcome for the client. Transformational practice is about recognising the diversity of different realistic choices, assessing the relative merits of each and constructing one of many viable routes through them. Alan Ayckbourn, a playwright based in Scarborough, England, has written a well-known play with multiple endings. In this, the four actors each play a part in triggering the choice of one route through a decision about a word or phrase. By making a small number of such decisions, the play diversifies into a great number of alternative outcomes. Nobody knows at the start of each performance which outcome will be reached.

This creative approach recognises the complexity of human situations and the uncertainty of the situations in which social workers practise. Social work practised creatively is analogous to such semi-improvised drama. The laws and procedures represent the script. But, the creative practitioner seeks transformations through previously unenvisaged approaches, leading to unpredictable, but possibly more positive outcomes for the service user, carer and others. Like weather forecasting, the further ahead we try to engage with the futures of people's lives, the more unpredictable their circumstances and the greater the range of different possibilities.

Transformational practice engages with the futures of people's lives. It is our responsibility as social workers to empower people, give them the means to consider options, explore alternatives, take choices, make decisions, reflect critically on experiences and evaluate outcomes for themselves. Ultimately, we may achieve transformation of the service user's situation, the setting for practice, the policy context and, not least, ourselves. In transforming ourselves, we enhance our capacities for self-awareness, self-evaluation and self-actualisation or personal and professional fulfilment.

Seeking new perspectives and approaches

Several authors in this book write from outside the context of English social work. Chapters 5, 15 and 19 are written from a continent outside Europe. This diversity reminds us that we cannot assume that there is one way of organising and working the partnership between academic tutor, practice teacher and student in what we call 'a placement'. We need to bear in mind diverse ways of structuring that partnership. Hugh Macpherson, head of the Northern College of Acupuncture, described to one of the authors of this chapter the struggle to find a professional body in the UK to validate the professional qualification for acupuncturists. The assumptions and values of Eastern practice are different to those in Western countries. In China, the acupuncturist does not learn from books but in practice. The university is not the sole holder of academic credibility, which lies in the traditions passed on from one practitioner to another, rather than being embodied primarily in the written word. In similar vein, many Eastern therapies emphasise not just the physical, but also the emotional and spiritual dimensions of practice. They are holistic. The first consultation with the acupuncturist typically is a diagnostic conversation that ranges beyond presenting symptoms. This approach has much to teach our Western approaches to assessment in health and social care. It has great implications for our view about where practice is taught and the respective roles of student, practice teacher and college tutor and how they interact.

The social work relationship

We are now in a position to return to the starting point of this chapter, namely, the basis for practice. It is assumed that social workers must form good relationships with service users for productive work to be done. This is fine as long as we recognise that the most productive social work relationship may not have much in common with other relationships such as those with work colleagues, friends and family. In these, the priority may be to maintain good relations and, perhaps, intimacy.

The social work relationship is a helping, enabling or empowering relationship. A good deal of confusion is possible between what constitutes helping, and what may be perceived as a helpful relationship. Paradoxically, the social worker who is regarded as everybody's helper may not be doing the best social work with people. One of the responsibilities of social workers is to make change possible. Change may entail a painful jolt out of present ways of coping. It may be the job of the social worker to give unpalatable, but necessary, feedback.

The social worker may find the role of enabler incompatible with being a friend. In psychotherapeutic work, the therapist is prepared for the client who develops a positive transference, or warm feelings, to the extent of wanting to embrace or even marry the therapist. Conversely, there is negative transference, where the client begins to hate the therapist. It is possible for these extremes of positive or negative feeling to be transferred from other relationships in the client's life. The fact the client loves or hates the therapist is significant, but should be interpreted in relation to what is going on in the therapy. This is why it is generally regarded as unethical and inappropriate for therapists to become emotionally involved with clients, while they are in therapy.

Similarly, service users' perceptions of social workers as unhelpful should be responded to with caution. The history of scandals has raised media, public and line managers' sensitivities to the possibility of malpractice and mistakes by social workers. But the fact remains that people on the receiving end of social work may not react objectively during the enabling process. A similar argument takes place over the best time to ask social work students to evaluate their professional training course. Is it four months into the course – the time of the notorious mid-course blues – when the honeymoon is over and the first wave of essay marks are returned? Is it on the last day of the course before practice commences, when the student never wants to see another list of required reading again and can't wait to walk out of the building a free person? Or is it two years into practice, when the course is a distant memory but a different valuation of knowledge and skills acquired might be judged in practice? There is no easy way of choosing between the value of the answer we get at these different times; they are all relevant but individually incomplete.

Practice paradoxes and dilemmas

Practice presents many paradoxes and dilemmas. A dilemma in Greek is insoluble, unresolvable. Greek tragedies from more than 2000 years ago are like modern social work. They often present on the stage a human situation to which there are alternative responses, none of which allows everybody to win. Quite the reverse. In one play, two brothers are separated in infancy and grow up in different countries. Eventually, as generals of opposing armies, they are faced with the dilemma of remaining loyal to each other and betraying their country, or leading their armies to fight each other and ignoring their loyalty to their family.

At the heart of such dilemmas are matters of value and belief. What do we value most – our sense of responsibility to our relatives, or our duty to the colleagues we work with, our employers, our country? Social workers have multiple accountabilities – to the law, the local authority, the line manager, the service user, the carer and, not least, to the profession, themselves and their own values. There are often conflicts between these different strands of accountability.

CONCLUSION

Our conclusions do not bring this discussion to a straightforward ending. That is entirely appropriate. The job of social work is beset with uncertainties. Our task is to bring to bear our knowledge and skills on situations, anticipating the likelihood that the complexities of people's lives will not make it possible to find a single path through their difficulties, a simple solution to their problems. On the contrary, every possible decision entails gains and losses, for them and other people involved in their lives – relatives, friends, carers and members of the public. We shall need to make judgements about these situations. At the heart of our decisions lies our commitment to our own values. We have proposed complexity thinking as a way of including the multiple aspects of any situation that social workers deal with. It incorporates critical reflexiveness in the reflective cycle of experience–reflection–action that allows practice to move towards different futures, for individuals, social work, policy and social relations.

The fact that social work touches our own values makes it crucial for us to examine these beliefs and assumptions in training and make them explicit. We have to question them self-critically and be prepared for their challenge by others. As we develop as critical practitioners, we have to adopt this self-critical, self-questioning approach as a way of work. Because our own values interact with our work, we have to accept that critical practice in social work isn't only a way of working; it's a way of life that affects our personal and professional activities and forms a crucial part of transformational practice in social work. This becomes part of our engaging in continuing professional development. Post-qualifying study is a necessary part of lifelong learning. Future practice, therefore, requires us to engage in continuing personal and professional development that enables these two aspects to progress side by side. Our minds, our emotions and our actions are affected. Our continuing learning, like the future development of our practice, is lifelong. It is transformational in that it extends that work into a variety of forms in future practice and the choices and dilemmas that accompany them. This book is a companion in that endeavour, perhaps a guide, but at least a starting point for change towards our futures.

FURTHER READING

On reflective practice

Jasper, M. (2003) *Beginning Reflective Practice* (Cheltenham: Nelson Thornes). A useful and practical general introduction to developing reflective practice, written for nurses, but very applicable to social work.

Payne, M. (2002) 'Social Work Theories and Reflective Practice', in Adams, R., Dominelli, L. and Payne, M. (eds) *Social Work: Themes, Issues and Critical Debates*, (2nd edn) (Basingstoke: Palgrave Macmillan, pp. 123–38). A brief account of reflection applied to social work, showing how to use reflection to be critical in the use of theory.

Schön, D.A. (1983) *The Reflective Practitioner: How Professionals Think in Action*. (New York: Basic Books). A classic argument for and presentation of the importance of reflective practice for professions working with people and their problems.

On critical practice

Payne, M., Adams, R. and Dominelli, L. (2002) 'On Being Critical in Social Work', in Adams, R., Dominelli, L. and Payne, M. (eds) *Critical Practice in Social Work* (Basingstoke: Palgrave Macmillan, pp. 1–12). A brief account of critical thinking in social work practice.

Pease, B. and Fook, J. (eds) (1999) *Transforming Social Work Practice* (London: Routledge). A useful collection of papers on taking a transformational approach.

Critical Social Work http://www.criticalsocialwork.com/ A useful internet journal reflecting transformational and critical approaches to social work.

PART

I

Social Work Process

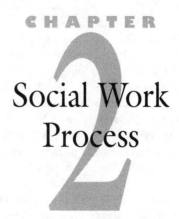

Social Work Process

Malcolm Payne

What is process?

Among my responsibilities in the hospice where I work is protection of vulnerable adults. A common situation is conflict between spouses, really angry exchanges between husband and wife. The multiprofessional team are sometimes uncomfortable about such events. Is a particularly violent outburst aimed at getting the spouse's own way emotional abuse? If so, our local multi-agency procedures for the protection of vulnerable adults say that we should take action to protect the person affected.

Our starting point is the present position of the family: we are involved with them because someone is dying and usually there are social consequences for their family members. Therefore, an outburst might easily be a reasonable expression of what they are all experiencing. But what view do we take if there is continuous hectoring? We might look into the history of the marital relationship. Perhaps this is a particularly edgy or tempestuous relationship, in which outbursts are accepted as part of the family culture. There are two ways of seeing this: we might say that both parties have accepted the continuing nature of their relationship; alternatively, we could see one spouse as the unthinking object of long-standing abuse. Another factor is the overall task that we are there to carry out. Our service aims to help people to maintain a good quality of life until they die, and assist family members with the process of bereavement afterwards. If we protect our patient by removing another family member, will we interfere with our main aim? What if the patient says they want their spouse with them, while we think they need protection?

I have set out some of the things going on in this situation in Figure 2.1. At least five factors are relevant. The patient is dying, which is part of a 'disease trajectory': the disease has built up from minor changes in their body, to physical changes that have produced symptoms. These have been treated, perhaps with some success, but eventually their illness is leading to death. How they die, however, is not only defined by the disease, but by their life history. Are they satisfied with their life and relationships? What is their view about death? Do they still have tasks to perform? Then there is the conflict that worries us, part of a marital and family history, constantly evolving relationships. It will continue until death and beyond it, because it will affect the surviving partner in all future relationships, looking back and perhaps reassessing the marriage continuously after the death. The illness and death and the conflict and the marriage interact with our multiprofessional services. Doctors, nurses, nursing assistants, chaplains, complementary and creative therapists, physiotherapists, social workers all have their duties and they are part of a philosophy of palliative care and treatment and care policies, regulated by the requirements of our funders and the government regulator of hospices. How these people interact together and how their occupations see their roles and activities constantly changes and develops as professional knowledge and policy decisions accumulate and interact with each other. Fourth, there is a reporting and investigation process on adult protection, following multi-agency guidelines set up and administered by our local authority, according to government guidance. These have been built up over time by the multi-agency working party, and are constantly monitored and developed. The fifth element,

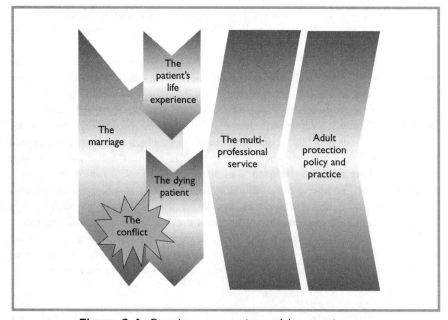

Figure 2.1 Complex processes in an adult protection case

the conflict, exists as part of these continuing streams of social relations. How each party perceives it depends on the social relations they are involved in. Their perceptions then colour how they will react.

At any one time, all these factors contribute to a 'situation'. We can try to understand their contribution and define what is going on in order to decide how to act. However, looked at over time each factor changes at its own pace, responding to the relationships and social changes that affect it. For example, the marriage may have been a rather edgy compromise for the spouses a few years ago, but constant conflict may have altered the balance of power between the spouses and turned one into an abuser. Another example, the multiprofessional team might have concentrated on the wishes of their patient a year ago, but have been forced to balance this with risks to a vulnerable adult by the development of the protection policy. We call those continuous changes 'processes'.

Process has several connected meanings. A *proces*sion brings to mind people in uniform or ritual dress entering to take up their positions. Industrial *process*es mix chemicals, or machines manufacture something. In offices, lines of clerks *process* application forms. More generally, *a process is a series of actions and the factors affecting them that go towards making or achieving something.*

This account of the idea of process suggests, first, that it refers to an accepted way of doing things. In the ceremony, there is an order of precedence; the office worker 'goes through' documents; inside a computer a 'processor' carries out a series of tasks in logical sequence, similar to the officials at their desks but more quickly. The formal church or academic procession, where people enter, go to their places and perform tasks has many features in common with the informal process of a family entering a sitting room and settling down to watch television. They go to their normal seats, settle down, agree about the programme to watch and fiddle with the remote control. In both, there is an accepted way of doing things that grows up in social relationships. In social work, this idea helps us to understand how a marriage, the experience of dying, the professional task or the organisational policy sets social expectations so that people know how to behave and how to react in different circumstances. The 'way of doing things' comes from both formal procedures and socially accepted conventions.

Second, process refers to complexity and connectedness. We do not see separate events but the connections between them. This is, of course, a human interpretation of events: it is how we *understand* connections and complexes that create process. In social work, people's stories or narratives of what has happened to them connects apparently separate matters together in their minds and the connections then affect how they act. For example, a woman dying of cancer may connect her weight loss with her husband's sudden lack of interest in sexual intercourse.

Third, process is time-based. Events and the factors that affect them occur in sequence, over a period of time. Seeing social work as a process, rather than, say, as a packages of services or as separate episodes in people's lives makes connections between events in the client's life and the social worker's assessments and reactions to them, and between what the worker does and the effects on their clients. For example, a package of services including a daily delivery of meals, visits by carers in the morning and evening, a daily visit by district nurses, twice-weekly shopping and domestic help are experienced by the service user as a sequence of stimulating and mutually supportive visits, or perhaps irritating interruptions to their own life sequence. The care manager may interpret them as a complex whole, covering different risks or needs, rather than separate events and services or a sequence. How people see the process may help or hinder them. For example, the care manager who sees a total package may not have thought to check that it works for a service user who sees it as a sequence, or an occasional visitor who may not realise that there is a care plan and thinks the support is random.

Fourth, a process is structured and organised. Part of the structure is the time-based sequence, but other parts of it may be the people involved, the place where they interact or the organisation that they are a part of and the accountabilities that participation in an agency and service involves. The process of deciding what to do about a family in conflict in a hospice involves various members of the multiprofessional team coming together. There is an acknowledged and partly written down procedure for doing so. For example, in my hospice if there is a worry about family relationships, rather than a ward management issue, a social worker will be called. If there is concern about abuse, I will be called. If there is concern about physical functioning, a physiotherapist might be called

Fifth, there is an outcome to processes. The procession arrives at its position and then events begin to happen, the factory produces goods, the office approval for actions to take place. The multiprofessional team will decide the best thing to do, people will take on tasks; plans will be made. These will then form part of a process of intervention, a new process, and the decisions and actions will begin to incorporate themselves into the longer running processes of dying and marriage.

Social work as a process

At a general level, social work as a whole is a process. Considering process makes social work a whole, one activity. Aim, starting point, process and interactions with other aspects of life are made whole by our interpretation of them as a process, rather than as separate events. Several writers have described it in this way: Table 2.1 outlines some of their contributions.

Process differs from content and outcome; the three integrate together as social work deals with the whole situation. Many writers referred to in Table 2.1 present an aim, such as critical social change or problem-solving, connected to a process for achieving it: helping, strengthening or releasing, for example. Process focuses on how to practise and what happens during practice, rather than the aims and outcomes of social work activities. Sheppard et al.'s (2000; Sheppard and Ryan, 2003) empirical research identifies social workers' thinking processes as they work. They make a critical appraisal of situations, focusing attention on important aspects of it, querying and evaluating information and then make causal inferences. This first stage then links to hypothesis generation. Partial case hypotheses proposed ways of understanding particular aspects of the situation: is a husband's aggressive behaviour towards his wife due to life stress or psychiatric illness, for example? Whole case hypotheses were propositions about the case as a whole: was it an adult protection case, requiring application of formal procedures,

Table 2.1 Social work as process: alternative interpretations

Type of process	Writer	Aims
Critical	Fook (2002); Healey (2000)	Move towards transformation of social relations through dialogical, shared relationships
Developmental	Smalley (1967)	Help people to 'grow' in understanding and skill
Ego-supportive	Goldstein (1995)	Strengthen people's will to plan and organise life
Empowering	Solomon (1976); Lee (2001)	Strengthen people's ability to overcome social barriers
Person-centred	Rogers (1967)	Release individual's capacity for self-actualisation
Problem-solving	Perlman (1957)	Help people to specify and overcome problems
Psychosocial	Hollis (1964)	Help people to identify and respond to psychological and social stresses
Process knowledge	Sheppard et al. (2000)	Make assessments and decisions through cognitive processes
Systems	Evans and Kearney (1996)	Phases that place work tasks in sequence, according to connections in time

for example? Finally, there are speculative hypotheses about proposed actions: could I persuade the husband to moderate his behaviour, for example?

Process describes social work generically, rather than referring to the content that the process deals with, for example child or adult protection, disability, ageing or family conflict. This suggests that social work is all three aspects of social work: to miss out process misses an important aspect of practice analysis. Aims and content can only be understood fully by including how it works, what it works on: critical dialogue, understanding, skill, the will to plan and organise, the ability to overcome barriers, self-actualisation, overcoming problems and responding to psychosocial stresses.

In social work, to set an outcome is not the end of the matter. If we want to improve someone's childcare skills, where do we start from and how are we going to get to our aim? If a single-parent father provides effective physical care to his daughter, but finds it hard to deal with her emotional needs, we start from a different place than if he can do neither. If he can learn through discussion, the process is different from the situation where he needs to practise interpersonal skills first. Another factor is that other processes will be going on in his life, as with the dying patient discussed at the outset of this chapter. If he is being criticised at work because he is taking too much time out for his family, the process of relationships with his boss will be proceeding at a different pace and in a different place from our attempt at helping, but will interact with it. The social work intervention has to take into account its interaction with other processes in his life.

All these processes are social. Doctors might be concerned about the body and its physical processes, with the mind and its mental processes, or teachers with developing personal knowledge and understanding. Social workers, on the other hand, are concerned with capacities to deal with other human beings and the social assumptions or relationships that follow from that and are required in order to do that.

Ideas about process

The idea of process as an important part of social work comes from a variety of different sources, both within and outside social work. It is useful to explore these because they bring to the surface some of the thinking that we sometimes take for granted or even are unaware of when we casually say that 'social work is a process'. In this section, I identify four important sources of process ideas in social work:

- Whitehead's process philosophy of science
- Psychodynamic social casework
- Groupwork
- Feminist and critical theory.

The mathematician and philosopher A.N. Whitehead saw process as a complex of factors that achieve unity through a distinct series of stages or changes taking place through a time dimension and an organised structure that we can understand and define. He proposed, in the early 1900s, contrary to many scientific approaches to knowledge at the time, that it is as important to think about reality as events and occurrences as well as being about objects and substances. So, what is important about a building or a human being is not only what they are made of or look like, but also what has happened to them, what is happening or might happen to them and how they might be used. Thus it opens up options and possibilities for change, rather than focusing on what simply exists in the present (Rescher, 2002). It is also about including holistically all the factors in a situation, as in our consideration of social work process.

Psychodynamic theories of social casework drew strongly on Whitehead's ideas. Discussing 'psychosocial process' in an early casework text, Hamilton (1951: 3–4) described social work as a 'living event' incorporating and integrating the person, their situation, social experiences and their feelings about their experiences. Functional casework theory sees process as central to achieving social work purposes that are expressed in the aims of the agency or service. Hofstein (1964: 15) defines process in the functional view as a 'recurrent patterning of a sequence of changes over time and in a particular direction'. Process ties together work with service users to indirect work with the agencies and people around them (Irvine, 1966; Smalley, 1967: 16–17), achieving unity of purpose between different aspects of the work. Smalley's (1970) principles for the practice process include workers using relationships to engage with and act on clients' choices, consciously using time phases – beginnings, middles and ends – and gaining direction, focus, accountability and clarity for the work from agency function. These aspects are integrated together by a constantly changing interaction with the client.

The importance that functional casework gives to relationships also emphasises the way in which social work requires the interpersonal as a basic aspect of its practice. Psychodynamic social work sees process as a cycle of interactions between worker and service users, tied together by growing mutual understanding in their interpersonal relationship (Perlman, 1957: Ch. 5; Ferard and Hunnybun, 1962: 48–81; Butrym, 1976: Ch. 5). Social work requires more than the superficial bedside manner. Workers' dealings with clients must have integrity, must therefore be integrated with their authentic personal reaction to the client and the situation. Communication of feedback between the worker and client on reactions to the other's actions and thoughts is a crucial part of process working. All these writers are putting forward a model of process in which the worker and client demonstrate their personalities and ways of behaving to each other. This then leads to an interpersonal engagement with each other, in which difficulties are raised and identified and ways of dealing with them planned and executed.

From its earliest days, groupwork relied on ideas of process. Mary Parker Follett (1918), one of the historical sources of groupwork ideas, writes about being part of a group:

> I go ... [to a group] in order that all together we may create a group idea, an idea which will be better than any one of our ideas alone, moreover which will be better than all of our ideas added together. For this idea will not be produced by any process of addition, but by the interpenetration of us all. This subtle psychic process by which the resulting idea shapes itself is the process.

Expressing this 'subtle psychic process', Thompson and Kahn (1970: 13–14) say:

> In order to try to understand ... [group] interaction, it is necessary to take all the individual pieces of behaviour, the contributions of each different member, and treat them as if they were part of a meaningful whole ... It is necessary to treat the group as a distinct psychological entity, but this does not alter the fact that it has no existence apart from the activity of its individual members ... If we are to assume that some connection exists between all the events taking place in a group, then we must also assume that, at some level, forces exist and exert an influence over every single thing that happens. To these forces we give the name of group processes.

This quotation emphasises that process always involves bringing together different elements and dealing with the differences that arise. This is clearer in groupwork than in other forms of social work, but it applies to all process. If social work is a process, it is, therefore, about trying to be inclusive when dealing with difference. A process seeks out and tries to respond to everything that affects what is going on. It is thus particularly relevant for anti-discriminatory and anti-oppressive practice, because these forms of practice examine and try to respond to difference.

Thompson and Kahn also make it clear that process is a metaphor, a human interpretation of what is going on in complex situations. It is treating events 'as if' they were connected and that 'forces exist and exert an influence'. The metaphor of process allows us to understand how events are connected, to make a 'story' or narrative that offers explanations that can be adapted to reflect more information as it arises during our engagement with the client and the situation as it changes.

This aspect of groupwork continues to have its influence. Mullender and Ward (1991) discuss self-directed groupwork as an endeavour to help to empower oppressed groups. They describe process as a development from workers setting up and starting the group, through a series of stages leading to the point where the group operating as a inclusive whole takes charge of its future. Here the process is not just a sequence in time, it is a sequence from powerlessness to empowerment, through learning self-direction in the group.

Critical and feminist theory (Fook, 2002) draws many of these different points together. Feminist theory emphasises a particular aspect of integrity and integration: between the personal and political. Politics is about groups contending for power. We experience power being used in relationships. Sometimes, this is to achieve personal ends. For example, the wife of a dying man prevents his children by the previous marriage from seeing him, by showing him that she is upset by the reminder of the previous relationship. They experience this as frustrating; a direct application of power against them. As well as personal power, politics is also expressed in our personal experience; through discrimination people experience personally how social and political divisions affect society. Personal experience is an expression of political relationships, but a political reaction, to form groups for mutual support or to seek change, also involves personal commitment.

Process in practice

Why should we use the idea of process in practice? There are three main reasons. First, the idea of process treats workers' actions with people as wholes, rather than separating different aspects of what they do. So, for example, when you ring the social security office to sort out entitlements, the idea of process tells us that this is part of a more general attempt to take the pressure off a single mother whose child has a serious disability. Better social security will make her feel that she is more in control of her weekly budget, and free her from some money worries to focus on caring for her child. Perhaps this is in the early stages of working with her, in which case getting her some practical help may improve your relationship with her and make her more willing to work with you in more emotionally difficult areas later on, such as her fear of letting her child gain more independence. We can see the connections, how everything affects everything else, and our planning (Chapter 4) identifies and makes use of those connections. The relationships with the other agency are also wholes: how they experience us in this case will affect how they respond to us the next time.

Second, process makes clear and takes into account the complexity of the connections between different aspects of the situations we are dealing with. Ideally, everyone should trust that a social worker will be of benefit to them, but most people want us to prove it before they will let us in on the more complex parts of their problems. So, a disabled woman will ask us to sort out her social security entitlements and, if we seem responsive, might be prepared to come up with more personal issues. Third, process allows us to connect theory with practice and practice with theory in a critical way. Identifying processes begins to make explanatory narratives about the client's situation and our intervention. As our connection-making continues, we see more and more aspects to the narratives that allow us to criticise our earlier explanations and adapt them to the new information. Thus, explanation becomes a process of making meaning from what we see and participate in, not deriving an assessment from a set body of information about the client and then acting on it (Chapter 3).

Although the idea of process comes from psychodynamic and critical theories, it is now used as a general idea in social work. We can use a range of social work theories (for example those discussed in the second part of the first of this series of books (Adams et al., 2002a), as ways of guiding our practice.

Connectedness, communication, context

Accepting that the idea of process may help us to practise, how can we use it? The definition of process given above, as 'a series of actions and the factors affecting them that go towards making or achieving something', offers a starting point. This definition draws attention to how we must bring together both the actions of various people involved, factors that affect those actions, movement towards achieving something and the outcome we want to achieve. My discussion of process so far sets the objective of identifying and bringing together as many relevant factors as possible. A good process identifies relevant people and agencies and brings them together in the interaction.

A social work process is one human event made up of elements. Figure 2.2 identifies a series of elements within the overall process, a sequence of social work activities. The elements are themselves processes, which draw different elements of the whole into the main. The overall social work process takes place in the context of the processes going on in the lives of the people and the agencies who take part. For the social worker, this might include their personal life, their professional development, the agency's policies and conventions. For example,

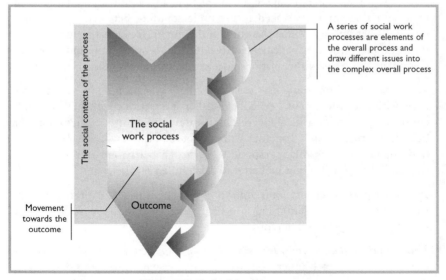

Figure 2.2 Social work process

they might not be prepared to work with the client late at night, and how they would behave would be different if they are a student rather than a seasoned worker. Clients' context might include continuing social relationships, the social environments they live in and the issues they bring to the social work process. Process brings together aspects of the environment through those elements as worker and client find or make connections between those elements, intellectually and in practice in our relationship with the people involved. They need to understand that we are taking the right factors into account, and our relationship will develop so that we can help them better if we can demonstrate our efforts to incorporate what they see as relevant factors.

The elements are connected in social work interventions (Chapter 5) by the following factors:

- *The context in which they take place* For example, I made a home visit to a couple recently, and the experience is socially different from when the wife visits my office in the hospice. Their involvement with our agency comes from his serious illness; this brings them to us rather than some other agency, and dictates the focus on their support for each other and relatively brief changes in relationship, rather than long-term family change. We sit in a group of comfortable chairs in both cases, but one environment is domestic and controlled by the clients, the other is professional and perhaps medical and is more in my control. Clothing is different, relationships are revealed differently.

- *Communications between the human beings involved* When the wife visits my office, she gives accounts of, among other things, marital interactions between her and her husband and I try to demonstrate, by interest, commitment to our time together and intelligent responses, that I understand something of her perceptions of the difficulties and value her interpretation of them. I try to get her to make plans to respond differently to some of the human communications. When I visit their home, I can see the interaction, although I am not party to all of it, and I am more balanced in my understanding between her and her husband's perceptions. When the nurse in the multiprofessional team visits, she focuses more on the management of the husband's symptoms, and therefore sees different aspects of the relationship and attempts different interventions.

- *The human understandings developed by the communications* My communications with the wife aim at her managing her interactions with her husband, choosing particular times for difficult interactions and controlling her behaviour, for example. Together with the husband, my work helps them to understand how each might respond to particular behaviours in the relationship and plan how it might be better to relate to each other.

- *Human reflection on the understandings* Seeing through experience what works better in the relationship also helps them to reflect on and see their long-term relationship differently.

- *Human action that communicates based on the reflection* As a result of changes in how they view each other's behaviour, they act with more consideration to each other.

The process elements, then, form a reflexive cycle: the context and what takes place in it affect (through communication, human understanding and reflection on that understanding) actions that communicate, changing the context and understanding of participants. This starts off another cycle. A sequence of cycles form the process; because it moves forwards it develops from a cycle into a spiral. The cycles change, during the sequence. Early on in the overall process, I was more inclined to explore, to try to understand how each party saw the relationship and how they wanted to change it. Later, I use the events of the process elements to try to change perceptions and reactions that may lead to changing behaviour.

As it is one event, a process has boundaries, which are defined by the context. Among important boundaries are:

■ The agency's responsibilities to its political or managing body, which may set its priorities and funding, and to regulators, who set standards of practice

■ The worker's (my) accountability to the people I am working with and professional regulatory bodies for professional standards of practice

■ The different personal identities of the individuals involved and as part of a family and community

■ The interests of other stakeholders, including individuals such as neighbours, and organisations, such as the client's employer.

Understanding boundaries is an important focus of this book because it is always important to how social workers exert professional control over their participation in other people's lives. Making boundaries clear helps people, both users of services and colleagues in other agencies, to understand and manage their interactions with the social worker. One boundary lies between the social worker as a professional and as a person. Social workers will disclose aspects of themselves as a person. Part of this will be natural, for example the way they pay attention to what clients say and express concern will enable clients to make judgements about what kind of person the social worker is, whether and in what ways they can be trusted. However, workers may also introduce information about themselves as a person. For example, they might talk about how they have experienced similar events to those of the client, as a way of helping the client feel that the worker has empathy with their experiences. However, it is easy to step across the boundary between disclosing similar experiences to achieve empathy for the client's benefit and disclosing information to feel good about ourselves for our benefit. Perhaps we want to see ourselves as open to and equal with the client, when the client is clear about our different status as a powerful professional rather than a friend. Worse, the client may be unclear and our disclosure may make it even more confusing.

Process requires us to take into account accepted ways of doing things. They cannot be ignored because they will have an important emotional and practical effect on the people involved. Accepted ways include the following:

■ *Social and emotional conventions and expectations* For example, when a family member dies, there will be a period of bereavement. The emotion and behaviour that people express will reflect what is expected of bereaved people in the family and culture (Smith, 1982).

■ *Legal and administrative requirements* For example, children must go to school during the years of compulsory attendance. Such requirements place pressures on families. Where there is a disabled single mother, for example, children in the family might be expected to care for her and this may conflict with the legal requirement to attend school.

■ *Agency requirements and procedures* For example, to provide help to a frail elderly person means that they must meet either the social services department's criteria for providing 'packages' of care in the community or the primary care trust's criteria for funding 'continuing care' packages.

Each system of social provision across the world has similar criteria fitting with their welfare system. For example, in the USA, a similar aspect of service is called 'managed care'.

Process brings together all the elements that might have an impact on the situation. Important elements that the worker will consider are the people and agencies involved. Often, these elements are lumped together as 'stakeholders'. This term implies that they are likely to be affected by the issues being dealt with in the process. How might they be identified? Factors might include their present participation, their relationships with the client or the issues involved and their official responsibilities. For example, one of the issues for the hospice multiprofessional team is referring cases of abuse of vulnerable persons to the local authority for investigation, under the local multi-agency guidelines. The local authority has a 'stake' in such matters, because of its role in government guidelines, but its staff often have no other involvement with a person to be referred, so they have no stake as far as the patient or other professionals are concerned. This means that careful arrangements for explaining and gaining consent for referral are important to maintaining the trust of the client.

Time, sequencing, structure

How process connects elements involves seeing a structure in the events that we take part in, how the different elements fit together. The structure may develop from a client grouping. For example, in the first volume of this series (Adams et al., 2002a), Adams discusses social work processes as established by present-day trends such as managerialism, competence-based practice and the 'contract culture', in which services are commissioned by public authorities, rather than provided directly. Various writers then divide social work into work with children and families, adults and offenders. This points to the agency whose legal and administrative roles form an important structure that constructs our work. Part II of the second volume in this series (Adams et al., 2002b) extends this by examining the special interests of particular client groups in a more detailed way. Other ways of looking at structure include using theories to decide how to connect the different aspects of cases together, and using a perspective such as feminism or the kinds of values discussed in the first part of Adams et al., (2002b) to identify connections within what we do.

A common approach to structure in social work, however, is sequencing. The following are examples of social work sequences and time phases:

1. Beginnings – middles – ends

2. Study – diagnosis – treatment

3. Intake – assessment – intervention – outcome – evaluation

4. Problem specification – contract creation – task planning – task implementation – ending

5. Assessing need – care planning – implementing care plans – monitoring – reviewing

6. Critical appraisal – hypothesis formation

The first of these is used in Golan's (1978) account of crisis intervention. The second was a common description of social work in the 1950s and 60s, and the third is a more managerial or research account of social work process sequences. The fourth is the conventional task-centred practice sequence (Reid and Epstein, 1972). The fifth is the sequence of care management described in the British government guidance on care management and assessment (SSI/SWSG, 1991). The final line reflects in outline the stages of process knowledge disclosed in Sheppard et al.'s (2000) research in process knowledge.

Although all these structures for social work process have been commonplace in social work at various times, and elements of the sequences connect, they each carry different implications. For example, ideas such as 'diagnosis' and 'treatment' imply connections with the medical assessment of patient; looking at tasks and problems implies a different approach. To focus on structures such as beginnings, middles and ends draws attention to the way in which workers and clients may behave differently at different points in the process. Both may be anxious or uncertain at the outset. They may have established a way of relating in the middle that may be difficult to break out of if change is needed. An end might imply anxiety about the future or a feeling of loss. 'Intake' implies an administrative and professional stage of taking a case into the agency as well as 'taking in' the implications of its initial presentation for the worker. Many accounts of social work sequences ignore this element of the sequence, focusing on assessment first. But the pathway by which the client arrives at the agency, how the agency treats them and how the worker reacts to them in the first instance can be important factors in how the rest of the process goes. For example, a family with relationship problems may come to a criminal justice agency and the initial focus will be on offences committed by one member, or it may come to a housing agency and the initial focus might be on their behaviour as tenants or the maintenance of their property. In either case, their social security entitlements may be an issue to remove the need to commit offences or give them resources to manage their property. Family relationships may become an issue or not.

Similarly, to refer to 'endings' implies a concern for the relationship aspects of finishing a process, while 'outcomes' refers more to achievements, measuring by evaluation or monitoring and review (Chapter 6). In between, activities such as planning, intervention and implementation form other activities of social work, designed to create change.

Although I have referred here to interpersonal social work, the same account of process may be applied to residential work, community work, groupwork and social care management. All involve processes made up of elements, and our understanding of them as wholes, overall processes, is crucial to making plans and interventions with purposes and aims. When we run a group, we organise a series of meetings with purposes, selecting members appropriate to the purposes within the context of the agency's practice. We see the connections between the different groups, consistencies between group members, connections between their behaviour in the group and behaviour in the community, and try to draw these together and make links for the groups' members. A manager or a community worker has a strategic sense of where they want to go with the activities they are organising. In the same way, therefore, they see themselves as taking part in a process.

CONCLUSION

Process is important in thinking about practice in social work because it provides a universal way of conceiving what we are doing as we practise. It allows us to think of the many different elements of what we are doing as connected, and therefore to make sense of them, both for ourselves and the people we work with. Most social workers do not think about particular theories or value commitments when they are working with people in everyday practice, but they do have plans and strategies that make sense of their work as a sequence or pattern of activity that will benefit the client.

Process has several important features as a way of thinking about social work practice:

- It makes clear that social work is not a series of episodes or 'packages' of service, but that it seeks to integrate them into a whole.

- It makes clear the continuing contexts, those things that are already going on in the life of the agency, the worker and the client, within which the work takes place. These move continuously. This does not mean that they necessarily progress in the sense of improving, but they do move on.

- It identifies the importance of structuring and sequencing practice so that many different factors can be incorporated into the practice we are undertaking.

- It emphasises that *how* we do things is as important as what we do and what the aim and outcome might be.

- It helps us to understand and deal with the complexity of the range of people, stakes, ideas and values that we usually have to struggle with.

This part of the book makes use of a conventional time sequence, starting with processes around assessment, moving on to intervention and then review. You can use the discussion in this chapter to examine critically what each author says about the element of the structure they are dealing with. For example:

■ How does an assessment or intervention integrate different elements?

■ How does it deal with contexts and their movements?

■ How does it use structures and sequences?

■ How does it deal with aims, processes and outcomes?

■ How does it include complexity and the range of potential stakes?

You can ask the same of your own practice.

FURTHER READING

Butrym, Z.T. (1976) *The Nature of Social Work* (London: Macmillan – now Palgrave Macmillan). Chapter 6 of Zofia Butrym's book provides a good account of 'traditional' views about process and is still a valid and useful account.

Compton, B.R. and Galaway, B. (1999) *Social Work Processes* (6th edn) (Pacific Grove, CA: Brooks/Cole). This widely used American textbook only minimally discusses the idea of process (on p. 7) (astonishing considering its title), but in its presentation of many aspects of social work demonstrates how social work processes may be understood in some complexity, and it is a current update of ideas that draw upon Perlman's (1957) account of casework as a problem-solving process.

Sheppard, M. and Ryan, K. (2003) 'Practitioners as rule using analysts: a further development of process knowledge in social work', *British Journal of Social Work* **33**(2): 157–76.

Sheppard M., Newstead S., Di Caccavo A. and Ryan K. (2000) 'Reflexivity and the development of process knowledge in social work: a classification and empirical study', *British Journal of Social Work*, **30**(4): 465–88.

These two papers report an empirical study about how social workers develop rules for thinking about what they are doing and show how this becomes a process for gaining understanding and making decisions about their work.

CHAPTER 3

Assessment

Norma Baldwin and Linda Walker

Introduction

Assessment is the foundation for all effective intervention: as such it needs to be grounded in evidence from research and theory in the disciplines such as sociology and psychology, which illuminate human needs. Evaluations of the effectiveness of practice will inform general approaches, but individual cases need to be assured of attention and sensitivity to their unique situations.

Where services are to be provided in situations of risk or need, accurate and realistic assessment of all relevant information needs to be undertaken before judgements and decisions are made about action and resources. A simple question for all professionals in social work, health and welfare services, who are engaged in caring, supporting or safeguarding vulnerable children and adults, is:

> What does this person need in order to maximise well-being in all key areas of his or her life?

This is the starting point for any assessment. The question may be simple, but solutions which match the reality of people's lives are likely to be complex. Key areas will vary according to age and stage of development, personal and social circumstances, aspirations and achievements and whether any risks are posed for or by the service user.

In this chapter we draw on an ecological framework to reflect the complexity, seeing individuals in context, taking account of the wide range of influences on any individual situation. We discuss the importance of an ecological approach in balancing the assessment of need and risk with the evaluation of strengths and resources, in order to determine the potential for and possible route to change. We consider how key principles of social work and other professional practice inform this approach.

Following a brief discussion of the underpinning theory, we set out a working model of assessment, which we elaborate through a case study. Whilst we have both had experience of working with adults and children, our recent experience has been concentrated on work with children and families. Inevitably this influences the references we draw on. We believe, however, that the principles, content and processes of assessment are broadly generic, and that specialist assessments for particular settings or groups should build on these, elaborating more fully and probing more deeply. Generic and specialist assessment should connect, recognising the uniqueness and expertise of each individual, maintaining their centrality in the process.

Whilst we focus on the assessment of individuals and families in this chapter, the logic of an ecological approach demands that the implications of individualised assessments will be looked at alongside population-wide assessments, informing the strategic planning process through children's services and health and community planning mechanisms, attempting to ensure that the pattern and range of services matches local needs and priorities.

Why is assessment important?

In social work services, workers are concerned with support, care, guidance and control. They have responsibilities towards some of the most needy, disadvantaged and vulnerable people in society and responsibilities for trying to respond to unmet personal and social needs and risks to and from service users. They deal with issues of public safety – through mental health services, the justice system, child protection and some aspects of community care. Drawing on best evidence from research and principled practice is essential in a systematic attempt to plan interventions which have the greatest chance of achieving success in these services.

The needs and risks in individual situations must be assessed in detail before judgements can be made about the most appropriate interventions, services and resources. There is increasing emphasis from government on the need for evidence-based practice (EBP) and increasing attention to what works in literature and research relating to all aspects of social work, social care and the justice system (McGuire, 1995; Little, 1997; Acheson, 1998; Buchanan, 1999; MacDonald with Winkley, 1999; Farrall, 2002). (See Chapters 16 and 20 for more discussion of EBP.)

Human situations, however, involve many interconnected variables, frequently changing, not all capable of accurate measurement. Black (2001), discussing the limitations of evidence, argues that not all situations lend themselves to the gold standard test of randomised controlled trials (RCTs), where a carefully measured and controlled treatment can be compared with a placebo or non-intervention. He emphasises the prior intellectual analysis of the problem (p. 33), a planned search for all relevant evidence and continuing review. He recognises that art as well as science is involved.

In circumstances where people's lives are complex, it is difficult to anticipate any particular outcomes, when attempting to balance the holistic assessment of their needs against the uncertainties of predicting future risks to them. The pressure to adopt an actuarial approach to the assessment and prediction of risk is not well supported by an understanding of the limits to our knowledge of human behaviour (Kemshall and Pritchard, 1997; Baldwin and Spencer, 2000; Munro, 2002). Where events of relatively low probability – such as child abuse or child homicide – are involved, Alaszewski and Walsh (1995) (in Warner, 2003) question whether it is possible to derive objective measures of risk. Baldwin and Spencer (2000), Munro (2002) and Reder and Duncan (2002) draw attention to the large number of false negatives and false positives involved in ensuring that screening covers all those potentially at risk. There are also ethical problems in relying on predictive tests which may label and stigmatise individuals and families.

McDonald and Marks (1991: 120), in their review of risk factors used in a wide range of risk assessment instruments, found that less than half the variables used had been empirically tested. They concluded that a common approach was to adopt and adapt an available instrument and put it into practice without testing. Even where extensive testing has taken place, predictive tests and screening instruments are likely only to be able to give a guide as to *proportions within a given population* where the risk may come to fruition, rather than pinpoint precisely the individuals where that risk will lead to harm. Yet social work and social care professionals have the responsibility to reach judgements about intervention, protection, safeguards and resources in a wide range of situations where evidence may be unclear or contested. This is the background to an emphasis on systematic, critically reflexive assessment, drawing widely on theory, research and professional judgement.

Other criticisms of a preoccupation with risks to the detriment of a wider process of assessing needs suggest that this preoccupation has been concerned with 'bureaucratic and organisational needs' (Department of Health, 1995), rather than those of the vulnerable service user. Calder (2003: 44), however, identified an apparent 'jettisoning' of the concept of risk and risk assessment in favour of needs-led assessment. He speculates that this may be due in part to the term 'risk' frequently being misused in social work because it focuses exclusively on the risk of harm, whereas in any other enterprise a risk equation also includes a chance of benefits (Carson, 1994). Calder draws attention to a shift from terms such as 'protection', 'abuse' and 'risk' to 'safeguard', 'promote', 'welfare' and 'need'. There is an uneasy tension between these trends, and social workers and others in caring professions have the task of managing them. An ecological approach, recognising a web of multiple, disparate, interacting factors, provides a holistic framework for understanding, analysing and acting on them.

Given the complexities of individual situations and organisational arrangements, it may not be surprising that there is a poor record in social work of high-quality assessment and purposeful planned intervention (Department of Health, 1995; Scottish Executive, 2000; Horder, 2002; Petch, 2002).

Munro's research into child abuse reports (1999, 2002) found that there was a lack of recognition of known risk factors and a lack of systematic investigation and assessment of all the available information. Workers tended to concentrate on the immediate, current incident or episode, rather than carefully evaluating both long- and short-term evidence relating to behaviour, risks and safeguards. She also found a reluctance to revise initial assessments in the light of new evidence. Workers were not drawing all the complex information together, documenting sources, considering the impact over time on the child and synthesising updated information. All these activities are core features of assessment.

The consequences of the inadequate assessment of need and risk are demonstrated in the numerous child protection inquiries held when things have gone tragically wrong (Reder et al., 1993; Laming, 2003; O'Brien 2003). There are similar examples from mental health, work with older people and people with disabilities. Often the result of inquiries into cases where there have been serious failures in the system and in professional practice has been an upsurge of criticism of agencies and individuals – a culture of blame which can lead to defensive practice and undermine the principle of user-centred assessment and intervention.

Our aim here is to encourage practitioners to increase their confidence, skill and professionalism in assessment as a basis for intervention, recognising it as a collaborative process, which is undertaken within a legislative and organisational framework. National standards (Scottish Executive, 2001; GSCC, 2002) identify the centrality of assessment to the social work task and link it with the core values of social work. We hope here to show that systematic, evidence-led assessment is a straightforward process, drawing on the core principles and skills of social work and social care.

Key principles

Human rights legislation such as the Human Rights Act 1998 and the *UN Convention on the Rights of the Child* (UN, 1989), mental health and community care and children's legislation provide a framework for the *Code of Ethics for Social Work* (BASW, 2003), the *Codes of Practice for Social Service Workers* (GSCC, 2002) and the *Codes of Practice for Social Service Workers and Employees* (SSSC, 2001). Underlying principles support assessment which is firmly based within an ecological framework, with the service user centre stage, a player in a collaborative interprofessional process.

Effective assessment should:

■ Be centred on the service user – not agency- or resource-driven

■ Be built on partnership: with individuals, families and across agencies

■ Recognise the service user within the context of family, material circumstances, culture and social networks

■ Respect dignity, individuality, privacy and human rights and adhere to social work and other professional ethical codes

■ Recognise conflicts of interest and power differentials

■ Seek alternative explanations, judgements

■ Balance protection and safeguards for the user and family members and members of the public with the right to autonomy.

An ecological framework

These principles are best supported by an ecological framework which addresses the context within which needs, risks and problems arise (Bronfenbrenner, 1977; Belsky, 1980; Garbarino, 1992; Acheson, 1998; Baldwin, 2000; Calder, 2003). This is a framework which takes account of research on human needs and is readily applicable in health and social work practice.

Individuals do not live in a vacuum, rather they exist within complex systems made up of their immediate surroundings, social networks, cultural communities, set within a wider social structure. An understanding of ecological systems will encourage systematic information-gathering, drawing on observations and factual evidence, taking account of intra- and interpersonal factors, alongside social, organisational and economic influences on situations where assessment is required. It allows the possibility of recognising the unique influence and relevance of the immediate environment and interconnecting systems on an individual's situation; how strengths within them may be mobilised to support positive change, as well as how deficits and problems may be addressed.

Figure 3.1 shows diagrammatically these interacting systems. The web of interacting factors influencing individual situations, the Department of Health Assessment Triangle and the guidance for Single Shared Assessment in community care follow this approach.

All three models illustrate the importance of not concentrating on single factors but rather recognising and understanding the complexity of any given situation and individual circumstance. The web illustrates how a complex range

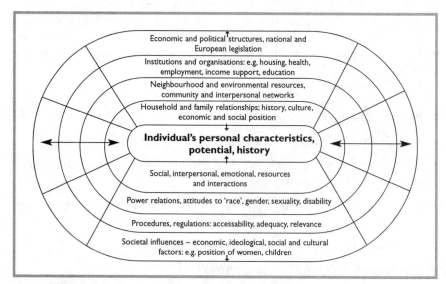

Figure 3.1 The web of interacting factors influencing individual situations
Source: Baldwin, N. (2000) *Protecting Children and Promoting their Rights,* reproduced with permission of Whiting and Birch

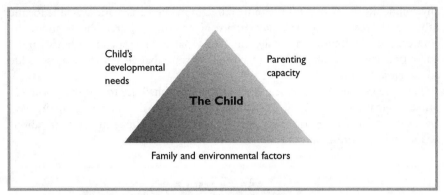

Figure 3.2 Department of Health Assessment Triangle
Source: DoH (2000a) Framework for the Assessment of Children in Need and their Families

of interrelated factors impacts on any individual's life and requires to be addressed within any assessment process. The Department of Health Assessment Triangle recognises how children's lives are not only influenced by their immediate environment but also by parenting styles and capacity, which in turn affects their developmental needs. All these factors require consideration within any assessment. Although expressed differently here, the Single Shared Assessment framework adopts similar principles by recognising that an interprofessional coordinated approach to assessment should capture and address the complexity of individuals' lives and allow those involved in the assessment to address issues from a wide range of perspectives.

The approaches in both the Department of Health Assessment Triangle and Single Shared Assessment are fundamentally interdisciplinary, assuming systematic gathering of information from diverse – but evidenced – sources, which will be critically evaluated and used to develop a structured, purposeful intervention plan.

Jack and Gill (2003) criticise the Department of Health Assessment Triangle, however, for not backing up the third side of the triangle – on family and

---

Single Shared Assessment:

1. is person-centred and needs-led
   relates to level of need
   is a process, not an event

2. seeks information *once*
   has a lead professional who coordinates documents and shares appropriate information
   coordinates all contributions
   produces a single summary assessment of need

3. actively involves people who use services and their carers
   is a shared process that supports joint working
   provides results acceptable to all agencies

Figure 3.3 Single Shared Assessment
Source: Scottish Executive (2000)

environmental factors – with the same range of materials as made available for the other two. This is particularly important, given what research shows about the connections between disadvantage, poor material and social circumstances and a range of harm. An ecological approach must ensure that all aspects of a user's life are taken fully into account.

Here we outline a brief case example, which we shall use to illustrate how key principles may support assessment within an ecological framework: gathering and analysing information, assessing needs and risks, reaching judgements about action and evaluating outcomes.

CASE EXAMPLE

Cathy (mother) 37, unemployed

Sanjit (Cathy's current partner) 35, unemployed

Dennis (Cathy's father) 69, retired

Gary (father of Jonny) 39, unemployed

Jonny (son of Cathy and Gary) 11, primary school

Jason (son of Cathy and Gary) 8, primary school

Zac (son of Cathy and Sanjit) 6 months, full-time local authority daycare

Cathy is currently living in local authority housing with her partner Sanjit and two of her children, Jason and Zac. Her third child Jonny lives with his father Gary (Cathy's ex-partner) and Gary's mother. Cathy is six-months pregnant.

Dennis, Cathy's father, also lives with her. Dennis retired from work on medical grounds when he was 52 and has lived with Cathy for the last four years. His health has deteriorated recently and he requires a wheelchair to get around the house. He does not go outside. His GP has expressed concern about his deteriorating mobility and restricted lifestyle.

Cathy and Sanjit are regular users of cannabis. Sanjit is suspected of supplying others.

Cathy left her previous relationship because of domestic violence which was frequently witnessed by the older children. There has been no suggestion of violence in her current relationship with Sanjit.

Cathy has previously sought help from the Drug and Alcohol Team at times when she has used alcohol as an escape from problems: she has recently contacted them again to ask for general support.

The health visitor has had concerns about Zac's overall development and has been talking to Cathy about the inadvisability of leaving the children – particularly the baby – in the care of her father Dennis.

We work from the starting point of a social worker from the Drug and Alcohol Team, responding to Cathy's request for support. However, the request could just as easily apply if it was a social worker from a Children and Families Team responding to a request by a health visitor to talk to Cathy about her support needs or a request from the GP to a Community Care Team in relation to Cathy's father's disability issues.

Collaboration with service users

Principles of respect and partnership are central to the social work task and must begin with the assessment process. The unique contribution which each service user can make to the process, in relation to their history, personal circumstances, feelings, priorities and understandings, needs to be fully recognised. A partnership approach can recognise an individual's rights to autonomy, safety, inclusion and having their voice heard, without denying power differentials.

In the case of Cathy and her family, with their diverse needs, as in any complex situation, substantial time will be needed to engage with the individuals and the family group. If all are to understand why professionals are showing an interest in their welfare, then they and the professionals involved need to understand the concerns as well as the resources and interventions available – honesty, openness and transparency cannot be achieved instantaneously.

The Single Shared Assessment and the *Framework for the Assessment of Children in Need and their Families* (Department of Health, 2000a) are based on these principles. The Framework for Children provides a good model for assessment, which those agencies under the umbrella of the Department of Health, the Department of Education and Employment and the Home Office, are expected to use. Yet critics suggest that its guidelines are being too rigidly applied, leading to set piece assessments being required, within unrealistic timescales, with the continuing problem that families will experience 'things being done to them', rather than being 'engaged' in a collaborative process (Calder, 2003: 25).

Some initial questions to address when engaging with the family within the case example might be:

- What are the strengths, aspirations and priorities of the individual members of the family?

- How do they – singly and collectively – characterise their current needs?
  - personal needs
  - interpersonal needs
  - social needs
  - material needs

- Do they identify any points of vulnerability or stress about their daily lives, routines, living arrangements?

- Has a professional – health visitor, social worker, teacher, carer, identified any reasons for concern: what are these specifically?

- Have they been shared previously with appropriate family members and any legal and resource implications discussed?

- Do they know why the worker is discussing these matters with them?

■ Do they understand the purpose of any further discussion, information-sharing, assessment?

■ If caring arrangements for the baby are a reason for concern, has the substance of this been explained, for example feeding patterns, sitting in arrangements?

■ If health and personal care of Dennis is a source of difficulty, has the worker had preliminary discussions with the appropriate team about how they may proceed in a coordinated way?

It would be possible to focus on any one member of the family in a narrow, discipline-related way, for example are there child protection issues for Zac? Are there issues about accommodation for Dennis? Are there problems of drug and alcohol abuse for Cathy? Targeted, specialist assessments for individual services would risk a one-dimensional, fragmented approach. An ecological approach – no matter which service initiates it – offers a broader and more realistic perspective.

Interprofessional collaboration

The development of a Single Shared Assessment in community care and the Department of Health's *Framework for the Assessment of Children in Need and their Families* have both been driven by the recognition of a need for joined-up approaches to common human needs and problems. Yet our health and welfare services are enormously complicated, often with labyrinthine bureaucracies and funding arrangements.

Many child protection inquiries have shown that a contributory factor to negative outcomes and sometimes irreparable harm to children has been the lack of coordination and cooperation between agencies (Reder et al., 1993; Laming, 2003; O'Brien, 2003). Assessment which engages with the complex realities of service users is an essential starting point in accessing appropriate services and ensuring that they operate for the benefit of users. When gathering and sharing information for an assessment, it is essential that professionals coordinate their efforts and cooperate with one another. Routes for prompt information-sharing – with or without consent – need to be clearly set out and agreed across agencies. Information should be held and shared in ways that best promote and safeguard individuals' interests. Human rights legislation rightly stresses privacy and confidentiality, but not to the extent of overriding safeguards for the vulnerable.

The format of record-keeping should be simple, flexible and useable across professional boundaries. Assessment and other records should be capable of expansion to take account of complex, changing needs over time and involvement of new agencies. However comprehensive the record-keeping system and sophisticated the guidelines about content, workers need to be clear that they are only tools to be used for the benefit of service users.

Interprofessional collaboration carries undoubted benefits in terms of improved coordination of consultation and decision-making. However, its hidden costs include the time required for professionals to begin to understand each others' ways of thinking and working and engage in the process of working more closely together (Hallett and Birchall, 1992; Hallett, 1995; Wilson and

Pirrie, 2000). Although current governments in Scotland and the UK demand joined-up working and promote integrated services through the provision of specific funding streams (Single Shared Assessment, Joint Futures, Changing Children's Services Fund and so on), there are practical problems in many areas about allocating the time necessary to support these collaborative arrangements, such as workforce and recruitment problems, inexperienced staff and managers and infrequent supervision.

Many have argued that from initial training onwards different professionals become embedded within their own 'camps' and are reluctant to look at alternative perspectives (Wilson and Pirrie, 2000). Others argue that professional jealousies, status issues and alternative value bases all contribute to frequently poor working relations between differing professions (Wilson and Pirrie, 2000; Leathard, 2003; Weinstein et al., 2003).

Any worker attempting to help Cathy and her family will need to be sufficiently aware of these issues to handle them constructively and engage with the family in assessing and meeting their needs. Initial issues to be addressed when working across professions are:

- Who has relevant information about the members of the household?
  - individual family members
  - health professionals
  - Drug and Alcohol Team
  - local authority carers
  - social worker
  - primary schools.

- Who needs to make information available?

- Who is the most appropriate person to coordinate information with the family?

- Who will deal with issues of confidentiality, consent for information-sharing?

- How will evidence, facts and observations be verified and separated from opinion?

- What timescales will be set for gathering and analysing the information and using it to arrive at an assessment of strengths, resources, risks and needs?

- Who will take responsibility for recording, updating, sharing the range of information with this family and professionals involved, ensuring their continual engagement in the collaborative process?

- Is there a local system of 'core group' advice, discussion and collaborative working which an individual worker can activate, or does the worker have to create the most appropriate mechanism to match the needs identified?

- Are there conflicting professional priorities which need to be made explicit and agreements made about resolving them?

■ Are there legal or funding issues which need to be checked out, for example child protection, arrangements about payments for community care?

Instruments and tools for the assessment process

Smale and Tuson (1993) describe three main types of assessment within social work. One is the *questioning model*, where a social worker will be seen as the expert, drawing out and processing information. A second is the *procedural model*, where a social worker gathers information to assess whether the service user fits predetermined criteria for services. The third is described as an *exchange model*, where all people are seen as 'an expert on their own problems' and the emphasis is on the exchange of information. The social worker attempts to help service users to mobilise internal and external resources to meet goals defined by them. This third model is the one which best fits the values and principles of social work. It recognises principles of empowerment of the individual, setting the service user at the centre of the assessment process. Principles of empowerment can be seen in the widest context – including issues of safety for and risk to others, power differentials and conflicts of interest.

Social workers have an enormous range of assessment tools to guide their work, some concentrating on general risk factors whilst others have an emphasis on specific aspects such as mental health, alcohol use, disability or domestic violence. Each of these instruments should be guided by the principles of social work and human rights legislation and located within the wider ecological framework. A positive aspect of such a diverse range means that methods can be closely aligned to an individual's situation. However, the diversity and range of methods and approach can lead to confusion about how they should be applied, or result in key principles of assessment being subordinated to the priorities of a particular method.

Which instrument to use, how to use it and how well it has been evaluated are all questions to tax individual workers and their organisations. Although clear guidance may be issued with an assessment tool (Department of Health, 2000a), this still needs to be interpreted locally within individual agencies and translated for staff in the form of training, policies and more specific guidelines. Calder and Hackett (2003) discuss further tensions arising from local training and guidelines, where there can be multiple interpretations of the method, and confusion on the part of workers in relation to the administration of the tools and their effective outcomes. We are not yet at a point in social work where the evidence base neatly points to the validity of a few all-encompassing assessment tools. The skill of workers in drawing systematically on the best evidence available relating to the general circumstances they are assessing will need to be backed up by skill in analysing and judging the unique situation and its specific strengths, needs and risks. The expertise of workers also arises partly from reflections on their own situation.

If workers are guided by the set of principles previously outlined in relation to assessment and locate their work within the wider ecological framework, then Maddock and Larson (1995) in Calder and Hackett (2003) suggest they also need to take cognisance of their own position within the assessment process. The worker has to address how and where the individual being assessed is located within an ecological framework and also 'pay attention to his own place in the total ecology of the client's presenting situation, choosing an appropriate ecological niche from which to make some useful contributions' (Calder, 2003: 33).

This allows all those involved to operate within a systems framework where conflicts of interest and tensions are commonplace and recognised as the norm within a complex set of interlinked relationships. The 'ecological niche' from which workers make their contribution will be affected by their ability to make sound professional judgements. These judgements are made against a backdrop of limited knowledge, time pressures, high emotions and conflicting objectives (Munro, 2002). In these circumstances assessment tools should be seen as working documents that should be transparent to all involved, with decisions and actions being continually measured against the available evidence and updated accordingly.

The fallibility of assessment tools needs to be recognised, however, as studies show that professionals seek certainty, have a tendency to choose one option rather than checking out several possibilities and dissent is often discouraged (Munro, 2002). A further criticism of some assessment instruments is raised by McCarrick et al. (2000), who argue that many of them rely far too heavily on verbal exchanges. They suggest that this can accentuate power differentials and fail to engage service users in genuine participation. They propose a wide range of interactive exercises and methods of observation as essential tools of assessment.

Following any system, or relying on a particular tool, will inevitably constrain the assessment process, reducing its flexibility. Here the issue of exchange becomes crucial – openness to the realities of the service user's situation demands critical flexibility in skill and professional judgement.

Supervision which supports critical reflection is a crucial part of the overall systemic approach to assessment (Morrison, 2001). Opportunities need to be provided for workers within complex cases to challenge and be challenged on their assumptions, question their decisions and analyse their understanding of information received.

Assessment as inquiry

Assessment itself can be seen as a method of inquiry, to be adapted to respond to the unique situations of service users. Professionals assess individual circumstances in relation to risk, need and potential change, from within organisations where tensions exist between the allocation of time and the time required for assessment. Workers require time not only to assess and intervene as appropriate in relation to potential risk and need but also, taking an ecological approach, to think about and question their decision-making. Such reflective practice is essential to the assessment process and decisions about intervention and the provision of services and resources.

We support Heron's (1996) model of inquiry that harnesses cycles of reflection and active participation to improve the assessment process. Within the process of assessment, workers are required to 'act' in relation to gathering information from a wide range of sources, through collaboration with others, and then intervene where appropriate. They need to continually 'reflect' on information obtained, on their judgements and decision-making based on it, then on any action to be taken as a result. They need to analyse, review and make sense of it. Figure 3.4 illustrates this inquiry process linked to assessment.

When reflection is built into each stage of the assessment process, any follow-up action taken by workers will be based on up-to-date information and grounded in current reality. Reflecting on information gathered allows workers and others involved to question their assumptions, challenge accepted givens, frame and reframe further questions and analyse information in a collaborative attempt to gain new 'common meaning structures' which lead to greater common understanding (Dixon, 1999). Within complex situations where there may be conflict, power differentials and space for misunderstanding, this mechanism is essential to provide clarity and transparency and deal with a diverse range of opinions about potential direction and possible outcomes.

Within any assessment process there are likely to be many cycles of reflective and active practice as workers seek to update information and obtain more pieces of what, at times, seems like a complex jigsaw puzzle. Coulshed and Orme (1998) suggest that assessment requires administrative and interpersonal skills. Parker and Bradley (2003) add communication and observational skills, and an ability to organise, synthesise and rationalise information-gathering. A cyclical model of reflection and action which allows time to process material in this way

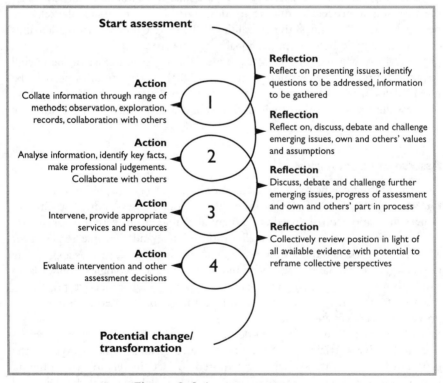

Figure 3.4 Assessment as inquiry

recognises workers' need to be reflexive, in order to help discourage bias in their assessment (Cooper, 2000). It can support holistic assessment, taking account of diversity, complexity and the need for a balanced approach.

The use of a cyclical model, which recognises the complexity of unique human situations, provides safeguards within which information can be continuously assessed, collective understanding questioned and potential intervention and outcomes revisited. It allows the possibility of the individual service user being centre stage, recognising the potential for individual and collective change through active participation in a process.

The first cycle within the assessment process requires workers, in partnership with service users, to set the scene and begin to frame the parameters of the assessment. Taking an ecological perspective, this should encompass the key principles of assessment as outlined previously, showing respect for individuals whilst recognising the imperative to address safety and immediate issues of risk to or from service users.

Questions to be addressed and action taken in cycle one might be:

Reflective phase

- What information is available at the outset?

- Is intervention required immediately or in the short term?

- What further information do we need?

- Where might this information be obtained?

- Who needs to be involved in a holistic assessment?

- What timescales are we working to?

- What systems of communication will be employed to keep everyone informed during the assessment process?

- What resources might we need to carry out this assessment?

- Who might need to be contacted regarding resource allocation?

- Where will supports come from for service users, carers, workers?

Action phase

- This requires active collaboration with individuals, families, wider groups and other professionals to obtain information through discussion, observation, reading records and collating photographic and other evidence.

Although within any assessment process, depending on the complexity of the situation and the number of variables involved, there are likely to be multiple cycles, within this example only the four key steps are shown to illustrate the model. Within each step, smaller cyclical processes will occur as information is gathered and ideas framed and reframed within the process.

Questions to be addressed and action taken in cycle two might be:

Reflective phase

■ What issues/concerns are emerging about disability, drug and alcohol use, pregnancy, developmental and health issues?

■ What evidence do we have?

■ Does the evidence match the emerging issues/concerns?

■ What value judgements are being made and by whom?

■ Where can these be checked out?

■ What mechanisms are in place to support, challenge and question, for example in relation to prejudice about race, disability, child development and parenting capacity?

■ What assumptions are being made and by whom, for example in relation to past requests for support, current circumstances, 'norms' and 'stereotypes'?

Action phase

■ Whilst continuing to collate information from a range of sources, this phase involves analysis of the presenting information obtained in collaboration with service users and other professionals. Professional judgements are made based on presenting evidence and evidence from research. Alternative judgements, of professionals or family members, are considered and recorded.

The reflective phase in cycle three provides ongoing quality assurance in the assessment process, by allowing workers to step back and assess the situation so far. Compton and Galloway (1999) caution that workers can never fully understand what others are saying, doing or feeling and should not attempt to do so. However, taking time to begin to make sense of information provided and seeking to understand the context within which it is located goes part way to gaining greater understanding. Similarly within the action phase active participation by family members in problem identification and solving recognises key principles of collaboration, partnership and respect.

Particularly in child protection cases, where workers are often faced with the 'resistant client', some degree of creativity and flexibility is required to skilfully engage the individual or family concerned (Calder, 2003).

Questions to be addressed and action taken in cycle three might be:

Reflective phase

■ Are the facts gained so far correct and how might we know this, for example in relation to Dennis's health, the mother and father's past and present drug and alcohol use, Zac's development?

■ Has everyone who needs to be included within the assessment been included and how would we know this? Has an opinion been sought from the GP, HV, other relevant health professionals, extended family members, nursery, school and so on?

- What changes do the individuals within this family want?

- What do they consider achievable and sustainable?

- What is your professional judgement and what do other professionals think?

- Have assumptions and 'givens' been challenged?

- What mechanisms exist to debate and question emerging issues and reframe thinking?

Action phase

- Intervention should by this stage be agreed and include a wide range of options for this family. Their inclusion in relation to identifying and solving problems is essential in achieving effective outcomes.

Within an ecological framework, cycle four emphasises the collaborative nature of the process, concentrating on collective perspectives through reframing in the light of specific current evidence and research evidence. Workers here need to review the information gathered and interventions made so far, checking that thorough attention has been paid throughout the assessment process. It has been suggested that in Samra-Tibbets and Raynes' (1999) stepwise model of assessment, workers frequently skip the planning stage to progress to a later information-gathering stage (Cleaver and Department of Health, 2000).

Questions to be addressed and action taken in cycle four might be:

Reflective phase

- Has the assessment process been completed to everyone's satisfaction (in relation to Dennis, Cathy, Sanjit and the children)?

- If not, what are the gaps or unresolved issues?

- Have issues of risk, need, problems, targets and potential change been identified?

- What mechanisms and resources will need to be in place for these to continue to be addressed?

- How will this be agreed and outcomes reviewed?

- Who will continue work with the individuals within this family, if continuing involvement is agreed – drugs team, school, GP, social worker, health visitor and so on?

- Has the coordination of professional contact been identified and agreed by everyone?

Action phase

- This stage requires workers to be very clear with individual family members and each other about future planning and expectations, agreeing specific outcomes, who will be responsible for particular actions, resources, review and assessment.

■ Transparent, honest communication both written and verbal is essential, which respects individual rights, confidentiality and privacy. This needs to be balanced with the imperative to have accurately assessed degrees of risk and need for all in the household and to have made clear what consequences may follow if agreed – or required – expectations for care and safety are not met.

CONCLUSION

Robust systems to support a process of assessment which can take all these factors into consideration are required across all sectors of care services. Professional judgements need to be made based on a balance of complex relationships between risk, need, safety and autonomy. An ecological framework provides a structure from within which workers can consider the impact which interconnected layers have on an individual's life.

Professional judgements are based on evidence relating to specific sets of circumstances unique to the individuals involved and from wider studies and perspectives. Inquiry processes that harness cycles of reflective practice and active participation provide workers with a model to collate and assess evidence systematically. All assessment processes, whether they be in relation to children, families or adults, should place the service user at the centre of the process, valuing their perspective as a contributing partner.

Professional support mechanisms, allowing time to reflect and encouraging the development of skills to evaluate and challenge practice, should be embedded within and across organisations, with active supervision being a vehicle to aid this process. Balancing risk, need and safety requires a complex set of skills, involving the cooperation and collective understanding of a range of individuals in seeking positive outcomes.

When workers have the opportunity to work collaboratively with service users and other professionals, to address power differentials and potential conflict through a systematic approach which draws together and evaluates strengths, needs, risks and the potential for change, the effectiveness of services is likely to be improved and the outcomes for service users more positive.

FURTHER READING

Calder, M. and Hackett, S. (eds) (2003) *Assessment in Childcare* (Lyme Regis: Russell House Publishing).

Hudson, B. (2002) 'Interprofessionality in health and social care: the Achilles' heel of partnership?', *Journal of Interprofessional Care* 16(1): 7–17.

Jack, C. and Gill, O. (2003) *The Missing Side of the Triangle: Assessing the Importance of Family and Environmental Factors in the Lives of Children* (Ilford: Barnardo's).

Kenny, G. (2002) 'The importance of nursing values in interprofessional collaboration', *British Journal of Nursing* 11(1): 65–8.

Loxley, A. (1997) *Collaboration in Health and Welfare* (London: Jessica Kingsley).

Worth, A. (2001) 'Assessment of the needs of older people by district nurses and social workers: a changing culture?', *Journal of Interprofessional Care* 15(3): 257–66.

Planning

Margaret Holloway

In the flurry of statements and definitions which emerged in the shake-up of social work training and the regulation of the profession in the UK at the turn of the century (QAA, 2000; Department of Health, 2002c; TOPSS, 2002), planning – once seen at best as a bridge between assessment and intervention – has been afforded an importance all of its own. Originally seen as primarily the province of the service manager, planning is now a central requirement for every practitioner. Key Role 2 of the National Occupational Standards for Social Workers (TOPSS, 2002) identifies that practitioners should be able to '*Plan*, carry out, review and evaluate social work practice, with individuals, carers, groups, communities and other professionals', and the Quality Assurance Agency for Higher Education's subject benchmark for social work states that students should develop the skills to '*plan* sequences of action to achieve specific objectives' (QAA, 2000). Moreover, the shifting emphasis from the Department of Health over the past decade on outcomes rather than process incorporates, often explicitly, the notion that these must be *planned* outcomes based on evidence from research. The National Service Frameworks published to guide the development, delivery and regulation of health and social care services for children and adults each contain within them a substantial emphasis on the notion of care which is planned and systematically reviewed (for example Department of Health, 1999d, 2001b, 2004), and the same notion underpins the Care Standards Act (CSA) 2000. In many ways this emphasis on what at first sight may appear merely a technical process is the automatic outcome of professionalising trends over thirty years, which have sought to establish social work as a logical, ordered and defensible activity. To many social workers, however, it appears that their skills in human relations, their flexible, intuitive use of mechanisms for change and their ability to respond at the user's pace are all being subsumed to the planning machinery. Yet when it comes to their day-to-day case management, these same social workers find themselves reaching for 'planning' as the tool which may help them to reduce a complicated, multifaceted problem to a manageable situation.

CASE EXAMPLE – PLANNING AT THE HEART OF PRACTICE

Janice is a 35-year-old woman with severe and multiple impairments. She has very limited verbal communication. She lives with her parents, now in their late seventies, and is supported by home carers who attend to her personal care needs. She goes to a social services day centre between Monday and Friday. Janice's overall care has not been properly reviewed for years. The last time a full day centre review procedure was conducted (two years ago), the resulting plan was subsequently withdrawn because it was deemed that hers was not a priority case for the more intensive social programme recommended. This was because, simultaneously, a programme of one-to-one working for the more 'able' users was being implemented, leaving insufficient staff resources to develop programmes for users such as Janice, whom, it was felt, would benefit far less from such dedicated resources. However, no alternative plan was put in place to address her identified need for greater social stimulation. Janice's parents, concerned about the future, contacted the social services area office for information to assist them in making plans. They express some dissatisfaction that the centre isn't working as well for them as in the past. Janice has developed a sore on one leg, apparently caused by the use of leg restraints, which staff argue is in the best interests of both Janice and other users as she is constantly kicking in an agitated fashion.

The weaknesses in Janice's care package and arguably her limited quality of life can be seen to stem from *systematic deficits in planning*:

- Her basic package of care developed in an ad hoc fashion, the home care having been originally funded from the Independent Living Fund and put in place by her parents. She has never had an overall assessment of need or an integrated care plan devised on the basis of that assessment.

- Previous care plans have been partial. The home care was targeted at her physical care needs and there was a failure to set any broader objectives relating to her social or emotional needs.

- There have been repeated failures to review her care and revise the care plan in line with her current needs. Thus, new 'problems' such as the agitated kicking, have been dealt with via an isolated response designed to contain the problematic behaviour.

- There has been no attempt to work in partnership with informal carers, or for the different formal carers to pool their knowledge and understandings to create the optimum caring environment. Janice's 'voice' is lost as she does not have the one-to-one attention which might help her communicate her needs and wishes.

In summary, in the words of the care manager picking up the parents' request at this stage: 'Each missing component of care management created a situation where services no longer met her needs but this was not detected.'

Planning and the policy–practice interface

The distinguishing feature of social work in the UK, and the one which has pushed the planning task to the fore, is the policy–practice interface. Although social work theorists in the UK have only relatively recently been particularly concerned with planning as part of the social work process, policy makers and service providers have for some time been increasingly preoccupied with its importance in social services delivery. The relationship between service planning and individual care planning is an important one which increasingly impacted on the work of the frontline practitioner throughout the 1990s. The Children Act 1989 highlighted the responsibilities associated with planning for children 'in need', particularly those in need of long-term care and those leaving care, and subsequent guidance detailed the procedures and skills to be employed by the social worker. The National Health Service and Community Care Act (NHSCCA) 1990 introduced care management as the 'cornerstone' of health and social care delivery, in which the production and monitoring of an individual care plan is a key task of the care manager. The Care Programme Approach in community mental health services preceded and has continued to run alongside care management, and the production of a care plan, which is periodically reviewed, is central to the approach. The 'modernising services' agenda of the late 1990s, combined with the drive for 'quality', has seen a series of policy directives giving increasing weight to the planning task for the frontline worker. Not only have practitioners found themselves increasingly planning their interventions within statutory frameworks and government guidelines, they also have to set objectives and make plans that can result in demonstrable outcomes and will be subject to regular review. The balancing act between professional considerations and management imperatives which the individual practitioner must achieve becomes crucially located within the planning task.

The core task

Planning as a core task can be simply stated. It involves the setting of objectives to meet the needs and/or address the problems identified through the assessment, followed by the development of a plan for intervention to realise those objectives. However, as already discussed, the complexities of the situations with which social work is concerned, and the relationships in which it must engage in intervening in these situations, make the reality of planning far less simple. Payne (1995) delineates six stages in the 'planning interaction': introduction, in which the relationship is established, assessment, formulation, agreement, implementation and operation. Hughes (1995) also emphasises the importance of preparatory planning, taking account of factors specific to this situation which are likely to be significant. Thus, to undertake the planning task, social workers must employ a range of analytical and human relations skills:

- assessment
- design
- creative thinking
- review

alongside the generic interpersonal skills of

- communication
- negotiation
- motivational/enabling
- sustaining.

The plan needs to specify purpose, requirements and timescale for each element. The mechanisms and schedule for evaluation and review should be built in. User groups emphasise that plans must be 'explicit, action orientated and practical' (National Schizophrenia Fellowship, 1992: 10). Importantly, the planning process should be shared by worker and service user and the objectives agreed or disagreements recorded. Finally, although planning is clearly a task whose execution requires the use of a number of core skills, it should never be conceived of as atheoretical. As Brown (1996) has pointed out, implicitly or explicitly social workers use knowledge and theoretical models all the time in planning their interventions, and this is better done as a conscious integrated process than one which exerts an unconscious and perhaps biased influence.

Multiprofessional and interagency planning

A growing emphasis in health, social care and criminal justice services since the 1970s has been the need for different professionals and services to work together. Without exception, the different types of plan discussed in the next section are built around the assumption of multiprofessional working. The most recent development – the Single Assessment Process – takes as its starting point that it is in the best interests of the service user for health and social care perspectives to be brought together at the earliest opportunity into an integrated assessment and 'treatment' plan. A series of policy initiatives have been concerned with creating the agency structures to achieve better joint working, with the White Paper *Modernising Social Services* (Department of Health, 1998) and the Health Act 1999 both introducing levers to promote joint working at interagency level. One such lever is the requirement to produce a joint plan specifying agreed aims and outcomes, the lead commissioning agency and delegated functions, in order to access new funding. When we come to consider the 'on the ground' implementation of these initiatives, and are returned to the core skills of the frontline worker, it also becomes clear that multiprofessional working is *primarily carried out through the planning task.*

Specific types of plan

The generic planning task, which as we have seen belongs to the ongoing intervention process, takes formal shape in a number of specific types of care plan in the UK at the present time. It is primarily through these frameworks that multiprofessional and interagency planning are conducted at practitioner level. These sorts of care plan fall broadly into two categories – need and risk.

Care planning and need

In both children's and adults' services, all intervention is to some extent built around the devising of a plan to meet assessed needs. The following tasks, however, formally devise a plan on the basis of a needs assessment.

Community Care Plans

Under the NHSCCA 1990 tailored packages of care are arranged for disabled or older adults or people with mental health problems on the basis of a needs assessment. The *Care Management and Assessment Practice Guidance* (Department of Health/Social Services Inspectorate, 1991) outlines seven stages in which the core tasks are carried out, of which Stages 4–7 are concerned with the design, implementation, monitoring and review of the care plan. It is the responsibility of the care manager, in conjunction with the service user and/or carer, to design and put in place this care package, which is formalised into a written care plan. A key feature of Community Care Plans is that each element has to be costed (Department of Health, 1994), and this costing may be included in the written plan. Another common element, favoured by disability groups, is the incorporation of a daily/hourly timetable (Gathorne-Hardy, 1995).

Single Shared Assessment

The Single Shared Assessment process, introduced between 2002 and 2004 in conjunction with the National Service Framework for Older People (Department of Health, 2001), may in time replace the community care assessment procedures for older people. There are four levels and types of assessment:

1. *Contact* (initiated at the first identification of significant health and/or social care needs)

2. *Overview* (encompassing all or several life domains)

3. *Specialist* (requiring one specific professional expertise)

4. *Comprehensive* (specialist assessments in all or most domains). Each level, however, is intended to produce a care plan which fully integrates health and social care needs, although the structure leads more towards health-led care plans than the social services-led care plans initiated under the NHSCCA. The significant factor from the point of view of the service user, however, is to what extent a more integrated assessment process results in holistic plans which meet their overlapping needs.

Person-centred planning

For adults who have continuing, life-long needs, such as those with complex, multiple disabilities and many people with learning disability, the emphasis on holistic care and life-long planning was retained alongside the introduction of care management. This has developed into a mode of practice termed 'person-centred planning' (Department of Health/Social Services Inspectorate, 1995, 1996; Burton and Kellaway, 1998). Although not governed by legislation in the same way as Community Care Plans, person-centred planning provides a widely adopted framework for supporting people in the community who have continuing and often intensive needs, grounded in the notion of developing short and longer term goals which are based on the things in life which are important for this individual service user in their particular social context.

Child in Need Plan

The Children Act 1989 laid down that a child may be deemed to be 'in need', whether as a result of neglect, abuse, deficiencies in their environment or their own special needs arising from physical or intellectual impairment. In such circumstances, the local authority has a duty to address those needs, employing a multi-agency, multiprofessional plan as appropriate (Department of Health, 1991a).

Care Plan for Looked after Child

A child in need who is looked after by the local authority has a care plan which must identify immediate and longer term objectives. Here the notion of 'permanency planning' is particularly important to reduce the risk of children drifting around the care system or in and out of care (Department of Health, 1991b).

Pathway Plan

A young person preparing to leave the care system will be involved in drawing up their individual Pathway Plan with a worker, usually in a specialist team, designated to work specifically with them on making that transition.

The above three types of plan, all stemming from the Children Act guidance, are designed to prevent children remaining in situations which fail to meet their needs, or which fail to foresee and prepare for their changing needs. They are examples of the way in which planning may be used to structure medium and longer term caring situations at the same time as introducing purpose and therapeutic potential.

Care planning and risk

The escalating concern about risk assessment and risk management in all branches of social work has brought with it the notion of 'risk planning' (Titterton, 1999). The dominant view, which derives from the concept of risk as 'bad', a threat, sees planning as an essential element in preventing and managing risk posed to a vulnerable party. This is essentially the approach in children's services, encapsulated in the Child Protection Plan (Department of Health, 1999d). Second, however, is the approach which sees risk as an essential part of life and the right to take risks as an essential part of taking control of one's own life. This approach incorporates the notion of informed choice concerning risk into care planning. In adult services we see a tension between the protection of vulnerable adults and their right to take risks. There has been little development of the concept of risk planning, nonetheless. For example, risk assessment procedures for older people commonly specify multiprofessional planning meetings, but these are largely concerned with managing risk as conceived as a threat to safety stemming from the service user's frailty or incapacity (for example Lawson, 1996). Relatively little account is taken of the risks posed to the service user from an inadequate support package.

CASE EXAMPLE

Geoff is a 51-year-old man who sustained cerebral damage following a heart attack, causing severe memory problems and visual impairment. As a further consequence of the cognitive damage, Geoff has limited insight into his difficulties and frequently puts himself at risk in everyday situations. He is divorced and has no children, but has been supported by his parents and a few friends and former colleagues throughout his period in hospital. He is now ready for discharge from the neuro-rehabilitation unit. The social worker joins the multidisciplinary team of doctors, nurses, psychologist and therapists who have been involved in his rehabilitation treatment to plan his discharge into the community.

The social worker has a dilemma at the heart of this care plan. Whilst his professional instinct is to balance needs and risks and utilise Geoff's own resources and strengths to the full, the priority given to risk management in local resource distribution means that he must emphasise the risks inherent in Geoff returning home, in order to activate a care package at the level which he feels is necessary to meet Geoff's needs. This may be concentrated on objectives which are not a priority for Geoff. He manages this dilemma by establishing the twin aims of risk management and the achievement of a degree of independence as of equal importance in delivering the desired outcome of Geoff's rehabilitation in the community. Thus it is possible to devise a plan which:

■ Establishes Geoff's eligibility for the service

■ Allows for a flexible, holistic approach but ties each element to an objective which may be monitored

■ Has the potential to achieve the desired outcome, which in itself is a shared objective for both the service user and service providers.

Without such a plan, there is a danger that risk management will dominate to the point of exclusion of other quality of life elements. To devise and implement such a plan, a range of skills must be employed:

■ Skills in communicating with other professionals, formal care providers, informal supports and a service user who has cognitive difficulties

■ Skills in negotiating between parties so that there is agreement on principal objectives and a shared understanding of the strategy to achieve these

■ The ability to think creatively, since Geoff has very particular needs and there is no dedicated community rehabilitation service available

■ Skills in setting up adequate monitoring systems for different components of the package

■ The ability to sustain a creative dialogue, in which the service user remains involved, about the effectiveness of the care package and the possibility of adapting the plan in line with changing needs.

Dilemmas in the planning task

The planning task appears to be a straightforward process on paper, but it is at the planning stage that most of the classic dilemmas in social work practice emerge.

The problem of inadequate resources

A common frustration expressed by practitioners is that undertaking a needs-led assessment is pointless when the care plan is predetermined by the available resources. Part of the problem here is that planning is perceived as a mechanistic activity, rather than a creative strategic process. Such thinking appears to ignore the challenge of harnessing the combined skills and resources of the worker and service user to engage in problem-solving. Thus it may be that within the planning stage alternative solutions can be devised, or a staggered response may be planned, which includes making use of the less than ideal, whilst pressing for the required resource. The policy–practice interface is not static, and, as already discussed, information from the front line is crucial for higher level service planning and resource distribution.

Overtaken by events ... crisis

O'Hagan (1986) argued that social services departments are characterised by crisis-driven responses in situations of danger and uncertainty. He goes on to argue that social workers have a duty to bring this 'dangerous chaos' down to manageable proportions, in which 'good' decision-making, on the part of both worker and service user, replaces the frequently 'bad' decisions which have long-lasting deleterious effects. The potential of planning to contribute to this chaos reduction, as both therapeutic and pragmatic process, should not be underestimated. All planning involves partialising the problem and setting boundaries of time and responsibility within which the situation will be managed. However, some practitioners feel that it was all for nothing when some external event causes the plan to 'fall apart' or at best appear redundant. This falls into the trap of viewing planning as a static event rather than a dynamic process subject to continuous modification. Many people become service users precisely because crises, or negative events over which they have no control, are regular features of their lives. To engage with them in developing the planning skills to manage these events is a crucial professional task.

Managerial versus professional objectives

It has been argued that through the 1990s managerialism triumphed over professionalism in the community care sphere in particular (for example Cowen, 1999). A culture in which quantitative, material outcomes override qualitative factors such as a 'good' working relationship has an immediate impact on care planning. The practitioner may assess an older person as grieving the death of their spouse and therefore neglecting self-care. S/he may wish to offer counselling and/or other forms of social contact such as a volunteer visitor, whilst monitoring the risk from neglect, but the GP's referral is for home care. One hour's home care per day is possible within current resources, demonstrates a response to the assessment made by another professional and contributes to area statistics as an identifiable outcome in a way in which ongoing emotional support does not. This is precisely where the skilled use of planning allows the merging of a number of objectives. The service user, previously very independent, may be happy to accept home care for a trial period since it represents some company. The care manager may use the planning process to allow the older person to ventilate their feelings about 'not wanting to be bothered anymore'. The home carer brings to the situation another listening ear. A planned review suggests to the service user that they may not always feel like this and can consider whether or not they need the service to continue; it allows the care manager to monitor the level of risk and whether the need continues, has changed or has now been met. What is important is that each of these elements is identified within the plan and that objectives are set which can be monitored and result in identifiable outcomes.

Problematic partnerships with users

The age-old problem of disagreement about the terms of the working contract between worker and service user becomes particularly acute when there is a requirement to draw up a written plan. However, the explicit nature of a plan is also its strength. So, for example, a Child Protection Plan, which is imaginatively put together and skilfully used in the ensuing interactions, provides the framework which both supports the worker in carrying out their statutory duty and provides a clear agenda for the parents. The 'contract' which is often incorporated in a plan provides an explicit basis for negotiation. Studies in Scotland found that service users appreciated a written plan and transparency about costings (Cameron and Freeman, 1996).

Disputed accountability/ responsibility between agencies and providers

Significant drivers in the development of joint working have been the problems of people 'falling through the net', confusion over blurred boundaries between agencies and tragedies arising from the failure of anyone to take responsibility for a particular situation at a particular point in time. Sadly, these problems persist, despite repeated calls for better working between professionals and across agencies (for example SSI, 1992). It is hard to see how this can be ignored in the planning process, or how problems can be addressed *except through* the planning process. A plan which fails to negotiate between fixed positions, which is applied inflexibly despite changes in the situation which were not originally anticipated or which deals only with those outcomes which are uncontentious, easy to demonstrate and do not challenge the rhetoric of anyone is unlikely to function as the facilitating tool in complex service delivery which we have been discussing here. One of the greatest causes of failure in joint working is the sabotaging of 'shared' objectives through hidden agendas. A carefully developed plan, which allows the dynamics of the professional and agency interrelationships to surface, offers *both a tool and a process* through which to address and manage disputed territory. Maintaining the centrality of the service user in establishing and holding on to the primary objective ensures that those concerned do not lose sight of the reason why the struggle is important.

CASE EXAMPLE

Lisa is 19 years old and has a daughter, Melanie, of 15 months. She had spent most of her teenage years in care. Lisa has a history of heroin use and is currently on a methadone maintenance programme, supervised by the Community Drugs Team (CDT). Six months ago Melanie was put in the care of the local authority because Lisa was leaving her alone at night whilst she worked as a prostitute. There are a number of workers involved. Lisa herself is supported by her key worker from the CDT, her GP, a tenancy support worker and a dependency support worker from the New Deal for Communities initiative. Melanie's case is carried by a social worker from the children and families intake team, but consideration is being given to moving her case on for permanency planning.

A number of formal plans have been, or are currently, in place:

1. A *contract* has been drawn up between Lisa and the CDT, which governs her continuing on the methadone programme.

2. Melanie was originally the subject of a *Child in Need Plan*, but now has a

3. *Care Plan for a Looked After Child.*

CASE EXAMPLE cont'd

However, the key to the overall management of this case, given the interdependence between Lisa and Melanie's welfare, the principle of involving Lisa in planning for Melanie's future and the interrelationship of health, social and emotional needs, is the plan agreed between the key worker and Lisa as part of the *ongoing intervention process*. It is from the perspective of the objectives of this plan, and the review of its progress, that the CDT worker will contribute her knowledge and professional assessment to multidisciplinary discussions, will support and empower Lisa to be actively involved in planning her own and Melanie's care, and will sometimes negotiate with other agencies on Lisa's behalf. Moreover, the relationship which develops between Lisa and the CDT worker as a necessary ingredient in the planning process has the potential to be, of itself, of therapeutic benefit and an agent for change.

The Plan

Aims

1. For Lisa to detox from methadone and ultimately become drug-free.

2. For Lisa to stabilise her lifestyle so as to be able to offer parenting to Melanie.

3. In the short term this means that Lisa should develop her understanding of Melanie's needs and contribute to discussions about Melanie's care options.

Strategy

- To identify 'risk' factors in Lisa's lifestyle and explore options for managing these.

- To identify activities which both act as a diversion and enhance Lisa's social networks and skills.

Actions

- The CDT worker identifies and introduces Lisa to a 'street' project working with women in the sex industry.

- Lisa begins to regularly attend sessions concerned with parenting young children at the women's drop-in centre run by project workers from the New Deal for Communities.

- Lisa identifies that she would like to attend a gym, both to increase her fitness and boost her self-esteem and hence confidence. The CDT worker agrees to explore options for funding this.

In the course of developing and implementing this plan, the worker has to draw on counselling skills and motivational interviewing techniques. Throughout, she offers constant encouragement and emotional support. However, despite a coherent plan, developed in partnership with Lisa, progress is hampered by a number of the issues and dilemmas identified in this chapter.

First, and most importantly, Lisa's case has to be managed in the context of national and local drug strategies. Thus, the outcome which is most important to Lisa – regaining a parenting role with Melanie – has to be related to the outcome which is of prime significance for the agency, that she should in the longer term become drug-free. Whilst the worker is able to use the aim of being seen as a responsible parent as a powerful motivating factor for Lisa to pursue the detox programme, it is also necessary to find shorter term objectives which could demonstrate outcomes which in themselves are of less significance for Lisa but important to the agency. So, for example, a counselling programme aimed at relapse prevention assumes priority over discussion of Lisa's feelings about herself as a parent. However, by focusing on Lisa's problems with low self-esteem, it is possible to integrate these two objectives to an extent.

Second, there is a clear conflict between rehabilitation objectives for Lisa and permanency objectives for Melanie. Melanie's review at six months had concluded that it was important to start planning for her longer term future now, whilst Lisa had at this point not long entered the methadone programme. It is necessary for the different professionals to work hard at using their specialist expertise as complementary contributions rather than competing perspectives. A compromise is negotiated in which the pursuit of the CDT's plan of intervention forms part of a contract between Lisa and the childcare team until Melanie's next review.

Third, the only suggestion volunteered by Lisa was that she would like to attend a gym. Despite this being linked to the boosting of her self-confidence, the worker is unable to obtain funding to enable Lisa to pursue this activity. To some degree this is compensated for by the worker liaising with the women's centre to identify other confidence-boosting activities and supporting Lisa in getting involved with these, but they lack the 'fun' element and access to a mainstream lifestyle which Lisa desires.

Fourth, whilst the roles and responsibilities between Lisa's key worker and Melanie's social worker remain clear, a degree of blurring and overlap of roles occurs between the other workers offering Lisa support and the CDT worker. This results in conflicting plans and advice being given on occasions, with the problem never being resolved completely since communication proves difficult and there is no forum in which these parties would automatically meet. In such situations, at minimum it is essential to clarify each set of intervention objectives and agree the primary goal. Keeping the service user central and continually checking out goals and reflecting on process is one way of doing this.

Planning and the reflexive practitioner

This chapter, and Lisa's case example, has emphasised that planning is much more than a technical exercise used to link assessments to interventions. Payne (1995) argues that it is a human interaction. It occupies the core ground in many frontline service delivery dilemmas and utilises a range of social work skills. The setting of objectives and agreement about desired outcomes requires a conscious reflection on the inherent value position and tests and stretches the practitioner's commitment to working in partnership with the service user. The creation of the elements in the plan and its implementation require a diverse knowledge base spanning human behaviour, social structures, policy frameworks and local resources. Thus planning is very much the business of the reflexive practitioner. It incorporates Schön's notion of 'reflection-in-action' (Schön, 1983) and demands the critical thinking skills of 'reflective scepticism' (which challenges the notion that there is only one way of doing things) and 'imagining and creating alternatives' (Brookfield, 1987). It does so cognisant of policy and social context.

CONCLUSION

Social work has at its heart the tension of intervening in a rational, ordered way, which can demonstrate what it has done and why, in contexts which are marked by instability and crisis at both individual and corporate levels. This chapter has discussed the planning task as one which facilitates the practitioner holding onto core values and essential objectives, while maintaining the goal of creative, empowering interventions in situations marked by constraint and dilemma. As such it holds the key to practice which is at the same time a reflexive, and a managed, response.

FURTHER READING

Department of Health/Social Services Inspectorate (1995) *Planning for Life: Developing Community Services for People with Complex Multiple Disabilities, No 3 Good Practice in the Independent Sector* (London: HMSO).

Department of Health/Social Services Inspectorate (1996) *Planning for Life: Developing Community Services for People with Complex Multiple Disabilities, No. 2 Good Practice in Manchester* (London: HMSO).

These two linked publications set practical models and examples of planning into discussion of the principles and values underpinning person-centred planning.

Johnson, L. (1996) *Social Work Practice: A Generalist Approach* (6th edn) (Boston: Allyn & Bacon). A detailed examination of the concept and generic skills of planning for the individual practitioner, which roots planning in the social work process.

Marsh, P. and Crow, G. (1998) *Family Group Conferences in Child Welfare* (Oxford: Blackwell). Deals with the development and evaluation of an important practice initiative for involving families in professional childcare planning.

Parker, J. and Bradley, G. (2003) *Social Work Practice: Assessment, Planning, Intervention and Review* (Exeter: Learning Matters). A handbook for practice, focused on the requirements for the new social work degree.

Payne, M. (1995) *Social Work and Community Care* (Basingstoke: Macmillan – now Palgrave Macmillan). Provides a detailed discussion of care planning in adult services following the introduction of care management, but, similarly to Johnson, locates this in a broad discussion of social work intervention, traditional social work relationship skills being described as the 'glue' which holds the care plan together.

Acknowledgement

I should like to acknowledge the contribution of Sheffield University DipSW (Adults Pathway, 2002 cohort) students in providing me with case study material from their assignments. The responsibility for adapting this material is, however, mine; I trust I have stayed close to their original meanings.

CHAPTER 5

Intervention

Siu Man Ng and Cecilia L.W. Chan

Introduction

This chapter presents intervention as more than simply the practitioner's response to a person's problems, but as a proactive means of enabling people to empower themselves to take action to improve their situation. The holistic approach proposed integrates the physical, cognitive and spiritual aspects of the person, with a view to develop strengths and enabling well-being rather than focusing on pathological problems. The aim is to build on harmony between the mind, body and spirit as a means of promoting growth and transformation.

Social work intervention to embrace holistic well-being

Although intervention follows assessment and planning, their relationship is not necessarily linear or sequential. As intervention is about making progress, there can be repeated reviews, reassessments and revisions in an intervention plan. In an ideal case, this spiral process as described in Chapter 3 can take intervention beyond reactive problem-solving. Through fostering growth and transformation, intervention may achieve the social work ideal of 'helping people to help themselves'.

The scope of social work intervention is extremely wide, ranging from the remedial to the developmental, and even the transcendental. We can conceptualise it as a four-level model, which is summarised in Table 5.1.

Table 5.1 Scope of social work intervention

Scope of intervention	Key intervention strategy	Social workers' primary roles
4. Holistic well-being	■ Responding to clients as an integrated whole ■ Achieving body-mind-spirit harmony ■ The SMART principle 　■ Strength-focused 　■ Meaning reconstruction 　■ Affirmation of self 　■ Resilience training 　■ Transformation	Coach and counsellor
3. Psychosocial distresses and pathology	■ Problem-solving and a task-centred approach ■ Psychosocial therapies 　■ Individual therapies 　■ Marital and family therapies 　■ Group therapies	Counsellor and therapist
2. Basic needs and physical illnesses	■ Mobilisation of resources 　■ Medical service 　■ Rehabilitation service 　■ Support for the underprivileged or disabled	Case and care manager
1. Personal safety	■ Crisis intervention ■ Exercising positional duties and statutory power in relation to: 　■ Child abuse 　■ Domestic violence 　■ People with mental disorders in an unstable mental condition 　■ Negligence in caring for people with mental incapacitation 　■ Victims of crime/violence	Official agent in implementation of welfare legislation

1. *Personal safety:* in cases where personal safety is under imminent threat, the primary objective of intervention is to ensure safety. A social worker's most prominent role is as an official agent who performs duties in line with their position and, if necessary, exercises the relevant statutory power. Common examples of such case scenarios are child abuse, domestic violence, dealing with people with mental disorders in an unstable mental condition and negligence in caring for people with mental incapacitation. Crisis intervention skills are often necessary in these situations.

2. *Basic needs and physical illnesses:* when basic needs are unmet and physical illnesses untreated, the primary objective of intervention is to ensure that the necessary resources are mobilised to address those needs. These resources can include medical services, rehabilitation services and other tangible support. A

social worker's most prominent role in such cases is that of case and care manager. Competence in case management is required in such situations.

3. *Psychosocial distresses and pathology:* in cases where individuals or families are experiencing distress, the primary objective of intervention is one of problem-solving and, if appropriate, treatment of the underlying psychosocial pathology. A social worker's most prominent role in such cases is that of counsellor and therapist. Competence in problem-solving training, task-centred approaches and various counselling and psychotherapy approaches is required.

4. *Holistic well-being:* many social workers may see this term as being non-specific. 'Holistic' refers to the integration of the whole in terms of the physical (body), the cognitive and emotional (mind) and peace of mind and life meaning (spirit). 'Well-being' refers to a positive state and growth, rather than pathological problems. The focus of intervention at this level is on strengths rather than problems, and on the whole person rather than a narrow interpretation of cognition or behaviour. The primary objective is to promote growth and transformation through achieving body-mind-spirit harmony. A social worker's most prominent role here is as a coach and counsellor.

Most social work textbooks cover levels 1 to 3 very well, but few of them provide information about specific intervention at level 4. Since one of the themes of this book is 'transforming practice', this chapter will focus primarily on intervention at level 4. In particular, we introduce the body-mind-spirit approach to therapy (Chan et al., 2001b). First, however, we briefly focus on levels 1 to 3.

Many social workers work under immense pressure and spend most of their time struggling with the problems of their clients at levels 1 and 2. Some more fortunate individuals can also afford to play a role at level 3. Level 4 is often regarded as something too impractical, idealistic and remote. Such a concept is incorrect. Strength and transformation-oriented intervention can speed up the recovery process and shorten the entanglement in problem-focused interventions. As is shown in the following sections, it is not as difficult as it seems to be, and can be incorporated into the intervention process early on.

Intervention is about inducing change in the client. Change can involve the reduction or extinction of the negative or the increase or synthesis of the positive. Research and clinical experience suggest that the former is far more difficult to achieve than the latter. It is easy to understand why. The negative factors, including emotional, behavioural or cognitive reactions, have usually been in existence for years and have become a habit of the client and a part of their whole system. Taking away the negatives will trigger homeostatic forces to restore the old pattern. By contrast, inducing positives is often rewarding, self-reinforcing and reinforced by the system. In return, in making positive changes, clients will gain more capacity to cope or live with the negatives. Therefore, adding level 4 intervention at an early stage can help to free social workers from the entanglement of intervention at levels 1 to 3.

Responding to clients as an integrated whole – body-mind-spirit interconnectedness

Mainstream psychotherapy focuses on the psychosocial domain, on emotions, behaviour, cognition and interpersonal relationships. As influenced by the evidence-based movement of conventional medicine, evidence-based practice is now a widely recognised goal in mainstream psychotherapy. The values of reductionism and objectivity are shared by more and more therapists. Many interventions are narrowly focused on a particular aspect of the client. Despite obtaining evidence of the efficacy of a measure in a controlled experimental situation, knowledge of its general application in a real clinical situation is often scant. A common fault in social work intervention is that of reductionism and a compartmentalised view of the total well-being of individuals and groups. Such an approach fails to address the multidimensional and interconnected nature of the problems, or bring about meaningful benefits to the clients' lives.

Traditionally social workers are shy of working in the bodily and spiritual domains. However, there is growing evidence that the body, mind and spirit are interconnected. This evidence includes research findings in diverse areas such as biofeedback, psychoneuroimmunology (Ader et al., 1991), holistic body work such as tai chi (Cheng and Macfarlane, 2001) and yoga (Panjwani et al., 2000; Manocha et al., 2002), mindfulness training (Baer, 2003; Kabat-Zinn, 2003) and spirituality in clinical care (Culliford, 2002). There is a strong indication that social workers should incorporate bodily and spiritual dimensions in their interventions so that they may respond to their clients in an integrated way.

Inspired by the conceptual framework of traditional Chinese medicine, Chan (2001) developed the Eastern body-mind-spirit approach, which aims at fostering a harmonious dynamic equilibrium within clients, and between clients and their social and natural environment. This approach has been applied to various target groups such as cancer patients, infertile couples, divorced women and adolescents. Systematic outcome studies were conducted for the approach, and evidence of its efficacy and its potential for generalisation are growing (Chan et al., 2000; Chan et al., 2001a; Ho and Chan, 2002).

The bodily processes that are highlighted in this model are not necessarily very complicated. Inspired by traditional Chinese holistic health practices, Chan (2001) developed one-second techniques that are simple to learn for counsellors and easy to follow for clients. Dialogue Box 5.1 provides some examples of these interesting techniques. By working with the body, the client can develop a sense of control because they are doing something to help themselves physically and emotionally. The mood changes as the clients focus on the physical movements and massage. Tai chi and qigong practice can also be used as a psychological distraction for clients who are troubled by an obsessive indulgence in pain.

DIALOGUE BOX 5.1: ONE-SECOND TECHNIQUES

Techniques of the hands

Health is in our hands. According to Chinese medicine, all the twelve meridians pass through the hands, feet and ears. Massage of the hands, feet and ears can activate our self-healing capacity.

1. *Palm rubbing:* with palms facing one another, fingers to fingers, palm to palm, rub the palms and fingers hard until they are warm. With palms slightly cupping and palms facing each other about six to eight inches apart, close your eyes and feel the tingling *qi* (invisible energy that circulates around our body through the meridians) sensation between the palms.

2. *Healing hands:* rub the hands until they are warm, then place the hands over the body parts that feel pain or discomfort. Pass the heat and healing energies of the hands onto the part of the body that needs nurture and love. Our hands have healing abilities which we do not utilise effectively. Put the hands on the abdomen when going to bed, imagining calming and soothing energies going into the body and go to sleep with such comforting energies.

3. *Clapping qigong:* for people who are prepared to work much harder on their hands, the clapping qigong is the simple single technique that one can try. With fingers and palms facing each other, hold the fingers upward with palms in front of the chest like hands folded in prayer. Open the palms to shoulder width and make loud forceful claps. The hands should feel the pain and may look blue for the first two weeks of practice. Do this for five minutes, three times a day for effective results. For people with acute grief or extreme anger, do it for half an hour twice every day.

4. *Open and close fingers:* put both hands on both sides of the body forming a straight line with the shoulders. With some force, stretch all the fingers out and fold them back into a fist, then stretch out again. Imagine that there is dirt on the tips of your nails, and while stretching your fingers, try to discard the dirt. Do this fifty times twice a day.

5. *Roll the wrists with hands like a lotus flower:* there are acupuncture points along the wrist which can be calming and stabilise heartbeat. Roll the wrists in big circles so as to stimulate the acupuncture points. Do the rolling of the wrists fifty times twice a day.

There are also techniques of the ears, eyes, mouth and feet in Chan's book.

Source: Chan, C. L. W. (2001) *An Eastern Body-Mind-Spirit Approach – A Training Manual with One-second Techniques.* Hong Kong: Department of Social Work and Social Administration, University of Hong Kong

---

Similarly, enquiring into the spiritual domain does not require a social worker to have had intensive training in a monastery deep in the mountains for decades. As spirituality is a natural part of every person, reflection on and sharing of spiritual issues should not be too alien to social workers or their clients. Reflections on growth through pain, as well as the search for a meaning of life are core spirituality interventions.

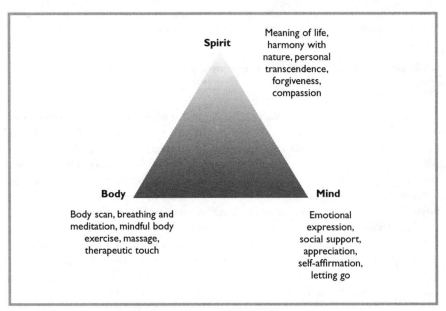

Figure 5.1 Body-mind-spirit transformation

In the following sections, the body-mind-spirit approach will be introduced in more detail. The essence of the model is represented in Figure 5.1.

The body-mind-spirit approach in therapy

Basic assumptions and therapeutic goals

Inspired by traditional Chinese medicine and philosophies, the model has a number of basic assumptions:

1. *Everything is connected:* human existence is a manifestation of physical, psychological and spiritual being. The different domains are interconnected and come together to form a whole. Human existence is also connected with the bigger world, in both the social and natural environments.

2. *Life is the eternal dance of yin and yang.* Life is ever-changing, and the interflow of energy maintains a harmonious dynamic equilibrium. The disruption of such harmony is the cause of life problems.

3. *Healing comes from within:* therapy aims to ignite the client's innate healing power that will bring them back to a state of balance. Intervention looks for strength rather than pathology.

4. *Restoring harmony* not only cures illness and resolves problems, it also opens up opportunities for growth and transformation.

While most existing psychotherapy interventions are problem-focused, the future of social work should be strength-focused and growth-oriented. It should go beyond coping and symptom reduction and aim for transcendence to a higher level of connectedness within the self, with others and with the universe.

Body processes and emotional healing

Body scan

The healing process can start with getting in touch with the body and connecting it with the emotions. Body scanning is a useful technique. In a relaxed and mindful state, clients are instructed to use mental imagery to scan through their whole body to check if any part is experiencing pain or discomfort. They are then encouraged to talk about the physical pain and discomfort, and explore the relationship with their emotions. The process enhances clients' awareness of their physical discomfort and emotions, and the connection between them.

Unlike Western medicine, Chinese medicine does not classify emotions as good (for example happiness) or bad (for example sadness): it sees all emotions as natural and necessary. Adopting a systemic perspective, Chinese medicine regards health as a state of harmonious dynamic equilibrium among the different emotions, maintained by the facilitative and repressive forces between the emotions. Through the meridians, the emotions and different systems of the body are connected into an integrated whole, but both an excess and a lack of certain emotions will upset the balance, and hence affect health. For example, excessive anger and fear damages the bodily functions and general health. A fully healthy person should be able to experience their emotions fully.

This systemic perspective on emotions is a reflection of the deep influence of the Yin-Yang Theory and the Five Elements Theory on Chinese medicine. Dialogue Boxes 5.2 and 5.3 give a brief account of these theories of ancient China.

DIALOGUE BOX 5.2: THE YIN-YANG THEORY

The Yin-Yang Theory and the Five Elements Theory were first described in the ancient book *Yi Jing* (also known as *I-Ching*, the *Book of Changes*, written around 7 BC) and had great influence in the conceptualisation of the original theories of Chinese medicine. Both theories propose a universal model to understand the pattern of change of all things in the world, from the microscopic to celestial phenomena. Firstly, they propose that all things in the world can be classified by broad categorical systems – the Ying-Yang System or the Five Elements System. Secondly, they propose that there is a universal pattern of interaction and change among these broad categories. Thirdly, by applying the knowledge of the universal model, one can understand the pattern of interaction and change between anything: for example, the relationships between the different bodily organs.

Yin and yang are opposites and are a mutually facilitating, but also a mutually repressing pair. Yin signifies substance, stillness, storage, darkness and softness. Yang signifies energy, movement, transporting, brightness and hardness. Examples of such yin-yang pairs are earth and sky, day and night, moon and sun, winter and summer,

DIALOGUE BOX 5.2: THE YIN-YANG THEORY cont'd

woman and man, and so on. The Yin-Yang Theory proposes a universal model depicting the pattern of interaction and change within a yin-yang pair. Some core relationships are as follows:

1 Yin and yang are mutually facilitating as well as mutually repressing. These two opposite forces together maintain an equilibrium.

2 Yin and yang are mutually dependent. They cannot flourish on their own.

3 Yin and yang are relative but not absolute concepts. For example, among a group of yin subjects, there can be subjects that are relatively yang, as well as subjects that are extremely yin.

4 At either extreme of yin or yang there can be sudden qualitative change, that is extreme yin changes to yang, or extreme yang changes to yin.

Yin and yang working in a harmonious dynamic equilibrium are considered to be fundamental to good health.

This classic yin-yang logo shows the mutually embedded nature, dynamic interflow and dual metamorphosis of yin and yang.

DIALOGUE BOX 5.3: THE FIVE ELEMENTS THEORY

The Five Elements Theory proposes the classification of everything into five broad categories: wood, fire, earth, metal and water. Each category is representative of a cluster of characteristics. For example, wood stands for growth, blossom, stretching and decongestion. Two normal forces – the facilitating force and the repressing force – work on each other among the elements. Wood facilitates fire, fire facilitates earth, earth facilitates metal, metal facilitates water and water facilitates wood. Meanwhile, wood represses earth, fire represses metal, earth represses water, metal represses wood and water represses fire. Each pair of forces working together maintains the dynamic equilibrium among the five elements, and prevents any element from becoming 'hypo' or 'hyper'. Such a state of equilibrium is considered to be essential for good health.

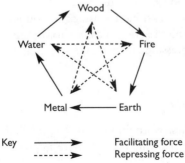

Inspired by the conceptual framework of these ancient theories, a social worker in the role of therapist may stimulate clients to explore their own body-emotion connections.

Breath is life

Breathing can be used as a powerful tool to bring stability to the body and mind. Mindful breathing helps us get in touch with our deep emotions, whether they be feelings of pain, fear, anger, joy or contentment. In deep breathing meditation, a person moves to a state of total concentration and consciousness. People in a state of supreme consciousness are able to connect with their internal self – body, mind and spirit – and the outer world – the social and natural environment.

During breathing meditation practice, a therapist may verbally guide clients to achieve harmony within themselves and with the external world. Values such as appreciation, self-affirmation, forgiveness and compassion can be cultivated in clients during this practice.

Breathing exercises do not necessarily have to be practised while the body is still, but can be practised along with movement and mental imagery. Tai chi, qigong and yoga are good examples of this type of body-mind-spirit exercise. Through mindful movement and breathing, clients get in touch with their true total being and develop an appreciation of themselves and their environment. Simplified tai chi, qigong and yoga are practical options for use in counselling work. If these exercises are practised in a group, they can provide the additional benefits of social support.

Acupressure and light massage

Acupuncture and *tuina* (therapeutic massage) were originally conceived based on the meridian theory of Chinese medicine. They aim to manipulate the flow of *qi* in the meridian system so as to restore the state of healthy balance. There is evidence that acupuncture and *tuina* are effective for a number of conditions such as insomnia, depression, migraine, pains and perimenstrual problems. For safety reasons, acupuncture and *tuina* need to be administered by qualified personnel. For social work intervention, acupressure and light massage are more appropriate alternatives. Chan (2001) simplified these practices into one-second techniques. Mastery of these techniques can help clients to regain a sense of control over both the body and the mind.

Prescribing acupressure and light massage to couples or families can help to enhance marital and family relationships, as massaging one another is a way of communicating and expressing concern and love. Sometimes it can work quicker and better than words.

The power of the mind

The corresponding Chinese word for mind is *Xin*, which literally means 'the heart'. We believe that the power of the heart is more important and ultimately greater than the power of the brain. When the heart is 'dead', a person cannot be truly living. Effective intervention must include the rekindling of the heart as a goal.

As such, the concept of mind (*Xin*) is a complex construct that encompasses willpower, vision, hope, emotion, human sensitivity, passion, cognition, or the whole of humanity in one word. Techniques for mobilising the power of the mind include mindfulness practices, meditation, letting go, forgiveness, compassion and loving kindness. The process of transformation in our body-mind-spirit model involves five 'A's – three of them related to the mind and two related to the spirit:

- Acknowledge vulnerability
- Accept adversity and the unpredictability of life
- Activate self-healing capacity
- Affirmation
- Appreciation

Acknowledge vulnerability: influenced by Buddhist and Christian teaching, we help clients to normalise suffering as part of life. By acknowledging our own vulnerability, we can face pain and loss with tranquillity. Trauma and loss can result in ultimate growth.

Accept adversity and the unpredictability of life: acceptance is different from resignation. Resignation represents the assumption of the role of victim, but acceptance is the peaceful understanding of the reality of a situation. 'Acceptance is not a passive surrendering, but rather an act of taking responsibility; it is not blaming oneself for having the disease, but working energetically to restore one's system to balance.' (Abramson, 2003: 20). Acceptance means fully embracing whatever is in the present. The yin-yang metaphor inspires us to understand that gains and losses are embedded in each other. People who embrace loss are more ready to appreciate gain.

Activate one's self-healing capacity: by letting go of intense emotional attachment, we can free our energy for self-healing. Buddhism teaches people not to cling to things or persons. Frustrations can be caused by unmet expectations. Letting go and genuine forgiveness are the ultimate solutions to our emotional problems. In our experience of working with Chinese cancer patients, bereaved widows and divorced women, we have found that clients' self-healing power is largely ignited from their determination to let go of the victim role and maximise their own healing capacity. We invite our clients to read aloud affirmation statements like 'I am determined to let go of the past and to live a new, independent life', and 'I choose to love myself and be the master of my own life'. If an individual can move through and beyond illness patterns and discover the inner self, they can regain a state of well-being (Wong and Mckeen, 1998).

Affirming spirituality and a new appreciation of life

The remaining two As are *affirmation* and *appreciation*: affirming the meaning of life and a renewed appreciation of life through suffering help recreate the once-disrupted harmony of body, mind and spirit. Traumatic events may shatter a person's world-view and self-identity (Fife, 1994; Janoff-Bulman and Berg, 1998). The cognitive reappraisal of a traumatic event, the search for meaning and the integration of the experience into one's life helps people to adapt to the loss brought about by the event (Taylor, 1983; Lazarus and Folkman, 1984; Fife, 1994; Janoff-Bulman and Berg, 1998). The reconstruction of meaning after loss involves the process of 'sense making', 'benefit finding' and 'identity reconstruction' (Davies et al., 1998; Neimeyer, 2000, 2002). We engage clients in a process of restorying their lives to develop a more coherent narrative of their life experiences. We help them to discover the positive in suffering. The body-mind-spirit model uses the concepts of impermanence and the unpredictability of life from Buddhism and Daoism to help patients to reconstruct their experience of illness or loss and make sense of their misery. Our recent study of cancer survivors confirms our belief that life affirmation (for example 'I can face life challenges with a peaceful mind') and appreciation of life (for example 'I enjoy life every day') are two important factors constituting spirituality (Chan et al., 2004).

While Western forms of therapy largely work to help patients better master, control and overcome their problems, Buddhist teaching encourages the individual to detach and let go so that they can flow with the here-and-now, the 'moment-by-moment experience', instead of being controlled by, or preoccupied with, desire. Paradoxically, one gains control by letting go of control. By practising emotional detachment and letting go, people find it easier to forgive. Forgiveness is the ultimate solution to emotional disharmony.

The SMART principle

The body-mind-spirit model is a multidimensional and holistic approach that can be used to guide social work intervention. Its uniqueness can be summarised by the SMART principle. The SMART principle is consistent with the theoretical shift from psychosocial pathology to positive psychology and empowerment interventions. The five SMART components are as follows:

- **Strength focused**

- **Meaning reconstruction**

- **Affirmative and Appreciative**

- **Resilience**

- **Transformation**

- *Strength focused:* intervention should focus on identifying, assuring and enhancing the strength of the clients. By actively identifying strength, a social worker can truly respect the healing capacity of their clients.

- *Meaning reconstruction:* the therapist may help their clients to emerge from the victim role, and obtain meaning from and transcend the suffering. The ability to find meaning in suffering can be a motivating force for perseverance and the generation of healing strength.

- *Affirmative and appreciative:* the therapist helps the client to affirm and appreciate themselves as well as the external world of both their social and natural environments. The process of downward comparison by the clients can also help them to mobilise energy to help other people.

- *Resilience:* this is not only about coping ability, but also about the ability to acknowledge vulnerability, accept adversity and unpredictability, recognise impermanence and let go.

- *Transformation:* this is a state of body-mind-spirit harmony that enables a person to live fully and completely. With transformation, individuals can develop a personal capacity of self-sufficiency in life and are able to formulate selfless goals to help other people and collectively benefit society.

Responding to new political, economic and social trends

The discussion so far has focused on individual and group interventions. Since individuals and families do not exist in isolation, social workers also need to consider the wider environment. Social workers need to be able to respond at both the micro- and macro-levels, and should take into account factors in the wider environment when performing individual and group interventions. In response to the key issues in the wider environment, they should also intervene at community level to help create a better world for all. Among major political, economic and social trends that are having a far-reaching impact at all levels of society are globalisation, information technology and terrorism.

Globalisation

Globalisation is speeding up due to advances in information technology and logistic systems, as well as the setting up of various regional and international trade organisations, such as the WTO and the EU. Globalisation enhances productivity and economic growth and encourages the interflow of money, resources and people. However, it also upsets the existing regional and international equilibrium, causes distress in the underprivileged, activates fierce competition and heightens tensions among different interest groups. The process of reaching a new point of equilibrium will be lengthy and, for some, even painful.

Social workers need to recognise that change is inevitable. To function effectively in the context of globalisation, social workers themselves need to develop an international vision, as well as competence in working in a multicultural environment. At the micro-level, social workers should provide support to the underprivileged so that they are able to adapt to changes in the wider environment. There are various ways in which this can be achieved – case and groupwork, retraining programmes, vocational support services, and so on. At the macro-level, social workers need to uphold the basic values of social work and initiate community work projects that advocate justice, equality, the protection of human rights and the promotion of family values.

The promotion of harmony is a key concept and should be striven for at all levels as follows:

1. *The pursuit of productivity versus the preservation of individual and family wellness:* productivity gained at the expense of individual and family wellness is not sustainable. For instance, the extremely low fertility rate in many economically developed cities is partly due to a lack of family-friendly policies.

2. *The pursuit of economic growth versus the preservation of nature:* sustainable economic planning must include reasonable policies for environmental protection to ensure that future generations will have access to fresh air, clean water and beautiful countryside.

3. *The pursuit of material comfort versus the preservation of spirituality:* quality of life does not necessarily come with an increase in material comfort. On the contrary, indulgence in the material world can lead to a loss of spirituality. Advocacy for the pursuit of spirituality is particularly relevant in highly developed cities.

Information technology

Organisations employing social workers, as well as those with which social workers engage, are subject to widespread major change as a consequence of the introduction of information technology (IT). Information technology not only transmits information, it also transmits values, culture, affection and trauma. To some extent, it is a virtual reality, as well as being a part of our reality. It changes many aspects of human life, including how social workers work.

Taking the New York 9/11 incident as an example, we can see that the ripple of trauma was transmitted widely and quickly in a way that was unimaginable in the past. Hundreds of millions of people around the world were shocked and people thousands miles away from the scene were emotionally affected. In the past, debriefing for such disasters was conducted in small groups (Mitchell and Everly, 2000), but such an approach is inadequate in the IT era. Social workers need to be innovative in this area to have a meaningful impact on society. Instead of focusing on symptomatology and the prevention of post-traumatic stress disorder, we may focus on post-traumatic growth. Other than conducting small debriefing groups, we may also run mass functions and make use of the media and the internet. The focus should be on meaning reconstruction, that is, deriving new meaningful purposes for society as a whole.

Terrorism and anti-terrorism

The global impact of terrorist incidents throughout the world has implications for social workers. Terrorism and anti-terrorism are forces that repress and facilitate each other at the same time. If history is predictive of the future, then this tragic cycle will linger for a long period of time. Moreover, the confrontation is not restricted to the national level. It can trickle down to the community, neighbourhood, family and individual levels. However, it can also be transformed into affirmative action and anti-discriminatory practice.

Social workers may not be able to contribute much to the resolution of international conflicts. However, social workers do have an important role to play in mediating conflict at lower levels – between individuals, families, neighbourhoods and communities. The key to successful mediation is to encourage the letting go of rigid positions and promote genuine understanding and respect. A mastery of mediation techniques is necessary in handling these situations.

In this area, social workers also have an important role to play in preventing and rectifying discriminatory practice. This can be achieved through advocacy, mass education and community intervention.

Evidence-based practice and the future of social work intervention models

In the nineteenth century, a small group of physicians in France started advocating evidence-based medicine (EBM). This started the EBM movement, which gradually picked up momentum and eventually had a far-reaching impact. After nearly two hundred years of steady development, EBM has now firmly established itself as the gold standard in medicine. This standard has been imposed, implicitly and explicitly, on professions and disciplines that interact with and complement medical science. To be respected in a healthcare setting, most disciplines have adopted similar standards and have promoted evidence-based practice (EBP), some examples being nursing, physiotherapy, occupational therapy, radiotherapy and clinical psychology. EBP has already become a gold standard in the health and social services. This is leading to a higher degree of merging roles among the caring professions. Since resources are always limited, all disciplines are under pressure to justify what they are doing. This can lead to crisis, but also to opportunity. To survive and grow from these challenges, the caring professions need to self-reflect and change.

To adopt EBP in social work intervention, social workers need to master practice research skills, and continuously keep up to date with the latest developments in evidence-based interventions, regardless of whether they originate from within social work or another discipline. As roles within the caring professions merge, social workers can maintain role differentiation by truly asserting basic social work values and objectives. At the same time, social workers need to maintain a critical attitude towards EBP (see Chapters 16 and 20 for further discussion of this).

CONCLUSION

All too often social work intervention is restricted to dealing with tackling issues of protection and personal safety, basic physical or emotional needs, or problems perceived as pathological. This chapter has proposed a much broader and holistic approach, based on a four-level SMART model of the scope of social work intervention.

This expands the conventional scope model to cover the holistic treatment of clients. The body-mind-spirit approach facilitates growth and aims to foster a harmonious equilibrium within clients, and between clients and their social and natural environment. The model illustrated in this chapter significantly enhances the conceptual coherence and completeness of social work intervention. We have seen how a strength-oriented holistic approach can speed up recovery and help to shorten the entanglement in problem-focused intervention.

FURTHER READING

Abramson, R.J. (2003) 'The unity of mind, body, and spirit: A five-element view of cancer', *Advances in Mind-Body Medicine* 19(2): 20–1.

Chan, C.L.W. (2001) *An Eastern Body-Mind-Spirit Approach – A Training Manual with One-second Techniques* (Hong Kong: Department of Social Work and Social Administration, University of Hong Kong).

Chan, C.L.W., Ho, P.S.Y. and Chow, E. (2001) 'A body-mind-spirit model in health: an Eastern approach', *Social Work in Health Care* 34(3/4): 261–82.

Engel, G.L. (1977) 'The need for a new medical model: a challenge for biomedicine', *Science* 196(4286): 129–36.

Ng, S.M., Cheung, K.Y.R. and Chou, K.L. (2004) Application of Chinese medicine yangsheng in community health service. Paper presented at the Fourth International Conference on Social Work in Health and Mental Health, 23–27 May, 2004, Quebec City.

CHAPTER

Review

6

Lorna Bell

Introduction

Reviewing often is presented as the terminal stage of the fourfold processes of assessment, planning, intervention and review, without recognising its embeddedness throughout practice. This chapter illustrates the crucial importance of reviewing and shows how the practitioner needs to move back and forth between reviewing and other activities, before, during and after the practice takes place.

CASE EXAMPLE

Sam, aged 4, lived with his mother, Judy Pitt, aged 27. She is a single parent and suffers from depression and takes non-prescription drugs. Sam was removed from the care of Judy a year ago after he had been found in the house alone on four separate occasions. Following an assessment by a social worker, Carol Forbes, and discussion at a child protection case conference, it was decided that he was a child at risk of significant harm and as Judy's family have rejected her and her son, he was placed in foster care. The intention was to rehabilitate Sam with Judy and she was encouraged to spend time with him and attend parenting classes. Judy was also receiving help from the Community Mental Health Team (CMHT), whose members were concerned about her depression and use of drugs.

➡

> ### CASE EXAMPLE cont'd
>
> After six months, it was noted that Judy had not been attending classes, visited Sam sporadically and did not engage with him when she did visit. Sam was getting increasingly upset by the visits. An interim care order was applied for and granted and Judy and Sam were provided with intensive family support. However, Judy has continued to show little interest in Sam and Carol is now considering placing Sam for adoption.

Reviewing before, during and after

The aim of reviewing is to ensure that practice is effective and efficient. Practitioners should be involved in reviewing before, during and after their work with service users. Before the process of assessment, planning, intervention and review begins, the practitioner gathers evidence about the efficacy of potential interventions so that he or she can negotiate the implementation of the most effective one(s) with the service user. This can be described as 'evidence-based practice'. During and after the work, the practitioner gathers evidence about the intervention that he or she is implementing, or has implemented, to assess its effectiveness. This can be described as 'reflective' or 'reflexive practice'.

Reviewing existing evidence

According to Hamer and Collinson (1999: 6):

> Evidence-based practice is about finding, appraising and applying scientific evidence to the treatment and management of healthcare. Its ultimate goal is to support practitioners in their decision-making in order to eliminate the use of ineffective, inappropriate, too expensive and potentially dangerous practices.

In other words, when the practitioner is about to begin work with a service user, he or she should start by searching for evidence about what has been shown to work and what has been shown not to work in similar situations. The practitioner should then critically appraise the evidence to determine what intervention is most likely to be effective and then negotiate the implementation of this with the service user. Thus, the decision to place Sam for adoption might be based on research that suggests that the younger a child is placed for adoption, the more successful that adoption is likely to be (Department of Health, 1999a).

There are a number of problems with evidence-based practice (see Calder and Hackett: 2003). One is concerned with the nature of evidence. Most social work practitioners are aware that academics and researchers have been engaged in a long-established debate about the relative merits of qualitative and quantitative methods of inquiry and the quality of the evidence generated by such methods and may well feel ill-equipped to engage with the controversy in order to appraise evidence from studies about an intervention. In Hughes et al.'s (2000: 50) study, the difficulty of making use of research when presented with contradictory findings was frequently cited by practitioners: 'There's tons of research published nowadays. Masses and masses of it and quite a lot of it conflicts … in the sense that it is quite difficult to use it as a signpost for practice'. Indeed MacDonald (2000: 121) asserts that 'practitioners are not equipped by qualifying and post-qualifying training to exercise the discrimination required to identify, critically appraise, and use research or syntheses of research'.

More comprehensive analyses of the debate can be found in Creswell (1994) and Oakley and Roberts (1996) but in essence it is concerned with conflicting views about the purpose of research, how data should be collected and how potential bias should be viewed.

For the quantitative researcher, the research process starts with theory from which the researcher develops hypotheses which are then tested. This testing involves collecting facts to confirm or disprove the hypotheses. The quantitative researcher assumes that there is an objective reality that can be uncovered by applying the same logic of inquiry to social science as found in the natural sciences. By following rational methods of empirical inquiry, the social researcher will find regularities and relationships and discover the cause of social phenomena. For example, a study by Isaac et al. (1986) found parental mental illness to be an important cause of children entering the care system and an important contributor to some children remaining in care for long periods. Thus truth can be established by the rigorous and systematic application of scientific investigation. The quantitative researcher makes every effort to reduce bias in research by maintaining a distance between the researcher and the researched, using methods such as surveys and experiments and employing systematic sampling techniques. Quantitative research is described as 'positivist, empiricist and hypothetic-deductive' (Clarke, 1999: 38).

The qualitative researcher does not begin with theory but with the collection of data. From the analysis of the data, broad generalisations about the phenomena being studied are developed. The aim is not to test a hypothesis but to gain understanding and insight and in order to do this the researcher gets close to the data to understand the actor's point of view and uses methods such as observation and in-depth interviews. For the qualitative researcher, there is no single truth because individuals and groups construct their own versions of reality and give their own meaning to phenomena. Thus, the task of the researcher is to ensure that the different versions of reality are accurately recorded and reported as, for example, in the personal accounts from adults who grew up with a mentally ill parent (Marlowe, 1996). Qualitative research is described as 'natural-istic, holistic, inductive, humanistic and interpretive' (Clarke, 1999: 38).

The same debate is reflected in the evaluation of practice, with, on the one hand, Hadorn et al. (1996) suggesting that there is a hierarchy of evidence, with systematic reviews being of most value and personal experience being of least value, and MacDonald (2000) regretting that the more scientific evidence that underpins evidence-based healthcare is not evident in social care. On the other hand, Everitt and Hardiker (1996) express their concerns about the emphasis on randomised controlled trials as the gold standard of research, while research designs most frequently used in social care, such as service user opinion studies, are seen as having limited value.

This often unhelpfully polarised debate can make it difficult for practitioners to engage in the critical appraisal of evidence.

Reviewing practice

The second type of review is conducted by the practitioner either during or at the end of his or her work with the service user. For this review, the practitioner 'researches' or 'evaluates' the way in which he or she had done the work and/or the effect that the work is having or has had on the service user. This requires:

> the application of a common core of research skills: in formulating research questions or hypotheses, in collecting or utilising data and analysing it in ways which address the questions, in interpreting the findings, and in communicating the results in writing or orally. (Fuller and Petch, 1995: 4)

It then involves the practitioner using the information he or she has gained from the research to inform his or her practice. The importance of this is highlighted by Laing (1969:4) who argues that:

> without time for critical reflection we may become dogmatic in theory and keep repeating ourselves in practice. We may even keep repeating a story about what we repetitiously do which does not even match what we do; especially if we do not have sufficient time to scrutinise what we are actually doing.

Combining evidence-based practice and reflection demonstrates how reviewing research before intervening and reflecting during and after intervening informs practice. (see Figure 6.1).

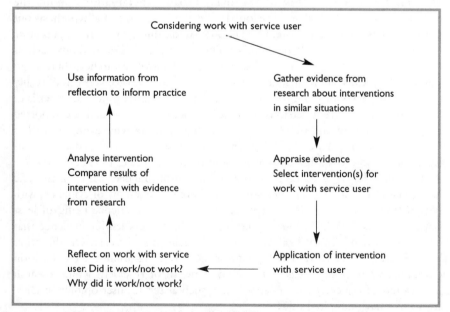

Figure 6.1 Combining evidence-based and reflective practice

Using research in practice

Despite the importance of research for practice, social workers often appear reluctant to use it prospectively or retrospectively to inform their practice. As noted earlier, this may be because they are made to feel confused and uncertain by the debate about methodology or they are sceptical about the process of research and the findings that emerge from it – seeing research as ineffectual, remote from the real world, exploitative of service users and politically naive. Or it may be because they feel daunted by research, intimidated by the language typically used by researchers and deskilled by the prospect of engaging in it. In their study examining the connections between research evidence and social care practice, Hughes et al. (2000) argue that the potential users of research were put off if:

■ The style of the research was not adapted to the audience

■ The report was overly long

■ The policy and operational implications were not made clear

■ It was not seen as immediately relevant to practice

■ The study produced inconclusive or conflicting evidence.

So, given the importance of evidence-based practice, how can practitioners be encouraged to embrace it more wholeheartedly?

MacDonald (2000), Hughes et al. (2000) and Sheldon and Chivers (2000) stress the importance of improving training and staff development in critical appraisal skills and understanding research on both basic and advanced courses. Where such training has been provided, such as the practitioner research programme at Stirling University (Fuller and Petch, 1995) and the programmes at the Centre for Evidence-based Social Services at Exeter University (MacDonald, 2000), the outcomes appear to be positive. Critical thinking and research-mindedness are likely to blossom where there are organisational cultures that support and encourage practitioners and managers to use and engage in research.

Hughes et al. also list practitioner-friendly strategies that research producers might adopt to make research more palatable, such as providing accessible summaries of research, like the Joseph Rowntree's *Findings*, National Children's Bureau's *Highlights*, Barnardo's *What Works* and the Department of Health's *Messages from Research*, using a combination of dissemination methods, such as websites, the media, seminars and targeted mailing and using language and a style of presentation which engages interest.

Reasons for reviewing

There are three main reasons why is it important for practitioners to review evidence before deciding on an intervention and to review the intervention they have implemented. First, it is unethical to intervene in the lives of service users without seeking to gain an understanding of how an intervention might affect them and how an intervention has affected them and to share this understanding, where appropriate, with service users. At the very least both need to know that the intervention will not harm or has not harmed the service user, particularly as ethical codes of practice (going back as far as the Hippocratic oath) demand that professional practice should not be maleficent – it should do no harm. Section 5.1 of the General Social Care Council's (GSCC, 2002) code of practice requires that social care workers 'must not harm service users'. The potential for doing harm to Sam is real. Research by McCluskey (2000) suggests that the eventual outcomes for children in care, in terms of educational achievement, health, self-esteem, employment and so on are worse than those for other children, so Carol needs to monitor Sam's progress carefully to ensure that he is not being harmed. Social workers and service users also need to know about the beneficial effects of the intervention, particularly as GSCC s.1.3. expects workers to 'support service users' rights to make informed choices about the services they receive'. For example, Judy is given advice about her alcohol consumption and the relative merits of abstinence and reduction programmes. Reviewing the effectiveness of interventions demonstrates what harms and benefits are being or have been experienced by the service user.

For practitioners, review provides the opportunity to determine whether or not what they do is worthwhile. To assess this workers ask questions such as:

- Did I reach the best decision in determining the intervention? Was the decision evidence-based?

- What effect, if any, has the intervention had on the service user?

- Have I been intervening well, or well enough?

The answers to these questions provide valuable information about what works and why it works and what does not work and why it does not work. Thus, if the answers to these questions are positive, workers can demonstrate their effectiveness to themselves and others, which is particularly important in a climate in which the values of professional practice are continually being challenged. If the answers to these questions are ambivalent or negative, then workers can recognise why they have not been effective, can take remedial action and modify or change their practice to make it more effective.

Second, there are requirements for social care workers to review their work. For example, s.6 of the GSCC's code of practice states: 'As a social care worker, you must be accountable for the quality of your work and take responsibility for maintaining and improving your knowledge and skills.' Reviews are also required by legislative guidance. For example, the decisions made about Sam and Judy at the case conference must be reviewed 'within three months of the initial child protection conference, and further reviews should be held at intervals of not more than six months' (Department of Health, 1999d), and the care of Sam in the foster placement must be subject to a first review within 28 days of placement; a second review within three months of the first review and third and later reviews within six months of the previous review (Department of Health, 1991d). Guidance also makes it clear what should be reviewed: 'The purpose of the child protection review is to review the safety, health and development of the child against intended outcomes as set out in the child protection plan' (Department of Health, 1999d: 60).

Third, there are government pressures towards reviewing. Social work intervention, whether directly by the social worker or indirectly by the commissioning of services from others, involves spending public money, and government at both national and local levels has a duty to ensure that public money is being spent wisely. Thus, there has been an increasing emphasis on ensuring that all public services provide 'value for money' and this is policed through a range of agencies, including the Audit Commission, the Social Services Inspectorate and the National Care Standards Commission (brought together as the Commission for Social Care Inspection in 2004). Shaw (1996:81) notes that:

> Cost-effectiveness, joint objective setting, strengthened accountability of welfare professionals, managerial effectiveness, explicit standards, performance monitoring and customer involvement, choice and satisfaction are recurring themes in the pleas and provisions for quality in the personal social services.

Clear objectives, standards or criteria for services have been set against which the performance of the service provider can be judged and there are guidelines regarding the content and process of review. For example, in 1998, the government launched its three-year Quality Protects programme which aimed to provide effective protection, better quality care and improved life chances for children. The key elements of the initiative included new national government objectives (eleven in all) for children's services which set out clear outcomes for children and in some instances gave precise targets to be achieved. For example, Objective 1 is relevant to Sam as it requires the local authority:

> To ensure that children are securely attached to carers capable of providing safe and effective care for the duration of childhood [by, for example] supporting families to help children in need be as successful as possible in their lives [or] helping children who need them find secure homes with adoptive parents (Department of Health, 1999c: 1).

For all social services provision, the most significant assessment of performance was introduced in 2000 with the launch of Personal Social Services: Performance Assessment Framework (PSS: PAF) which aimed to ensure 'best value' – 'the duty to deliver services to clear standards covering both cost and quality, by the most effective, economic and efficient means available' (Department of Health, 2002b). As part of this initiative, 50 performance indicators were developed to provide a tool for managers and councillors to identify where they are performing well and where they should be focusing future efforts to improve performance. The indicators also provide a statistical overview of social services' performance, allowing comparison between councils and over time, and where central government feels that councils are not providing best value, then they have powers to intervene. Indicators against which Sam's progress might be measured would include 'A1 Stability of placements of children looked after', and 'C23 Adoptions of children'.

National Service Frameworks (NSFs) have also been developed since 1998 to set national standards and identify key interventions for an identified service or care group and thus raise standards in service provision. There are a number of current frameworks, for example frameworks for cancer, mental health, older people and children. In the NSF for Mental Health, standards have been set in five areas: mental health promotion; primary care and access to services; effective services for people with severe mental illness; caring about carers; and preventing suicide. As part of the promotion of better mental health within the locality, Judy is receiving help from the CMHT because research suggests that for people whose alcohol consumption exceeds recommended guidelines, brief primary care interventions, such as an assessment of alcohol intake and provision of advice, can help to reduce it (NHS Centre for Reviews and Dissemination, 1997).

These government initiatives might seem remote from individual practice and review but they are significant at an individual level because the objectives, indicators and targets provide a template against which the performance of an individual worker or a group can be measured, and the worker or group needs to review to understand why his, her or its performance has exceeded, reached or failed to reach the standard. If Sam has experienced more placements than other children, Carol needs to know why this is the case in order to reduce the number of placements that Sam has in the future. Furthermore, the data provided for and by government tends to be quantitative and describes 'how much' but does not provide much data that provides a context and explanation for the figures. Frontline workers are in an ideal position to collect this qualitative data.

Practitioners do not always experience these formal review processes positively. They are frequently seen as the blame culture or the suspicious organisation checking up on staff and attempting to 'find them out' – part of the 'checklist and truncheon' approach (Reid, 1988: 45). The evidence that they produce is seen as highly suspect because it is based on what happens during the review, not what happens in real life. For example, prior to the review, which is advertised in advance, managers ask practitioners not to work with service users but to ensure that their case files are up to date as the latter will be measured by the reviewers. Shaw (1996: 88) refers to this type of formal review as 'Evaluation with a big "E"' and he speculates that this strict management by effectiveness approach creates

> a self-defeating threat to the development of practitioners evaluating in practice competencies [and that] management by measurement risks producing a concentration on easily measurable aspects of practice; organisational behaviour will change in order to score well on measurable criteria; agency performance requirements will take precedence at the expense of the service user and the professional role of the social worker will be put at jeopardy by management by measurement.

For example, Carol was irritated because she struggled to complete the initial assessment within seven days, as specified in the *Framework for the Assessment of Children in Need and their Families* (Department of Health, 2000a) but her professional view was that, because of the complexity created by Judy's mental health and drug abuse and the involvement of a number of healthcare professionals, this was too short a period within which to complete a competent assessment. Nevertheless, she was encouraged to complete it within seven days because this is a measure used to assess the effectiveness of local authority childcare services (see SSI, 2002).

Social care workers are also suspicious about the interpretation of the evidence collected by 'evaluation with a big "E"' and the use that will be made of it. The Social Services Inspectorate Report (SSI, 2000) suggests that only 39 per cent of initial assessments are completed within seven days. Social workers may believe that this will be interpreted as evidence that they are not performing their tasks efficiently and their work will be policed even more rigorously. However, other interpretations might be that it is impossible to complete 'good' assessments within seven days and time limits should be increased or scrapped altogether, or that social workers' workloads are so large that they have not the time to complete the assessments and more staff should be employed to reduce workloads.

What to review

Although the review of practice comes after work has started with the service user, thinking about and planning the review must be included at the beginning, as at this early stage there needs to be clarity about what will be reviewed and how it will be reviewed. What will be reviewed is determined by setting objectives for the intervention against which the inputs, outputs and outcomes of the intervention can be assessed. As noted by Fook (2000: 165) in her discussion of evaluating social work interviews: 'An interview cannot be understood and therefore effectively evaluated without an appreciation of its function within a particular context'. The easiest objectives to be reviewed are those that are SMART – they are specific, measurable, achievable, relevant and time-limited (for SMART criteria that are set for the development of performance indicators in mental health, see Department of Health, 1999b: 97). For example, the work with Judy aimed at enabling her to provide for her son's needs. A SMART objective derived from this would be that she would visit Sam at the foster placement twice a week for six weeks and would spend no less than an hour playing with Sam on each visit. A number of questionnaires and scales have been developed for practitioners using *The Framework for the Assessment of Children in Need and their Families* (Department of Health, 2000a) so that practitioners can, for example, measure the performance of families at the beginning of an intervention and then measure the performance at the end and thus identify any change. In working with Judy, Carol might use the 'Parenting Daily Hassles' scale which aims to assess the frequency and intensity/impact of 20 experiences that can be a hassle for parents. The scale indicates whether the difficulties lie in the behaviour of the child or in the burden experienced by the parent in trying to meet the child's needs.

Some objectives, particularly those that focus on exploring what happened during an intervention, are much more difficult to specify and measure. For example, trying to measure how effectively Carol has worked in partnership with Judy.

Furthermore, setting objectives can be problematic as the various stakeholders involved in a social work intervention may have different views about what the objectives of the intervention are. For example, in Sam's case, some of the stakeholders are Sam himself, Judy, Carol, the foster parents, Judy's CMHT, the social services department and the Department of Health. In terms of objectives, Judy's main objective is to have Sam back at home with no more involvement from social services but this conflicts with social services' objective which is to be able to demonstrate that Sam is safe and his needs are being met. The conflicting objectives of parents and social services departments create tensions, particularly as the objectives of the most powerful, social services, are more likely to set the agenda than the objectives of parents, despite notions of working partnership. Efforts to redress this balance can be seen in the development of family group conferences (Marsh and Crow, 1998), in which professionals are excluded from the decision-making process and families determine the objectives against which outcomes can be measured (although where there are child protection concerns, the family's objectives require the approval of professionals).

Professionals can also have conflicting objectives. The objectives that Carol has are strongly influenced by her duty to act in the best interests of the child and she believes that, in this case, his interests may be best served by adoption. Although Judy's CMHT must also act in the best interests of the child, they are also influenced by the requirement, under the NSF, to 'strengthen individuals to enhance their psychological well-being' (Department of Health, 1999b: 15) and see Sam's rehabilitation with Judy as crucial in helping her to regain her self-esteem, confidence and motivation. Such conflicts between childcare and mental health professionals have been explored by Stanley and Penhale (1999: 34) who note that collaboration between mental health professionals and social workers was sometimes lacking and that might be due to 'the way in which the problems of mothers and their children are conceptualised by different services'.

Clearly, there are problems in reviewing and assessing the outcomes of interventions with service users if there are disagreements about the objectives. If the objectives are set by professionals and the outcomes are measured by professionals, the intervention may be seen as effective. However, the service users might see the intervention as ineffective because it was not what they wanted anyway. As a parent who had approached social services because of the behaviour of her son put it: 'We went to [family therapy] ... everything was directed at me. He was just drawing a picture. It was a waste of time. I had better things to do' (Department of Health, 2000b: 68).

Furthermore, there is a danger that the indicators used to assess the achievement of an objective may be used because they are measurable rather than because they truly reflect the underlying objective. Thus, measuring the amount of time Sam's mother plays with him does not provide a measure of the quality of that play. In their study of local authority indicators in relation to children looked after, Oliver et al. (2001) note that:

> Staff frequently challenged the extent to which selected performance indicators represent a suitable measure of good social work practice. For example, a good piece of social work practice, a baby moved from hospital at birth to a foster placement then on to her adoptive family, all within a year ... appeared as a negative statistic under the proxy measure of 'stability', that is, number of placements in a year.

How to review practice

In considering how to review practice, practitioners need to consider what it is that they want to find out and how they will find it out. Smith (1996) and the NSF for Mental Health (Department of Health, 1999b) suggest that there are three major areas that evaluators want to find out about:

1. Inputs, such as the resources that have been put into an intervention

2. Process, what happens during the work, what is the throughput?

3. Outcome, which includes output and the value of the output.

Examining inputs provides some information about the efficiency of the work and encourages a consideration of whether or not the outcome of the intervention was worth the cost of the input and whether or not there were more efficient ways of achieving the same output. There appears to be little evidence that, in their evaluations of their work, practitioners consider the cost of inputs (usually their time) against the value of the outcome, and the review by the Audit Commission (1994) noted that even health and social care organisations were not always aware of the costs of the services they were providing.

The second area for evaluation is concerned with the process of the intervention and seeks to discover what was done, why it was done and how it was done. For example, Lonergan (2000) provides a detailed description of his work with a young man who is moving from foster care to independent living. This type of evaluation is usually linked to a qualitative approach.

The third area for evaluation is the outcome which is made up of the output from an intervention, for example Sam's weight increasing since he went into foster care, and the value of that output, which, from the social worker's perspective, might be that this demonstrates that Sam's safety and welfare have been enhanced. This type of evaluation more usually adopts a quantitative approach. For example, MacDonald (1999) describes a randomised controlled trial that aimed to assess whether an intensive, natural parent-focused service would enhance placement outcomes for children.

The methods available to evaluate or review social work interventions range from carefully controlled experiments or surveys to single case studies or reflecting on practice (see Alston and Bowles, 1998). Information can be gathered through observations, questionnaires, interviews, discourse analysis and the analysis of documents.

Concerned with the lack of progress in relation to Judy, Carol decides to have a thorough one-off review of the case because although there have been regular formal 'reviews', these have not fully explored her work with Judy and Sam. Carol could use a review pro forma as described by Cheetham et al. (1992) but such forms can be formulaic and generally do not capture the complexity of practice. Instead she decides to embark on a summative case review using a 'research map' developed by Layder (1993). He argues that 'planning and designing research (or evaluation) projects involves consideration of the different levels of social life, [each] closely interrelated, but which for analytic and research purposes can be scrutinised separately' (Layder, 1993: 71).

The research map serves as a reminder of the complexity of the intervention as it explores the intervention from macro- to micro-levels:

- *Context*, including values, traditions, social and power relations such as class, gender, race relations

- *Setting*, including the immediate environment of social activity such as school, family, team, project, community group

- *Situated activity*, including interpersonal relations and the dynamics of face-to-face interaction

- *Self*, including biographical experience and social involvements as influenced by and interacting with the above.

Thus, in relation to her intervention with Judy, Carol can generate evidence from practice to answer, for example, the following questions:

- *In relation to context:* What general distribution of power and resources in society is relevant to the analysis of state intervention in Judy's life? What values, ideas and ideologies encourage or discourage certain forms of behaviour on the part of Judy in her role as a mother?

- *In relation to the social setting:* What forms of power, authority and control are there in the organisations providing the interventions (between staff, such as Carol, her manager, the voluntary organisations providing the parenting class and the intensive family support, and the service users; and between men and women and between different ethnic groups)?

- *In relation to situated activity:* Who is doing what to whom in the parenting classes and in the intensive family support? What forms of communication are being used, verbal and non-verbal? What are the relationships and interactions between Judy and the workers who are providing services?

- *In relation to the self and situated activity:* What are Judy's subjective feelings associated with the parenting class and the intensive family support: feelings of disempowerment, low self-esteem, hopelessness, distrust/dislike/fear of authority?

Carol also decides to involve her supervisor in the review using Smyth's (1991) model of supervision, which includes describing, informing, confronting and reconstructing, as an aid to reflecting on her practice. In *describing*, Carol provides a description of her practice and outlines the confusion, ambiguities, contradictions and concerns that she has; in *informing*, she explores the meanings, theories and values that help to make sense of the description; in *confronting*, Carol thinks about how and why the case has developed in the way that it has and reflects on who has gained and who has lost throughout her work with Sam and Judy; and in *reconstructing*, Carol works out how further involvement with Judy and Sam may be developed in different ways in the direction of 'good' practice and how Judy can be empowered by that practice. Everitt and

Hardiker (1996: 155) argue that 'this supervision provides ways in which to interrogate practice, to make explicit evidence of practice, and to tease out the thoughts, values, intentions and aspirations of the actors involved'.

Following this review, Carol decides to recommend continuing work with Judy but the approach will be different. She will adopt an 'action research' approach which will include Judy throughout the process. Hart and Bond (1995: 3) argue that the

> combination of enquiry, intervention and evaluation which powers the action research cycle mirrors the iterative processes involved employed by professional staff in assessing the needs of vulnerable people, responding to them and reviewing progress (see Figure 6.1).

The main attraction of an action research approach is that it can be used to make changes in non-hierarchical and non-exploitative ways.

Together, Judy and Carol will:

- Define the problem(s) and explore ways in which the problem(s) might be addressed

- Agree on a way to address the problem(s)

- Set objectives for work on the problem(s) and agree how objectives will be measured

- Work on resolving the problem(s)

- Review the work being done and assess the extent to which it is meeting or has met the objectives

- If the work *has met* its objectives, consider tackling another problem or close the case; if the work *is meeting* objectives, continue with the work; if the work *is not meeting* objectives, agree a different way of working

- Continue reviewing the progress of the work until the case can be closed.

CONCLUSION

Good reviewing is more complex than is implied by many of the formal review mechanisms because it explores the process, output and outcome of social work practice from a range of perspectives, including those of the social worker and the service user. Nevertheless, despite its complexity, it is essential that practitioners review their work, not merely because government or agencies require it but because effective practice is built on the learning gained from the practitioner's own past practice as well as the past practice of others.

Reviewing is as critical a part of social work practice as assessing and intervening and good, competent, effective practitioners will have developed understanding of and skills in reviewing, alongside understanding of and skills in assessing and intervening. For, as stated by Williams et al. (1999: 94)

Social work is not an exact science but this does not make it an art to be performed on the basis of flair, intuition and affiliation to a particular school. In the absence of a more certain practice it is important that social work interventions are based on the best available understanding and the best available information about what works.

FURTHER READING

Clarke, A. (1999) *Evaluation Research: An Introduction to Principles, Methods and Practice* (London: Sage). Clarke introduces the reader to the fundamental principles of evaluation by demonstrating how a wide variety of social research methods can be applied in different evaluation contexts in imaginative and creative ways. He outlines some of the conceptual, methodological and practical problems that might be encountered by the would-be evaluator.

Everitt, A. and Hardiker, P. (1996) *Evaluating for Good Practice* (Basingstoke: BASW/Macmillan – now Palgrave Macmillan). Everitt and Hardiker argue that the increasing evaluation of social work and social care practice by government and organisations has turned evaluation into a mechanism for managerial and financial control. They go on to suggest ways in which this trend can be countered by practitioners conducting evaluations that will contribute to the development of 'good' practice and empower service users.

Shaw, I. and Lishman, J. (eds) (1999) *Evaluation and Social Work Practice* (London: Sage). The first three chapters of this book provide an overview of research and evaluation in social work practice. The remaining chapters are written by a range of contributors who provide examples to demonstrate how social workers can review their practice. This 'applied' aspect of the book makes it relevant to practitioners.

Social Work Practice

Working Within and Across Boundaries: Tensions and Dilemmas

Robert Adams

Introduction

Three features of social work make an understanding of working within and across boundaries even more important for social workers than for many other practitioners. Firstly, the raw material of social work is people's everyday lives, from which none of us can detach ourselves. Practitioners unavoidably share the life course with people receiving services, including many of the problems involved in growing up and growing older. Of course, divisions and inequalities in society privilege some of us and protect us from poverty, discrimination and harm. Also, we can maintain boundaries between us, the worker, the professional, and us as the private person. From time to time, though, our thoughts and feelings are bound to 'leak' back and forth across these boundaries. We need to acknowledge the impact of this on our practice, as life events such as illness and bereavement affect us in our work with other people. Secondly, the problems many people experience are not like illnesses which can be cured. We cannot 'solve' the situation of an abused or bereaved person, any more than we can make decisions which, in a conflict-torn family or other group, will satisfy everybody. Sometimes, service users, their carers, family and friends are in conflict and one person's solution is another person's nightmare. Thirdly, partly because of the previous point, people's lives are often complicated and uncertain.

These three features of social work lead us to expect that practitioners cannot provide resolutions to the complex difficulties of people's lives, any more than any of us can be assured of simple answers to the questions posed by life itself.

One consequence of this complexity and uncertainty is that social workers are called upon increasingly to do two things: reflect and work across boundaries of many kinds. *Reflecting across boundaries* arises from the different disciplines – areas of knowledge such as social policy, law, sociology, psychology, anthropology and so on – on which social workers draw in their practice. The most obvious *work across boundaries* is in settings where multiprofessional and multidisciplinary teams are involved. Social workers are not unique in this. Other practitioners in the health and social services, such as occupational therapists, health visitors, community physicians and nurses, in their work with social workers share many common perspectives on work with people. In such circumstances, boundaries between organisations, professions and disciplines may be crossed, or even shift.

Social work offers a distinct and, on occasions, unique view, however. By definition, social workers occupy boundary positions between people and diverse views of their situations and different choices about what they should do next. Boundaries arise in every aspect of practice. In social work with children and families, social workers intervene in situations where families are divided by force of circumstances, such as exclusion or armed conflict leading to emigration of refugees or asylum seekers. More locally, when partners separate, for example, complex situations may arise involving contact between children and adults, especially where there is disagreement, violence or abuse between family members. Social work is intimately involved at these pressure points in people's lives. In the process, global, ethnic, cultural and religious boundaries all may be encountered.

In work with adults, social workers contribute to decisions involving health and social care practitioners about the care that people receive from a range of services, ranging across boundaries between residential, day and community care services.

Of course, social workers do not have a monopoly over ideas about boundaries – they are embedded in all human affairs. Biologists, psychologists and sociologists rely on the notion of boundaries to distinguish between individuals, groups and communities, as well as to refer to commonalities and interactions. It is also apparent that boundaries do not always divide. They may clarify differences and encourage communication and joint activity. This is important, not least because social workers can exploit it to enable people to change their lives.

So it is inevitable that when we consider boundaries and the idea of separating one area of activity from another, we are also implicitly acknowledging the importance of connectedness and the idea of practitioners making connections across boundaries. This inherent paradox reminds us that boundaries are profoundly ambiguous, with the consequence that practice may encounter tensions and dilemmas.

This chapter examines the notion of boundaries and boundary crossing in two parts. First, we consider the idea of boundary, and in particular the ambiguities at its heart. Later, we shall examine tensions and dilemmas arising in the practice of working within and across boundaries.

Boundary: an ambiguous concept

We may grumble about a boundary such as a fence denying us access to something we want. We may applaud a boundary we perceive as serving a useful function: distinguishing our territory, or serving as protection from threats to our health or safety. In part, our differing view may depend on which side of the boundary we are, how we construct its meaning and whether we are privileged or excluded by it. Some boundaries, such as legal and organisational limits, may seem clear-cut and less ambiguous in their meaning, but it is probably safe to assume that no boundary or limit will be agreeable to everybody. So, it is realistic to remain ambivalent towards most boundaries. This is more uncomfortable, since it means that we recognise their strengths as well as their weaknesses. It is a critical view, appreciating the complexity of the situation.

We sometimes view boundaries as a symbol of safety and personal or group security; at other times they may be an irritation, as we seek to cross them or tear them down. We most obviously encounter the notion of boundaries when working in organisations. The fact that organisations have boundaries, yet at the same are interconnected is an incontestable reality in situations where services have to be organised and delivered. Social work services are delivered through increasingly complex arrangements involving a growing diversity of providing organisations and agencies working together. Where do the ambiguities arise? Quite simply, working together – whether liaison, cooperation, coordination or collaboration – is not just complicated but problematic as well. Organisations and ways of organising can be both liberating and oppressive. The implications for people – managers, practitioners, service users, carers and member of the general public – are complex and take some teasing out.

Sometimes, our boundary crossing affects not only our tasks, but our sense of who we are: our definition of ourselves as worker or service user becomes blurred, fragmented or contradicted by circumstances. One of the more obvious examples of boundary crossing occurs when a social worker becomes a client, or becomes the main carer for a relative who is a 'client' of social services. Kathleen Jones, when professor of social policy at York University, told of the confusion of some nursing staff when several years earlier she was carrying out research at a hospital as 'Dr Jones', became ill, was admitted and treated as an inpatient. Sometimes people with a strong professional identity will play this down in order to be treated as just another client.

These examples remind us that our experience as practitioners may contrast with what we feel when we become users of those same services. If we become a carer for a relative or spouse, in addition to our role as a practitioner in health and social care, we may have to manage tensions between our identity as practitioner and our identity as service user or carer.

In order to illustrate the interplay between boundary crossing, the complexity of situations and associated practice tensions and dilemmas, we shall use a case example.

CASE EXAMPLE PART 1

Kis, a man aged 65, has been married for more than 30 years to Kati aged 59. Kis has suffered anxiety and depression and for many years has had a drink problem. Kati finds

---

CASE EXAMPLE PART 1 cont'd

it increasingly difficult to cope with Kis, but is unwilling to consider alternatives which would give her respite. She leaves the house only for short periods, for essential shopping. Kati and Kis were refugees from Eastern Europe and, although having lived in England for many years, have a limited command of English. This makes Kati less confident when dealing with health and social services agencies.

The couple come to the notice of social services when Kis has a fall and Kati goes to the local social services department to ask if she can borrow a wheelchair. The duty officer recognises the complexity of the situation. She invites Kati to talk to a female social worker, Mari, from a similar ethnic background. Mari is able to appreciate the extent of Kati's problems because Mari's mother, who has suffered from dementia for several years, has just been admitted to a nursing home. Mari is faced privately with the decision about whether to sign the consent form for her mother to have a potentially life-saving, but also risky and life-threatening, operation. Shortly afterwards, Mari and a community nurse from the community-based, multidisciplinary Mental Healthcare of Older People Team visit Kati and Kis at home. Their needs are assessed, with their full participation. As a result, respite care is organised for Kis, who is admitted to a hospital ward, linked with a day centre.

This summarised case example illustrates the complexities of situations which may face social workers. It is instructive to try to identify as many types of boundaries as possible, recognising that different people will perceive them differently and a comprehensive list is probably unattainable. However, the following list makes a start.

Types of boundaries

1. *Global and ethnic boundaries* The multidisciplinary team takes responsibility for allocating a Gujarat social worker to work with Kis and Kati, as a way of crossing ethnic boundaries between agency service providers, service users and carers.

2. *Boundaries of language* Mari, the social worker, is aware of the language boundaries preventing Kis and Kati having full enough access to other people, services, groups and communities. She takes responsibility for facilitating communication across these boundaries.

3. *Boundaries of culture and religion* Mari, who is from a Muslim background, is aware of religious and cultural differences between her and Kis and Kati, who are Christians.

4. *Community, group and family boundaries* In the multiethnic, multifaith locality in which Kis and Kati live, they are aware of different kinds of boundaries between them and other families, groups and communities.

5. *Individual boundaries* It is not uncommon for some practitioners, like Mari, to be juggling multiple roles, across the boundaries between their personal and professional lives, between their responsibilities as workers and their personal circumstances, as carers, or, less commonly, as service users.

6. *Organisational boundaries* Mari, as the social worker, has to engage with a range of organisations outside her own employing agency, including the local hospital, primary healthcare team, residential home and day centre, quite apart from visiting different practitioners in their work settings in the NHS trust. Any decisions taken by social workers in multiprofessional or multidisciplinary teams to involve Kis and Kati in particular ways in the assessment, planning, implementation and review of the work done with them will affect the work of other practitioners with them, such as community nurses and occupational therapists.

7. *Professional boundaries* Mari's collaboration with different professionals such as occupational therapists and community nurses necessitates interaction back and forth across boundaries between differing professional values, approaches, methods and skills.

8. *Disciplinary boundaries* A clinical psychologist working with the Community Care Team has a very different perspective on the family to that of the social worker. Mari works with the psychologist, although the disciplines informing their practice are different. The disciplinary boundaries between the psychologist and the social worker are maintained, but they collaborate across them.

Sceptical practice: the need for self-critical reflection

There is a need for Mari to maintain a self-critical approach to her own work. We can use the term 'sceptical' to describe this, as long as it is not taken to imply a lack of commitment. She needs to use this scepticism as a way of examining her practice critically and not simply evaluating what has happened, as though this is independent of her and other practitioners. All the practitioners involved could ask many questions. Here are three key questions to encourage this process of critical reflection:

1. What have I learnt from this piece of work?

2. In what ways could the situation have worked out better for Kati and Kis?

3. In what ways could I have practised differently so as to achieve these better outcomes?

Delving further into the ambiguities of boundaries

According to Mike Walsh (2000: 107), in his study of nursing practice, boundaries are 'lines of demarcation that help us make sense of the world by separating entities such as territory, occupations or objects from one another.' This statement clarifies one aspect of boundaries, their function as organisational and professional lines of division. The concept of boundary is value-laden, ambiguous and multifaceted. Consequently, one group of managers and practitioners may regard professional and organisational boundaries as needing to be crossed to improve the coordination and integration of services. On the positive side, Walsh notes that interprofessional boundaries help people receiving services to distinguish between different practitioners and enable professionals to know what roles the different practitioners are performing. However, he reminds us that professional boundaries may become positions to defend, in which case they become negative and harmful to people receiving services, as different professions spend time in conflict with each other rather than fighting ill-health and disease (Walsh, 2000: 107). Gareth Morgan (1986: 170) describes how individuals, groups and departments in another setting may regard it as necessary to work defensively to maintain boundaries around their practice. In this way they may hope to avoid the threats they perceive to their autonomy, maintain their independence and defend their existing ways of working.

Boundaries are complex, even contradictory in their character. An experienced residential childcare manager said to me that setting boundaries was integral to his practice. Exemplified in various major and minor rules, they provided an adolescent with an important symbol of authority. But with great insight, he said that they were intrinsically ambiguous, both a source of frustration and support to teenagers. The manager used the analogy of the cage. The young person could lean on the bars when day-to-day life was too much, but might also grab them and shake them furiously when they seemed to represent a barrier to desired satisfaction.

The above example shows how practitioners can use their authority creatively and supportively and not merely as a controlling means of enforcing compliance. Such ambiguity is central to the concept of the boundary. When I first began work in a prison, I was under the illusion that HM Prison Pentonville was an archetype of Goffman's total institution (Goffman, 1961), an island in the middle of London, entirely cut off from it by high walls. The reality was far more complex. The wall represented a physical symbol of the social, psychological, spiritual, political, economic and values boundaries between the institution and the rest of the world. But people crossed these boundaries in both directions all the time. There was a huge amount of this traffic between the so-called 'total institution' and the neighbourhood, between London and other parts of Britain. Some of the transactions across these boundaries – like trafficking and escape attempts – were less manifest and less approved than others. Others – like the links between prisoners and their families – were fragile but often desirable and necessary to rehabilitation. But the ambiguities, the strength and the fragility, of the boundaries were there. The social, physical and psychological walls were high and thick, but they were undermined and breached in so many ways. In *Stigma*, Goffman (1963) explores some shifting boundaries around negative, undesirable and excluded aspects of people's lives. He demonstrates how stigmatised people, including disabled people, may have to suffer the indignity of having their private lives subjected to wide, public review, as they become a case for social workers (Goffman, 1963: 136). The prison, of course, is the ultimate paradox: simultaneously separate from society to facilitate its goal of segregating offenders privately behind bars *as a punishment*, but seeking to be part of society's public disapproval of crime and setting out to ensure that offenders are not imprisoned *for punish-*

ment. Paradoxically, the further *outside* the boundaries of the prison its critics and visiting professionals are, the less their chance of reforming its detailed practices. On the other hand, the more they become *insiders,* the more their freedom as critics is compromised. As suggested elsewhere (Adams, 1981), members of prison Boards of Visitors are the archetypal outsider-insiders. However, social workers in hospitals, schools and similar institutions may experience similar tensions in their outside-inside roles.

Boundary crossing: an elusive goal

We might imagine that the only real boundaries are like those prison walls – physical barriers round the perimeter of geographical entities, organisations or total institutions. But boundaries can exist in so many ways. They can manifest themselves in barriers *within* organisations or communities, sometimes in negative ways. One classic contemporary example involves boundaries around personal space. For instance, there are tensions between preserving people's rights to privacy under the freedom of information and human rights legislation and ensuring that agencies can communicate intelligence about assumed risks to adults and children posed by people with a history of abuse.

Brigham refers to the identification by Mary Douglas in her classic study of taboo and pollution (Douglas, 1966: 123) of four categories of social pollution by people as a threat or danger:

1. *By infringing on external boundaries* – people categorised as unfit to breed or parent, being regarded as a danger to the next generation

2. *Through trespassing across internal boundaries within the system* – people being regarded as crossing from one category to another

3. *On the margins of boundary lines* – people such as those regarded as psycho-pathic killers, serial sex offenders or very low in intelligence and seen as on the border of what is regarded as humanity

4. *Through internal contradictions* – people with profound learning difficulties or major psychoses as being both unreachable by virtue of extreme problems but as holy innocents or eternal children, and also having access to a serene inner world from which so-called 'normal' people are excluded (Brigham, 2000: 33–4).

Having established how difficult it is to arrive at a single, simple idea of what a boundary is in the health and social care field, we can appreciate the even greater problems which arise in discussing any changes in boundaries. Four kinds of movement are possible involving boundaries: boundary intensification, boundary abolition, boundary movement and boundary crossing:

1. *Boundary intensification* occurs where the barriers between organisations, professions or people are made more definite

2. *Boundary abolition* takes place when boundaries between organisations and

professions are dissolved and people share roles, sometimes in novel, meta-professional activity

3. *Boundary movement* happens when one organisation or profession acquires new territory or roles at another's expense

4. *Boundary crossing* comes about when collaboration achieves joint working.

Yet, attempts are made all the time to identify the barriers to crossing boundaries and the aspiration towards permeable boundaries. In organisation theory, the coordination of people and resources has proved to be one of the most intractable problems. Many other problems may be identified as *the* problem: rigidity in the organisation, the leadership roles or management styles of managers, conflict and competition between collaborating staff and apathy on the part of staff.

Government policies emphasise the need for joined-up thinking. Organisational approaches such as systems perspectives have been adopted as one way forward. Others include lateral thinking, creative thinking, or what Gareth Morgan (1986) calls 'imaginisation', critical reflection and the contextualising of practice. There have been attempts to control, punish, eject and, more positively, train practitioners out of the problems.

Behind many of these activities lie fairly persistent assumptions, notably that organisations have fixed or stable boundaries and unique characteristics which means that this workforce has a culture and a repertoire of skills which cannot be gained by that workforce, no matter how closely they may be working together.

On the other hand, contemporary research in health and social care often regards boundaries between, say, community and residential care as intrinsically permeable. People are encouraged to cross some boundaries. Research into redrawing boundaries between hospital and home care of acutely ill people refers to the 'changing balance of home and hospital care' (Marks, 1991: 7). But whilst the idea of the 'hospital without walls', as the report makes clear, can be found as far back as 1961 (in New Zealand), progress towards minimising inappropriate hospital admission and promoting paediatric home care has been sporadic and slower than desired (Marks, 1991: 7).

Widespread assumptions about boundaries may be challenged by critical theorists and practitioners. It is necessary, for instance, to challenge the assumption that boundaries – such as the boundary around assumed 'normality' – are fixed. Over the past two centuries, increasing numbers of people have been excluded from 'respectable' society, on grounds of the threat they represent. This may be in terms of their criminal behaviour, mental health problems, disability or other aspects of their differences. Thompson (1998) shows how, in the early twentieth century, the social construction of women shifted from being in need of protection from temptation and corruption to being a threat to the moral health of the community. Let us be clear, not all changes in such boundaries are negative. A large voluntary agency in Scotland traditionally provided residential care for people with disabilities and now offers a range of residential, day and community outreach schemes for them. It aims to:

- Provide a safe, protective, homely environment
- Give care and support to individuals, families and groups
- Encourage people to achieve their desired lifestyle
- Empower them to form relationships and achieve independence.

Staff in its group care settings work as multidisciplinary teams. They work in partnership with individuals, their carers, families, social workers, health and education services. The roles of the workers span key worker, supporter, carer in one-to-one work with service users and carers, involvement in teamwork, groupwork and advocacy and in work with other professionals and agencies. This is a powerful illustration of the ability of some formerly residentially based organisations to reframe their work by recasting boundaries between the institution and associated community networks. It is all too easy for organisations to function as though the organisationally based group is at the 'core' of practice and external groups are at the 'periphery'. This may be part of the reason why vulnerable individuals and groups continue to be marginalised and excluded. Continual vigilance is needed to prevent this happening.

Shifts in policies and practices concerning disabled people need to be appreciated in their wider social and political context. Brigham discusses how, in the late nineteenth century and early twentieth centuries, people with learning disabilities came to be regarded as a threat. Women were targeted by policies directed at controlling their sexuality, restricting their fecundity and curbing their alleged immorality. In the process, boundaries between public and private domains, social classes, 'races', men and women and normality and abnormality have been redrawn (Brigham, 2000: 27–42). These changes have taken place in the context of changing attitudes to the public and private spheres of society and the production and consumption of goods (Hirschman, 1998: 13–17). Boundaries exist between public and private, inclusion and exclusion, selfishness and selflessness, individualism and the collective, the personal and the social, possessions and shared ownership, trespassing and migration.

Whilst boundary crossing may be associated with positive or negative ideas, often social policy has made it difficult for refugees, asylum seekers, travellers and others dispossessed and seeking new opportunities to migrate.

In all these areas, the question is how far it is possible for social workers to assert and advocate on behalf of excluded individuals and groups, when social work's boundaries are being configured and reconfigured. In other words, social work is part of the wider context of health, welfare and other services and issues concerning how practitioners respond are linked with legal, policy, organisational and managerial decisions about how responsibilities are assigned to different professional groups.

Practice tensions and dilemmas

Let us move on now to examine the extent to which boundary crossing practice may involve associated tensions and dilemmas.

First we need to distinguish between tensions and dilemmas. A tension is a resolvable problem, whereas a dilemma is insoluble. A dilemma is a situation presenting a choice between two equally problematic or undesirable alternatives. In practice, the social worker may manage the dilemma by choosing the alternative which seems least harmful to the service user and carer. We return to consider the case of Kis and Kati, listing some of the main tensions and practice dilemmas raised by this case example (neither list is exhaustive).

Tensions

■ The work needs to be done by the social worker and other members of the team, with the full involvement of Kis the service user and Kati his carer. Nevertheless, the more the social worker involves them, the more this creates expectations which other members of the multidisciplinary team will need to match.

■ There is a need to balance risks against quality of life. There is a risk that if Kis continues to live at home, he will be less inconvenienced but will suffer a quicker deterioration in his health. On the narrow criterion of reducing risks, he would be safer in a residential setting. On the other hand, if he stays at home, perhaps his quality of life will be sustained for longer. There is no 'answer' to this. It depends on your vantage point.

■ From Kati's point of view, she experiences relief that Kis is in hospital, but also mourns his absence.

■ The uncertainties are inherent in the complexities of everyday life which many people encounter, and from which Mari as a social worker cannot be exempt. Mari has to manage the tensions between her work as a practitioner and her identity as a carer. There is a tension between Mari's aim as a carer to enable her mother to remain as independent as possible and the priority to manage her situation so as to minimise risk. Practice is not about assessing a case and finding the technical means to 'solve' problem situations. There may be no 'solution'. Whichever decision is made, there may be gains and losses for the different involved people.

Dilemmas

■ Kati is in a double-bind. She wants to continue to care for Kis at home but she wants him to be treated successfully and his condition to improve.

■ Kis is in a dilemma. He wants relief from his long-term depression and finds his drink problem debilitating, but does not want to go through the stressful and painful process of treatment.

■ Mari faces a dilemma. Should she sign the form giving permission for her mother to have the operation and run the risk of her dying during the operation, or do nothing in the knowledge that without the operation her mother will die within a short time?

Crossing boundaries and transforming practice

What ways forward exist that will offer prospects of surmounting the kinds of practice tensions and dilemmas faced by Kis, Kati and Mari? On one hand, it seems uncontroversial that social workers should establish clear boundaries around their practice. On the other hand, there are many circumstances in which social workers should practise more effectively with others, across professional and organisational boundaries. Surely boundaries are clear, whether as markers around organisational territories, activities, roles or meanings, or as ways of demarcating and defending best practice. The closer we examine these ideas, the easier it is to dispel illusions of simplicity and certainty around the ideas of boundaries and boundary crossing. We need to explore how these difficulties are manifested in social work and how practitioners may be better equipped to tackle them. The goal is to help us to deconstruct the idea of boundary crossing and enable a more constructive engagement with the meaning of boundaries in our practice.

Contemporary policies aspire towards seamless services, so as to meet people's complex psychological, medical, emotional and social needs in a coordinated way. This implies that a range of health and social services managers, professionals and practitioners work together. Cable (2002: 2–3) points out how policy in the UK since the mid-1980s has converged with publications by the WHO. In 1973, a WHO committee asserted that benefits in terms of increased job satisfaction as well as more effective, holistic care would result from greater interprofessional integration of healthcare services (WHO, 1973). In 1979, the WHO supported the need for an emphasis on the distinct organisation of primary, secondary and tertiary health and social care services (WHO, 1979) and a decade later argued for improved interdisciplinary teamwork in the interests of the holistic care of people (WHO, 1988).

Health and social care policy in the UK since the late 1980s, based on the Griffiths Report (Department of Health and Social Security, 1988) and enacted in the National Health Service and Community Care Act 1990, reflected this consistent emphasis on improving coordination between, and integration of, health and social care services. Cable (2002: 5) argues that these aspirations have not led to 'the development of clear and coordinated policy in relation to either global directives or local need'. He refers to a catalogue of potential conflicts: care versus cure; central control versus local control; bureaucracies versus collegiate structures; managerial versus professional dominance; public versus private funding of services; and the integration versus the separation of particular health and social care services, professions and practices.

In order to tackle these intractable problems, it is vital that all employees and volunteers in all participating organisations take responsibility for their work, across organisational boundaries. It is also vital that the agencies set up a partnership agreement in which all participants are accountable for the service. This involves sharing tasks and taking responsibility for managing and delivering the service.

Let us revisit the case of Kis and Kati for a view about how Mari the social worker may use the ideas of boundary crossing in developing positive practice.

CASE EXAMPLE REVISITED

The situation improves. The social worker contributes to a multidisciplinary community care assessment of Kis's circumstances. Kis's anxiety and depression begin to ease. The team agree to a discharge plan following a discharge care plan approach meeting, attended by Mari, ward staff including the ward manager and psychiatrist and nurses, as well as staff from the day hospital, following guideliness for discharge planning and aftercare. As part of this, it is recommended that Kis spends alternate nights at home. Three weeks later, he is discharged from the ward. The social worker sets up an arrangement with the GP, community nurse and pharmacist in the local primary care unit that Kis's medication will be monitored to ensure that he continues to take it. The social worker also contacts a local voluntary organisation offering visitors to older people with drink problems. A volunteer begins to visit Kis and Kati regularly, to act as a bridge between them and services they need and empower them to deal with their difficulties.

This example shows how Mari, the social worker, works effectively within and across the following kinds of boundaries:

- Aiming to provide a seamless service, to enable carers and people using services to cope better, achieve change and improve their life chances

- Providing continuity of services as service users and carers move between hospital, community and continuing care day and residential settings

- Providing multidisciplinary assessments, reassessments and reviews

- Working with individuals, families, groups and communities.

Let us reflect on some wider lessons raised by this boundary crossing case, under three main headings of identifying potential boundary crossers, networking and developing skills.

Identifying people with potential as boundary crossers

Sometimes boundaries are crossed, sometimes they are blurred, shift or disappear. There are unavoidable contradictions and dilemmas for practitioners. In order to tackle these, social workers need to draw on critical perspectives on geographical, conceptual, value-based, organisational, disciplinary and professional boundaries between different areas.

It is necessary to identify reticulists, both agency staff and volunteers, with the ability to facilitate interagency working. (Reticulists are people with responsibilities and skills in bridging organisational and professional boundaries.) In some circumstances, working across boundaries is essential to achieving particular goals which are desirable for people receiving services. Evidence (Lart, 1997) suggests that it is difficult to impose boundary crossing on the organisation or team, from above.

Rule-following may be customary, accompanied by the beliefs and assumptions which support this (Morgan, 1986: 128–30). Significant change in established ways of practising and thinking is necessary. Any change is likely to require unlearning and relearning. Rachel Lart (1997) evaluated the Wessex Project, which introduced planned discharge for prisoners with mental health needs, using the Care Programme Approach (CPA) where appropriate. The project began in a context where no other agency saw this area of work as their particular responsbility. Lart examined the vital sharing of tasks and responsibilities in the multi-agency team, and the key role played by reticulists, in situations where crossing professional boundaries is essential to the continuance of day-to-day practice.

Networks and boundary crossers

The failure of welfare policies to meet the needs and wants of the people who should receive services is, in part, a failure of organisation and service delivery. Donald Schön (1971) developed the analysis that transformations are needed in the model of government responses to these failures. Schön (1971) argues it is fine for policy-makers to govern change from the centre, but power needs exercising by people at the 'periphery', where services are actually delivered, to ensure that they meet needs. The complexity and variety of local needs contradicts the requirement for uniformity at the centre, where general policy is formulated and administered. Even regionally and locally, formal bureaucracies managing services, to the extent that they replicate this 'centre-periphery' model, impose restrictions and control, rather than abolishing need, acknowledging diversity and ensuring justice. Schön states: 'The need is for differentiated, responsive, continually changing but *connected* reaction' (Schön, 1971: 189). His argument is for mechanisms encouraging systems at the local periphery to transform themselves and connect with each other. This depends on two contributions: from leaders and through networks. If informal networks are strong, they support a nuclei of leadership and local arrangements hold together without any necessary central direction or support for the transformations (Schön, 1971: 189–90). Whilst formal networks exist to serve the management of an organisation – purchasing, processing, advertising and delivering – Schön is writing of informal networks here. These, he states, are 'the informal or "underground" networks connecting persons, groups and organisations. These are used to circumvent, supplement or replace the operations of formal organisational systems' (Schön, 1971: 191). Such networks often are ad hoc, remedying shortcomings between the large providers of services and local problems that people perceive as requiring services. These networks may have a short life or, if poor conditions persist, may acquire permanency. Schön (1971: 192) instances poor, black communities where informal networks of so-called 'nannies' look after young and sick people. He coins the term 'shadow network', to refer to the informal arrangement 'filling the gap between fragmented services and a more highly aggregated functional system' (Schön, 1971: 195).

Other writers have emphasised the key contribution of workers, not all senior line managers or even employed staff, as crossers of boundaries and networkers.

Sarason and Lorentz (1998), in their study of the informal mobilisation of support for schools in the USA, identify people with a flair for boundary crossing as the key to more effective coordination. They argue that these people may not be staff occupying senior positions. They may not be employed by the organisation, but may work in the community, occupying key positions in networks and maintaining significant relationships. Sarason and Lorentz discuss the need for recognition of the essential, although usually informal, contribution of the coordinator. They view coordination and drawing people together as taking place not in formal organisations and meetings, but in the neighbourhood, communities and informal networks. Much of their book is taken up with examining the five elements which they regard as essential if this is to be successful:

1. Regarding, and drawing on, people as resources

2. Recognising obstacles to redefining resources

3. Accepting the unique contribution of networks and networking to making the most of resources

4. Building on the particular character and role of coordination through networks

5. Identifying how resource exchange energises and reinforces collegiality and a sense of community (Sarason and Lorentz, 1998).

Recognising qualities, developing skills

We can recognise many social work qualities and skills in the four aspects of the role of the coordinator identified by Sarason and Lorentz (1998: 95):

1. Developing a real, authentic knowledge of the territory, through 'curiosity', rather than through knowledge passively obtained

2. Scanning, that is, seeking commonalities, with fluidity, that is, easily and speedily recognising commonalities, and imaginativeness

3. Perceiving assets and building on strengths

4. Using power and influence as well as selflessness.

We can go further than this in identifying the kinds of skills that social workers need, in order both to use and work within, as well as transcend, boundaries in their practice. According to Sarason and Lorentz, coordinators possess a constructive way of thinking (p. 115), that is, the ability to avoid focusing on people's deficits and see opportunities for connecting between people and organisations that to others may seem entirely separate. This enables them to contribute effectively to a range of partnerships in their work with others. In order to flourish, these partnerships need to:

■ Be flexible and able to make use of new and unexpected opportunities

- Be open-ended, so they produce benefits now and in the longer term

- Go beyond simple mechanistic arrangements where services are provided in exchange for information from the service user, and become true collaboration where the participants create genuine 'added value'

- Be dependent not solely on line management in the organisation but also supported by local networks and interpersonal relationships.

An example of how to transform practice

The above different research findings should encourage us not just to replicate existing practice but to develop a transformational practice. We can show how this could work, by inventing an agency and speculating first on a worst-case scenario and then on a best-case scenario where practitioners are motivated and are given the scope and power to tackle problems creatively.

Prime Serve is a fictitious not-for-profit organisation contracted to provide community care for adults in Midshire. Among other activities, Prime Serve employs staff to coordinate a large number of volunteers working with multidisciplinary staff in different local agencies.

Several problems have arisen among agencies in partnership with Prime Serve. A number of meetings have been held to examine these. All these meetings have agreed that improvements are necessary, but so far little progress has been achieved. The reasons for this are not clear to the staff involved. An already long list of possible reasons has been added to at each meeting.

In the worst-case scenario, procedures may dominate. Care managers in the local authority are clear about the problems. A senior manager produces an organisation chart to demonstrate that the problems lie 'out there', are not his responsibility and he cannot be held accountable for them. The organisation chart view of the situation prevails. The job descriptions of staff state that they carry out the procedures prescribed and do not go beyond these. They are taken as forbidding staff to cross boundaries, or only cross those authorised by management. Boundary crossing in other areas, such as networking, is perceived as a threat.

Now let us consider the transformational, best-case scenario. In this, a consultant or practitioner colleague advises the agencies on how to surmount the difficulties which have arisen. The consultant discusses the issues with staff in agencies and the volunteers working for Prime Serve. The consultant suggests a series of informal dialogues and informal and formal meetings between people working for local agencies and Prime Serve, to examine how to improve collaborative working. Staff are empowered to use their initiative to go beyond the boundaries of their job descriptions, the role of their employing organisation, seek and tackle problems they identify, recruit local workers and through them promote networks to maintain improvements in services. Reframing what practitioners are coordinating is not considered 'out there', and is brought within the scope of the practitioner. This may involve disengaging with embedded perceptions and practices and being willing to embrace new practice. This is an intrinsically anti-oppressive, equality-driven, non-stigmatising, person-valuing process. It involves non-directed, flexible, imaginative interaction, such as networking, which fosters interdependence. It necessitates that managers and practitioners grasp how boundary crossing works, formally and informally, at different levels and in different sectors.

CONCLUSION

It is common to write of boundaries as though they are mainly organisational and managerial, but there are many different kinds. In particular, social work straddles boundaries between geographical, religious, ethnic and cultural, value and disciplinary divides. In many ways, social workers occupy unique positions in complex situations, where other practitioners work within a designated professional territory and social workers draw on a variety of disciplines and have the capacity to work across many different kinds of boundaries.

Whether social workers positively regard boundary crossing and the associated challenges posed depends on the extent to which they are committed to developing beyond procedurally bound practice and seek to change practice significantly. Boundary crossing may be more creative, but is more demanding. It requires more commitment to work with all parties towards outcomes which aspire to empower service users and carers, but en route may be more stressful and resource-consuming.

Practitioners setting out to meet the diversity and full extent of people's needs can use notions of boundary crossing to engage in work which is more capable of being transformational. The remainder of the chapters in Part II of this book illustrate the major practice challenges of social work which engages with the complexities of achieving this.

FURTHER READING

Banks, S. (2001) *Ethics and Values in Social Work* (2nd edn) (Basingstoke: Palgrave – now Palgrave Macmillan). A good source of discussion on practice involving ethical dilemmas.

Payne, M. (2000) *Teamwork in Multiprofessional Care* (Basingstoke: Palgrave – now Palgrave Macmillan). A rich source on aspects of boundaries and boundary crossing.

Sullivan, H. and Skelcher, C. (2002) *Working Across Boundaries: Collaboration in Public Services* (Basingstoke: Palgrave – now Palgrave Macmillan). A source of much material on aspects of joint working.

Acknowledgement

My thanks to Juliette Oko for her comments on an earlier draft of this chapter.

Risk and Protection

Viviene E. Cree and Susan Wallace

Introduction

We are living in a 'risk society' (Beck, 1992). Wherever we look, we are faced with the dangerousness of life in the early twenty-first century. But there is a paradox here. Just as we are confronted by risks at every corner, so we have come to expect that we should be protected from risk as never before. Within the field of social services, there is an increased expectation that risk should be controlled so that vulnerable children and adults are protected. When social work or health agencies fail in this endeavour, the public outcry is characterised by hurt and anger. The underlying message is clear: 'We trusted you, and you let us down.'

This chapter will begin by considering the meanings of risk and protection, before going on to explore a series of broad considerations which are fundamental to risk and protection, including legislation, values, rights and responsibilities. Drawing on evidence from literature and our own work experience in children and families' and criminal justice social work, we will discuss the two key concepts of 'risk assessment' and 'risk management'. We will argue that although these concepts are undoubtedly central to what social workers do (and have always done), we should not be lulled into a false sense of security – into thinking that somehow we have 'covered' the risk or guaranteed protection. In offering suggestions for good practice in social work, we are acutely aware that there is no 'quick fix' solution to the uncertainty and unpredictability of life. Our achievement, at best, must be that we behave in a professional, ethical manner, working alongside service users and other professionals to share the responsibilities and challenges that real life brings.

Understanding risk and protection

A quick search of any sociological database tells the same story: risk is 'big business' (Adams, 1995). From chemical accidents, to low birth weight infants, nuclear terrorism, environmental protection, flood risk, HIV prevention, data protection, consumer risks and child protection, research studies implicitly (and sometimes explicitly) take it for granted that the world is more unsafe than it was in the past, and that something must be done about it.

One of the most influential writers on risk is Ulrich Beck (1992, 1999). He argues that there has been a major shift in the way that we view risk. In 'traditional' or 'pre-modern' societies, disasters such as famine, disease and flood were viewed as acts of God, or accidents of fate; there was little that anyone could do to either prevent catastrophes or protect themselves from future adversity. Industrialisation brought with it a new, 'modern' outlook, which presumed that human beings could and should seek to control such misadventure. But, Beck (1992) argues, industrial society did not remove risk; instead, it created new and more damaging risks. While 'modern' industrial society brought wealth and 'goods', it also created 'bads', or threats, including environmental problems such as pollution, and social problems such as unemployment and family breakdown. These were not simply 'negative side-effects of seemingly accountable and calculable action' but rather they are 'trends which are eroding the system and delegitimating the bases of rationality' (Beck, 1999: 33). Risks have become more difficult to calculate and control; they are global and at the same time local, or 'glocal' (1999: 142). 'Risk society' therefore equals 'world risk society', in which human experience is characterised by unintended consequences and in which greater knowledge does not ease this state of affairs; instead, more and better knowledge often leads to more uncertainty (1999: 6). Thus 'expert' and lay voices compete with one other as the outcomes of modernity are challenged on all fronts, in a process Beck calls 'reflexive modernisation'.

Beck's thesis has been hugely influential; however, we believe that it may have contributed to a sense of pessimism in how we view risk and protection. While Beck has provided a language for something which has deep resonance for many people, he plays down the contradictions, ambivalence and complexities which are an inevitable part of the individual's response to risk; moreover, Tulloch and Lupton (2003) suggest that Beck fails to pay sufficient attention to the roles played by class, gender and 'race' in constructing different risk knowledges and experiences. In their recent comparative study of attitudes to risk in Britain and Australia, Tulloch and Lupton found that early 'modernist ideas' about the control of risk still dominate people's ideas, as do some pre-modern notions about 'fate'. Although many risks were indeed categorised as 'uncontrollable' by individuals, this was not because they were incalculable or global. Instead, fate or the actions of others were seen as beyond the individual's control (2003: 37). What is more, Tulloch and Lupton point out that risk is not necessarily negative. People choose to take risks all the time, for personal gain, excitement or self-actualisation, or 'simply as part of the human project'. A life without risk may be perceived as 'too tightly bound and restricted, as not offering enough challenges' (2003: 37). Risk-taking is therefore part of the process through which human beings create themselves as individuals; it is a 'practice of the self' (Foucault, 1988).

Risk, protection and the law

Legislation shapes and determines what social workers do, so this is our starting point in considering risk and protection. It will not be surprising, given the discussion already, to learn that there is no explicit legal definition of risk in either English or Scottish law, although it will often be pertinent to both civil and criminal matters in all aspects of social work. Given the absence of a precise legal definition, the onus is on the social worker or probation officer to familiarise themselves with applicable primary legislation and procedures in children and families' social work, community care and criminal justice social work. Social workers must also be aware of secondary, procedural legislation as it applies to specific work activities. For example, the Criminal Procedure (Scotland) Act 1995 Section 210A(1) requires that the author of a social enquiry report (known as a pre-sentence report in England and Wales) produces a risk assessment of any potential harm a violent and/or sex offender may cause, so that the judge can make a decision about whether to impose an extended sentence. In such a situation, the social worker must know the type of case which could legally result in an extended sentence being imposed, the type of offences which fall into this category (and those which do not) and the type of court procedure which is being used.

Social workers must also be knowledgeable about key governmental policy directives, and these often emerge as an outcome of a high-profile case where protection has failed. National standards are currently being developed throughout the UK for child protection work and will be applied across all agencies – health, education, social work and police – to encourage better joined-up working and approaches which will deliver improved outcomes for children (see, for example Social Work Services Inspectorate, 2003). Social workers also need to know about internal departmental procedures which may apply. Failure to follow procedural guidelines has been highlighted as a contributory factor to 'things going wrong' in cases where children involved with social services have been killed (Butler-Sloss, 2003).

Adherence to the relevant legislation, policy and procedure thus provides three corners of a working framework which should anchor good practice in relation to assessing and managing risk and protection. The fourth corner must be attention to rights.

LEGISLATION	POLICY
PROCEDURE	RIGHTS

Risk, protection and rights

In considering issues of protection and risk, it must be recognised that those we consider to be 'at risk' and those whom we believe may present a risk equally have rights; social workers have duties to observe the rights of others and advise them about their rights (Wallace, 2000). Just as Article 19 of the *UN Convention on the Rights of the Child* (1989) assures a child the right to protection from abuse and neglect, so the Human Rights Act 1998 (which came into force in October 2000) guarantees all citizens certain absolute and qualified rights, which all public bodies in the UK (including social services, social work and probation departments) must adhere to when dealing with the public (Walden and Mountfield, 1999).

The Human Rights Act guarantees basic civil, political, social and economic rights. Some are absolute, for example, 'Article 3: Freedom from Torture'. Others are subject to some limitations and qualifications, and in such cases, the Act seeks to balance the rights of the individual against other public interests (Harris, 1995). For example, 'Article 8: The Right to Respect for Private and Family Life' has a proviso that interference by a public body is permissible, if it is in the interests of preventing a crime or protecting the rights and freedoms of others. However, before a public body can overrule an individual's rights in such a situation, five issues must be considered: proportionality, legality, account-ability, necessity/compulsion, subsidiarity (see Walden and Mountfield (1999) for a fuller discussion on these principles). Any infringement by a public body or an employee of another's rights must therefore be justified and transparent.

Given the uncertainties and grey areas which abound in assessing potential risk and questions of protection, social workers must develop a good working knowledge of the European Convention on Human Rights 1950 and the Human Rights Act 1998 and ensure that protocols and practice are compatible with the Convention. This should include making recipients of social work services aware of their rights in a meaningful fashion, not only in terms of a narrow reading of the Act, but also that they reach a deeper understanding of what they can expect as a recipient of a social work service and what recourse they may have, if they are not happy with the service they are receiving (Wallace, 2000). A rights-based framework should ensure sharper, more open and transparent decision-making with clear lines of accountability. The concept of the 'defensible decision' is especially useful here: if you were to hand over your case notes to another profes-sional, would they act in the same manner as you had, because you had taken the correct steps and acted ethically in the process (Kemshall, 2002a)?

Risk, protection and responsibilities

Alongside rights, inevitably come responsibilities. There are commonly two sets of responsibilities to be considered: the responsibilities of the client, service user or offender and his/her contacts, and the responsibilities of the social worker or probation officer. When a tragedy occurs and a child or vulnerable adult is hurt or dies, thoughts turn very quickly to blame: to whom can responsibility be attrib-uted? Who is to blame? Sir Louis Blom-Cooper, who has chaired many inquiries into abuse, including homicides, states that the purpose of inquiries is 'to examine the truth ... what happened ... how did it happen, and who if anyone was responsible, culpably or otherwise, for it having happened?' (Blom-Cooper, 1993: 20).

But what is 'the truth'? Whose 'truth' are we to believe? In an examination of the role of the public inquiry in welfare scandals, Butler and Drakeford (2003: 219) argue that the inquiry is itself 'a player in the contested terrain, contributing its own voice to the construction of the original events'. Furthermore, the 'truth' which inquiries seek to uncover 'is influenced by the institutional framework within which the seeking-after is constructed ... If scandals are constructed, then, they are manufactured with a purpose' (2003: 221). The purpose, Butler and Drakeford assert, is to manage the immediate consequences of the scandal and, in so doing, leave the wider institutional order intact. Public attention is thus diverted from organisations onto individuals, and larger questions of historical and structural significance are avoided.

In thinking about the ways in which inquiries focus on the actions of individuals, Peay (1996: 11) tellingly asks: 'subject to this level of analysis, which of us would be likely to be found completely without fault?' The following case example, which describes a real scenario from practice, demonstrates that responsibility cannot be held by a social worker alone, or even by a team of professionals. Parents, relatives, neighbours, friends, health, education and social care professionals and society as a whole must share some responsibility for keeping children safe. All names have been changed to protect anonymity.

CASE EXAMPLE – VIVIENE

A health visitor referred a 28-year-old white, single mother to the voluntary sector children and families' agency where I worked. Joan was isolated and depressed following the break-up of her marriage, and wanted information about welfare benefit entitlements, as well as an opportunity to talk with a social worker about the marital breakdown. The health visitor also made a referral to the local children's centre for part-time provision to enable Joan's children Lisa (aged 2 years) and Robert (aged 4 years) to enjoy some quality time away from Joan.

As our relationship developed, Joan gradually told me the story of her life; the violence in her marriage and her father's sexual abuse of her when she was a child – abuse which had continued, sporadically, into her adult life. She was eager to try to understand what had happened to her and, with my support, she began to write her story down, and write poems which she shared with me. I introduced her to a local incest survivors' group, and she began to grow in confidence as she heard the stories of others. One day, her son Robert began to draw scary pictures at the children's centre, and speak about a 'night monster with a prickly chin' that sometimes came to his bedroom and climbed into his bed. On questioning, he told the daycare worker that the night monster was 'Pappa' (his name for his grandfather). A case conference was called, and Joan had to confront the reality that her father may have abused her son and perhaps also her daughter.

> **CASE EXAMPLE – VIVIENE cont'd**
>
> It emerged that while Joan had been making such strides in her own life, her father Peter had continued to play an important role with the family, supporting Joan financially and helping her with everything from decorating to babysitting. It should be stated that, aside from Robert's story (which he retracted a few days later), there was no evidence at this time that either Robert or Lisa had been sexually abused. The case conference recommended that voluntary measures of care should remain in place, and that all those working with the family should continue to monitor the children carefully. Joan assured the case conference that she would never again leave the children alone with her father, and that she would restrict his contact to occasional visits.
>
> The postscript to this case is that six months later the police were called at 1am to Joan's house. The 10-year-old son of a neighbour had been sleeping in Joan's house (this boy was unknown to the agency) and had telephoned the police to report that he had been attacked by Peter and had defended himself with a knife. Peter was subsequently taken to the police station for questioning and all sheets in the house were removed for forensic examination. I was called out to the house and arranged for the children to be placed temporarily in foster care; Joan was nowhere to be seen and had been out all night at a party. Following a children's hearing, the children returned home under a statutory Supervision Order; meanwhile, there was insuffi-cient evidence to pursue any complaint against Peter. I continued to work with Joan alongside a local authority social worker until I left the agency the following year. No further action was taken against Peter.

This case highlights a persistent reality in social work practice: that even when we have done everything possible to protect those with whom we are working, we cannot, with any certainty, know what is going on in a family when we are not present. Two options had been available in this situation, and neither had been in any way palatable: Viviene could seek to remove the children for their own 'protection' from a mother whom they loved and who loved them; or the children could be left at home, albeit with supervision, where sexual abuse may occur. Because of the lack of 'hard' evidence of abuse, only the second option could ever be realised, and the children continued to live at home with as much support and monitoring as was possible. But this could not remove all risk of harm from the children.

Risk, protection and values

As this case demonstrates, the whole process of dealing with risk and protection is fraught with moral and ethical dilemmas for social workers, primarily as a result of the uncertainty of outcomes. There are no 'right' or 'wrong' answers in most cases; assessing risk is not an exact science (Bottoms, 1977), and if the wrong decision is reached, this can have grave and profound implications. In any assess-ment of risk, there are four possible outcomes:

	Prediction	
Outcome	A	B
	True Positive Prediction	False Negative Prediction
	C	D
	False Positive Prediction	True Negative Prediction

Source: Kemshall (2002b: 14)

- In box A, it is predicted that harm will occur and it does
- In box D, it is predicted that there will be no harm and it does not occur
- In box B, it is predicted that there will be no harm but it does occur
- In box C, it is predicted that there will be harm but it does not occur

From this representation, the two outcomes which clearly present most difficulties for social workers, service users and the public at large are B and C. In the case of box B, vulnerable adults and children may be harmed or killed, and their agencies may be brought into disrepute; box C raises significant ethical dilemmas for practitioners and those concerned with civil liberties (Kemshall, 2002b: 14). MacDonald and MacDonald (1999) assert that we frequently over-emphasise low-risk, extreme outcomes (for example, child death), and argue that what is needed is a revisiting of the moral assertions made about risk. They assert that 'our untutored, intuitive perceptions of risk are likely to be systematically misleading, so that we must use 'a more stringent, scientific approach in the future' (1999: 43). This is self-evidently a worthwhile goal. But the reality is that all of us must make decisions under conditions of 'manufactured uncertainty, where not only is the knowledge base incomplete, but more and better knowledge often means more uncertainty' (Beck, 1999: 6). Furthermore, 'to be free to act well, is to be free to act badly' – autonomy brings risk, inevitably (Caddick and Watson, 1999: 66).

CASE EXAMPLE – SUSAN

Matthew was a 24-year-old white man subject to a Supervised Release Order, having spent 18 months in custody for a series of car crimes. Three special conditions were attached to Matthew's Release Order: firstly, he should reside at an address approved by his supervising social worker; secondly, he should seek employment; and thirdly, he should undergo drug counselling.

I had not met Matthew until shortly before he was due to be released from prison. He had a long history of involvement with the social work department as a child due to a rather chaotic home life, which resulted in him being taken into care. As an adult, he was also well known to the criminal justice system and had served a number of prison sentences. Stealing cars and driving without a licence were his main type of crimes. Departmental records indicated that mental health personnel had seen Matthew on a number of occasions. He had never been diagnosed as suffering from a recognised mental illness, however concerns had consistently been expressed regarding his mental well-being. He impressed as a very troubled soul with a history of self-harm and suicide attempts.

Matthew moved into supported accommodation after his release from prison. As the weeks went by, I became increasingly concerned about Matthew. He acknowledged that he was drinking a lot and using drugs, and he appeared incredibly distressed. I arranged for Matthew to be assessed by a psychiatrist but subsequent events took over. Matthew walked into a police station one evening in November stating that he did not want to carry on and wanted to die. He was taken to A&E where he was seen by the duty psychiatrist, who reported that because Matthew did not suffer from a recognised mental illness, he could not be admitted to hospital for assessment/treatment. The psychiatrist was clearly of the opinion that he needed help, but the system was not able to avail him of this.

A few days later, Matthew's solicitor contacted me. Matthew had been arrested the previous evening for stealing a car. He was due to appear in court later that morning. Whilst in custody, Matthew had bitten his arm very badly and his solicitor was concerned about his state of mind. I shared my own concerns with him. The solicitor decided not to oppose any moves that Matthew should be remanded in custody. This was an unusual action, but we both felt that given his fragile state of mind and inability to access an admission to a psychiatric hospital, prison may well provide a secure and safe environment for him to be monitored.

Matthew was remanded into custody. Discussions immediately began with prison social work and health services. A case conference was convened and the decision was taken that Matthew should be placed under suicide watch and he should undergo assessment and receive support. A week passed, Matthew appeared to be stable and had not caused himself any further injury. On Christmas Eve, Matthew asked to see a nurse. He explained that he was feeling much better and was desperate to be moved into one of the regular remand wings in the prison. He was very persuasive and the duty nurse agreed to his move, although this contravened established protocol which stated that such a decision should only be taken by a reconvened case conference. A few hours later, Matthew was found dead in his cell.

This case again highlights profound issues about risk and protection. It demonstrates that, in spite of the willingness of social work and health professionals to work together, Matthew 'fell between two stools', in this case, between the mental health and criminal justice systems. Susan was forced to accept that the only way Matthew could be protected from himself was in prison; but even this was not sufficient to prevent the eventual outcome. The case also shows that where procedures and protocols exist, they should be rigorously followed; the decision to take Matthew off suicide observation should not have been taken by one person, and the nurse's actions left him open to accusations of blame. But does this make him responsible for Matthew's death? Who has the right to interfere with an individual's choice to determine whether to take his or her own life? These are ethical and moral questions which go far beyond a common-sense reading of risk and protection.

Risk assessment

All social work practice, implicitly or explicitly, involves an assessment of risk. But risk measurement is no easy task, and what might work well in one setting may not readily transfer to another. 'Risk assessment is a process of analysis, not a specific kind of research and not a result, and it must be viewed as a process that is subject to much uncertainty' (Bailar and Bailer, 1999: 285). Although writing about risk relating to chemical hazards, these sentiments equally apply to risk assessment in social work. The one certainty in social work that does exist is that there are *no* certainties, at best probabilities. In thinking about risk assessment, we need to be clear what the risk is, who presents the risk and to whom. Parsloe usefully separates out three different kinds of risk:

- Risk to service users from other people, usually their own relatives
- Risk to users themselves from their own behaviour
- Risk to known or unknown others from service users (1999: 11).

Two methods are currently used in assessing risk in social work: actuarial and clinical methods.

Actuarial method in risk assessment

The actuarial (or statistical) method has its roots in the insurance industry; it involves statistical calculations of probability, in which an individual's likely behaviour is predicted on the basis of the known behaviour of others in similar circumstances. This method is in common usage in mental health and criminal justice social work, largely because it has been found to have greater accuracy than clinical methods in terms of assessing the probability of a behaviour occurring (Farrington and Tarling, 1985). This method is also easy for social workers to use, since it presents them with a fixed set of questions to ask and a simple way of calculating level of risk (they simply add up the number of 'high risk' responses).

There are, however, major methodological limitations in transferring information about the behaviour of a group to an individual risk assessment. For example, in the field of criminal justice social work, where actuarial tools have been employed for several years, many of the risk assessment tools currently in use have been developed using male prison populations. These do not readily apply to other groups such as female offenders, or specific types of offender (Kemshall, 1997; Silver and Miller, 2002). There is also a recognised problem with cultural transferability, when tools developed in one sociocultural jurisdiction are employed in another culture. Many of the risk assessment tools being employed in the UK today have their origins in US and Canadian populations. Smith and Vanstone (2002) indicate that this can lead to deep-rooted problems which may require much more than merely tipping the cap to 'cultural sensitivity' when using imported materials. Moreover, Silver and Miller (2002) note how easy it becomes for those conducting risk assessments to depersonalise the subject of their assessment so that they come to see the person merely as a collection of 'risk variables'.

Clinical method in risk assessment

Clinical assessment is the traditional and more familiar method used in social work practice, and employs diagnostic assessment techniques relating to personality factors and situational factors relevant to the risky behaviour and the interaction between the two (Prins, 1999). It is highly dependent on the interaction between the social worker and client or service user; interviewing and direct observation are the key components used to collect information on social, personal and environmental factors associated with the problematic behaviour. Its main usefulness has been in terms of making sense of an individual's risky behaviour, by shedding light on the attitudes, motivations and precipitating factors which led to the risky behaviour and assessing their likely responses to 'treatment' (Prins, 1988; Kemshall, 1997).

The clinical method has serious limitations as a predictive tool. Clinical assessment is a highly subjective process, which is affected by the individual background, values and beliefs of the assessor (Kemshall, 1997). In this uncertain world of risk assessment and prediction, the most promising and productive practice would seem to be to draw on a combination of actuarial and clinical assessment methods (Kemshall, 1997). By combining clinical assessment (with all its potential for eliciting 'rich' information relating to an individual) with actuarial information (developed from broader populations with higher predictive accuracy), risk assessments are likely to be stronger, more focused and more useful than simply using one method.

But this does not go far enough. Social work values promote the worth of the individual and the uniqueness of human beings in their social and cultural contexts. By channelling all our energies into the assessment of risk, we may lose sight of social work's traditional values, especially when the service user is regarded by society as 'dangerous', or when his/her behaviour is seen as abhorrent, such as in the case of sexual offenders (Harris, 1999). Risk assessment methods illustrate a wider process in social work in which tasks are becoming increasingly routinised and performed in often highly prescriptive ways. McBeath and Webb (2002) assert that accountability, quality control and risk management dominate social work today, with an accompanying emphasis on duties and regulations. This has led to the development of defensive forms of social work, which, they argue, are uncongenial to the development of human qualities likely to promote engagement in discussion of what counts as good practice in social work.

This is a good place to start in terms of a rethink about risk assessment. If the assessment of risk is, as we have stated, at the heart of social work practice, it provides an opportunity to work with service users in an empowering rather than oppressive way. Regardless of whether the service user is a willing recipient of care (for example an older woman who has had a fall at home) or an 'involuntary client' (such as a young parent under investigation for neglecting their child), those whom we are assessing should feel part of the process of assessing risk (Trotter, 1999). This means at the outset that attention must be paid to the relationship between the worker and the service user. This is not about encouraging service users to see us as their 'friends'. Instead, it is about being clear with service users what our role is, what our responsibilities and obligations are, what the service user can expect from us and the organisation and what may happen in the future. Only then will service users be able to make informed decisions about the risks they are prepared to take (and not take) and the protection they may require.

Risk management

Risk assessment is not and should not be an end in itself, but is best considered as part of a wider risk management strategy. There have been occasions in the past when the process of registration, for example, at a child protection case conference or a sex offender registration conference, has been treated as an end in itself; it has become an administrative procedure, rather than the opportunity to address the future management of risk as part of an ongoing process (Kemshall and Maguire, 2001). This has had disastrous consequences (Butler-Sloss, 2003).

Risk management, like risk assessment, brings its own dangers. An investigation of risk management in the world of business draws interesting parallels with risk management in social work. Traditionally, risk management in business was concerned with assessing how and why a company experienced losses, with a view to minimising those losses. However, heightened sensitivity to risk exposure has led to a huge elevation in the importance of risk management. Instead of being a useful tool, it starts to become 'an unnecessary self-regulation', and companies become far too cautious (Hunt, 2003: 93). This is undoubtedly a real possibility in social work, as workers become afraid to show creativity and initiative, and become procedure-driven and overly concerned with self-protection.

Davis (1996) points out that risk management is often interpreted simply as a risk minimisation strategy. In terms of mental health, this means locating risk 'in a deficient and potentially dangerous minority of individuals who need to be identified, registered and managed by medication and surveillance' (1996: 113). In doing so, real issues for the majority of service users are often ignored, and little attention is paid to the ways in which 'social, economic, cultural and interpersonal environments influence vulnerability as well as a potential for violent, harmful and self-neglectful behaviour' (1996: 114). Davis thus shifts attention from the 'dangerous' individual to the wider context, including the relationship between the service user and the agency, the locations where practice takes place, the different agencies involved and the organisational structure. Mental health service users must be empowered to take risks to be whole human beings. In order for this to happen, workers must be adequately supported and supervised in their own organisations.

But there is another important point here. Social workers are never alone in carrying the management of risk (although it may feel like this at times) and it is vital that there is a clear sharing of tasks and responsibilities between all those in an individual's social network. This is likely to include formal supports (through social work, health professionals, teachers, police) and informal supports (through relatives, family friends, local community groups and so on). Most children, Beckett (2003) indicates, look to their parents for protection first and then to neighbours, friends and other family members. This means that social workers must be prepared to work in partnership at all levels and appropriately share information and responsibility, in such a way that service users know what is happening and why.

Checklist for good practice

We have considered some of the general themes underpinning risk and protection in social work. These raise a number of fundamental questions for practice:

- What is the risk? Is it positive or negative, and for whom?
- What is the relevant legislation?
- What procedures and policy frameworks apply to the situation?
- Whose rights and whose responsibilities need to be safeguarded?
- What values issues need to be considered?
- What methods of assessment should be used and why?
- How can decision-making and tasks be shared between agencies?
- What support systems are in place for you as a worker?
- What are the lines of accountability? How can these be shared?
- How will the work be monitored and reviewed?

CONCLUSION

In reviewing this chapter, a number of themes emerge. Firstly, we have argued that risk and protection are a huge preoccupation in social work, as they are in society as a whole. Massive sums of money have been earned by North American companies that have tapped into this preoccupation with risk, seeing a gap in the market to produce risk assessment tools which have eagerly been snapped up in the UK. Our questions remain: how far have these actually met the needs of the situation? And more provocatively, are these tools in fact a 'smoke screen' to convince ourselves and others that we are doing something positive in a situation over which we may have little control?

But this seems overly pessimistic. Our second thesis is that although risk is everywhere, it is not necessarily negative. Social work should be about much more than minimising risk; it should be about maximising welfare (Munro, 2002). This means that in some situations, we will be encouraging people to take risks – to continue to live at home in spite of physical or mental frailty, join a self-help group, go to school, apply for a college course. Social work is in this way a balancing act in which we encourage service users to take risks and learn by their mistakes. *Messages from Research* (Department of Health, 1995) attempted to shift the agenda in social work with children from child protection to child welfare, yet still the emphasis today in social work with children and families remains on the few 'high risk' cases, and local authority social workers complain that they have little opportunity to carry out preventive social work with families. Each new child abuse scandal becomes another 'nail in the coffin' for preventive practice. This must be resisted at management and organisational level (Spratt, 2001) if social work's core values and skills are to be upheld.

Thirdly, we have argued that while 'risk' and 'protection' may be social constructions, perceived differently by different people at different times, this does not make them imaginary. On the contrary, as our two case examples demonstrate, risk can have serious consequences for individuals and their families. Social workers must therefore work from the basis of a sound understanding of legislation, policy, procedure and rights. They must be prepared to examine their practice from a moral and ethical perspective and work from the basis of theories which aim to challenge, not support oppression, in other words, they must act with integrity (Cree, 2000: 209). Lastly, they must seek to work in real partnership with service users, other professionals and members of society to ensure that the risks which are taken have positive outcomes and that protection allows vulnerable children and adults to live creative, full and, if at all possible, 'safe' lives.

FURTHER READING

Beck, U. (1992) *Risk Society: Towards a New Modernity* (London: Sage).

Kemshall, H. and Pritchard, J. (eds) (1996) *Good Practice in Risk Assessment and Risk Management* (London: Jessica Kingsley).

Parsloe, P. (ed.) (1999) *Risk Assessment in Social Care and Social Work* (London: Jessica Kingsley).

Prins, H. (1999) *Will They Do It Again? Risk Assessment and Management in Criminal Justice and Psychiatry* (London: Routledge).

Tulloch, J. and Lupton, D. (2003) *Risk and Everyday Life* (London: Sage).

Troubled and in Trouble: Young People, Truancy and Offending

Angela Grier and Terry Thomas

The behavioural 'problems' of young people are nothing new. Successive genera-tions see the latest group of people moving through adolescence as more 'problematic' and more 'threatening' than the last one (Pearson, 1983), and devise various ways of managing that problem and threat. Over the last thirty years social workers have been drafted in to assist in that management.

Social workers work with young people who are truanting from school, and are engaged in criminality and other antisocial behaviour; that work now takes place largely in multi-agency Youth Offending Teams (YOTs) alongside police officers and others working with young people. Social work interventions are made within the context of these teams and within the extensive legal frameworks and national standards that now circumscribe social work with young people who offend. It all takes place against a political backdrop that is often hostile to young people:

> one of the biggest challenges we face is how to deal with young offenders who believe that their age makes them untouchable, who flout the law, laugh at the police and leave court on bail, free to offend again. The public are sick and tired of their behaviour and expect the criminal justice system to be able to keep them off the streets.
>
> (Home Secretary David Blunkett, quoted in Home Office, 2002a)

In this chapter we seek to explore the changing nature of work over the last twenty years with young people who offend, from a position of 'welfare' and 'minimalism' to today's more directed and authoritarian 'interventionism'. Four areas of work are singled out for particular attention as examples of the 'popular punitiveness' currently directed at young people: the identification and interventions to deal with truancy, antisocial behaviour, young people who commit sexual offences and the persistent young offender.

'Popular punitiveness' is a phrase coined to describe the way in which politicians, using the umbrella of the rhetoric of 'law and order', have been 'tapping into, and using for their own purposes, what they believe to be the public's generally punitive stance' (Bottoms, 1995: 40). Garland (2001: 13) has elaborated on the idea:

> A few decades ago public opinion functioned as an occasional brake on policy initiatives: now it operates as a privileged source. The importance of research and criminological knowledge is downgraded and in it's place is a new deference to the voice of 'experience', of 'common sense', of what 'everyone knows'.

From 'welfare' to 'minimalism' to 'interventionism'

The history of youth justice policy between the 1960s and the early 1990s has been divided into two phases: that of 'welfare' and that of 'minimalism' (Pitts, 2003).

The welfare era reached a peak in the late 1960s and early 1970s. The social sciences, through social work, appeared to offer a means to resolve social problems and therefore associated behaviour such as youth offending. When questions were asked about whether these new approaches actually worked (Martinson, 1974), the optimism of welfare was deflated and followed by an era of minimalism; the 1980s saw crime as almost a 'routine activity' for young people who were best left alone wherever possible to 'grow out of it' and practitioners were best occupied in trying to divert them away from the criminal justice system.

When New Labour came into power in 1997, a new era of 'interventionist' youth justice came into being. For many observers it was simply a case of more of the same because:

> in the run up to the 1997 general election, it was difficult to work out who would make the most right-wing home secretary, the then holder, Tory Michael Howard (not noted for his kindness towards law breakers), or Labour's Jack Straw.
>
> (Driver and Martell, 2002: 58)

The Crime and Disorder Act 1998 defined, for the first time, the 'principal aim' of the youth justice system which was 'to prevent offending by children and young persons' (s.37). Critics were quick to point out that this definition said nothing about any 'welfare' component of the work to be carried out, even though the Children and Young Persons Act 1933 s.44 still required courts to 'have regard to the welfare of any child or young person' brought before them.

The Crime and Disorder Act also created for the first time a national body in the Youth Justice Board (YJB) to have oversight of the youth justice system; as before, most activities would remain localised but the YJB would promote good practice, issue national standards, provide funding and commission research. Research was back on the agenda for practitioners in terms of their practice being evidence-based to ensure that it 'worked' and their work became more liable to evaluation.

The Act restructured youth justice services at the local level by creating Youth Offending Teams (YOTs). Social workers were to be relocated from the social services department into the multi-agency YOT to work alongside seconded probation officers, police officers, education workers and (sometimes) healthcare professionals. The presence of social workers in the YOTs presumably meant 'welfare' was still seen as important but it would have to take its place alongside other practitioners from different backgrounds and cultures, and with possibly different aims and objectives. Any concerns social workers might have had about 'confidentiality' and the sharing of personal information were allayed by s.115 of the Crime and Disorder Act, which in essence said it was alright to share such information as long as it was for purposes of the Act.

CASE EXAMPLE

Alan is aged 15 and lives with his mother and brother in a rural area. A few months ago, following an argument with his mother's 'boyfriend', he 'stole' her car and drove it around a supermarket car park at 2am in the morning. Nearby residents called the police who arrested him. No one was hurt but £500 worth of damage had been caused to the car's bodywork. A reprimand was considered insufficient and prosecution followed.

The social worker in the YOT wrote a pre-sentence report (PSR) for the Youth Court and proposed an Action Plan Order (APO) as the best way forward. Alan was assessed as being very remorseful and unlikely to reoffend; the APO (lasting three months) was considered to be sufficient intervention to bring home to him the risk to himself and others. Alan had no previous convictions, attended school regularly where he was described as 'industrious' and had no apparent social 'deficit' that needed meeting.

However, the Youth Court imposed a two-year Supervision Order. Alan met with his supervisor (the author of the PSR) twice a week (as required by the national standards). The supervision was seen as somewhat perfunctory and with no real aim. Plans were in hand to apply for a revocation of the Supervision Order after 12 months.

The social work role appears almost non-existent in this case example; the court ignored the options outlined in the PSR and work on improving credibility in the courts might be needed; and the resulting imposition of top-down national standards was clearly inappropriate and denied any professional discretion to the social worker.

The Crime and Disorder Act left the age of criminal responsibility unaltered at ten years. It did, however, introduce the Child Safety Order (CSO) that allowed interventions with children *under ten* who behaved in such a way that they would have committed offences had they been over ten. For some this effectively meant that we had no age of criminal responsibility at all (NAPO, 1998). Social workers could be involved in applying for these orders and supervising the children on them; failure to comply could lead to care proceedings and a Care Order – in effect a back door route into care, bypassing the 'significant harm' tests of the Children Act 1989 which requires evidence of ill-treatment or the impairment of health or development.

The 1998 Act also removed the common law protection of 'doli incapax' for young people which required proof in court that children aged 10–14 knew the difference between right and wrong. With 'doli incapax' now repealed these children were now presumed to know the difference and became *more* responsible for their actions (Bandalli, 1998). At the same time the Act introduced Parenting Orders which, paradoxically, emphasised the responsibilities of parents for their children's actions; the contradiction appears to have been lost on the government. Parenting Orders could require parents to attend counselling classes and even residential classes (after amendments by the Antisocial Behaviour Act 2003) to make them better parents and meet the perceived 'parental deficit' (Goldson and Jamieson, 2002).

It is only possible here to give a flavour of the Crime and Disorder Act and its initial moves towards greater interventionism; we consider the Act's Antisocial Behaviour Order in more detail below. Some of the Act's provisions did give space for more social work input within them.

The Drug Testing and Treatment Order accepted a welfare role was needed with offenders who used drugs, and the Reparation Order and Action Plan Order allowed for the first glimpses of restorative justice into the youth justice system to be followed a year later by the Referral Order.

On the other hand, reprimands and final warnings continued the authoritarian movement by replacing the old non-statutory police cautions with a new statutory version, limiting their frequency and including their existence formally into a person's criminal record. The police had their discretion to deal with things informally reduced; they could only now do this in 'exceptional circumstances' (Home Office/Youth Justice Board, 2002: para. 4.1). Unlike cautions, parents and children no longer had to consent to reprimands and the police no longer had to consult with anyone before administering them. The whole process taking place behind closed doors lacked transparency and 'due process', and the police were found to be keeping even *less* formal justifications for their decisions than in the days of cautions (Evans and Puech, 2001).

In the following sections we consider the interventionism introduced into four particular aspects of young people's behaviour: truancy, antisocial behaviour, the young sexual offender and the persistent young offender.

Young people who engage in antisocial behaviour

One new direction now taken by New Labour was that towards combating antisocial behaviour. What exactly antisocial behaviour is and how it differs from criminality has always been a matter of debate. It has variously been described as 'sub-criminal', 'low-level disorder' and 'public nuisance' but others have pointed out that this can also mean behaviour that is non-criminal; on the other hand, if it includes criminal behaviour why call it just antisocial?

The developing idea of antisocial behaviour appears to have started not with the police or social workers but with housing officials. Elizabeth Burney (1999) has carefully documented the early history of antisocial behaviour from the mid-1990s. Beset with problems and complaints landing on their desks, housing officials lobbied for new laws to tackle this seemingly growing behaviour that included noise, abuse, graffiti and inconsiderate behaviour. New Labour's Crime and Disorder Act tried to deal with it in many ways but most directly by introducing the Antisocial Behaviour Order or ASBO.

ASBOs are a form of injunction applied for in the civil courts by police or local authorities. The applicants have to prove *not* that a specific law has been broken but that someone or a group of people have experienced the behaviour as 'harassment, alarm or distress', and only an ASBO will protect those persons (1998 Act s.1). The recipient of the ASBO is given a list of activities they must desist from and sometimes a geographic area they must stay out of. It is estimated that 'juveniles represent nearly 60 per cent of those attracting an antisocial behaviour order' (Pollard, 2003).

If a young person subject to an ASBO fails to comply with its conditions, they may be returned to court but this time the court is a criminal court and sentences replace injunctions. It meant that two young people in a city could be acting in exactly the same way but one – subject to an ASBO – now faces the criminal court and even a possible custodial sentence, whilst the other one – not subject to an ASBO – may not necessarily have broken any criminal law at all. No longer 'equal under the law', some young people could start to experience a separate 'jurisprudence of difference'.

Social workers were amongst those practitioners initially hesitant to be involved in applying for the new orders (Burney, 2002). The government's belief in this head-on approach appeared to leave no space for social work, which, if anything, was being left behind as having 'failed' (Jerrom, 2003). Worse than that there were implicit suggestions that the non-judgemental welfare approach of the past had even contributed to the present problems, and that the Blair government was now ready to 'abandon long established taboos on judgementalism and on discussions of personal behaviour' (Deacon, 2002: 105). This seemed like an extension of the 1980s New Right agenda that stigmatised social work as symptomatic of all that was wrong with the welfare state. In the communitarian rhetoric of the times, if you had 'rights' then you had 'responsibilities' and could not hide behind welfare 'hand-outs' and 'acceptance' of everything you did.

This hesitancy caused the first Labour home secretary to write to all local authorities urging them to use the ASBO (Home Office, 1999) and his successor went further to suggest that 'professionals working to reduce antisocial behaviour who fail to use new powers afforded to them ... should be sacked' (*Community Care*, 2003a). By late 2003 some 1330 ASBOs had been made on adults and young people (Blears, 2003).

One of the most difficult aspects of the ASBO for the social worker was that of the publicity that could attend the making of a successful application. Social workers, used to a veil of confidentiality falling over their work with young people in the Youth Courts, now realised that no such veil fell over ASBOs. The courts listening to applications were the Magistrates Courts where there were no automatic reporting restrictions, and the press duly provided names and addresses and sometimes photographs of young people. On top of that some local authorities decided to produce their own publicity leaflets to distribute door to door in an offender's locality to let the community know who was now subject to an ASBO (see Grier and Thomas, 2003, where examples of leaflets are reproduced). Some parents sought to challenge this publicity against Article 8 (the 'Right to Privacy') of the European Convention on Human Rights (*Observer*, 12 October 2003).

Social workers were also aware of the *UN Convention on the Rights of the Child* 1989 that said a young person involved in criminal proceedings had the right 'to have his or her privacy fully respected at all stages of the proceedings' (Art. 40(2)(b)(vii)). The irony was that ASBO applications were not criminal proceedings but as a 'lesser' form of civil proceedings they allowed more publicity to fall on the recipient.

Young people who do not go to school

New Labour has set out a new authoritarian approach towards non-school attendance and truancy. The education welfare officer or education social worker recognised that some truants had problems at home or were even phobic about schools, while for others truancy may have become just another 'routine activity'.

In the past there were limits to interventions that could be made in public places where children of obvious school age could be seen, when they should have been in school. The police were having to turn a blind eye because not going to school was not a criminal offence for the young person involved. On the other hand, if you believed truancy to be a precursor to youth crime, perhaps 'something should be done' in the name of crime prevention; the parliamentary debate on the Crime and Disorder Bill heard that 5 per cent of offences committed by children were said to occur during school hours (Hansard HC Debates, Standing Committee B, 9 June 1998, col. 778.)

Some police forces had tried rounding up truants, usually in collaboration with education welfare officers, making joint patrols through city centres (see for example *Guardian*, 13 June 1988; *Independent*, 18 September 1989). Critics pointed out that the problem for the police was having no real legal powers to intervene when they saw a possible truant (Thomas, 1994).

The Crime and Disorder Act 1998 (section 16) resolved the problem. Not going to school was not made into a criminal offence but in future the police, in collaboration with the local education authorities, could put in place patrols which did have the power to pick up truants. This use of police power was *not* an arrest, and the law was unclear on exactly what degree of force could be used by the police. The powers were also to be time-limited and for a given geographic area, rather than an all-encompassing blanket provision. The new powers did take the police into new areas that were primarily civil rather than criminal. Having removed the child to designated premises or the school in question, the police handed over to the education social worker for follow-up work.

The only criminal offence connected to non-school attendance is committed not by the child but the parent. Unless parents are exercising their right to educate their child at home, they have a legal duty to register the child with a school and then ensure regular attendance; failure to do either is an offence. Social workers working with families have always been aware of this final sanction but their interventions sought to avoid it. Now the sanctions were to get heavier.

Parents failing to secure the attendance of their children became liable to a fine of £2500 and/or three months in prison. Much publicity surrounded the imprisonment of an Oxfordshire woman in May 2002 (*Guardian*, 14 May 2002) and the government later proposed new 'fast-track' arrangements to bring parents to court within 12 weeks in cases of truancy. The Anti-social Behaviour Act 2003 section 23 went further with its provisions to introduce on-the-spot fines for parents of truants.

Although all these punitive sanctions would no doubt be discussed between education and social workers before implementation, the rising levels of authoritarianism may question just how much the social worker is being drawn into what is about to befall the family they are working with.

Marginally more welfare-oriented and supportive are the Parenting Orders (Crime and Disorder Act 1998 section 8) and Parenting Contracts (Anti-social Behaviour Act 2003 section 19), both available as a court disposal where elements of truancy have been identified. Social workers may be implementing both of these initiatives. The Parenting Contract is not a legal contract but any non-compliance might be used as evidence for further court hearings; it formalises earlier initiatives by social workers and others known as ABCs (Acceptable Behaviour Contracts) (see Maye-Banbury and Walley, 2003) and builds on a well-established tradition of using contracts in social work (see for example Corden and Preston-Shoot, 1987).

Young people who commit sexual offences

Most of the concern about sexual offenders in recent years has been directed at adult offenders who target children and young people as their victims. It has, however, long been recognised that young people may themselves commit sexual offences. Guidance accompanying the Children Act 1989 advised that where young people have abused other young people or children 'the appropriate child protection procedures should be followed in respect of both the victim and the alleged abuser' and that 'such adolescent abusers are themselves in need of services' (Home Office et al., 1991: para. 5.24.1–2; see Department of Health et al., 1999: para. 6.31 for latest guidance).

The extent of the problem of abuse by young people was explored in an influential NCH report which estimated that a third to a quarter of all sexual offending could be by young people under 21 (NCH, 1992). Since this report social work services to young sexual offenders have improved and spread across the country. Early into the field were such therapeutic agencies as Barnardo's 5A Project in Liverpool and G-MAP in Manchester. In early 2004, researchers at the University of Durham set out to map the full extent of social work and other services to this group of offenders (Coombes, 2003).

At the same time as this acceptance of social work help to young sexual offenders, there have been contradictory policies made that have sent shots across the bows of a welfare approach. In 1993 the law was changed to make it easier to prosecute young sexual offenders by lowering the age at which it was thought possible to rape, from 14 down to 10. Within a year it had been used for the first time (*Independent*, 23 June 1994).

Critics bemoaned the English desire to punish rather than help young offenders:

> the real concern is that the 13 year old boy prosecuted for rape is just another example of the law turning its back on a sympathetic approach to young children by treating them as criminals and putting them through the same justice system as adults.
>
> (Rhead, 1994)

Later research revealed the new laws to be little used and not particularly helpful; the research accepted that rape could be committed by those under 14 but believed that the original claims of a 'widespread problem' seemed likely to have been exaggerated (Soothill, 1997).

When the sex offender 'register' was introduced in 1997, young offenders, convicted or cautioned, had their names included alongside adults; they, or their parents, were required to notify the police every time they changed name or address, with non-compliance leading to a criminal sanction. The only concession given to young people was that the time period for which they had to register would be half of that imposed on adults.

From the outset, the inclusion of young people on the register was challenged as being unhelpful in terms of a welfare intervention (NSPCC, 1997). Although it was not supposed to be part of the punishment, the idea that juveniles should be on the register for only half the time imposed on adults seemed to come more from the justice sphere of thinking than from any welfare orientation; arguments might even be made that young people should be on the register *twice* as long as adults if welfare provisions were being made to prevent them becoming adult sexual offenders in the long term. The arguments continued (see for example Myers, 2001) and the government responded by taking a focused look at young sexual offenders when it reviewed the working of the register and its legal framework, and a number of welfare options were proposed that included taking young people off the register (Home Office/Scottish Executive, 2001: 28–9).

These welfare-oriented options were welcomed in many quarters and the majority of respondents opted for some change along the lines now put forward (the responses were not formally published but are to be found at www.sexual offencesbill.homeoffice.gov.uk). At this point, however, the government seems to have got cold feet and quietly refused to countenance any changes to the present regime.

The White Paper that followed the review and its consultation exercise simply ignored the position of young people who commit sexual offences (Home Office, 2002b) but it did show, once again, the authoritarianism of New Labour, because the legislation based on the White Paper did include provisions to make life harder for the young registered sex offender.

The Sexual Offences Act 2003 s.91 introduced a custodial sentence for young people not complying with registration requirements to strengthen the existing non-custodial sanctions. Why this new sentence was needed was even more of a mystery because compliance was never a problem. For all registrants, of whatever age, compliance was reported to be as high as 97 per cent and 'steadily improving' (Home Office/Scottish Executive, 2001: para. 4) and on top of that the Home Office had admitted that it did not even know how many of those on the register were under 18 (ibid.: para 3; see also Thomas, 2003)!

Young people who persistently commit offences

If criminal activity was seen as fairly normal for some young people and even a 'routine activity' that would eventually be left behind, others posed a more serious problem. In the early 1990s, the 'persistent' young offender had been identified as someone responsible for an inordinate amount of crime.

In 1993 the Home Secretary's announcement of the new Secure Training Orders were premised on the idea that they were needed for 'that comparatively small group of very persistent juvenile offenders whose repeated offending makes them a menace to the community' (Hansard HC Debates, 2 March 1993, col. 139). The 'persistent offender' was also offered up as part of the explanation for why youth crime statistics were actually falling at this time:

> one explanation for the apparent discrepancy between ACPO's (Association of Chief Police Officers) picture of greater juvenile offending and the decline in the number of juvenile offenders is a growth in the number of persistent offenders.
>
> (House of Commons 1993, para. 15)

The press would name such offenders as 'blip' boy, or 'rat' boy to suggest that they were different from other offenders and caused their own 'blips' in the crime statistics; if these young people offended whilst on bail they were called 'bail bandits'. More considered research, however, found the 'persistent young offender' somewhat hard to pin down (Hagell and Newburn, 1994) and raised the possibility that this was another form of 'folk devil' emerging from a 'moral panic'. Either way, it did not stop the introduction of secure training centres through the Criminal Justice and Public Order Act 1994, and a range of subsequent punitive measures to deal with the 'persistent young offender'. The 1994 Act, for example, introduced new powers to detain children as young as twelve in police custody if considered necessary and gave the police powers to arrest any young person in breach of bail conditions.

The change of government in May 1997 did not change the focus on persistent young offenders. Fast-tracking was to be encouraged by the Crime and Disorder Act (Part Three) to get young offenders through the courts quickly because 'there is a real urgency in dealing with all young offenders, and especially persistent offenders, really promptly' (Lord Chancellor's Dept, 1997; see also Graham, 1998). Whether fast-tracking meant skating over the needs of welfare and justice was an unanswered question in the race to bring punishment closer to the initial offending.

The Youth Courts already had the power to remand violent and sexual offenders aged over 15 years and those who had offended when absconding from local authority accommodation; in 1998 the age criteria had come down to 12.

The problem was that 'persistent' young offenders did not usually commit violent and sexual crimes, and were not necessarily absconding from anywhere. The response in 2001 was simply to lower the criteria for direct remands to cover 12–16-year-olds 'who commit persistent, *medium low level offences* and who courts believe continue committing offences whilst on bail'; the absconding criteria was repealed (Home Office, 2002c, emphasis added; Criminal Justice and Police Act 2001 section 130).

The use of a custodial sentence for young people – renamed as a Detention and Training Order by the Crime and Disorder Act – has remained an option for the Youth Courts. The role of the social worker, whether in a YOT or other part of the social services department, has been to track these young people through their time in custody and back into the community at the end of it. Social workers needed to be particularly aware of the difficulties this return may entail for young people. From a position of being 'degraded' as a person who has lost their normal rights and responsibilities, as well as their liberty, they need help to realise a 'regraded' position back into the community.

The UN is amongst the critics of the UK's high use of custody for children and:

> particularly concerned that more children between the ages of 12 and 14 are now being deprived of their liberty (and) ... deeply concerned at the high and increasing numbers of children in custody, at earlier ages for lesser offences
>
> (UN, 2002: para. 57)

The arguments that custody was damaging and brutalising in itself for young people seemed to have been lost along the way, until a rude reminder was brought home by a High Court ruling in the winter of 2002. The case had been brought by the Howard League, concerned that young people detained in the prison estate appeared to be outside of the remit of the Children Act 1989. In particular they were outside of the Act's child protection provisions should they suffer abuse within custodial settings; a Prison Order actually stated that the Children Act was not applicable to young prisoners.

The courts ruled that this 'disapplying' of the Children Act to certain children was simply 'wrong' in law. Local authorities with Young Offender Institutes (YOIs) and secure training centres in their area had to start talking to each other about how child protection provisions in particular could be made manifest in custodial settings (Wise, 2003). This official denial of welfare had been going on for ten years before it was put right. When 16-year-old Joseph Scholes hanged himself in Stoke Heath YOI on March 24 2002, he was the twenty-fifth young person aged 15–17 years old to have killed themselves in prison custody since 1990 (Inquest, 2003).

One attempt at avoiding the negative aspects of custody has been the adoption of the Intensive Supervision and Surveillance Programme (ISSP). The ISSP was specifically aimed at the persistent young offender, to bring structure into often chaotic lives (Home Office, 2001). The ISSP is not an order of the court but may be built in to other orders as part of remand arrangements, a Supervision Order or a condition of aftercare supervision following the custodial part of a Detention and Training Order. As its name suggests, the ISSP offers rigorous community-based surveillance, with up to 25 hours a week contact with a young person in the initial part of the Programme that generally lasts six months in all. The ISSP was limited to certain areas to start with, but went nationwide in 2003; according to Home Office Minister Hazel Blear: 'we must have tough programmes like ISSP in place to punish persistent and serious young offenders' (YJB, 2003).

Intensive Supervision and Surveillance Programmes and some remands for young people can now also be accompanied by electronic monitoring and the wearing of an ankle tag. Any misgivings that these might be stigmatising and unhelpful 'Orwellian' additions to the youth justice system appear to have disappeared. Indeed the Home Office was even happy to adopt Orwell's terminology and, without any trace of irony, proudly reported the new developments as 'a Big Brother-style approach to dealing with persistent offenders' (*Crime Reduction News*, April 2003: 4).

Trials on the use of tags with young people started in Manchester and Norfolk in January 1998 (*Guardian*, 10 January 1998) and became available for 12–15-year-olds on bail or on remand to local authority accommodation in March 2002, with the implementation of sections 131–2 of the Criminal Justice and Police Act 2001. The Act talked of 'a recent history of repeatedly committing imprisonable offences while remanded on bail' (s.132) which was the latest manifestation of the 'persistent young offender'.

CASE EXAMPLE

Robert is 15 years old and comes from an inner-city area of a large conurbation. He is currently the subject of a 12-month Detention and Training Order (DTO) and residing in a local authority secure children's home; he was considered too vulnerable for a custodial setting. Robert has committed offences of criminal damage, assault, sexual assault and burglary; he has 39 previous convictions of a similar nature.

A meeting has been convened to discuss Robert's care for the second half of his DTO which will be served in the community. Robert was made the subject of a Care Order seven years ago and has had numerous placements during that time. Before coming into care Robert was brought up by his grandmother and believed his real mother was his sister; he was physically and sexually abused by various male visitors to the home. Robert has three siblings in care.

The meeting is attended by the YOT's social worker who will be supervising Robert for the six months of his DTO in the community and by the social worker who will be finding him suitable accommodation; placement with his mother is considered unrealistic. Robert's behaviour is considered unpredictable and even 'dangerous'; he is 6ft 2ins and weighs 18 stone. The education authority is seeking a school for Robert; he has a statement of special educational needs. A psychiatrist reports being unable to help because Robert has an 'untreatable' personality disorder.

The meeting was inconclusive as no placement or school exists as yet for Robert. A six-month ISSP was considered inappropriate because it would be too demanding for

> ### CASE EXAMPLE cont'd
>
> him. The possibility of further secure accommodation under the Children Act s.25 will be looked into; Robert leaves his present secure accommodation in eight weeks' time when the DTO ends.

This case example illustrates the damage that can accumulate within one child by ineffective social work interventions; the outstanding work now required is almost overwhelming and leaves the social worker with almost nothing but a 'containing role' whilst awaiting a new crime or other event to take place. The requirement to 'protect the public' that is now placed upon social workers through national standards and other guidance is both nebulous and unrealistic, especially when accompanied by a lack of resources and a wariness from other agencies and professionals.

CONCLUSION

Contemporary social work with young people takes place in the shadows of new 'popular punitivism' and authoritarian interventions. Social work and welfare is offered to children and young people up to a point and then punishment falls in on them from the sky; once labelled as offenders it is hard for us to see them as children first. As Dame Elizabeth Butler-Sloss, president of the Family Division of the High Court has said:

> as a society we are highly protective of children for so long as they remain innocents. Once those children get into trouble, however, society becomes unforgiving.
>
> (cited in *Youth Justice Board News*, July 2003: 9)

The police have moved into new areas such as truancy, antisocial behaviour and 'criminal' behaviour by children under ten. Social workers in YOTs now share offices with police officers and probation officers and we are told that 'we've got out of the mindset that you're either in welfare or in law enforcement' (Home Office Minister Paul Goggins, cited in *Youth Justice Board News*, December 2003: 6). Whether or not social work in YOTs is surviving intact only time will tell, as they balance social work help to children in need at the same time as assessing risks and trying to reduce crime. Some social workers in YOTs feel driven by the process of their activities rather than being able to engage in 'real' social work.

Other elements of the 'new youth justice' give more optimism to social work. Restorative justice may be able to find space in Reparation Orders, Action Plan Orders and Referral Orders. Restorative justice sees offending and antisocial behaviour as a 'wrong' committed on an individual or the community that needs to be put 'right' as a problem-solving exercise (Johnstone, 2002). Early reports look promising, suggesting 'against the expectation of many commentators ... Referral Orders seem to come remarkably close to providing the basis for constructive and thoughtful youth justice' (Earle et al., 2003).

The requirement increasingly put on social workers to be evidence-based in their work, mindful of research and ready to have work 'evaluated' may be a double-edged blessing. On the one hand, it can constrain creativity and autonomy but, on the other, it might prove useful in combating the excesses of 'popular punitivism'.

Social workers are otherwise in an unenviable position working with young offenders. As the criminal justice agenda gets ever more interventionist in family life, it does so at the expense of more generalised family support. Criminal justice strategies become the preferred way of resolving – or repressing – social problems and social workers could get caught up in the undertow. Already some critics of the new directions have reported how members of the YJB have told them to 'get on board' and stop 'carping on the sidelines' (Pitts, 2003). Having just achieved a level of recognition, with degrees for qualification and their own General Social Care Council, the social work profession may also be expected to 'get on board'. If so, the future of social work may really be standing on the edge.

FURTHER READING

Crawford, A. and Newburn, T. (2003) *Youth Offending and Restorative Justice: Implementing Reform in Youth Justice* (Cullompton: Willan Publishing).

Garland, D. (2001) *The Culture of Control: Crime and Social Order in Contemporary Society* (Oxford: Clarendon Press).

Hagell, A. and Newburn, T. (1994) *Persistent Young Offenders* (London: PSI).

Johnstone, G. (2002) *Restorative Justice: Ideas, Values, Debates* (Cullompton: Willan Publishing).

Pitts, J. (2001) *The New Politics of Youth Crime: Discipline or Solidarity* (Basingstoke: Palgrave – now Palgrave Macmillan).

Thompson, N. (2002) *Building the Future: Social Work with Children, Young People and their Families* (Lyme Regis: Russell House).

Sexuality: Social Work Theories and Practice

Stephen Hicks

Introduction

What challenges face social workers working with lesbians, gay men or bisexual people? How has social work theorised questions of sexuality? Are contemporary ideas really all that helpful? These are the questions that this chapter seeks to address via an examination of the ways in which 'sexuality' has been constructed in social work theory and practice. The chapter will focus mainly on lesbian and gay issues within social work and welfare in the UK, but will inevitably also be concerned with the ways in which sexual 'normality' is both produced and maintained.

I have organised the chapter into an overview by decade, looking at the 1970s through to the current day. This is a structural device only and is not meant to suggest a sudden switch or change of ideas. In addition, this is not a progressive narrative, working from the 'dark ages' through to an enlightened present. Actually I intend to show how some ideas about sexuality have changed very little over the past thirty or so years, and there is a great danger in assuming that our contemporary view is the more liberated. Readers should also remember that this chapter is not an impartial account and I shall try to make my own preferences obvious. I begin with a discussion of 'sexuality as discourse', before moving on to give an overview of each decade. I relate theories to social work practice implications, taking the question of lesbian and gay parenting as my exemplar. The final section reviews the status of social work knowledge in this field and asks what happens 'after sexuality'.

A 'discourse' approach to sexuality and social work

The very term 'sexuality' is itself problematic because it is usually taken to refer to something possessed by a person, as in, 'what is your sexuality?' This, of course, relies upon a way of thinking which divides bodies, desires, actions into a series of discrete 'types' such as 'the lesbian', 'the gay man', 'the bisexual' or 'the hetero-sexual'. However, while these terms appear simply to describe the way people are, 'lesbian', 'gay' and so on are actually socially achieved ideas that are part of a wider set of sexual discourses that regulate what can and cannot be known or said. They specify particular ways of thinking about sexuality, but it is important to remember that there have been, and will be, other models. In addition, these terms are not simply different and equivalent because discourses of sexuality are also linked to questions of legitimacy and power. Thus heterosexuality is privileged and normalised while homosexuality is accorded an 'abnormal' and lesser status. Therefore it is assumed that everyone must have a 'sexuality' (Heath, 1982) which is organised into a series of types, hierarchically related, and in which heterosexuality is promoted as the norm.

I intend to take a discourse approach to sexuality in this chapter (Mills, 1997). The word 'discourse' is here used to refer to groups of statements which are regulated but which also have effects. That is, a discourse of sexuality regulates what can and cannot be known, allowing some ways of thinking but attempting to exclude others. It also forms the objects of which it speaks. Julianne Cheek provides a helpful definition of discourse as follows:

> Discourses create discursive frameworks which order reality in a certain way. They both enable and constrain the production of knowledge in that they allow for certain ways of thinking about reality whilst excluding others. In this way they determine who can speak, when, and with what authority, and conversely, who can not.
>
> (Cheek, 2000: 23)

Taking this kind of approach to sexuality and social work will be new to, and may even frustrate, some readers. This is because I do not present a 'how to work with lesbians and gay men (or indeed heterosexuals or bisexuals)' model for a number of reasons. Firstly, I am critical of models that assume an obvious set of sexual types with their attendant characteristics. This kind of approach tends to suggest that social work merely needs to determine the 'special needs' of lesbians and gay men in order to avoid discrimination. I intend to argue that 'anti-discriminatory practice' (Thompson, 1993) adopts this model, and instead I suggest a more reflexive approach to the very idea of 'sexuality' and social work. Secondly, people who use the terms 'lesbian' or 'gay' to refer to themselves are so diverse that to specify 'their needs' is to reduce that very complexity to a limited, and dominant, version of those categories, not least in terms of race (Lorde, 1984). Finally, like Chambon and Irving, I think that the role of social work theory is not to present 'how to' guidance, but rather to challenge 'the boundaries of our vision' (Chambon and Irving, 1999: xiv). Succinctly, instead of asking, 'how do we work with lesbians and gay men?', I ask, 'how does social work produce the very categories "lesbian" and "gay"?'

I ask this because social work is a profession in which sexuality is constituted as an object of inquiry and classification, and in which expert status is used to define people's sexuality in ways that they may not agree with. For example, social work practice is capable of enforcing the view that some people ought not to be sexual (disabled people, older people) or that their sexual behaviour should be curtailed. And this is because social work is an activity that constructs ideas about people and their 'needs' through the operations of discourse. A person's 'needs', their 'sexuality', the very idea that they have needs or have a sexuality, are all defined through negotiations between the social worker and the client or service user, a situation which involves the operations of power.

The 1970s

Much of social work theory during the 1970s was completely silent on questions of sexuality (for example, Pincus and Minahan, 1973), but, where addressed at all, the dominant response was to define homosexuality as a 'pathology', meaning a disease which is studied, debated and defined through professional discourses. Homosexuality was a problem in need of help (in extreme form, a sickness requiring cure), or a danger which threatened the welfare of others, especially children and other vulnerable adults. The features of this discourse of pathology are exemplified by the 1975 National Council for Civil Liberties' survey of local authority social services committees' views on homosexuality. This noted that authorities saw homosexuality as a form of disability, criminality or illness (Ferris, 1977: 32). Thirteen authorities reported active discrimination to prevent homosexuals working in residential settings, with children or the 'mentally handicapped' (the term that was then used):

> It is one of the more worrying findings of this survey that three authorities specifically mention the fear of sexual involvement with children as a reason for discrimination against homosexuals, while the replies of several others ... seem to imply a lingering belief that homosexuals are likely to be sexually predatory either towards children or more generally.
>
> (Ferris, 1977: 19)

There is little recorded evidence of a liberal equality position on sexuality and social work during the 1970s, and this did not gain prominence within social work theory until the 1980s. However, Val Carpenter's account, as a lesbian in the youth service of the 1970s, does highlight liberal views and the ways that those who held them were threatened by any real challenges to heterosexual superiority. She recalls how heterosexual workers implied that she was 'always "pushing lesbianism down their throats"' (Carpenter, 1988: 172), and notes that lesbians' work to challenge heterosexual privilege was interpreted as a threat, since liberals preferred to see sexuality as a private and individual matter.

In response to models that tolerated homosexuality at best, and pathologised it at worst, radical social movements made very different arguments. Lesbian feminists developed various analyses of what they termed 'heterosexual privilege', in which they argued that heterosexuality, far from being 'natural', was a political institution designed to restrict the sexual behaviour and choices of women and deny the lesbian possibility (Rich, 1980). Similarly, the gay liberation movement, questioned the supposed normality of heterosexuality, and argued that tolerance of homosexuality did not represent true liberation. Instead, gay liberationists stated that lesbians and gay men should 'come out of the closets' and openly declare their sexuality (Young, 1992[1972]).

These lesbian feminist and gay liberationist ideas strongly influenced the development of radical social work theory in the 1970s, which argued that part of the role of the social worker should be, in fact, to challenge 'heterosexual superiority' (Milligan, 1975: 96). The *Case Con* editorial collective, for example, stated that versions of homosexuality as a sin, sickness or vice were 'ideologies perpetrating the supremacy of heterosexual norms and the oppression of homosexuals' (Charing, et al., 1975: 2). Thus, radical social workers rejected the pathology models of homosexuality so prevalent in social work theory of the time, also arguing that expert psychiatric help was actually a contributor to such oppression. Remember, for example, that homosexuality was listed as a classifiable 'mental disorder' by the American Psychiatric Association until 1973. Radical social work also rejected the liberal tolerance model, calling this the 'cultural submission of the minority to the majority' (Milligan, 1975: 100), and made the important point that social work theory and social work practitioners cannot, and should not, be neutral on questions of sexuality. Neutrality was not seen as possible or even desirable, which may come as something of a shock to generations of social work professionals brought up on the idea that they should always be 'non-judgemental' and 'accepting of the person'.

Lesbian custody

CASE EXAMPLE

Sharon was married to Dave for ten years and they had two children. Towards the end of their marriage, Dave had an affair and the relationship ended in divorce. Sharon subsequently met and started a new relationship with a woman called Marcia. For some time, she tried to keep this from Dave as she was worried that he would try to take the children away from her. When Dave found out about Sharon's relationship with Marcia, he was very angry and instigated legal proceedings to win custody of the children. He argued that lesbianism was unnatural and he didn't want his children living in such a household.

During the 1970s, what was then called lesbian 'custody' of children was a key area in which issues of sexuality were very much to the fore. Social workers, lawyers, psychologists and other professionals were involved in cases in which the 'fitness' of lesbian mothers to care for their children was in dispute, and in which lesbians' children were removed from their care purely on the basis of their sexuality. For example, lesbians were regarded as unfit to care for children, and expert psychiatric or psychological opinion was used to reinforce the idea that lesbianism was a form of sickness or mental disorder.

Not all lesbians lost custody of their children, but in cases where they won, it is possible to detect models that display liberal tolerance. For example, courts made distinctions between a lesbian 'preference' and 'practice', requiring those who were awarded custody of their children to be discreet about their sexuality. In one case, a lesbian was directed to live apart from her partner (Hunter and Polikoff, 1976: 698), and courts judged that political activism in relation to gender or sexuality was inappropriate. Radical models of sexuality emerged mainly in feminist commentaries and articles rather than in the court arena itself (Hunter and Polikoff, 1976).

Practice implications for social work

Social work practitioners should think about:

- How they can challenge discrimination based on sexuality within their practice, including work in the field of childcare

- How they can challenge pathological views of lesbians and gay men

- The evidence that they can draw upon to show that sexuality is no determinant of parenting skills (Golombok, 2000), alongside the need to ensure that children are protected from harm

- Ways to recognise that being lesbian or gay is a political choice made in the face of 'compulsory heterosexuality', and not just a private or irrelevant matter

- How they might link these ideas to a commitment to an anti-homophobic and pro-feminist social work practice

- How social work can be used to challenge anti-lesbian and anti-gay ideas as part of a wider commitment to social change.

The 1980s

In the 1980s, sexuality issues acquired slightly more prominence in social work theory. In the US, for example, major texts dealing with lesbian and gay issues appeared for the first time (Schoenberg et al., 1984; Hidalgo et al., 1985). However, it is important to be clear that pathologising models of sexuality did not disappear. In addition, much standard social work theory was still completely silent on questions of sexuality (for example Howe, 1987). Liberal equality models dominated where sexuality was addressed at all.

Steven Epstein (1987[1998]) has characterised liberal approaches to sexuality in the 1980s as being dominated by what he calls the 'ethnic model'. In making arguments for equality on the basis that they were a minority group, lesbians and gay men relied upon an '"ethnic" self-understanding' (1998: 140) in which those categories seemed to describe a distinct type. The consequences of this model are a tendency towards 'essentialist' views of sexuality categories, the prominence of 'identity' models and liberal equality agendas.

Essentialist views of sexuality categories rest on the idea that terms like 'lesbian' or 'gay' refer to fixed, obvious and identifiable 'types' of person. In addition, these types are seen as unchanging across both time and place, so that 'lesbians' and 'gay men' are imagined to have always existed throughout history and across all cultures. Within the social work literature, for example, Steve McMillan (1989: 31) argued that sexuality was an 'essential ingredient' of people, while Jeannine Gramick (1983: 139) suggested that homosexuality had existed within ancient Greek and Roman cultures and that it was a 'natural phenomenon'. The notion of a distinct gay or lesbian identity was present in Bernie S. Newman's work (1989), and in articles which considered the development of 'stable personhood'. These claimed that political analysis of lesbian and gay oppression was a 'militant' or 'aggressive' phase which must be resolved in order to reach a state of 'self-acceptance' (Lewis, 1984).

There was also a marked prevalence of liberal equality models in the social work literature. Diana D. Dulaney and James Kelly (1982: 180), for example, argued that 'gay or lesbian individuals who accept their own lifestyle and are acutely aware of the daily injustice confronting those who are not heterosexual may need help in learning the efficacy of gentle education and positive modeling in influencing people's attitudes'. McMillan (1989) said that social workers should accept the equal validity of homosexual and heterosexual lifestyles.

However, it was during the 1980s that two neologisms began to appear in the social work literature. 'Homophobia' was originally defined by George Weinberg (1972) as an individual dread of, or revulsion towards, homosexuals. During the 1980s, Wisniewski and Toomey (1987: 455) surveyed 77 social work staff and found signs of homophobia amongst a third, whilst Decrescenzo's (1984) study of 140 mental health professionals found that social workers had higher homophobia scores when compared with psychiatrists and psychologists. However, this literature treated 'homophobia' as if it were an easily detectable, and therefore preventable, state. Tievsky (1988: 58), for example, lists a series of 'signs and symptoms' to detect homophobes. This is a problem for a discourse theory of sexuality which would see homophobia as an enacted set of practices and ideas, rather than a condition or fixed set of attitudes.

The word 'heterosexism' also came to prominence in the 1980s, and this was used to refer to a form of social relations in which 'heterosexuality is assumed to be normal, and everyone is assumed to be heterosexual' (GLC Women's Committee, 1986: 5). Thus heterosexism was used to define the oppression of lesbians and gay men as more than just an individual fear or reaction, but rather as a system in which heterosexuality was promoted as natural, preferable and normal. This concept was used by Anthony Hillin (1985) to explain why many lesbian or gay social workers were not open about their sexuality at work, or by McMillan (1989) to show why questions of sexuality were rarely, if ever, addressed by social workers in assessments of need.

Nevertheless, 1980s' social work literature showed little sign of what was perhaps the most important debate within lesbian and gay studies of the time, the 'social construction' of sexuality. Social constructionism is a broad term that covers a diverse set of ideas that share an important purpose, the rejection of the essentialist models of sexuality discussed earlier. This is summed up in Jeffrey Weeks' statement of a social constructionist perspective:

> My starting point was the rejection of any approach which assumed the existence, across cultures and across time, of a fixed homosexual person. On the contrary, I argued then, as I argue now, that the idea that there is such a person as *a* 'homosexual' (or indeed *a* 'heterosexual') is a relatively recent phenomenon, a product of a history of 'definition and self-definition' that needs to be described and understood before its effects can be unravelled. There is no *essence* of homosexuality whose historical unfolding can be illuminated.
>
> (Weeks, 1985: 6)

Instead of assuming a continuity to the very idea of the 'homosexual', the social constructionists pointed out that sexual acts are given very different meanings at different times. Thus sexual categories, like 'bisexual', 'heterosexual', 'lesbian' or 'gay', are ways of making sense of, and indeed constructing, the world. Such categories perform important functions of producing and enforcing particular views of 'sexuality'.

Section 28, foster care and adoption

CASE EXAMPLE

Rajinder and Mark had been together for about six years when they decided to apply to their local authority to foster a child. Their social worker, Sam, told them that no gay men had ever been approved by the panel before, and so recommended that the couple consider respite foster care for a disabled child in the first instance. Rajinder and Mark were unsure about this but went along with it because they felt they might be rejected otherwise. Sam did not talk to the couple much about their sexuality, which meant that they were ill-prepared for potential problems that might have arisen at the panel, matching, introductions or placement phases of the process.

During the 1980s, a new right-wing discourse suggested that homosexuality was being actively 'promoted' by some local authorities. The Conservatives implemented Section 28 of the Local Government Act 1987–88 which prohibited the 'promotion of homosexuality' by any local authority and outlawed the 'teaching in any maintained school of the acceptability of homosexuality as a pretended family relationship'. This impinged directly upon the question of lesbians and gay men as foster carers and adopters. (Section 28 was repealed in Scotland in 2000 and England/Wales in 2003.)

Jane Skeates and Dorian Jabri's *Fostering and Adoption by Lesbians and Gay Men* (1988) devoted a chapter to what they called 'myths and stereotypes about lesbians and gay men'. These included the idea that lesbians and gay men were deviant, unable to provide correct gender role models and a sexual risk to children; that children of lesbians and gay men would automatically become gay;

and that lesbians and gay men were not 'natural' parents (pp. 20–1). Skeates and Jabri referred to these ideas as 'a false set of assumptions' (p. 18), but a discourse approach would consider them as versions of the categories 'lesbian' and 'gay' which perform the work of asserting and maintaining hierarchical ideas about sexuality. That is, they are not just 'myths' to be replaced by a 'true' set of ideas about lesbians and gay men, but rather are part of discourses about sexuality that aim to define 'normal/abnormal' relations.

One consequence of such ideas was that many social services departments blocked or refused applications from lesbians and gay men to care for children. Accounts by lesbians and gay men who applied to local authorities in the 1980s indicate that many experienced homophobic ideas, a focus on their sexuality to the exclusion of all else, psychiatric tests and even outright rejection (Hicks and McDermott, 1999).

Practice implications for social work

Social work practitioners should think about:

■ How homophobic practices are ever-present, even within social work itself

■ Ways in which they can examine how heterosexist ideas and practices operate within everyday social work (for example within assessment procedures for potential foster carers and adopters)

■ The various points at which discriminatory ideas about lesbians and gay men can operate within social work processes (for example within the field of foster care and adoption this might include recruitment, assessment, the views of individual family placement social workers, panels, the views and practices of childcare teams and social workers, meetings with birth parents, the legal arena and so on)

■ How the 'social construction' model of sexuality can be used to challenge essentialist views of lesbians and gay men as types with fixed 'needs'

The 1990s

Issues of sexuality continued to be debated in 1990s' social work theory, but were still absent from core texts. Even *Radical Social Work Today* (Langan and Lee, 1989) ignored sexuality. Instead, lesbian and gay concerns found a minority voice within the field of 'anti-discriminatory practice' theory, and full discussion in a series of specialist texts (Logan et al., 1996; Appleby and Anastas, 1998; Brown, 1998a; Hunter et al., 1998; Mallon, 1999).

Anti-discriminatory practice became a key theory in social work during the 1990s and remains the dominant approach to sexuality. Thompson's key text, however, devoted just five pages to 'sexual identity', whilst giving whole chapters to 'gender and sexism', 'ethnicity and racism', 'ageism and alienation' and 'disability and social handicap' (Thompson, 1993). Indeed, Thompson (1993: 33) defined anti-discriminatory practice as seeking 'to reduce, undermine or eliminate discrimination and oppression, specifically in terms of challenging sexism, racism, ageism and disablism ..., and other forms of discrimination or oppression encountered in social work'.

In most versions of anti-discriminatory practice, then, sexuality was marginalised or placed at the bottom of a hierarchy of oppressions. In addition, lesbians and gay men appeared to be a group separate from disabled people, women or black people, which had two effects. Firstly, there was a tendency to forget that lesbians and gay men could also be black, disabled, women, older or working class. Secondly, anti-discriminatory practice did not analyse the ways in which our ideas about sexuality also draw upon ideas about gender, race and so on. A classic example here is the way in which lesbians and gay men have been understood as 'gender deviants' (Terry, 1999). Further, anti-discriminatory practice promoted a particular version of sexuality categories that rested largely on the notion of sexual identities. Thus 'lesbians' or 'gay men' were seen as types with 'special needs' (Thompson, 1993: 139), and social workers were encouraged to understand them better. An equality model was therefore used in which it was argued that lesbians and gay men were not deficient but 'just different' (Thompson, 1993: 139).

Other texts also employed the 'ethnic identity' model of sexuality in which practitioners were advised to acquire 'knowledge of the history, culture, traditions and customs, value orientation, religious and spiritual orientations, art, and music, of gay and lesbian communities' (Mallon, 1999: 23). Understanding the special characteristics of lesbians and gay men, in this way, allowed social workers simply to employ 'lesbian- or gay-affirmative practice' (Appleby and Anastas, 1998: 396; Mallon, 1999). In fact, readers were assured that social work theory did not need to change in relation to lesbians and gay men (Appleby and Anastas, 1998: 396), and these writers promoted the view that the job of social work was to help 'different others' assimilate into mainstream society (Appleby and Anastas, 1998: 102; Mallon, 1999: 33). Overall, lesbian issues were subsumed under a general model of homosexuality that tended to focus on gay men, and there was little, if any, attention given to theories that question or resist heterosexuality including forms of lesbian feminism.

However, an interesting parallel development within lesbian and gay theory of the 1990s was work that questioned and rejected such assimilationist or liberal equality models. Urvashi Vaid (1995), for example, argued that a mainstream or liberal rights approach to lesbian and gay politics, that is, asking for the right to be included in what are normative structures, would amount only to 'virtual equality'. This is because a mainstream civil rights strategy would lead only to toleration of lesbians and gay men within an otherwise unchanged or heteronormative system and the acceptance of a narrowly defined set of beliefs about lesbians and gay men ('not deficient just different').

Helen Brown's work on sexuality was important because she suggested that social work knowledge was itself problematic. She said that social work knowledge was 'never neutral', and that attention should be given to an evaluation of ideas about lesbians and gay men (Brown, 1998a: 19). Brown listed pathological views of lesbians found in some social work theory (1998: 68), and the absence of any serious discussion of lesbian issues within most feminist social work texts (1992: 204). Brown (1992: 201) also questioned the tendency of some social workers to treat sexuality as an 'all or nothing' issue, that is, focusing on it to the exclusion of all else when dealing with lesbian or gay clients, or instead refusing to discuss it at all. Brown did not adopt a discourse approach, but the importance of her work is in its insistence upon reflexivity with regard to social work knowledge.

Lesbian and gay foster care and adoption

PRACTICE EXAMPLE

Sue was a single lesbian who applied to adopt a child aged six years or under. Her local authority had already approved a number of lesbian adopters and had worked alongside a lesbian and gay parenting organisation to develop some practice guidelines on assessment. Sue's social worker, Helen, incorporated discussion of Sue's sexuality into the assessment as a whole, and spent time talking to her about how she viewed her lesbianism, how others viewed it, how it might be handled with various people involved in the adoption process, potential pitfalls and how Sue had dealt with homophobia and other forms of discrimination.

Helen Brown's work on foster care and adoption argued that social workers should be helped to feel more confident in assessing lesbian and gay applicants. She pointed out that the dichotomy of 'gay rights versus children's needs' was a false one, stating that no adult has a 'right' to be a foster carer or adopter since all must be adequately assessed and approved, but that it would be wrong to exclude people arbitrarily on the basis of sexuality (Brown, 1991). She also encouraged social workers to look at a range of issues specific to being lesbian or gay when assessing such applicants. This was important because some social workers had felt unable to ask lesbians or gay men specific questions about their sexuality for fear of being seen as 'discriminatory' and applying extra standards. On the contrary, most lesbian or gay applicants wanted to talk about their sexuality and how it impacted upon the fostering or adoption process.

Based upon interviews with lesbians and gay men who had applied to foster or adopt, I have argued that, in many cases, a position of 'tacit acceptance' was in place. Here, agencies accepted lesbian or gay carers, but on the understanding that their sexuality should be a private or discreet issue, and that they should take only the most disabled or 'hard-to-place' children, that is, lesbians and gay men were to be used only as a 'last resort' (Hicks, 1996). Later I argued that risk-based objections to lesbian or gay applicants (that is, the idea that lesbians or gay men posed risks to the gender, sexual, psychological or social development of children) were actually based upon the need to reinforce traditional views of gender and the family (Hicks, 1997). I argued for assessment practices that recognised the need to address lesbian and gay sexualities explicitly, but as a part of the whole assessment, not as the sole focus.

Practice implications for social work

Social work practitioners should think about:

■ The full range of theories of sexuality (Weeks, 2003), rather than relying upon anti-discriminatory practice models

■ How they can question a hierarchical or additive approach to the range of oppressions

■ The need to develop a reflexive approach to social work theories of sexuality

■ The areas of everyday life particular to being lesbian or gay in contemporary societies that are important to discuss with lesbian/gay service users

■ How they can recognise that lesbians and gay men are already disadvantaged within social work systems (such as foster care or adoption) and work to challenge heterosexist practices.

CONCLUSION: AFTER 'SEXUALITY'

The picture of sexuality and social work in the present century is mixed. Liberal equality views are dominant where sexuality is addressed (Hardman, 1997), while others argue that lesbian and gay issues are still absent from much of the social work theory, practice and education agenda (Langley, 2001; Logan, 2001, Manthorpe, 2003). Sexuality is still seen as a sexual 'preference', as a part of the personality and ultimately as an identity (Holwerda, 2002). Some practitioners continue to hold homophobic views (Ben-Ari, 2001), as demonstrated by the case in which two workers agreed to be transferred from children's services after refusing to consider lesbian or gay adopters (Pearce and Smith, 2003). Pathological views of lesbians and gay men are being promoted by various Christian right-wing organisations that have developed well-organised campaigns to oppose all forms of lesbian and gay parenting (Hicks, 2003). It is therefore possible to see that many of the arguments from earlier decades remain, even though they take new and different forms.

I have argued for a discourse approach in order to interrogate the ideas about sexuality promoted within social work (Hicks, 2000; Hicks and Watson, 2003). Michel Foucault (1978[1976]) argued that discourses have defined and specified a range of sexual types, so much so that sexuality is now taken to be something that can reveal the 'truth' of our selves. However, in doing so, sexuality itself was constituted as 'a possible object' (p. 98), as something which appeared to have a legitimate and factual status. Instead, Foucault (1978[1976]: 105) said that 'sexuality' in fact refers to 'a historical construct'. Queer theories, too, have asserted that 'sexuality' refers not to an identity, a being or a set of descriptive labels, but is a system of knowledge that frames ideas into moral and political hierarchies (Turner, 2000). The very categories 'heterosexual/lesbian/gay/bisexual', for example, are claims that involve the operations of power and result in the establishment of normative frameworks. Queer theories have also asked why heterosexuality currently exists as a privileged subjectivity that has the ability to define sexual knowledge. Why, for example, does heterosexuality occupy such a 'natural' or taken-for-granted status that it is so rarely commented upon? Contemporary feminism, too, has challenged biologically determinist views of sexuality and the privileging of heterosexuality (Jackson and Scott, 1996).

Social work is implicated in all of this because it too is involved, through a series of complex practices and statements, in specifying sexual subjects. We have seen that the versions of sexuality promoted in social work theory, for example, are of a limited type. I have argued that, when it is addressed, sexuality is theorised in the terms of anti-discriminatory practice, and that this results in the establishment of a series of discrete sexual types with their attendant 'needs'. The concept that 'sexuality' is actually just a set of ideas is rarely acknowledged within social work, and other sets of ideas – those found within lesbian feminism, gay liberation, queer and other social constructionist theories – have yet to make a significant impact. This is no mere accident or oversight in my view. Social work discourse operates to define and specify what can and cannot be known about sexuality, and this means that some 'radical' ideas are organised out.

Foucault (2000: 460) reminded us that we should not search for 'a sexuality' but rather ask, 'under what conditions something can become an object for a possible knowledge'. Social work has not done much of this, but instead prefers to replace past 'myths' about sexual types with present enlightened versions. The problem with this, however, is that it retains the idea that there is an object called 'sexuality' that is possessed by individuals. In addition, it does not recognise that homophobic discourses cannot be challenged solely by the assertion of 'better truths'. This is because homophobic discourses take many forms and are part of a wider privileging of heterosexuality as 'the normal' that defies the need for rational explanation.

Instead of creating more 'accurate' versions of sexual categories, social work would do better to ask how it contributes to the legitimation of some subjects over others. This would, therefore, entail moving beyond the view of 'sexuality' as describing a series of discrete types to consider not what lesbians and gay men are, but rather what they are expected to be and what they might instead become. After 'sexuality', social work might ask difficult questions about the forms of sexual knowledge that it perpetrates. Then it can begin to recognise and even contribute to the many ways that people resist hetero-normative ideas and practices.

FURTHER READING

Brown, H.C. (1998) *Social Work and Sexuality: Working with Lesbians and Gay Men* (Basingstoke: Macmillan – now Palgrave Macmillan). This is the best introduction to lesbian and gay issues in social work.

Turner, W.B. (2000) *A Genealogy of Queer Theory* (Philadelphia: Temple University Press). This discusses queer theory.

Weeks, J. (2003) *Sexuality* (2nd edn) (London: Routledge). This is a helpful introduction to the subject.

Acknowledgement

My thanks go to Jodie Barber, Dharman Jeyasingham, Peter Massheder and Katherine Watson for help with the ideas in this chapter.

Frailty and Dignity in Old Age

11

Helen Gorman

Is it possible to be old and frail, yet live in a dignified way? For some older people with supportive networks and enough money to pay for their care this may be so, but for many others, in a society that favours the productive over the unproductive, it may be difficult to live a dignified life where your needs are met and you are esteemed. Unfortunately, mental frailty is stigmatising both for the individual and their family. In *Iris*, John Bayley's tribute to his partner Iris Murdoch, which describes their later years when he became her carer, he discusses how:

> These days I find myself proclaiming to others, and to myself as well: 'She seems to want to go to bed about seven' … Who is this *She* who has made an appearance, and with whom others and myself are so familiar? We are familiar because we are seeing her from the outside. She has indeed become a *She*.
>
> (Bayley, 1999)

As the above quotation indicates, the relative that one knew is not there any more in quite the same way, potentially becoming a problem instead. This can be the reality for family members and also health and social care agencies, who often become involved when carers cannot cope. One could say that the honesty of this statement is a blessing, stating what others might find difficult to articulate, but at the same time, if interpreted in an oppressive way, it could mean a restriction on the rights of a person who has become frail and old.

The language that we use when talking about older people reflects the society in which we live. Demeaning words are often used incidentally to refer to older people as if they are not people to be reckoned with, but peripheral to important current events. The above quotation illustrates the dehumanising of an older person when she or he becomes frail, in this case mentally rather than physically. Yet it would be wrong to assume that we can use the word 'frail' casually, as if there is a common understanding of the term. Frailty can mean being weak, delicate and infirm, yet the term also relates to fallibility and foibles as in moral weakness. To be frail may mean to demand sympathy; however, it could be a term used to indicate fragility in the sense of wrongdoing or omission through weakness.

Maintaining dignity is more than keeping up appearances: it relates to self-respect. It is a significant value because it is fundamental to human rights and how individuals relate to one another. Being in control in our society is synonymous with behaving as a worthy person should, for displays of uncontrollable behaviour tend not to be culturally acceptable. Despite the fact that Western society today is made up of many cultural norms and patterns of behaviour, being out of control or losing one's dignity is still associated with a lack of personal honour: a predominant norm is breached and the offending person is characterised as having weakness of mind or character, or at worst is deemed to be mad. Loss of dignity, often associated with bizarre behaviour, can be scary.

Social work and social care are about helping others to manage their lives so that as far as is possible their needs are met. By 'needs' we mean not only physical ones but emotional and spiritual needs as well (Maslow, 1954). 'Need', however, is a slippery concept; it is socially constructed and will vary in different cultural contexts (Langan, 1998). In addition, those who practise social work and may be assessing older people's needs are not exempt from being influenced by the dominant values of society today, which have been expressed as 'materialism', 'individualism', 'sensualism' and 'externalism' (Wolfensberger, 1994). The impact of such predominant values can manifest itself in many ways, including the use of language, routine and mechanistic practice and, at worst, abuse. Malin et al. (1999) relate these dominant values to the notion of 'community care', illustrating how their influence can affect service users and also those who construct theory through their practice.

The pervasive influence of ageism, which is an offshoot of those predominant values mentioned above, can influence our behaviour on a conscious and subconscious level. Thompson (1995) outlines aspects of the rapid increase in the higher age groups, the 'old old', an increase in persons of pension age and a decrease in numbers in the younger generation who would normally be expected to care for them. The need for anti-ageist practice to become established is correspondingly important (Thompson, 1995). Despite the experience of illness and disability, having self-respect and autonomy is part of human rights. The Human Rights Act 1998 means that breaches of human rights can be followed up in the UK courts. Social workers and healthcare professionals can now link their good practice to human rights in order to reinforce anti-oppressive practice.

Frailty and dignity: an example from practice

In the real world of practice there are often no correct answers, but rather complicated dilemmas, for no individual may have the right solution. Consider the following case example.

CASE EXAMPLE

Mrs Mary Flynn is 89 years old and lives with her son David aged 66 in a maisonette on a council estate in a major city. Her husband Ray died some ten years ago. David is divorced and has no children.

Mrs Flynn is becoming forgetful: she has left saucepans on the cooker until they burn and on one occasion the fire brigade had to be called out. Last week she told a neighbour that a thief had come and stolen her pension book. Later it emerged that she had hidden the book and forgotten about it, although some money had gone missing. It is difficult to hold a conversation with her because she repeats herself and makes inappropriate remarks. One neighbour is concerned about Mrs Flynn's continual accidents with the gas cooker and refers the matter to social services who have had some short-term contact with the Flynns in the past. Mrs Flynn has enjoyed good health most of her life but has recently developed leg ulcers that are being treated by the local community nurse.

David has been unemployed since his industrial accident in his early thirties left him with the loss of one arm, one eye and serious damage to his back which limits his mobility. With Mrs Flynn's increasing frailty, the household has become chaotic.

David visits the GP and tells him about his mother's forgetfulness and the incident with the burning pans on the cooker. The GP visits Mrs Flynn and suggests that she is referred to a psychogeriatrician. He recommends to David that he controls his consumption of alcohol, for David is known to have a drink problem. The GP suggests to David that social services might help with his mother, but he does not make a referral because David does not want social services to call. Mrs Flynn does not mind seeing the GP but is reluctant to see anyone else, 'especially anyone from the workhouse up the road' (the local hospital has a psychiatric wing built on the site of the old workhouse).

The social worker makes a brief visit but is not warmly welcomed by David. She holds a brief conversation with Mrs Flynn who shows some signs of distress at her own forgetfulness and inability to do the housework.

The following comments are the initial observations of those involved:

- *General practitioner* – Mrs Flynn has dementia, she has had mild Alzheimer's disease for the last few years and it has been managed so far. It is possible that she may have suffered a series of small strokes, so part of her dysfunction may be multi-infarct dementia. Her condition appears to have worsened recently. Refer to psychogeriatrician.

- *Community nurse* – Treated Mrs Flynn's leg ulcers, some improvement in healing. She may have had a slight stroke, I observed right-side weakness.

■ *Social worker* – Initial visit made to Mrs Flynn who appears to be forgetful and confused. Home conditions have deteriorated since our last visit a year ago. Mrs Flynn's son David is hostile to social services intervention. A neighbour reported that David may be stealing from his mother to buy alcohol. It has been confirmed that David has a problem with alcohol dependence; this has been noted before and confirmed with the GP. Mrs Flynn appears to have difficulty in communicating her needs. A full multidisciplinary assessment is required to explore support for Mrs Flynn and prevent further deterioration.

■ *Psychogeriatrician* – Completed the IO sub-test and the MMSE (see below). Evidence of cognitive impairment and clouded consciousness. Clinical judgement is that patient is suffering from dementia. Patient not overagitated and no evidence of wandering. Mood appears within normal range. Monitor. No specific drug therapy required.

■ *Mrs Flynn* – I am confused about what is happening; why are all these strangers calling to see me ...?

■ *David Flynn* – Why don't they mind their own business?

The initial diagnoses by the professionals show similarities and differences. The differences are related to professional culture; each professional's focus depends on his/her professional judgement based on training and past experience. However, another aspect worth considering is the use of language and the power of terminology. Each professional appears to be using language that may be important in determining outcomes and yet may be difficult for users and carers to understand. For example, the IO is an information/orientation sub-test: a diagnostic tool in the form of a questionnaire commonly used to diagnose dementia. The MMSE (Mini-Mental State Examination) is a similar test. All tests vary in their sensitivity, specificity and positive predictive value (Hall et al. 1993: 173).

Communication

A key issue is communication between the various professionals involved. In this case, like so many others involving older people, when professionals make their diagnoses, they rarely communicate them to colleagues involved and, more significantly, they do not communicate them to the persons directly concerned. Mrs Flynn's reaction is not untypical: she knows something is up because of all the visits and questions she is being asked. She might also be afraid that she is going to be taken away, that others may have the power to control her life. She refers to the callers as 'strangers'. Why should she communicate details of her personal life to strangers? Why does being old and frail give people the right to intervene in your life? One could say that the frailty and dignity of Mrs Flynn is already being compromised; her frailty is exposed by the professionals involved, but she herself may not know what is wrong, so she feels afraid. The problems of communication may also reinforce David's dislike of authority and fear that his lifestyle may be changed.

One role of the social worker is to be alongside, to explain and answer questions from service users and carers. It is hoped that the person who arrives as a stranger to help becomes someone who can be trusted. But one person alone is not going to solve the difficulties; the case requires a team approach. Better collaboration between agencies at the diagnosis stage is greatly assisted by organisational systems that are set up to allow appropriate transfer of information. Effective collaboration is unlikely to happen unless systems are set up within and between agencies (Ovretveit, 1993). GP practices with attached social workers and/or multidisciplinary teams comprising health and social service personnel can often assist in facilitating the transfer of information in the early stages. It is wrong to assume, however, that being in physical proximity is enough; it is vital that communication systems exist and work effectively. Being open and honest about boundary limitations and respective roles is fundamental to good communication between professionals. Payne (2000) reminds us that failures in communication become power issues because the essence of cooperation and participation is effective communication. Without communication between professionals, boundaries and roles are unclear, leading to power struggles.

Could the social worker have assisted in easing communications at this stage? Possibly: if she or he had access to appropriate systems of communication, recognised the need to communicate effectively and was skilled enough to help. Let us look more closely at issues of communication with sufferers of dementia. Dementia can be defined as the impairment of higher mental functioning including the loss of memory, problem-solving ability, the use of learned skills, social skills and emotional control. The consciousness of the sufferer is not impaired. The condition is both progressive and irreversible (Victor, 1991). Communicating with people with dementia is difficult and frustrating for all concerned. A quotation from *Iris* illustrates this dilemma:

> When Iris wakes the daily grind of non communication begins ... She does not ignore me or pay no attention; she seems to be listening to a garbled message. On the radio-telephone in the army the operator would have been saying 'I am not receiving you' or 'Receiving you Strength One'.
>
> (Bayley, 1999)

Hepworth (2000) discusses how if the processes of interpersonal communication break down, the individual sense of selfhood can be seriously threatened. He gives examples of where confusion and loss of memory are described through the eyes of the person with the condition in contrast to the external perceptions of family members. Dementia is described by the sufferer not as a blanket condition but one that moves erratically, with the dementia sufferer being aware of the change in perception and the inability to exercise self-control. Acknowledging such a change in one's abilities is a difficult and frightening prospect, and all the more so if the people wanting to know about it are those perceived to be powerful professionals who could remove one's dignity, emphasising and making public one's frailty. Hepworth (2000) considers that a central feature of an interactional model of dementia care is the recognition of the role of social approval in the maintenance of self-esteem in later life. Communication that involves a link with a 'can do' rather than 'can't do' approach can assist in helping an older person with dementia to cope with the illness. Breaking down the dichotomy between 'us', the professionals who are outside the dementia, and 'them', who are inside it as the manifestation of the disease, is discussed by Kirkwood (1998). Suggestions for improving communications include counselling and therapy built around the assumption of a positive identity.

There is also the issue of communication with David, who is hostile to social work intervention. He may be difficult to communicate with for a number of reasons possibly related to fear. He may not be ready to acknowledge that there are problems, and/or he may have difficulty relating to a female social worker; there may be a range of barriers to effective communication between the social worker and David. In this case both Mrs Flynn and her son are frail. David, as a man of pensionable age, may be exploiting his mother who is very elderly; his frailty may be the abuse of power that he wields over his mother which takes the form of financial abuse. However, in old age, nastiness, vengefulness and exploitation can be a two-way process, and to assume that the state of being old is aligned to virtue is a myth. Vincent (1999) outlines in detail some of the power structures that can exist in the personal politics of identity issues and goes on to link these dimensions with macro-issues relating to professionals, state welfare, financial structures and cultural attitudes embedded in intergenerational relationships.

It is often a crisis that brings matters to a head, for this is when actions are taken and decisions are made. The case example now moves on: it is two weeks later.

CASE EXAMPLE REVISITED

Mrs Flynn has a fall and appears to have had a stroke; she now has significant right-side paralysis of her arm and leg, her speech is impaired and her cognitive abilities have been further weakened. She is admitted to hospital under the care of a geriatric consultant. David remains in the house alone; his drinking is getting worse. When the social worker calls at the house, he is abusive to her. After a month in hospital Mrs Flynn's physical condition improves: she can now walk unaided. Physiotherapy has eased the paralysis in her arm and she can just about care for herself. Her dementia, however, appears to have got worse. A case discussion is held.

The various opinions of the professional staff are as follows:

- *Geriatrician* – The patient is now mobile and being assisted by physiotherapy which should continue at home. Patient is ready for discharge.

- *Ward sister* – Mary has been assessed in the rehabilitation unit and can just about manage herself. Medication is now sorted out.

- *Discharge liaison nurse* – Mrs Flynn is referred for discharge. I have contacted the social work department who have been to see the patient on the ward. I have also contacted the community social work office and filled in the discharge details for a Section 2 notice Community Care (Delayed Discharges) Act 2003.

■ *Hospital social worker* – I have visited Mrs Flynn on the ward. I am concerned about two main aspects of her situation. Firstly, her mental state appears to have worsened since her stroke and, secondly, her home circumstances are difficult. Mrs Flynn is keen to go home. The community social work office will need to be informed of the decision if discharge is to go ahead.

Other professionals involved but not at the case discussion have also made notes:

■ *Psychogeriatrician* – Visit made to ward. Mrs Flynn's condition appears to have worsened since I last saw her. Completed an abbreviated test with her and this showed a poor response. There is some evidence of behavioural disturbance. Nocturnal restlessness could be helped by temazepam. Residential care should be considered.

■ *Community social worker* – Message received from duty officer that Mrs Flynn's discharge takes place today. Not enough notification was given of pending discharge so emergency care package to be put in until full assessment completed. Mrs Flynn wants to go home and her son David says he wants her back. The case notes indicate there may be concerns that David is financially abusing his mother, but this has not been followed up owing to Mrs Flynn's hospital admission and David's lack of cooperation.

■ *Physiotherapist* – Mrs Flynn tries hard to regain her mobility. She scored reasonably well on the test in the rehabilitation flat, but her mental condition restricts her ability to understand instructions.

■ *Occupational therapist* – Assessment required for aids and adaptations on discharge.

These notes and comments reveal the concerns of the professional staff involved in this case. They also reveal some lack of coordination and collaboration because unfortunately organisations and professionals often operate in a way that does not put the service user at the centre of decision-making. The person most involved is often at the periphery and what happens is often determined by factors other than the concerns of the user. In this case some delay in assessment from social services, pressure to use a medical bed, the lack of coordination between branches of the medical profession and lack of communication between key players such as nursing staff and social services and allied professionals are dominating factors that demonstrate the use of power. Ideally, in a situation such as this, Mrs Flynn's case could be referred to an integrated care system where her concerns could be discussed and met in a coordinated way by all those involved in her care. Such an integrated multidisciplinary system is particularly important in cases where both physical and mental disabilities exist.

Yet evidence suggests that collaboration for the care of vulnerable user groups will continue to be a problem because needs are relatively unpredictable, best practices are unclear and different groups advocate different care models or underlying professional values (Johnson et al., 2003). Partnership working envisaged by the Health Act 1999 could enable locally based multidisciplinary teams to manage the care for older people with dementia. The existence of a single source of funding, single management and clearly articulated goals would help to establish such a service. Interestingly, a recent study on the operation of the Health Act 1999 flexibilities has shown that trust is an essential element of success (Hudson et al., 2001). Trust is a basic human need, the necessity of which should not come as a surprise, yet lack of it appears to be a major stumbling block to working effectively. It is an essential requisite for collaborative endeavour across agencies, between individual practitioners and between practitioners, service users and carers.

Yet within the health and social care system the potential for conflict is omnipresent. The pressure to free up medical beds is a critical issue in the care of older people. Recently, policy makers have taken a hard line on hospital discharges because they wish to encourage social services to use the period following admission to assess a patient's or carer's need and arrange discharge. When notice of likely need has been given to a local authority from the hospital under Section 2 Community Care (Delayed Discharges) Act 2003, the social services must then assess and, after consultation with the NHS body, determine what services they will provide for a patient or carer. Statutory requirements, if not complied with, form a trigger for payment as a delayed discharge. One problem that can be envisaged in the case of Mrs Flynn is when her needs cross boundaries; she has some physical health problems but also some mental health ones that significantly affect how her needs will be met.

The final scenario...

CASE EXAMPLE REVISITED

The social worker, Pat Smith, who is also the care manager, makes arrangements for an emergency care package for when Mrs Flynn arrives home. She is discharged from hospital back home but when the social worker/care manager arrives to complete a full community care assessment she finds complete chaos in the house. The domiciliary care agency refuses to continue with care because of the state of the house and the difficulty of communicating with Mrs Flynn. David is nowhere to be found and the neighbours think he has not been living in the house for the past week. Pat is faced with the decision about how to manage the immediate situation because it is apparent that the conditions at home are not suitable for Mrs Flynn. Pat manages to communicate with Mrs Flynn to some degree and it appears that she is pleased to be back home but oblivious to her own vulnerability within it. She decides to negotiate with an agency to clean the house and for domiciliary care to start immediately. In the meantime, she arranges for Mrs Flynn to go to a local daycare centre until the evening, when she will return home and be assisted in getting into bed by the care agency staff. Pat intends to call the next day to find out how Mrs Flynn is coping and assess whether the services are meeting Mrs Flynn's needs.

> ### CASE EXAMPLE REVISITED cont'd
>
> When Pat gets to work the next day there is an urgent message. Mrs Flynn was found wandering on the motorway in her night clothes. The police found her and took her to the police station. The out-of-hours duty team were called out and Mrs Flynn was admitted to the psychiatric wing of the local hospital as there were no residential care places available. Pat visits Mrs Flynn the next day and finds her in a sorry state. She appears to have behavioural problems and is very agitated; she has been given a tranquilliser by the hospital staff. Pat visits the Flynns' home and finds David there. He appears to be the worse for alcohol and although concerned about his mother's welfare, says he cannot cope with her at home. As Pat leaves he says: 'Mind you she'll hate it up there at the hospital, she used to call it the old workhouse.'

The next sections discuss the issues in the case and offer concepts and theories that explain and put into context some of the problems that emerged.

Care management and early intervention – systems and individuals

Does care management as it is practised really involve care and management? This debate was raised by Gorman and Postle (2003) and evidenced by research carried out in the late 1990s. It was found that very often crisis management was prevalent and organisational structures were dominated by managerialist approaches. This meant that managers' views about meeting organisational requirements predominated over meeting the needs of Mrs Flynn. This contrasts with work that maintained a balance between individual, community and societal needs. Professional decision-making is bounded by a range of factors including cost containment, dependence on family and informal carers, changing professional roles and defensive practice. The care manager, usually the social worker, has to operate in a climate of role conflict and ambiguity. In our case example, planning did not take place early enough; Mrs Flynn's case was not perceived as important enough for intervention that may have prevented breakdown. Mrs Flynn's home set-up was less than perfect, but if appropriate help had been offered and accepted earlier she may have remained at home with David as the main carer supported by domiciliary care. Being old and frail may have influenced others' perceptions of their need in this case. Working with older people with dementia requires time, patience and skilled help; unfortunately, in this case, Mrs Flynn's needs were not put centre stage and she became a victim of 'the system'.

Older people as carers

David was a difficult person to work with; indeed his frailty as an older person was that he had personal problems related to his industrial accident. He was unwilling to cooperate, but maybe a relationship could have been established with him to develop enough trust to allow appropriate help to be accepted. His needs were mostly ignored, for as an older man with drink problems he did not demand the care and attention that 'more deserving' users could receive. He was frail in the sense that he appeared morally weak. There was an indication that David might be abusing his mother by using her money to buy drink. This aspect needed careful investigation and could trigger an adult abuse enquiry as part of the whole assessment of the case.

Looking to carers' needs is an important aspect of care in the community, especially as it is becoming more commonplace for elderly children to be caring for their even older parents. Carers' rights are recognised in the Carers (Recognition and Services) Act 1995 and in the Carers and Disabled Children Act 2000. Carers can be assessed in their own right for community care services. It is, however, important to recognise that carers' needs may differ from service users' needs and there is a potential for conflict.

Coordination and collaboration between agencies, professionals and service users

Working together has become a vital part of health and social care, although it may have taken time over recent years for both agencies and their managers to recognise the importance of this. The integration of this concept into policy and legal requirements has helped to reinforce professional good practice. The pressures against collaborative effort need recognition to enable barriers to be crossed; these include economic factors translated into competition between agencies, professional tribalism and differences in the priorities of individuals working in health and social care. Both organisational and individual strengths and weaknesses play a part in success or failure of collaborative work (Gorman, 2000a). Leathard (1994) outlines the main advantages of interprofessional work in practice as more effective use of staff, efficient service provision and a more satisfying work environment.

To work in collaboration with service users means being aware of the values, skills and knowledge that they possess, to work as co-workers with them. Yet this is not as easy as it might seem. Research shows that older people tend not to complain and are most likely to express satisfaction (Bauld et al., 2000). They may receive a poor service and have unpleasant experiences but do not want to make a stressful situation worse by complaining about a service or lack of care that they perceive as unalterable. Poor communication, lack of respect and failure to understand the living situations of people in advanced old age were reported to be widespread among hospital and primary healthcare staff. Ageism appeared to be common and to contribute to the experience of poor service (Wilson, 1995). Staff who have a philosophy of user empowerment can help to improve practice by influencing the systems that operate and convincing their colleagues of the value of collaborative work.

Social workers need particular skills

What sort of skills did the staff involved in the Flynns' case need in order to improve outcomes for them? Research has shown that there are a number of skills required in care management with older people: these include coordination, collaboration and networking, negotiation, teamwork and conflict management. Analytical and reflective skills, especially when used in evaluative processes, are particularly necessary and these are developed with experience (Gorman, 2003). Recognising the significance of emotional labour, which is the management of feelings performed as part of paid work, affects the state of mind and/or the feelings of another person. This concept has been applied to care management work in terms of how relationship-building is often missing from work practices in favour of more mechanistic approaches to the assessment and planning of care (Gorman, 2000b). Working with service users, when translated into how Mrs Flynn and David perceived the outcomes of intervention from health and social services, becomes a critical issue related to quality of outcomes.

It is important that money for care is spent wisely and effectively, and the systems are in place to enable the movement from hospital to the community to work efficiently. However, it is important to ensure that the process of work and the use of expertise in context are recognised as equally important, because quality outcomes depend upon it. Staff need to be offered professional development as part of a continuing process within health and social care organisations. Recognising this need and doing something about it is a challenge for agencies involved in work with older people (Gorman and Postle, 2003). Training approaches require a great deal of thought because blanket acceptance of competency-based approaches to social work have been criticised as contradicting anti-oppressive practice (Dominelli, 1996). In the same vein it has been argued that such approaches can be reductionist, relegating the consideration of values, critical evaluation and the deployment of frontline knowledge to second place (Adams, 1998). The Flynns' case is a difficult one and waving a magic wand to restore Mrs Flynn's mental capabilities is an impossible dream. However, it is possible to improve the quality of Mrs Flynn's life and that of her son David. Confident and skilled professionals who are trained to negotiate and work collaboratively stand more chance of success.

Reconsidering frailty and dignity – the human rights agenda

Whether it is using a carrot or a stick, consideration of human rights by public sector organisations and those who work closely with them is now essential. Acting in an anti-oppressive way, being mindful of the potential for discrimination against older, mentally frail people and making sound judgements that can be evidenced and supported by good recording practices are what human rights are about. It is important that staff in health and social welfare encourage service users and carers to be aware of their rights. Challenges in welfare are most likely to be claims under Article 8 of the Convention for Human Rights (UN, 1950) which requires authorities to take positive measures to secure respect for private or family life. There are other convention rights that can be the source of challenge such as Article 6 related to procedural fairness. Delay in performing duties, failure to recognise a carer's needs and cases in which there was a great deal of stress and anxiety are all situations in which there could be a breach of human rights and a claim for damages against a local authority (Bernard and another *v.* Enfield LBC 25/10/2002).

CONCLUSION

Frailty is a multifaceted concept that needs to be considered in the context of human weakness, both physical and mental. Much depends on individual perceptions: losing one's dignity can be a matter of personal perception but one that goes to the core of a person's identity – it can mean the end of the quality of life. Social work is about ambiguity and managing situations that are problematic, so often there are no right answers but there could be better outcomes.

We can make some suggestions as to how practice could have been improved in the Flynns' case:

- *Putting the user and carer at the centre of the decision-making.* Neither Mrs Flynn nor her son were involved in decisions. Mrs Flynn could have been more involved at the earlier stages of the case and when she was ready for hospital discharge. Working with unwilling clients such as David can be difficult, but more attempts could have been made by the social worker to find out what his needs were, especially if with help he could undertake the role of carer.

- *Better and more effective communication with people who suffer from dementia.* Using time to communicate effectively with Mrs Flynn may have built up relationships and trust that could have led to more successful outcomes.

- *Ensuring a balance between social and medical perspectives in determining well-being.* Tensions between medical and social aspects of a case can become polarised because the professionals involved do not recognise the strengths and contributions of others. It is important that social workers can articulate to their colleagues the significance of the social aspects of people's lives.

- *Greater awareness of the human rights of older people and the procedures that apply to challenge abuses.* Social workers need to be aware of the potential for human rights challenges and the significance of providing evidence to back up the decisions they make.

- *Earlier multidisciplinary assessment of the needs of the user and carer.* Opportunities were missed to harness the skills of professional staff for the well-being of the service user and carer. Everyone involved has a responsibility to share relevant information.

- *Better partnership working between practitioners and with user agencies.* All the professionals involved were ploughing their own furrow. The systems were not in place to enable collaboration, a basic element of which is establishing common goals. When systems are in place they need to be utilised effectively.

- *Professionals need to update skills and learn new ones* in a context of continuing personal and professional development. There were several skills that could have been used in this case. Negotiation is an important skill that is underused and undervalued. Coupled with effective communication and a collaborative approach, the hospital discharge could have been managed more successfully. The lack of collaborative work meant that the discharge home had little chance of success.

Nowhere in the case example did we really get to know what Mrs Flynn wanted or what her interpretations of maintaining her dignity meant. Putting the service user at the centre of planning and intervention should help, but unfortunately systems that appear to prioritise other factors still dominate in our hospitals and social services departments. Maintaining a perspective that reinforces social justice and awareness of human rights can help to bring about change in organisations. Looking to improve one's practice through self-evaluation, careful appraisal of one's own practice, reflexivity and research-mindedness is a desired approach. A word of warning, however, about the fashionable stances of welfare practice that purport to follow a policy of social inclusion, the reality of which can be engagement on our terms. Our intentions may be good, but they can be perceived by the service user as patronising. Really listening and taking advice from elders is a positive vision for the future (Simey, 2000).

We cannot always make things right, but with skilled social work intervention, we can help to ease the burdens of older people who have become frail and are in danger of losing their dignity. Becoming old should not be synonymous with a poor quality of life. The challenge for social workers with frail older people in today's work environment is to trust themselves, the service users and their health and social care colleagues much more.

FURTHER READING

Gorman, H. and Postle, K. (2003) *Transforming Community Care: A Distorted Vision?* (Birmingham: Venture Press) Chapter 4: Decision-making about community care services – dithering as an art form? Chapter 5: Empowerment.

Payne, M. (2000) *Teamwork in Multiprofessional Care* (London: Routledge) Chapter 6: Power issues in open teamwork.

Simey, M. (2000) How and Where I Found Independence in Simmons, M. *Getting a Life, Older People Talking* (London: Peter Owen/Help the Aged) pp. 133–8.

Wilkinson, H. (ed.) (2002) *The Perspectives of People with Dementia: Research Methods and Motivations* (London: Jessica Kingsley).

Risk, Rights and Anti-discrimination Work in Mental Health: Avoiding the Risks in Considering Risk

Liz Sayce

Disabled people in general and mental health service users in particular are accustomed to being stopped from doing things on grounds of potential risk – sometimes overtly, sometimes more subtly. This chapter looks at the grounds on which this occurs and considers how rights and anti-discriminatory practice can stop it from happening unfairly.

A few twenty-first century examples give a flavour of the way risk can be used to constrain people. The examples cover different groups of disabled people, not only those with psychiatric disabilities, in order to learn from the range of potential policy and practice approaches that may help to increase autonomy and social participation for people with psychiatric disabilities. The chapter also explores how to avoid using risk-thinking as an excuse to limit opportunities.

The risk to others: care staff, service users, the wider public – and cats

The risk to cats

Emma Stevens, from Blackburn, Lancashire, was turned down by the Cats' Protection League as a potential cat owner on the grounds that, being deaf, she would not be able to hear the cat if it was in distress. A spokesperson for the Cats' Protection League said she was well placed to judge as she had experience of working with deaf children. A deaf person living alone could not look after a cat – 'the cat comes first' (*Lancashire Evening Telegraph* 24 December 2003). The deaf woman said 'I felt offended.' She planned to find a cat from another source.

The risk to care staff

Two women with physical and learning disabilities challenged East Sussex County Council's policy that staff should not get involved in manual lifting and handling. Disabled people's requirements to be helped in and out of bed, or the bath, presented a risk to the staff's backs; so policies preventing staff from manual lifting and handling were put in place. Following the case, other examples emerged, including one in which Ms Wolstenholme from Milton Keynes had slept in her wheelchair for months, apparently because staff were not permitted to lift her. Ms Wolstenholme weighed 7 stone. She stated that when five health officials visited her to decide if they could use slings or hoists to lift her, she fell. 'I asked them for help. They did not. They watched me crawling on the floor.' The *Sunday Telegraph* (14 September 2003) commented:

> This is the horrible terminus of an obsession with health and safety: 'carers' who are able to stand aside and watch as a desperately ill woman struggled on the floor – because they have been indoctrinated into believing that it would violate health and safety regulations.

In other instances, elderly relatives noted that they lifted the disabled person in and out of bed whilst care staff stood by. K. Maddison of Dewsbury managed to secure home care for his wife, but writes:

> We soon found out that we were paying more than £5 an hour for a service that was completely useless because of the tasks the carers were not allowed to do. Banned tasks included lifting the patient; giving the patient a shower (even though we have a special wheelchair and shower); administering prescribed medication (over the counter stuff was OK); moving patient's position in chair or bed; opening or closing a window above head height; assisting patient with toileting.
>
> (*Daily Mail,* 16 September 2003)

The risk to service users

Wright and Easthorne (2003) found that disabled students trying to enter nursing encountered barriers based on fears for the health and safety of service users. Deaf people were assumed to be a health and safety risk as they might not be able to hear alarms. Students with dyslexia were seen as a risk in administering medication. Students with mental health problems were thought to pose a potential risk of violence. Following nurse Beverly Allitt's murder of children in her care, many NHS trusts introduced the infamous 'two-year rule', requiring anyone entering nursing or working as a nurse to have been free of psychiatric treatment for two years. This has since been lifted.

The risk to the wider public

When a woman jogger was stabbed to death in London, in 2003, Philip Johnston wrote in the *Telegraph* (10 December 2003):

Police were astonished to find at least 30 care-in-the-community hostels, containing more than 400 ill people close to Victoria Park in Hackney where she was murdered. None of these institutions is secure. This is the legacy of one of the great scandals of modern times: the abject failure of care in the community.

These comments were made before any arrest. It seems it was not necessary to have any evidence that the murder had been committed by one of the '400 care-in-the-community patients' before interpreting the murder as a community care failure. There still appears to be no taboo against viewing 'psychiatric patients' as guilty until proven innocent.

Some cases are more complex. Ms Brazier, who has a diagnosis of psychosis, was threatened with eviction after causing a nuisance to neighbours. This raises the question, is it reasonable to evict someone who poses no threat, but does cause disturbance, due in part to a mental health problem?

The risk to self

Mr Paul had long-term depression. He applied for two part-time jobs with the probation service – a community service supervisor and a handyman. He was offered the handyman man post but turned down for the supervisor post on the grounds that it was thought too stressful for him. This decision was made without consulting him, his psychiatrist or the organisation with whom he had successfully been volunteering for some years.

Tom White has diabetes. At 16 he was refused permission to go on school trips in case he had a glycaemic attack.

The simultaneous risk to self and others

On 17 January 2004 the *Mirror* reported:

Eleven friends were ordered to get off a packed holiday flight seconds before take-off – because they were deaf. The pilot claimed the group was a liability to the safety of the plane. One passenger said 'The pilot thought that because we were deaf we would not be able to follow emergency instructions'. The humiliated passengers are now seeking compensation from easyJet.

In 2003 Anthony Ford-Shubrook, who has cerebral palsy, got the GCSEs he needed to study IT at the only sixth-form college in his area offering the courses of his choice. But the IT department was on the first floor and there was no lift. His parents offered to buy a 'climbing' wheelchair. The college refused him entry, as the wheelchair would be a health and safety risk (to Anthony and other students).

Discussion: is risk approached fairly?

Some academic commentators have argued that an ever-increasing focus on risk makes us excessively risk averse. Children spend all their time sitting at home or being driven from one place to another, for fear of the danger of the streets. Government demands for risk assessment and accountability at a micro-level distort the activities of public services, de-emphasising positive and imaginative developments in favour of defensive practice to avoid disaster. For instance, Rose (1998: 180) argues that society has become overpreoccupied with preventing dangers:

> Some go as far as to claim that we live in a 'risk society', which is no longer structured by belief in progress and concerns over the distribution of 'goods' (wealth, health, life chances and so on), but rather is saturated with fear and foreboding, and structured by concerns over the distribution of 'bads' or dangers.

O'Neill (2002: 46) refers to the increasingly centralised policies concerned with risk management:

> A look into the vast database of documents on the Department of Health website arouses a mixture of despair and disbelief. Central planning may have failed in the former Soviet Union but it is alive and well in Britain today.

It is undeniable that in some circumstances risk-thinking is used unfairly in relation to disabled people, including people with mental health problems. There are instances of institutionalised, not individual, unfairness, for example, no lifting policies in local authorities and the 'two-year rule' that in the past stopped mental health service users from entering nursing (but see below for its recent demise). There are also themes running through the examples that are confirmed by research, case law and health and social care practice.

Firstly, the tendency of decision makers to see an impairment as a fixed problem – posing risks – rather than thinking first how to resolve the apparent problem has been reported in numerous consultations and surveys of the experiences of disabled people (Barnes, 1991; Campbell and Oliver, 1996; DRC, 2004). To give one example, 60 per cent of deaf people report that they find primary care inaccessible (Knight et al., 2002), for instance, because they do not know when their appointment comes up or cannot communicate with the GP. If the appointments are shown on a visual screen and GPs learn to speak directly to someone who lip-reads or work with British Sign Language interpreters, what seemed a fixed problem can disappear. Imagination is required rather than a reflex response that 'this is not possible'.

In relation to the examples above, if an IT department is moved to the ground floor, a wheelchair user can study the A levels of his choice. If hospitals have flashing lights as alarms as well as sirens, or arrangements that colleagues will alert deaf people to the emergency, then deaf people can practise in nursing without danger. If someone is unable to travel in the rush hour due to panic attacks, the answer is not to refuse them the job but to explore whether the hours can be changed or some home working permitted. This is simple good practice under the Disability Discrimination Act (DDA) 1995 – which requires employers and service providers to make reasonable adjustments, so that disabled people are not treated 'less favourably'.

Secondly, judgements about potential risk to others are used to disadvantage disabled people – especially those with psychiatric disabilities – in ways that would never be considered acceptable in relation to non-disabled people. It has often been noted that a mental health service user can be compulsorily detained for a level of risk of violence which – if it were applied to young men who drink alcohol – would mean thousands of young men detained in advance of committing any crime (Sayce, 1995). There is no actuarial basis for allowing preventive detention in advance of crime for people with psychiatric disabilities and no one else. Moreover, when a mental health service user is deemed a 'high risk of violence', for instance because he or she has allegedly hit someone, she or he has not had the opportunity to be tried in a court of law. She or he might be innocent but has no way to prove it.

Although 'community care' has facilitated greater autonomy for people with psychiatric disabilities and is preferred by them to institutional care (Leff et al., 1996), it is often considered a 'failure'. Frank Dobson, when secretary of state for health, famously stated that 'community care has failed', seemingly on the grounds of a number of high-profile homicides during the 1990s. This assessment ignores the important evidence that the proportion of homicides committed by people with mental disorders actually went down steadily over the period of deinstitutionalisation – from about 35 per cent in 1957 to 11.5 per cent in 1995, according to Home Office figures (Taylor and Gunn, 1999). Evidence that could be used to reach fair judgements can be ignored in favour of populist reactions. These feed into policies that appear to expect health and social care staff to reduce risk virtually to nil. This is extremely hard to achieve without significant encroachment on human rights.

Mental health law itself – including the Mental Health Bill of 2004 – discriminates against psychiatric service users, in allowing them (but not other citizens) to be treated without consent even when they are legally 'capable' of making decisions for themselves. Organisations including the Royal College of Psychiatrists and the Disability Rights Commission have argued instead that a threshold of 'capacity' should be used, with only those demonstrably lacking capacity being treated without consent (DRC, 2002):

> Suppose I have two patients, one with schizophrenia and one with cancer. Both patients recognise that they are ill, that their illnesses can be treated and that there would be consequences to not receiving treatment. They both have the same level of understanding of their illness and the proposed treatment – in legal terms they are both capable. The patient with cancer may refuse my treatment and if I go ahead with it I will be committing an assault. But I will have a legal duty to impose treatment on the patient with schizophrenia ... If my patient has both conditions he will be able to refuse treatment for the cancer but not for the schizophrenia. This is unfair, absurd and makes the mentally ill lesser citizens.
>
> (Dr Tony Zigmund, Royal College of Psychiatrists, writing in the *Independent on Sunday*, 30 June 2002)

In 2002–4, the British government planned the introduction of both a Mental Capacity Bill and new mental health law. Some mental health organisations proposed that government could seize the opportunity to base all new legislative developments on the key principle that those capable of making decisions for themselves should be enabled to do so. Despite the Mental Health Bill of 2004 this view has not yet prevailed.

At the level of practice, commentators have noted that much higher standards can be expected of mental health service users than other citizens. Sometimes these expectations come from staff themselves, for instance people have to be exemplary rather than 'good enough' parents to retain involvement with their children (Sayce, 1999). Sometimes the expectations are from anxious neighbours, for instance:

> They want people using the facilities to have no history of drinking, taking drugs, committing crimes; to be paragons of virtue. How many of them could put their hands on their hearts and say they would fit those standards?
>
> (NHS trust manager, quoted in Sayce and Wilmot, 1997)

These patterns of unfair judgement about risk to others mean that social goods – community living, parenting, work – can be jeopardised (Sayce, 2000).

Thirdly, the notion of risk to self can be just as pernicious as the risk to others. Corrigan et al. (2001) found that what they called the 'stigma of benevolence' towards people with mental health problems was as much associated with discriminatory public attitudes – including authoritarian responses and a desire for social distance – as was the assumption that people were a risk to others. Protecting 'vulnerable' people from harm – though well-intentioned – can be stifling. The 1970s disabled people's movement began in Britain when people with physical impairments living in residential homes broke the rules that kept them safely inside after the typically early institutional supper and wheeled themselves to the pub (Campbell and Oliver, 1996).

Attempts to prevent mental health service users from taking up stressful jobs – as happened with Mr Paul, above – is widespread. One study found that of people with mental health problems who were working, about 40 per cent had been told by mental health workers that they would never work again (Rinaldi and Hill, 2000). A 1995 MORI survey found that the public was most likely to accept people with mental illness as road sweepers, actors, comedians or farm workers and least likely to accept them as doctors, child minders, police officers or nurses. It seems that madness co-exists in the public mind with the most menial and the most creative jobs – but not with jobs requiring responsibility. In reality, decision makers from Winston Churchill to Alistair Campbell have had mental health problems. The attitude that mental illness is incompatible with responsibility may, however, help to explain why people with mental health problems so often work at levels below their qualifications and capacity, if they are working at all.

People with mental health problems are less likely to be in work than any other group of disabled people, partly because of extreme employer prejudice. A 2001 evaluation of the government's ONE programme, designed to increase employment opportunities for people excluded from the labour market, found that despite acute labour shortages only 37 per cent of employers said they would in future take on people with mental illness. This compared to 62 per cent who would take on physically disabled people, 78 per cent long-term unemployed people and 88 per cent lone parents (Department for Work and Pensions, 2001).

A joint study by the Health and Safety Executive and the DRC found that health and safety is sometimes used as a 'false excuse' not to employ disabled people. A review of case law concludes that stereotyped views, wrong decisions and excessively cautious risk assessments may all act as unnecessary, but still sometimes lawful, barriers, so long as they do not give rise to decisions so perverse as to fall outside the range of responses open to a reasonable employer (DRC and HSE, 2003). Case law shows employers are particularly likely to use health and safety justifications when defending against charges of discrimination brought by people with psychiatric disabilities (DRC, 2003).

Apparently benevolent concern for health and safety can also be used to reduce people's responsibilities. As one corporate senior manager put it to me recently after returning to work following mental ill health:

> They gave my junior most of my job, so I wouldn't be 'stressed' – I think they actually thought they were being helpful. They didn't think to ask me how I might react to that. I did point out that a Disability Discrimination Act case from one of their senior managers might not put the company in too good a light.

This brief review shows that risk is not applied neutrally to disabled people. Disabled people are seen through a lens of risk. As Dea Birkett put it, in an article in the *Guardian* (4 April 2003), after her wheelchair-using 10-year-old was refused a ticket to a film because of fire regulations:

> Being portrayed as a threat to health and safety is a battle every person with a disability has to contend with. But disability is not a danger. The real danger is sanctioning exclusion by the misguided application of health and safety regulations.

There is evidence of systemic patterns of discrimination in decision-making based on risk in Britain – across fields including employment, education, transport and health and social services. Assumptions about risk to self and others go untested, often they are exaggerated and then applied unfairly, in ways that restrict people's autonomy and in some cases their human rights.

People with psychiatric disabilities are viewed as particularly high risk to others, but also as risks to themselves. They might be unable to cope, or a job may be too stressful for them. The discourse of risk is the justification for severe constraint on social participation.

Within the risk-dominated stereotypes, there is precious little attention to the (very high) risk of social exclusion. In reality a concentration on risk in terms of violence and vulnerability leads to social exclusion, as people's autonomy is denied and the wider public's tendency to desire social distance is magnified. A mark of respect towards mental health service users would be to stop subjecting this group to a different set of assumptions and rules on risk than that which applies to other citizens. Without risk, there can be no autonomy, no social participation and no achievement.

Clinically, Repper and Perkins (2003) have noted that risk is essential for recovery – for resuming roles and attaining hope. No one can do anything without risk of failure, they argue. Every new relationship means the risk of rejection, every job application means the risk of not getting it, every outing means the risk of being run down by a bus. But without risk there is also no hope –

confidence is eroded and opportunities limited. It is the job of mental health workers to support people in taking risks – not systematically avoiding them.

What can be done to challenge discriminatory approaches to risk?

Some of the individuals in the examples at the beginning of this chapter have – or could have – challenged discrimination or human rights abuses under existing legislation.

Tom White argued that it was discriminatory to stop him going on school trips, particularly without doing an individualised assessment of the risks. He took a case under the DDA 1995 and won. This sent a message to schools and colleges that blanket bans – on the basis of assumptions or stereotypes – are not acceptable. The key is to assess individually and make adjustments (like providing extra support) where necessary. The failure to do so is discrimination and is illegal.

Anthony Ford-Shubrook took a DDA case and won. The health and safety 'justification' for excluding him from the college of his choice was rejected by the Tribunal. The local Learning and Skills Council then worked with the college to make sure he could attend IT courses. He settled into the college successfully.

Mr Paul took a DDA case and won. The Employment Appeal Tribunal ruled that the employer could have scrutinised the occupational health assessment with more care, obtained specialist advice from Mr Paul's consultant, spoken further with Mr Paul himself and looked at adjustments to the job to enable Mr Paul to do it. Again a blanket ban on the basis of diagnosis – and the assumption that depression meant he could not do this job – was not acceptable. It was discriminatory. The probation service was instructed to provide Mr Paul with the next available suitable vacancy and he therefore obtained the work he wanted, as a community service supervisor.

Ms Brazier took a case against North Devon Homes, who were seeking to evict her following complaints by neighbours about her behaviour. The Court found that her disability was the cause of much of her conduct and that to evict her would be to discriminate against her under the DDA. This discrimination could not be 'justified' because, although the neighbours had experienced and were still experiencing discomfort, there had at no point been a danger to anyone's health or safety. Subsequent cases have concluded rather differently, so the law is evolving in this area.

It would be possible for a deaf person to challenge being rejected as a cat owner – on the grounds that she appears to have been treated 'less favourably' by a provider of services, arguably without justification. It is not yet possible for deaf people to challenge being thrown off an aeroplane, as transport is not yet covered by the DDA, although the government is committed to plugging this legal loophole.

There is a pattern in these judgements: health and safety 'justifications' for refusing someone a job, an education or a service cannot be based on assumptions or stereotypes. There has to be an individual assessment and it has to meet certain standards, for instance employers have to take some care over it, and look at whether reasonable adjustments could enable the person to do the job.

The Disability Rights Commission (DRC, 2003) has pointed out weaknesses and limitations in the Disability Discrimination Act 1995, especially in relation to mental health service users who – although they make up 23 per cent of those using this law in the employment sphere – are somewhat less likely to win at Tribunal than other groups of disabled people. As a result, the Disability Rights Commission has urged government to strengthen the Act. The following recommendations are particularly important for people with psychiatric disabilities:

- No questions about disability in recruitment except in highly specified circumstances. This would prevent, for instance, an employer from doing an occupational health check before deciding which person to appoint to a job and rejecting the person with a history of depression.

- Improved definitions of disability, to better cover people with psychiatric impairments, for instance a definition of 'day-to-day activities' that reflected problems in social interaction, and self-harm, on a par with problems in walking or seeing.

- Removal of the requirement that a mental health problem must be 'clinically well recognised' to count as a disability: this does not apply to physical impairments and therefore introduces discrimination into the face of law itself. In 2004, the government agreed to make this change.

The DDA can be very influential even without anyone actually going to court or a tribunal. The 'two-year rule' used in some NHS organisations, to prevent people with current or recent use of mental health services from training or practising in nursing, has been scrapped by the Department of Health. Following advice on the DDA, the Department issued new guidance in 2002 which stated that:

> As the largest employer in the UK, the NHS should set an example showing that discrimination is taken seriously and will be eradicated ... It is extremely unjust, a waste of human potential, a great cost to society and potentially unlawful to exclude anyone from employment simply because that person has experienced or experiences mental health problems ... The '2-year rule' ... is no longer to be used in the NHS.
>
> (Department of Health, 2002a)

Formal investigations can also be undertaken under the DDA – establishing systemic patterns of discrimination in particular organisations or sectors and requiring action to tackle it. And the government is committed to introducing a disability equality public sector duty – requiring the public sector actively to promote equality of opportunity (rather than waiting for discrimination and tackling it only after the event). The DDA is becoming a strong lever to encourage changes in policies and practices, to ensure that organisations do not discriminate against people with mental health problems or other disabled people.

The Human Rights Act (HRA) 1998 can also be used by practitioners to challenge unfair application of risk-thinking to disabled people. The two disabled women who encountered East Sussex County Council's 'no lifting' policy took the Council to judicial review. The judge ruled that the dignity and independence of disabled people is so important that some manual lifting is an inherent and inescapable feature of the task for which care workers are employed. An approach is required that attends to both staff health and safety – which can be addressed through training and agreed protocols – and the independence and dignity of disabled people. The judgement prompted reviews of policies beyond East Sussex:

> When Charles Dickens's Mr Bumble said that 'the law is an ass' he obviously hadn't encountered East Sussex County Council. Or witnessed the good sense of the Honourable Justice Munby. What on earth would Mr Bumble have made of the council's asinine decision to rule out manual handling by care workers in all circumstances? ... Whatever the reason, it's hard to understand and harder still to condone the blatant disregard for the human rights of two severely disabled women who brought the case – and all the other disabled and elderly people who must have suffered silently and unnoticed in the 'care' of this local authority or any other council to have introduced wholesale prohibitions on manual handling. It's good to know that – thanks to the good justice Munby – it is now 'likely to be unlawful' to leave disabled or older people lying on the floor in their own excrement while a hoist is imported to their home.
>
> (*Therapy Weekly*, 27 February 2003)

Challenging the stereotypes that underpin unfair risk-thinking in mental health

Legally driven remedies alone are not enough. It is also important to change the stereotypes that underpin discrimination (Sayce, 2003), not least because people go beyond mere compliance to best practice when they understand the point of doing so.

The *National Service Framework for Mental Health* opens with an introduction from the then secretary of state that talks promisingly about 'combating discrimination' and 'promoting positive images of mental ill health' (Department of Health, 1999b). But it goes on to talk of people with mental health problems in two groups: the minority who are 'a nuisance and a danger'; and the larger group who are 'vulnerable', 'presenting no threat to anyone but themselves'. It is worth noting that this description is utterly permeated by risk-thinking: if people are not a risk to others, then they are a risk to themselves.

The academic literature on how to reduce discriminatory attitudes towards people with mental health problems shows that it is necessary to go beyond seeing people as a risk to self or others and instead break the link with both violence and incompetence. Discrimination, or stigma, has four components (Link and Phelan, 2001):

1. Distinguishing between and labelling human differences

2. Linking the labelled persons to undesirable characteristics

3. Separating 'them' (the labelled persons) from 'us'

4. Culminating in status loss and discrimination that lead to unequal outcomes or life chances.

There is a particularly strong evidence base for how to interrupt component 3 – by stopping separating 'them' from 'us'. Attitudes improve as a result of contact or familiarisation with a person/people with experience of mental health problems (Corrigan and Penn, 1999; Alexander and Link, 2003). Opposition to mental health facilities disappears once the facilities open and neighbours 'see service users as people' (Repper et al., 1997). Contact appears to reduce fear of the 'other' and increase empathy. Contact affects attitudes whether or not the contact is voluntary (Desforges et al., 1991; Corrigan et al., 2001). Contact can be retrospective or prospective, in other words, engineering contact as an anti-discrimination intervention promises to be effective (Couture and Penn, 2003).

It is vital that contact is between people as equals. Other key factors are that people should be brought together in situations where stereotypes are likely to be disconfirmed, where there is intergroup cooperation, where participants can get to know each other and where wider social norms support equality (Desforges et al., 1991; Corrigan and Penn, 1999; Hewstone, 2003). Where people with psychiatric disabilities have ongoing significant roles as employees, bosses or teachers – or are trainers, with status – this is likely to impact positively on the attitudes of those around them.

Inclusion itself is a powerful way of changing non-disabled people's beliefs. Recent British research finds that the group with the highest DDA awareness and the most inclusive attitudes about disability are people who 'know someone who is disabled at work' (DRC, 2002b). Inclusive schools also influence non-disabled children to hold more accepting attitudes towards disabled children (Gray, 2002).

A key challenge is thus to make it safer for disabled people to assert the right to participate. It is encouraging that a recent American survey of professionals and managers with mental health problems (from across industries and sectors) found that the vast majority (87 per cent) had disclosed at work and most (61 per cent) had no regrets. One of the factors significantly associated with disclosure was awareness of the Americans with Disabilities Act 1990. Anti-discrimination law can encourage confidence and at best deliver greater safety to disclose (Ellison et al., 2003).

The other significant body of evidence relates to the messages that are used to interrupt component 2 in the stigmatising process – linking the person to undesirable characteristics. When setting out to replace undesirable with more desirable associations, evidence shows it is essential to test whether the new proposed characteristic actually is viewed as positive by people with psychiatric impairments and the intended audience. It is all too easy to replace one stereotype with another.

One type of message that 'works' is one that disrupts the link between mental ill-health and violence (Penn et al., 1999; Read and Law, 1999). This matches the finding that the association between dangerousness and mental illness is 'the core' of stigma (Link et al., 1999). People who associate mental illness with violence are most likely to hold discriminatory attitudes (Link et al., 1997) and where educational interventions break the link with violence, discriminatory attitudes wane. The more the message is spread that mental health service users are generally not violent the better.

Another promising message focuses on the contribution of mental health service users as employees, community leaders and so on. The New Zealand Like Minds campaign profiled people with mental health problems working and succeeding, including a well-known New Zealand rugby player, as well as more ordinary citizens. This emphasis may have been a factor in the campaign's success in measurably improving public attitudes (New Zealand Ministry of Health, 2003). It appears to have helped to replace the stereotype of helplessness and/or dangerousness with images of people with something to offer. This message tackles the view – perhaps as pernicious as the assumption of violence – that people with mental health problems are incompetent. It is therefore likely to be helpful to convey examples of mental health service users who contribute.

Beyond these areas, evidence for the effectiveness of particular messages is much less clear-cut. It is troubling that many anti-stigma campaigns worldwide are using, or even relying on, messages for which there is no clear evidence base. One of the commonest is the message that 'mental illness is an illness like any other' (or is a brain disease). There is no body of research that supports the effectiveness of this 'illness' message – or any message focusing on the causes of mental health problems. Causes are not the point when it comes to combating discrimination.

The illness message does not disrupt the link between mental illness and violence. In popular culture, 'sickness' co-exists readily with evil – as 'sick monster' tabloid headlines attest. The disease model also does not break the link between mental illness and incompetence and it can reinforce it (Read and Harre, 2001; Sayce, 2004). As one American service user put it:

> People used to be called crazy and lunatic. A lot of hatred was directed at them. NAMI (National Alliance for the Mentally Ill) stepped in and said 'No, don't hate them, they're sick. Pity them.' Now we're stuck with a lot of pity. I wish someone had had more foresight and substituted something different for the hatred.

Illness also means one is excused from social roles which may be exactly what the individual does not want. There is a powerful need to create images of possibility that go beyond the two models put forward in the National Service Framework – of mental health service users as either dangerous or a risk to themselves. The new images of possibility are needed by people with psychiatric disabilities themselves, and the staff who work with them, and decision makers like employers, and the wider public.

It is not possible to overthrow discriminatory attitudes as long as people are seen through the lens of risk. Instead people with psychiatric impairments need to be viewed as equal citizens who can and do contribute. Where risk needs to be assessed, that is one activity, not something that should define people as individuals or dictate society's response to them. Mental health service users are far more than a bundle of risks.

Implications for mental health professionals

Mental health practitioners need to:

1. Gain an understanding of how people with psychiatric disabilities, and disabled people more broadly, can be subjected to unfair risk assessments across different life domains, for instance employment, education, housing, health and social services. Accounts of disabled people's own lives provide a very different focus, one that goes far beyond a focus on risk to looking at people's hopes, disappointments and the barriers they face to realising their aspirations (Leete, 1989; Deegan, 1994). Often these barriers take the form of other people's attitudes, including – at times – the attitudes of those providing services to them. It is important to think about the opportunities in people's lives and how barriers might be overcome and not to get sucked into thinking only about risk, which can restrict opportunity and even wipe hope out of the dialogue altogether. Hope is essential to recovery. Mental health practitioners can help to foster it.

2. Think through how people with psychiatric disabilities can be supported to take risks. For instance, who will encourage the person if he or she goes for a job and ensure support is in place in the recruitment process and the employment itself if needed? Who will remain encouraging whether they get the job or not and support them in taking further risks rather than giving up?

3. Inform people with psychiatric disabilities of their rights under the DDA and the HRA. Enable people to understand that they can negotiate for adjustments, for instance if you are working or seeking work, you can ask for a 'reasonable adjustment' ranging from time off for appointments with a mental health worker to some change in the hours or specific job tasks. For further details of the type of adjustments that can be sought – in employment and beyond – see the Employers Forum on Disability, 1998 and Sayce and Boardman, 2003. People do not have to settle for the unimaginative view that because you have mental health problems, you are 'unable' to do all types of things. Just as deaf people can look after cats (see above), so people with psychiatric disabilities can work, achieve educationally and raise families – if the right adjustments are put in place. People need to know that they have rights to negotiate for such adjustments and to complain if they are not provided.

4. Aim to ensure that in mental health practice, risk does not distort decisions or the quality of relationships. For instance, if the individual wants to raise their child, it is good practice to judge parenting abilities just as a non-disabled person's abilities might be judged, that is, without discrimination, and also explore what supports might enable them to be a good enough parent. This should happen before making any long-term decisions on whether the child can safely stay with this parent. The approach should be fair: not expecting more of this person just because she or he is a mental health service user; and not making assumptions based, however unintentionally, on stereotypes of dangerousness or incompetence. Try to estimate risk accurately – not exaggerate it – and balance risk against opportunities and the desirability of

social participation and valued social roles (such as parent). It is worth noting that under forthcoming disability discrimination legislation, public authorities' decisions will be covered by the DDA, so the requirement not to discriminate will need formally to be addressed alongside the best interests of the child.

5. Be aware of the tensions between an anti-discriminatory approach and certain legal or policy requirements, for instance discriminatory elements of the Mental Health Act 1983 or, following the death of Victoria Climbié, greater requirements to track parenting by people with mental health problems than other citizens. Where possible, within legal constraints, ensure that you avoid discrimination. Feed back to managers or policy makers where this tension is most problematic.

6. Familiarise yourself with the evidence on risk. For instance, employment is far better for your mental health than unemployment (Warner, 1985; Link et al., 1997). Do not assume that the stress of work will be damaging – being unemployed is likely to be far worse for a person's mental health. Not having control at work is stressful – so the more junior jobs are usually more stressful. Do not fall into the trap of assuming a more responsible job will be particularly stressful – the reverse is more likely to be true. Do not feed into people's low expectations by discouraging people with psychiatric disabilities from roles that might be 'stressful' – let them decide and support them to take risks if they wish to.

7. Consider the 'risks' for the person of being kept in a safe cocoon, with no risk, no job, no major activities and no life at all. Remember that risk assessment can dominate dangerously and lead to risk-averse, overcautious behaviour, by clinicians and disabled people alike. Do not let assessment of risk seep through all aspects of a helping relationship. Do not let risk obscure opportunities. In doing a risk assessment, keep it in proportion – risk is only one aspect of the person's life. Overdoing risk aversion can make the life not worth living at all.

8. Involve people with psychiatric disabilities in thinking about risk. For instance, many people who sometimes feel angry or violent recognise their own triggers. Others know when they are becoming unwell and may be likely to neglect themselves. Talk with service users about risk assessment and how best to respond when triggers happen or the person is becoming unwell. Writing a risk assessment without reference to the person is not usually a good idea.

9. Become an advocate for the huge national priority to reduce discrimination. Familiarise yourself with the evidence on what works to change attitudes, make the law work and raise awareness in others. Talk about the DDA, the HRA, the need for people with psychiatric disabilities to know and use their rights, the need to support disabled people in challenging discrimination and negotiating for rights. And talk about needing to replace old stereotypes with genuinely new messages – not illness and incompetence, not violence, but contribution and opportunity.

10. Work for the goal of users and survivors of mental health services leading programmes to reduce discrimination. Discrimination is only effectively challenged when power is addressed. This means users and survivors of mental health services taking positions of power, leading change initiatives.

CONCLUSION

Risk has become a powerful driver of both policy discourse and practice and it is used in discriminatory ways to restrict opportunities and recovery for people with psychiatric disabilities. There are promising ways of challenging these forms of discrimination and risk aversion: including using the Disability Discrimination Act and Human Rights Act to change systems for the better; disabled people securing their rights; and replacing old stereotypes with hopeful messages of social participation and equality. Mental health professionals have a critical role in achieving change on this basis, operating as allies to people with psychiatric disabilities who need to set the agenda and be in the lead.

FURTHER READING

Deegan, P.E. (1994) 'Recovery: the lived experience of rehabilitation', in Spaniol, L. and Koehler, M. (eds) *The Experience of Recovery* (Boston: Center for Psychiatric Rehabilitation).

Link, B.G. and Phelan, J.C. (2001) 'On the nature and consequences of stigma', *Annual Review of Sociology* **27**: 363–85.

Repper, J.M. and Perkins, R.E. (2003) *Social Inclusion, Recovery and Mental Health Practice* (London: Balliere Tindall).

Royal College of Psychiatrists (2003) *Employment Opportunities for People with Psychiatric Disabilities*. Council Report (London: Royal College of Psychiatrists).

Sayce, L. (2000) *From Psychiatric Patient to Citizen: Overcoming Discrimination and Social Exclusion* (Basingstoke: Macmillan – now Palgrave Macmillan).

Social Work with Asylum Seekers and Others Subject to Immigration Control

Debra Hayes

Introduction

We have been familiar for some time now with scare stories and panic-stricken headlines about asylum seekers. These stories present predominantly male images of asylum seekers as feckless, bogus, criminal, terrorist, illegal and diseased. At this particular historical point, we are also in the midst of a dangerous escalation in the brutality of these messages. The global concern with terrorism, which has constructed the Muslim as the dangerous interloper in the West, is having a profound influence on the lived experience of many within our communities, some of whom are asylum seekers, many of whom made much earlier journeys before such a label was constructed. One of the consequences of this bombardment is the dehumanising of those forced to leave their home, homeland, family, love, support, shared language, culture and identity. We can then accept without flinching a system of immigration controls and an asylum infrastructure which revels in its purpose – to exclude, deter, separate and impoverish. The question at the centre of this chapter is whether social work itself has become so enmeshed in that culture of suspicion that we have lost sight of some of our central principles, namely, human dignity and worth, social justice and service to humanity (BASW, 2003). This chapter will focus on the changing role of social work in relation to asylum seekers and others subject to immigration control, considering tensions and ethical issues and offering examples of good practice.

My personal journey regarding these issues began over ten years ago when I was a probation officer in an inner-city borough. I was to be shaken out of my naivety, ignorance and complacency when a black prisoner I was working with was served with a deportation notice. 'That can't be right', I thought, 'he's lived here for 14 years, has a wife and children who were born here, has a job, a mortgage, a community.' Mr X was in fact serving a five year prison sentence for importation of heroin and whilst the court did not recommend deportation at the point of sentencing, he was subsequently served with a notice of intent to deport mid-sentence on 'conducive to public goods' grounds. I came later to understand the significance of these processes and will return to them later. I had not, of course, received any training on anything close to these issues during my social work course and spent subsequent months considering more thoughtfully what exactly the response of a worker in such circumstances should be. Mr X was eventually deported, leaving a divided family, fatherless children and a distraught wife and mother behind. I came to learn that in the UK, just like most other rich parts of the globe, there are many long-term residents who are not 'illegal', who are settled within communities, but who do not enjoy full citizenship rights, which has consequences when they break the rules. This 'lesser' status confirms the position of these predominantly black residents as 'other', as 'outsider' and creates a particular and inferior relationship with the state, and, for our purposes, more significantly with the local and welfare state of which social work is a part.

A history of discrimination

Whilst it is essential that we explore here the particular position of asylum seekers in a separate and inferior welfare system and the knock-on effects for them as users of social work services, I start with the above example to illustrate that there is a much wider community of residents in the UK who are excluded from equal access to both citizenship rights and welfare, as a result of their immigration status. From my experience of working with practitioners and students alike, it is necessary to contextualise contemporary immigration policies and practices in order to understand their role and purpose. In integrating immigration and asylum matters into the curriculum of a social work degree, it has been the *grounding* of students in the history and ideology of immigration, which has created the foundation for understanding the law, policy and practice in relation to those subject to immigration controls.

Whilst the movement of people around the globe is part of human history, the *control* of that movement is very much a modern phenomenon (see Hayter, 2000). In the UK this has a track record of around a century. At each of the key moments in that history, calls for restrictions have been posed in racist terms, marked by the Aliens Act 1905:

> It was the poor Eastern European Jew who was to become the focus for control and in the run up to the first piece of immigration control in 1905, 'alien' became synonymous with 'Jew'.
>
> (Hayes, 2002: 31)

Black and Asian Commonwealth immigration came under scrutiny in the period following the Second World War. Culminating in the 1962 Commonwealth Immigrants Act, anti-immigration lobbying was based on an open hostility to 'coloureds'. 'In the last forty years the main objects of anti-immigrant racism in Britain and elsewhere have been, and are, people of African and Asian origin' (Hayter, 2000: 4).

Contemporary constructions of asylum seekers also rely heavily on racist stereotypes. As Liz Fekete from the Institute of Race Relations states: 'Government policies and practices aimed at asylum seekers have educated a whole nation into racism' (*Guardian*, 2001). A historical framework allows for the unpacking of this seemingly inherent connection between immigration control and racism:

> Although controls formally discriminate on grounds of nationality, racism has fundamentally informed the construction of immigration controls. The ideological justification for control has been a racialised nationalism, and the practice of control by the state has been directed at racialised groups.
>
> (Mynott, 2002: 13)

Nowadays, we use words like 'asylum seeker', 'refugee', 'economic migrant' and in the past words like 'immigrant' or 'alien'. These different words do not necessarily represent different types of people, they simply reflect the changing political purposes to which the categories have been put across time and space. Today's asylum seeker may well have been previously constructed as an immigrant. For example, nationalities currently topping the asylum statistics (see Heath et al., 2003), namely Iraq, Zimbabwe, Somalia and Afghanistan, all had a particular colonial relationship with the UK. Waves of immigration restrictions since have changed the status of former colonial subjects, turning many who had a strong allegiance to 'Mother England', into nothing more than 'aliens':

- The Commonwealth Immigrants Act 1962, which took away automatic rights of entry to Commonwealth citizens by introducing work vouchers

- The Commonwealth Immigrants Act 1968, which systematically removed citizenship rights overnight to UK passport holders, unless they, a parent or a grandparent had been born, adopted or naturalised in the UK

- The Immigration Act 1971, which created 'patrials' who were largely white being born in the UK or having parents or grandparents who were, and 'non-patrials'. This effectively ended immigration for settlement for people from the Caribbean, the Indian subcontinent and Africa

- The British Nationality Act 1981, which amongst other things abolished automatic rights to citizenship to those born on British soil, establishing the bloodline as the key factor.

Since the 1980s, migration for settlement has been difficult to obtain, as we have changed the goalposts and increasingly restricted entry. This process has continued in most of the richer parts of the world, leaving a divided globe with very few *legal* means by which the poor can enter the richer and *safer* territory (see Harding, 2000). It is also important to understand that attacks on settlement are attacks on family reconstruction. The richer parts of the globe will always need labour, different skills for different times, what we don't want is to pick up the tab for the broader social costs of settlement – education, health, social security, social housing and so on.

Obstructions to family unity are institutionalised now, to the extent where many long-term residents find it difficult to unite their families, even for short-term visits and holidays. Our colleagues at work, students and social work service users have differing access to family networks. The significance of this should not go unnoticed in a profession which looks predominantly to that institution, the family, to find solutions to problems. I was struck by the enormity of this recently when a student, who happens to be an asylum seeker, experienced the death of her father in her homeland. Distanced from his death, she was also distanced from family support and the rituals we associate with bereavement. It was enormously difficult for her to access those rituals here, they were and are specific to her country and culture. Working with those subject to immigration control, we are already in an arena dominated by loss. It seems to me that listening to those stories can inform our own practice enormously and usefully challenge the complacency with which we construct 'family' in our professional arena.

The current focus, then, is on asylum seekers and the debate is posed in terms of genuineness. What is clear from those asylum statistics is that the countries dominating the list are in crisis. Despite the relentless media machine's presentation of asylum seekers as scroungers (see Refugee Council, 2002), it is global crisis which forces people across boundaries and within that context it is meaningless to differentiate between a flight from crippling destitution, war or persecution. The 'economic migrant' may be constructed as bogus, but with few legitimate routes to survival open, it may be that leaving family is the only way to support them.

Controlling welfare

Throughout all this is a common thread, a concern with ensuring that the resources of the *nation* are not spent on the wrong people. 'Outsiders' are, of course, by their nature the wrong people:

> Who those 'outsiders' are remains the product of racism, but no longer a racism simply targeted at black people, it now encompasses new layers of the world's poor and dispossessed.
>
> (Hayes and Humphries, 2004: 13)

So, whilst immigration controls over the course of the century have concerned themselves with who *gets in*, their other central purpose has been control over those who do and the conditions under which they live. The social cost of these newcomers is always presented in entirely negative terms, with scant attention to the taxes, labour and skills contributed by them. It is this powerful and distorted ideology around social cost, which runs throughout the history of immigration control, which has forced the drive to oppressive internal control of non-citizens. It has been astonishingly easy for the Far Right to make best use of this because the foundations for the argument are already there. Protecting the public purse from abuse from the outside is a popular position for most mainstream politicians on the left and right of the political spectrum. It encapsulates an acceptance of certain taken-for-granted ideas, for example that belonging to a nation should bring some security and support and being outside of it should not.

One of the most powerful media representations of asylum seekers is that they are the ones unfairly accessing public resources and are coming precisely to do so (see Refugee Council, 2002). It is not simply the Far Right who struggle to see humanity globally and are influenced by an idea of nation, which makes it appear natural for us to restrict *our* resources to *our* own. In my experience of working in higher education, black, white and Asian students alike have a sense of allegiance to other UK citizens when they are pitted against the needs of new arrivals. The idea of *contributing* in order to have rights to welfare is connected and equally powerful.

In fact, those *outside* 'nation' have also always been constructed as *outside* 'welfare'. The centrality of nationality for claims upon welfare existed long before large-scale black migration to the UK and is rooted in the very purpose of welfare (Cohen, 2001, 2003). Key players in the development of welfare reforms in the early twentieth century saw its purpose as very much connected to stopping the alleged deterioration of the British 'race'. Philanthropists and reformers during that period, such as Beatrice and Sidney Webb, William Booth, Seebohm Rowntree and Marie Stopes, were all preoccupied with improving the condition of the working class and wanted a population fitter for both work and war. The purpose of welfare is therefore precisely to improve the quality of *our* nation, in particular, in relation to *other* competing nations. A preoccupation grew with rooting out both the undeserving poor and foreigners who are both unwelcome and, by their very nature, not entitled to welfare support.

It can be argued that welfare exists to improve the ability of the nation to compete with emerging rivals in both global markets and global conflicts, and should, therefore, be for those *deserving* citizens who can help in this particular venture. Those calling for the control over the entry of largely Jews, escaping persecution in Eastern Europe at the turn of the last century, stood side by side with welfare reformers in this. The enormously influential welfare programme of 1906–1914, introduced by the Liberal government, included the Old Age Pensions Act 1908 and the National Insurance Act 1911. Both Acts contained residency and citizenship requirements, ensuring that Jewish entrants had no access to the provisions contained within them, because:

> it might be that crowds of foreigners of the age of 45 or 50 might come over here in the hope that, having resided in this country for the required time, they might get a pension.
>
> (MP Arthur Fell in 1908, cited in Cohen, 2003: 91)

Familiar-sounding arguments took hold concerning whether Jewish refugees were really fleeing persecution or attempting to access a better life at *our* expense (Hayes, 2002). Not only that, as they moved into the only affordable and accessible urban areas, they were blamed for the emerging social problems associated with the cities. In the battle for the first immigration control, the question of 'means', that is, whether those entering would be able to support themselves without accessing public money, was crucial. From the beginning, immigration control was constructed as a mechanism for deciding *who* would be beneficial to the British nation and *who* might be a burden. The Aliens Act 1905 only applied to those in third-class travelling conditions, that is, the poor. The Act allowed for refusal of entry where an alien immigrant was considered to be undesirable. The most common reasons for undesirability were as follows:

(a) If he cannot show that he has in his possession or is in a position to obtain the means of decently supporting himself and his dependents; or

(b) If he is a lunatic or an idiot, or owing to any disease or infirmity appears likely to become a charge upon the rates or otherwise a detriment to the public.

(Aliens Act 1905, cited in Englander, 1994: 279)

Decisions about undesirability focused predominantly on who might be costly, both socially and economically. If families could not support themselves without access to public monies, they simply could not come in. This concept has remained in immigration control since and there is a powerful reminder of this in the current immigration rules, which prevent entry to anyone likely to have 'recourse to public funds' (see Seddon, 2002). This illustrates the strong link between immigration control and the delivery of welfare and illuminates one of the central purposes of immigration controls – to target and control welfare spending. The state then uses a dual approach, firstly, by creating immigration controls at borders and internally which debar those who might require assistance and, secondly, by building into welfare, arrangements to exclude the *outsider*.

Post-war welfare

In the five years immediately following the Second World War, commonly associated with the development of a comprehensive welfare state, welfare was seen as part of a hopeful new world where ordinary people could look forward optimistically to universal healthcare, social security, education and affordable and good quality housing (see Thane, 1996; Timmins, 1996). These improvements created a sense that the 'post-war Labour Government had established something qualitatively new: a new approach to the use of the power of the state consciously in the interests of social justice for the mass of the population: a welfare state' (Thane, 1996: 249). This period also coincided with a period of mass migration, which was encouraged to help in this era of economic and social reconstruction. These predominantly black immigrants, unlike the Jews before them, did have citizenship rights as Commonwealth subjects, as well as a strong emotional and ideological connection with 'Mother England'. Would these citizens have access to the new world of welfare like any other Commonwealth subject?

This group were treated as short-term labour, migrant workers who, it was assumed, would return home to their families and not require the benefits of long-term settlement. Only when they began to present for services did the question of entitlement emerge. For example, in the post-war housing boom, Ginsburg (1989) showed how black citizens were not considered for the new council housing, but were left to the mercy of the private market. Whilst

Commonwealth citizens technically had rights to access the NHS, there were well-documented examples of illegal exclusions and requests for passports. In 1979 the DHSS issued guidelines to London hospitals entitled Gatecrashers, calling for restricted access for immigrants: 'it is feared that if they obtain this treatment without difficulty it might encourage others to come over and try their luck' (cited in Cohen and Hayes, 1998: 15). Eventually the 1982 NHS Charges to Overseas Visitors regulations were imposed, restricting treatment to those 'ordinarily resident' in the UK. This began a process whereby more and more mechanisms have been introduced in the NHS to police recipients of free services.

Similarly, in terms of social security, research by Gordon and Newnham in 1985 showed that black immigrants were being excluded from basic safety nets, even when they had entitlement as citizens. The practice of requesting passports was shown to fall mainly on black claimants:

> What developed during this period was a system in which discrete and separate agencies of the state were advised or encouraged to play a part in the enforcement of immigration controls.
>
> (Gordon and Newnham, 1985: 70)

These authors pinpoint here the shift to the inclusion of not only the police and immigration officials *internally* policing immigration, but also workers in welfare. This should be a major cause for concern for social workers and related professionals as this process has escalated since. As the immigration legislation in the 1960s, 70s and 80s, described earlier, reconstructed just who the citizen was, the need to 'gatekeep' access to state welfare resources has intensified. What the above examples illustrate is that layers of long-term residents, some with citizenship rights and some without, find themselves having to account for their status when they are at the point of accessing services. The full implications of this for social work are dealt with below.

It is also important to consider that anyone without citizenship with the right of abode is subject to the immigration rules and at their centre is the issue of maintenance and accommodation. Just as Jewish refugees at the turn of the twentieth century had to prove they could support themselves and their families without needing relief provided by parishes or charities, applicants wishing to stay or join family now must show that they 'will be maintained and accommodated adequately without recourse to public funds' (Seddon, 2002: 328). The list of things considered public funds is an ever-increasing one and currently includes income support, job seekers allowance, housing benefit, council tax benefit, working families tax credit, local authority housing, child benefit, disabled persons tax credit, attendance allowance, severe disablement allowance, invalid care allowance, disability living allowance (Cohen, 2001: 49). Here we see the absolute centrality of protecting public resources within immigration control. To underline this, long-term residents of the UK, many of whom in the past would have had citizenship rights, must satisfy these conditions if they are to reunite their families or stay long term. A Home Office circular in 1996 further illuminates government thinking. The circular (Home Office, 1996) was a response to a 1993 'Efficiency Scrutiny' which looked at key central and local government bodies and their relationship with the Home Office Immigration and Nationality Directorate (IND). The government had grasped that much of the information about immigration status and claims on welfare was in the hands of other agencies and not the IND, agencies such as the NHS and the DSS or housing departments. How useful it would be to access that and the scrutiny explicitly made agencies accountable for

> identifying claimants who may be ineligible for a benefit or service by virtue of their immigration status; and to encourage local authorities to pass information to the IND about suspected immigration offenders.
>
> (Home Office, 1996)

Entering the asylum

As described earlier, forty years of legislation, which has restricted rights of entry, even for those with previous citizenship rights, has left few avenues for entry open. Seeking asylum from war, persecution, famine and other consequences of global crises, has become the remaining route of entry. The asylum seeker, then, is a modern construct, as migration for settlement has become all but impossible. All focus is now on asylum, with little reference to others subject to immigration control as described above. Nevertheless the language and ideas from previous periods have been taken forward into the contemporary construction of the asylum seeker. They are seen only as poor, burdensome and socially costly. The velocity and force with which this ideology has been constructed has gained such momentum that it has been possible to go much further than previously. No more tinkering at the edges of welfare restriction, but the creation of a completely separate and inferior system. The Immigration and Asylum Act 1999 removed entitlement to a range of non-contributory, family and disability benefits to this group, extended the use of vouchers and created a system of compulsory dispersal. A centralised agency, the National Asylum Support Service (NASS) was created. NASS enters into arrangements with both voluntary organisations and local authorities regarding arrangements for asylum seekers in dispersal areas. Subsistence is by way of money or vouchers to the value of 70 per cent of basic income support. Asylum seekers, therefore, live well below the level considered as subsistence. Housing is organised via a consortia of local authorities and voluntary organisations to accommodate the asylum seekers being dispersed to zones on a no choice basis.

What we now have, therefore, unashamedly, is a 'welfare' scheme, deliberately separate and inferior, making no attempt to even offer subsistence-level support and which manages and moves human beings without offering any choice or indeed any consideration of individual need. As a profession, social work is now part of that machinery administering this system. In local authority Asylum Teams, which sort out accommodation, money, vouchers, GPs, schooling and so on, there is little room for more in-depth practical or emotional help for this vulnerable group. Having separated them from the normal welfare arrangements and mainstream services, social workers are operating in a system which discriminates, excludes and fuels a climate of hostility. The Nationality, Immigration and

Asylum Act 2002 further confirms a government strategy which breeds popular nationalism and hostility to asylum seekers. The measures contained in it were initially outlined in the government White Paper *Secure Borders, Safe Haven: Integration with Diversity 2002* (Home Office, 2002d), commented on in the Refugee Council briefing of December 2002 (Refugee Council, 2002). The requirement for applicants to pass an English test and the introduction of a citizenship ceremony involving an oath of allegiance illuminates the government's thinking. As learning English is often a priority for asylum seekers themselves, it would be easy to see this policy in entirely benevolent terms. In debates on the imposition of English testing, it is instructive to ask groups who can speak more than one language, in my experience, it will almost always be predominantly black and Asian participants who can, which adds a further dimension to the debate. Asylum seekers have far higher language skills and educational qualifications than the average UK citizen (*Guardian*, 2001), illustrating that we seem unable to focus on strengths and continue to present the group as deficient. Government plans for the separate education of asylum seeker children in accommodation centres, making it harder to integrate and access everyday language, asks further questions of the real agenda here. Parts of the Act which withdrew even subsistence-level support for some asylum seekers have come under legal challenge, but it is worrying for a government purposefully to create legislation which makes vulnerable people destitute. In 2004, the Asylum and Immigration (Treatment of Claimants) Bill proposed powers for the social work profession to take into care the children of failed asylum seekers in order to speed up the removal of their parents. These proposals breached the fundamental right of children to live with and be cared for by their parents and are against the spirit of the *UN Convention on the Rights of the Child*, as well as the Children Act 1989 which informs much social work practice with children and families.

The shift in the role of local authorities in the management of asylum seekers has had further significance for social work, for example in the community care arena. Many care in the community functions depend on immigration status, with exclusions for those 'subject to immigration control'. Research by Harris and Roberts (2002) shows the consequences for disabled asylum seekers of not accessing mainstream services. They point to the need for community care assessments to be done to ensure full access to a range of benefits and services. It has taken Appeal Court rulings to 'persuade' local authorities of their responsibilities (*Community Care*, 2002a). Refugee Council research has shown how social services departments have been failing to provide help to asylum seekers being discharged from hospital because of financial considerations (*Community Care*, 2003b). It has by no means been easy, therefore, for this group to access community care resources. And further, whilst school-age, asylum-seeking children are entitled to education, including free school meals, travel and uniform, some social services departments have argued that they cannot offer this, including special educational needs assessments where relevant (*Community Care*, 2002b).

Accessing suitable healthcare remains problematic for asylum seekers (Burnett and Fassil, 2002). Worryingly, many asylum seekers are healthy on arrival and their health deteriorates as a consequence of dispersal, poverty and poor housing.

Many do, unfortunately, have physical and mental health conditions as a result of the situations from which they escaped. The popular debate concerning asylum and health, though, has again not focused on need, but resources. Exaggerated claims regarding the burden on the NHS, outlined in the Refugee Council's (2002) analysis of press myths, replay the debates in previous periods outlined before. Asylum seekers are not only seen as responsible for bringing in disease, but are seen to get preferential access to resources.

Implications for social work

The experience of restricted rights and poor access to welfare for long-term residents subject to immigration control has for decades gone largely unnoticed in social work. Whilst the restrictions on access to housing, health, education and benefits have impacted greatly on people's lives, social work has intervened only minimally. We have also seemingly not noticed that many of our service users in this category are living in divided families, which has consequences in so many ways. What has forced the issue onto the professional agenda has been this separating out of the category 'asylum seeker' and the scale of the enforced destitution. There is now an inescapable reality, as social work is faced with individuals and families with enormous needs, sometimes in geographical areas without an infrastructure or history of support to such groups. The work is now emerging in and across a full range of social work contexts and workers are simply not prepared for it, practically, ethically or emotionally.

In attempting to improve service delivery to asylum seekers and others subject to immigration control, the context of hostility, racism and grinding poverty has to be acknowledged. This climate has reached a point where it is almost accepted without question that our existing arrangements are satisfactory and reasonable. For our purposes, the question is how far social work as a profession has become uncritical of these arrangements and complicit in their delivery. Social work seems to have largely occupied itself with concerns over gatekeeping resources, rather than responding to need (see Hayes and Humphries, 2004). The issue of asylum is asking questions of the social work profession, which shed light on its role, function and values. We are compromised by budgetary constraints and resource control and have lost sight of some of our central purpose. However, the asylum issue offers an opportunity to reflect on this and retrieve something from an alternative perspective for those concerned to work within a profession committed to supporting the poor and the oppressed and willing to offer challenges to the social order.

There appears to be widespread uncertainty, confusion and abstention within social work teams concerning this work. A key theme, which has emerged time and time again, concerns contention around responsibility between mainstream teams and Asylum Teams. The idea that 'the other team do that' is exacerbated by the conflicting status of asylum seekers. Asylum seekers are not just that, they might also be children, families, old, disabled and a range of other things, which contribute to them being passed from pillar to post. More worryingly, it appears that workers have been steeped in the negative culture described above and have absorbed these stereotypes, which contribute to a deserving/undeserving dichotomy (Sales and Hek, 2004) Given that they are working in a culture which prioritises resource control and involves decisions about desirability and deservedness, this should be of some concern. Hostility towards asylum seekers *within* social service offices, with teams in conflict with voluntary/community refugee organisations, is certainly a situation we need to take stock of.

The voluntary sector is not immune from these difficulties. As the sector has to chase money and resources for future survival, it is not surprising that monies have been accepted with conditions. Conditions concerning surveillance, control and cooperation with the Home Office are not uncommon now for organisations working with asylum seekers and refugees. Alarm bells should be sounding about the implications of this, particularly as the government has assigned reception support and one-stop services to this sector. Working within NASS arrangements seems harmless enough if you accept it is essentially a 'support' service, but less comfortable if you accept that its primary function is to control spending and control people's place in our communities. In addition, involvement in a system which allocates accommodation and money means withdrawing that when the end of the asylum process arrives. It seems to me that we have had very few conversations as a profession about our role at that end of the process. The majority of these service users will not be moving on with the security of refugee status, they are moving on to destitution. This is not to say that workers will not struggle with sending individuals off into the abyss, but to acknowledge that this is a long way off our vision of the role and function of social work. In such circumstances we become at risk of constructing a culture of suspicion and blame to justify the unjustifiable.

Social workers' involvement in the internal control of immigration is of most significance. Being required to identify immigration status in order to ascertain eligibility raises serious ethical questions and colludes in the racist questioning of service users. Research within a London Asylum Team by Sales and Hek (2004) indicates that asylum seekers understood clearly the role of state employees and were unlikely to trust them completely. Given many of their personal histories, this is an extremely worrying place for social workers to be. In organising the first national conference for social workers on immigration and asylum in 2004, I was asked by a group of young unaccompanied asylum seekers if they could provide a workshop. Their unsolicited offer was to focus on their experiences – not of the Home Office, the police, or immigration officials but of social workers.

CONCLUSION: POSITIVE WAYS FORWARD

Social work as a profession, though, does have a history of work with the poor and oppressed and historically has grappled with its dual care and control functions (Humphries, 2004b). It is better placed than many other professions within social care to take on this challenge because it still holds up social justice and respect for individuals as core values. The social arrangements we have established for asylum seekers both increase need and risk. These are familiar concepts to social workers, there is a knowledge base around risk conditions which should be used to argue *against* current arrangements on both an individual and political level. The conditions in which we are placing asylum seekers are precisely those we know to contribute to risk – poverty, isolation and hostility.

For qualified workers there are models of good practice to look to. Save the Children's research on unaccompanied children (Stanley, 2001) called for Section 20 assessments under the Children Act, rather than Section 17, to ensure a full package of *appropriate* accommodation and support. Mainstream teams need to begin to pick up responsibility for assessments which can lead to accessing services, rather than having to be legally challenged to do so. Social workers have the skills and training to produce good-quality reports for immigration tribunals, but are neither encouraged nor resourced to do so. Child Protection Teams need to accept responsibility for asylum-seeking families with children and not simply turn their back on protecting these children because of their status (see Grady, 2004) and good-quality advocacy and support organisations can be set up which are not reliant on Home Office money (see Fell, 2004).

When decisions are made and the asylum or deportation process is over, there remains the question of campaigning. How far is it legitimate to become involved in campaigns for, alongside or on behalf of service users? In the UK there is a long history of anti-deportation campaigns, which have included social workers, doctors and teachers, who have been influential in some success stories (see Gibbons, 1999). Irrespective of the individual outcome, campaigns also serve to highlight the inhumanity of immigration laws and offer an alternative set of ideas to the powerful media presentation of the issue.

Similarly, there is a need for thoughtful consideration of aspects of the work which the profession might withdraw from. Being involved in NASS systems which are fundamentally discriminatory and oppressive needs to be a focus for this debate. Social work has at times stood up against racism and been influential in noting discriminatory practices, and although this has become a weakened position, we have the opportunity now to refocus that discussion. These conversations about refusal and withdrawal can present as abstract and naive. Non-compliance/non-cooperation is certainly confrontational and requires union support, but the alternative is simply to collapse into informing the Home Office concerning immigration status, interrogating service users concerning their status before offering services, enforcing homelessness and withdrawing financial support at the end of the asylum process.

Immigration and asylum law and policy can be a daunting arena for social workers. We are likely to have been poorly equipped in our training pre and post qualification and feel a sense of impotence concerning how to intervene. The development of good practice, though, is always possible, and to return to the original case example, workers can become equipped with good skills of intervention. My first experience with Mr X and family taught me that understanding the law, policies and procedures is the necessary first step. I learnt that there are two possible routes to deportation for non-UK citizens committing criminal offences, one at the point of sentencing on the criminal matters and one during imprisonment on 'conducive to public good grounds'. Understanding this can help in preparation for both the criminal court case and report-writing and also in preparing and supporting the defendant and family. I learnt that certain offences were more of a trigger than others, for instance drugs offences, which can also inform your work with the defendant. In Mr X's appeal against the deportation I was able to produce a report to describe his place in his family and community. Whilst in this case the outcomes were negative, I became aware that social workers and probation officers could be putting their report-writing skills to good use in immigration appeals and tribunals if encouraged to do so (see Brown, 2004). I also learnt the limits of individual casework and in Manchester in the years that followed a collection of practitioners began to explore and develop the professional role in relation to mainly black prisoners and deportation. This culminated in the construction and delivery of training materials and a user-led voluntary organisation offering support to families in this situation. In addition the organisation led and supported anti-deportation campaigns locally, some of which were successful in challenging removal. What this example illustrates is that we can improve our individual interventions with this service user group, but we also need to look beyond the casework to developing collective professional and community-based responses to oppressive immigration systems.

FURTHER READING

Cohen, S. (2001) *Immigration Controls, The Family and the Welfare State* (London: Jessica Kingsley).

Cohen, S., Humphries, B. and Mynott, E. (eds) (2002) *From Immigration Controls to Welfare Controls* (London: Routledge).

Harding, J. (2000) *The Uninvited: Refugees at the Rich Man's Gate* (London: Profile Books).

Hayes, D. and Humphries, B. (eds) (2004) *Social Work, Immigration and Asylum: Debates, Dilemmas and Ethical Issues for Social Work and Social Care Practice* (London: Jessica Kingsley).

Hayter, T. (2000) *Open Borders: The Case Against Immigration Controls* (London: Pluto Press).

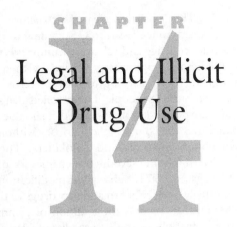

CHAPTER 14

Legal and Illicit Drug Use

Fiona Measham and Ian Paylor

Introduction

This chapter will consider current concerns relating to social work and illicit drugs in the UK, focusing on the debates surrounding changing patterns of illicit drug use and related attitudes, and recent developments in government policy and drug service provision. Particular attention is paid to the implications for social workers of multi-agency collaboration between drug workers and the criminal justice profession, through a consideration of the complexities of multi-agency collaboration responding to local and national agendas, against a backdrop of rapidly changing public drug-related attitudes and behaviour.

Contextual factors

The last fifteen years have seen rapid socioeconomic, technological and cultural change in the UK, exemplified in the field of illicit drugs. Social workers are operating within and have to respond to this world of enormous change: in patterns of availability, consumption, wider attitudinal change of both drug users and non-users and, in terms of policy, enforcement and service provision at the local, national and international level. An international shift from the American-led prohibitionist 'war on drugs' policies to a European-influenced new managerialism (Dorn and Lee, 1999) has to be set against the growing critique of a UK legal framework which has changed little in the last thirty years. The key piece of legislation governing psychoactive drugs is the Misuse of Drugs Act 1971 which came into force in 1973. This legislation created a structure whereby psychoactive substances were classified from Class A to C according to the specified drugs' perceived potential for dependency and relative harmfulness (for individuals and society), and their medicinal usage was governed by their segregation into Schedules One through to Five according to their perceived clinical value and consequent availability for use. Schedule 1 controlled drugs include heroin, ecstasy and cocaine and are deemed to have no medicinal value, whilst Schedule 5 drugs can be purchased over the counter at a pharmacy without prescription and include well-known cough mixtures and painkillers. The classification of individual drugs also determines the severity of penalties for offenders convicted under the Misuse of Drugs Act 1971. Subsequent modifications to the Misuse of Drugs Act have most usually been either to add new drugs to those considered to have the potential for misuse (such as the addition of gammahydroxybutyrate (GHB) and four types of anabolic steroids to the list of Class C drugs under the Misuse of Drugs Act in 2002) or to reclassify specific drugs according to a perceived increased or decreased risk of misuse and/or harmfulness (such as, most recently, the depenalisation of cannabis from Class B to Class C in January 2004). However, as Shiner (2003) has noted, such minor modifications do not affect the overall thrust of the Misuse of Drugs Act which remains framed within a medical model of drug misuse. Indeed, the medical profession has had a significant input into British drug policy throughout the last century, from the Rolleston Committee of 1924–26 and the subsequent establishment of drug controls to the 'British system' of heroin prescribing prevalent from the 1920s to the 1960s (Berridge, 1999[1981]).

Drug-related attitudes, patterns of availability and the use of drugs controlled under the Misuse of Drugs Act 1971 have changed enormously since its introduction. Levels of availability, experimentation and the use of illicit drugs increased rapidly throughout the 1990s and now appear to be plateauing at unprecedented levels. If we look at the broad trends across the 1990s, we can see from the official statistics that drugs offenders have quadrupled from approximately 26,000 in 1987 to 104,000 in 2000 (Corkery, 2002). Although official statistics are inevitably in part a reflection of police targeting and enforcement policy and practice, this escalation in illicit psychoactive drugs is supported by national figures on experimentation available from alternative sources such as self-report surveys. The British Crime Survey, a national annual household survey administered by the Home Office which includes a small number of questions on self-reported drug use, also indicates increased experimentation and use of illicit drugs across the 1990s. Amongst young adults under 30, rates of lifetime prevalence of illicit drug use have increased from 43 per cent in the 1994 British Crime Survey to 50 per cent in the 2000 British Crime Survey. Past year use of any illicit drug by young adults has increased from 23 per cent in 1994 to 25 per cent in 2000 (Ramsay et al., 2001). The most recent comparable figures for the British Crime Survey suggest that reported past year use of any drug for adults aged 16–59 has increased, from 10 per cent in 1994 to 12 per cent in 2002–03 (Condon and Smith, 2003). We might suspect, however, that a general national survey of private households such as the British Crime Survey might underestimate the levels of experimentation and use of drugs for a range of methodological reasons.

Specifically focused, sensitively administered self-report studies of drug use have found even higher levels of experimentation and use of illicit drugs than national household surveys: with the national schools survey conducted by Balding (2001) finding rising levels of drug use amongst school pupils across the 1990s.

Two large longitudinal studies of teenage drug use across the 1990s also found considerably higher levels of drug use than the British Crime Survey, alongside almost blanket access and availability of illicit drugs to young people by their late teens. A longitudinal study of young people in the northwest of England found that by the age of 18, over nine in ten young people reported having been in 'offer' situations where drugs were available to them either free or for money, nearly two-thirds of them reported having tried drugs at least once in their lifetime and over a quarter could be considered regular drug users (Parker et al., 1998). A separate longitudinal study of young people in the north of England found not dissimilar levels of self-reported experimentation and drug use (Aldridge et al., 1999). The body of empirical research from these (and other) studies by the three authors led to their development of the 'normalisation' thesis (see Parker et al., 1998), which suggests that there has been both a quantitative and equally signifi-cant qualitative shift in relation to recreational drug use in the UK in the last fifteen years, with significant changes in the degree of knowledge and understanding of illicit drugs and related behaviours by both users and non-users, the acknowledgement of the existence of such behaviour and the broader actual and symbolic role of drugs in the sociocultural terrain. Of further significance for those working in the field of drugs is that these longitudinal studies found that gender, ethnicity and socioeconomic background were no longer significant predictors of, or protectors from, illicit drug use, with levels of experimentation spreading across the social spectrum thus challenging conventional images of drug users. (This is not to suggest that there is no longer any relationship between social exclusion and drug use. As Gilman (2000: 23) has noted: 'drug *use* may well be an equal opportunity recruiter. Drug *addiction* is highly discriminatory' (emphases added). Thus recreational drug use has burst into the public domain in recent years, adding a new political and professional relevance for social work.

CASE EXAMPLE

Social services is contacted regarding a young woman of 15 whose school non-attendance is linked to suspected family problems. Alongside sporadic attendance at secondary school, the pupil is frequently late for school and her performance and concentration are poor when she does attend, but her parents seem unconcerned when these issues are raised with them. In discussion with the school head, parents and a social worker about where the young woman goes during the daytime, it comes to light that the young woman, along with two school friends from the same school, spends her time at a friend's house whose parents work during the week. Whilst the details of these visits are explored with the three young women, cannabis use by the group is revealed as occurring on a regular basis during the day, both on and off school premises. The three pupils are temporarily suspended whilst the head conducts a full investigation according to school policy on drug use.

Research and policy

The growing overall level of availability and experimentation with illicit drugs across the 1990s has been accompanied by an increasingly diverse repertoire of pharmacological possibilities, a willingness to experiment with a range of legal, illicit and prescription drugs to achieve altered states of intoxication and an involvement in drugs which has touched schools, families, friendship networks, pubs, clubs and workplaces across the country and across the social spectrum (see Measham, 2004). Contemporary drug use is scattered across a kaleidoscope of possibilities which range from dependent and daily usage to occasional and casual usage, resulting in professional imperatives to define what counts as problematic consumption to warrant or justify agency intervention. Simplistic characterisations of drug users as 'junkies', 'ravers' and 'dopeheads' are no longer possible. Furthermore, the increased number of young women and men of child-bearing age experimenting with illicit drugs will result in more drug-using parents, as well as and including more drug-using social workers (see, for example, Measham, 2002). For social workers this means that their professional intervention may well relate not to whether or not drug involvement exists in a particular case but the complexities of the assessment process and their own subjective experiences drawn from personal contact with drugs. As Harbin and Murphy note in relation to parental drug use and childcare:

> The crucial dilemma during the assessment process is ... what types/levels/ complexities of substance misuse, in what kind of family systems, will lead to significant harm or impairment, to which types of children? Conversely, what types of substance misuse, in what kind of family systems, will lead to minimal harm to children? Furthermore what types of professional interventions will help reduce this harmful impact on children? (2000: 6)

At a time of increased drug use in the UK, we have also seen a move towards a more child-centred approach in child welfare. The Children Act 1989 specified that agencies should aim to work in partnership with parents in childcare cases: with an assumption throughout the Act that children are best looked after by their parents, it follows that active involvement by parents is recommended to facilitate the process. The Act expects professionals to involve parents in plans for children; it also expects those parents to have the child's best interest in mind. Thus parental responsibility is seen by the Act to be more than a definition of rights. The concept of partnership with drug-using parents and the no order principle (that is, the courts should make no order unless it is in the interest of the child to do so) means that social workers have begun to look beyond the consumption of a substance to the development of an understanding about the wider context of that consumption, including the recognition that it is not enough to label all drug-using parents as bad, nor is it enough to say that drug use puts the child at risk. Thus social workers are required to develop an understanding of whether and how drug use might put a child at risk and also develop an understanding of how they can work with drug-using parents to reduce that risk.

The key to any such development is the SCODA guidelines (Standing Conference on Drug Abuse – now Drug Scope) on drug-using parents, first published in 1987 and recently updated and revised. The concept of 'good enough parenting' offers an important guide to work with drug-using parents. Is the parenting good enough despite the drug use? How can staff work with parents to reduce harm and help to make their parenting good enough? For social work practice this means:

- Developing an understanding of drugs and their effects on people

- Having an understanding of the context of drug use

- Knowing about the range of support services that are available for people who use alcohol and drugs

- Developing an understanding of the nature of drug problems to avoid placing unnecessary pressure on parents

- Developing an understanding of harm reduction in relation to substance use, so that realistic goals can be set and worked towards with the parents.

As Gilman (2000: 23) has warned, social workers need 'to be wary of a tendency to overreact to recreational drug use and underreact to problematic drug use'.

The spectrum of drug involvement has expanded not just in relation to the use of illicit drugs but also in relation to the supply of drugs and here too there can be a danger of overreaction by welfare and criminal justice agencies. Contemporary government drug policy is underpinned by a polarisation of users and suppliers, in the face of a growing body of research on the complexities of the retail drug trade in the UK and the hierarchies of the manufacture and supply chains which implicate the majority of drug users (Dorn et al., 1992; Parker, 2001). Research suggests that many users will obtain their supplies by buying in bulk for economies of scale, sometimes combining resources with other users to save time, money and risk in drug transactions, or users may buy drugs to sell on to friends or acquaintances to subsidise their own consumption. Whilst technically supplying others according to British legislation, the lowest levels of the retail trade are quite different to the middle market and top-level distributors outlined in the work of Pearson and Hobbs (2001), leading to the Runciman Report recommendation – alongside the suggested depenalisation of cannabis, ecstasy and LSD – of a new drug offence which recognises low level supply between friends which may not necessarily be for financial gain (Police Foundation, 1999).

It may well be that social work professionals come into contact with clients with criminal convictions for the possession, manufacture and supply of illicit drugs from across the range of possible levels of involvement. With 67 per cent of drug offenders in the UK having been cautioned or convicted of the unlawful possession of cannabis for personal use, and 62 per cent of herbal cannabis seizures and 48 per cent of cannabis resin seizures involving amounts under one gramme in weight, however, we can see that the majority of the 100,000 plus people caught up in the criminal justice system each year are at the lower end of the spectrum of drug involvement (Corkery, 2002). Such convictions may have significant implications for educational and employment opportunities, parenting and so forth and yet, given the high levels of experimentation with illicit drugs and the high level of continuing police activity in relation to this experimentation, the convictions themselves may provide no indication of the scale of drug involvement. For social work researchers and practitioners, as for wider society, the challenge is to identify and intervene when illicit drug use becomes problematic for the users, their families, friends and communities, in a climate where definitions of problematic drug use are historically, socially and culturally context-specific (Harbin and Murphy, 2000). Problem drug use is most usefully considered across a spectrum of possible patterns and consequences of use – physical, psychological and social – rather than as a simple dichotomy of problematic versus recreational usage, with the concept of drug careers helpful to a consideration of appropriate interventions (Measham et al., 1998; Heather and Robertson, 2003).

CASE EXAMPLE REVISITED

If we return to the head's investigation of the three 15-year-old young women, a key question considered by the school is the source of supply for the cannabis being smoked by the school pupils during school hours. The three young women revealed that they regularly pooled their part-time earnings for one of them to buy £20 bags of herbal cannabis or 'grass' from a friend of a friend, raising the issue of social supply to peers. Given that the young woman in question admits to technically supplying cannabis, a controlled drug under the 1971 Misuse of Drugs Act, to her school friends, the head has no choice but to implement the school policy on the supply of drugs and permanently exclude this pupil from the school, whilst reinstating her two friends who are not believed to have supplied the drug to fellow pupils. This example is repeated across the UK, where pupils buy an illicit drug without realising the grave consequences of seemingly rational consumption patterns and bulk purchasing between friends. The pupil's parents launch an appeal to the school governors at the perceived overreaction to their daughter's cannabis use and the disparity in treatment of the three pupils. In the meantime, the young woman remains at home and receives no formal education, compounding her earlier unauthorised absences from school and missing a significant portion of her GCSE classes. The social worker explores the 'liberal' attitude of the parents to both their daughter's cannabis use and her non-attendance at school, discovering the parents' recreational use of cocaine and ecstasy at weekends. The parents consider it preferable that their daughter is smoking cannabis in the safety of a friend's house to drinking alcohol on the streets with some other teenagers, or taking dance drugs in clubs. Given that cannabis is no longer an arrestable offence and the parents consider it to be relatively 'harmless', in both legal and health terms, they do not share the school's concerns about their daughter's drug use. The parents also view their own drug use as equally unproblematic, despite its admitted impact on family life, both financially with the considerable amount of money they are spending on Class A drugs, and emotionally with their 'comedowns' at the end of a weekend partying. Whilst the parents' drug use could not be considered daily, dependent or chaotic, it raises the issue of 'good enough' parenting and 'bad enough' drug use for intervention by the case worker.

Agency responses and practice issues

There has been a fundamental change in agency policy towards intervention since the emergence of HIV/AIDS in the mid-1980s. Concerns that injecting drug users who continued to inject (and therefore, by implication, could also be continuing to share injecting equipment) might be instrumental in spreading the infection led to a change in political and agency priorities. Prior to the emergence of HIV/AIDS, most agencies had seen their client base consisting primarily of those who had decided to modify, or abandon altogether, their use of drugs, with a smaller number who had not yet reached that decision being offered soup kitchens, day shelters and detached work provision. Subsequently the priority shifted to make and maintain contact with those drug users (often deeply suspicious of specialist drug services) who were at greatest risk of continuing to share needles, in other words, those who had little or no intention of stopping.

With harm reduction strategies established in the mid-1980s and the forecasted HIV/AIDS epidemic averted, recent policy has moved away from a primary focus on public health, at least at the national level. UK drug policy emphasises utilising the criminal justice system to target drug-using offenders and exploiting the legislation to coerce suitable candidates into treatment. Previously the criminal justice system has been used to tackle drug use punitively, by increasing the associated costs, with the aim of deterrence (Hough, 1996). In current drug policy the criminal justice system is instead viewed as a mechanism for diverting offenders towards appropriate treatment interventions, with the secondary aim of reducing drug-related crime (Pearson, 1999; Hughes et al., 2001).

A wide range of initiatives has been piloted and introduced at all stages of the criminal justice process to facilitate implementation of the current drugs strategy (Edmunds et al., 1999). Firstly, Arrest Referral schemes were launched in 1999 and are now operational in many police custody suites across England and Wales (Mair, 2002). Arrest referral schemes involve drug-misusing offenders being referred to a drug worker who encourages them to take up an appropriate treatment programme. Involvement with the scheme is voluntary and it is not an alternative to prosecution or due process. They aim to exploit the opportunity provided by arrest to encourage problem drug users to access treatment services. Schemes vary in their content, from the provision of information about drugs services to the opportunity for arrestees to be assessed by a drug worker based in the custody suite. Offenders can then be referred on to specialist drug treatment services (Edmunds et al., 1998). Recent statistics from the Arrest Referral National Monitoring Programme on the arrest referral scheme in England and Wales, collected between October 2000 and September 2001, show that 48,810 individuals were interviewed by arrest referral workers in England and Wales and 58 per cent of all arrestees interviewed were voluntarily referred to a specialist drug treatment service (Sondhi et al., 2002).

Secondly, the Crime and Disorder Act 1998 brought an alternative form of intervention within the criminal justice system, in the form of Drug Treatment and Testing Orders (DTTOs), introduced as part of the government's attempt to break the links between problem drug use and persistent acquisitive crime. DTTOs are community sentences which enable a court to order an individual who is 'dependent on or has a propensity to misuse drugs' to undergo an intensive treatment and rehabilitation programme for a period of between six months and three years, which includes weekly drug testing, counselling, groupwork and contact with a probation officer (Hales, 2002). DTTOs have subsequently been extended to include a less intensive treatment and rehabilitation programme for offenders with less serious offending and drug use.

Finally, the prison service set out a programme for tackling drug use amongst prison populations (HM Prison Service, 1998). A major strand of this was the establishment of CARAT (Counselling, Assessment, Referral, Advice and Throughcare) schemes, which are now operational in every prison in England (Hamer, 2002). The aim of these schemes is to assess prisoners who have problems associated with their drug use and ensure that appropriate treatment services are available to them. CARAT workers might therefore generate referrals to detoxification programmes, prison-based therapeutic communities or community drugs services where an individual is approaching release (Hughes et al., 2001). As a result there has been an unprecedented increase over the last five years in the number of drug workers employed within criminal justice settings and a parallel increase in the number of offenders accessing community-based drugs services (Harman and Paylor, 2002).

The involvement of criminal justice agencies with drug service providers has required significant cultural shifts on both sides (Rumgay, 2000). The move towards a partnership of the statutory and voluntary sector drug agencies with those in the criminal justice system has been hindered by differences in their objectives, values, organisational culture and operational systems. Organisational goals and values have often developed over significant timescales and define an organisation's identity and purpose. They impact upon practice at every level and can be resistant to change (Gibbs, 2001b). In the case of drug agencies and criminal justice agencies, a number of their fundamental values and objectives appear to be opposed. This potential incompatibility may be a barrier to effective partnership and has implications for social workers working in the field (Rumgay, 2003).

Consider, for example, the different value placed by each on the right of the individual drug user to choose whether to access treatment. Drug agencies typically provide treatment services which users access voluntarily. This approach has been adopted for both ethical and practical reasons. Firstly, compulsion into treatment poses ethical dilemmas which challenge the value base shared by many voluntary sector drug agencies, that is, the belief that it is an individual's right to choose whether or not to access treatment, at what point in time and what type of treatment (Newburn, 1999). Secondly, in terms of effectiveness, it is widely believed by drug workers that individuals who are coerced into treatment are less motivated to change and treatment is less likely to be effective (van Brussel, 1998). In contrast, criminal justice agencies are, by their nature, agencies of control and have the ability to coerce offenders into accessing treatment services. Even where coercion is not explicit (that is, offenders do not have to decide directly between punishment and engaging in drug treatment), offenders may feel under pressure to access treatment services. Turnbull et al. (2000: 6) expand on this with reference to arrest referral schemes, highlighting 'the pressures on arrestees to demonstrate compliance and to show the intention of "turning over a new leaf" in advance of court'.

Since around the turn of the twenty-first century UK drug policy has identified as a strategic aim the coercion of drug-using offenders into treatment services. For drug workers, the implication is that they will be required to adapt some of their methods of practice to enable them to work effectively in partnership with criminal justice agencies and this will be vital to drug agencies if they are to secure government funds. An example of this is the effect that partnership working is likely to have on the organisational policies of drug agencies regarding confidentiality. Where treatment is entered into voluntarily, the primary obligation of a drug agency is to the service user and client confidentiality is assured. Where an offender is coerced into drug treatment through measures in the criminal justice system, however, the treatment provider is additionally held accountable to the referring agency and may be required to share information regarding the service user with relevant criminal justice professionals (Hough, 1996). Such cultural differences in the goals of voluntary drug agencies and those of agencies within the criminal justice system evidently have the potential to cause conflict over the way in which treatment is provided to drug users. Drug workers operating within and alongside the criminal justice system may find that their role is constrained or they are forced to modify their practice, as a result of conflicting or divergent objectives.

The primary roles of voluntary sector drug agencies vary significantly to those within the criminal justice system. Typically, drug services aim to support and empower individual drug users, while the primary function of the criminal justice system is law enforcement and protection of the public. Although in reality agencies have multiple and overlapping functions, there is likely to be a divergence in opinions regarding the priority that should be accorded to each (Edmunds et al., 1999). This is illustrated by the change in emphasis of different treatment outcomes that has occurred, with the pendulum swinging between a public health and criminal justice-driven national drug policy. Since the 1980s, voluntary sector drug agencies have embraced a wide range of treatment goals, ranging from abstinence at one end of the spectrum to the reduction of drug-related harm at the other. However, although harm reduction strategies have been widely accepted and often prioritised at the local level in community health and welfare services for drug users, they do not fit readily within the context of national government policy and the criminal justice system, where the criminal and control aspects of drug use are viewed as paramount (Keene, 1997). This has resulted in tensions between national criminal justice-driven drug policy and the local public health agenda, for example when recommendations for harm reduction strategies in prison environments were rejected on the basis that they could be viewed as the criminal justice system condoning illicit drug use (Hough, 1996).

In addition to the scope for role conflict between criminal justice agencies and voluntary sector drug service providers, there is the potential for problems to arise from differences in their organisational structure and working practices. Criminal justice agencies are statutory agencies, with clearly defined, hierarchical structures of accountability. In contrast, drug treatment services are often (although not exclusively) small and localised, and typically adopt more flexible organisational and management arrangements (Edmunds et al., 1999). In the UK, drug services have tended to develop in response to localised needs, with a notable absence of any 'national standard' for evaluating their effectiveness. This is all to change with the arrival of the National Treatment Agency (NTA). The NTA is a special health authority, created by the government in 2001, to provide *national* guidance on model treatment services in England. It has yet to fulfil that remit but even at such an early stage caution needs to be expressed here. As McGrail (2003: 7) points out: 'good policies can be hampered by "one size fits all" models of implementation because local services work best with local delivery'.

Edmunds et al. (1999) also identify that differences in working style between these two types of organisation can be a barrier to effective partnership working. Specifically they highlight the procedure-led approach adopted by probation officers and contrast this with the client-centred approach which drug workers more usually employ (Edmunds et al., 1999). Difficulties can arise for drug workers employed within a criminal justice context if criminal justice agencies expect or require them to align to their own working practices. For drug workers to be able to operate effectively in partnership with criminal justice agencies, drug services cannot simply be viewed as 'add-ons' to criminal justice services. There is clearly a need for drug workers and those employed by the criminal justice system to develop joint service provision initiatives, rather than one agency taking a 'control' role and the other forced to align with them. The recent developments in drug policy and the emphasis that has been placed on the criminal justice system as a vehicle for directing drug-using offenders into treatment make clear the government's intention that drug agencies and criminal justice agencies will work in partnership.

One of the key objectives for successful partnership working is clarity in the roles of the different agencies involved. Turnbull et al. (2000: 83) identify the need for 'a clear division of labour which exploits the strengths of each discipline, but also allows for collaboration on key decision-making areas such as the assessment process and treatment plan'. In the case of liaison between drug workers and criminal justice agencies, there is a need for clarification of the responsibilities and role limitations of each party, particularly with respect to issues where there is the potential for conflict in objectives or practice. Take, for example, the issue of enforcement. Where drug treatment is provided within a criminal justice context, offenders may be reluctant to talk openly and honestly about their drug use and associated lifestyle, and drug workers may need to maintain a level of independence from criminal justice services in order to work effectively with clients. However, if the limitations to this independence in terms of information-sharing and confidentiality have not been established and agreed with the appropriate criminal justice agency beforehand, there is the potential for inconsistency in practice and for criminal justice workers to view drug workers as inappropriately collaborating with offenders, resulting in feelings of non-cooperation on both sides.

Newburn (1999) additionally identifies the need to clarify roles to ensure that the work of criminal justice workers and drug workers does not overlap significantly. This is particularly relevant in the case of offenders serving community sentences under probation supervision. Drug workers may work with clients in a holistic way, looking at a range of issues rather than focusing solely on an individual's drug use. If this approach is taken, however:

> the risk is run that the overlap between the role of the drugs worker and the [youth] justice worker will not only be considerable but will be problematic and the burden on the [young] offender concerned unjustifiable.
>
> (Newburn, 1999: 617)

For partnership between agencies to be successful it is vital that good working relationships are developed, whereby the expertise and strengths of each are recognised and respected. Interagency rivalry has been identified as a potential barrier to effective partnership between drug workers and criminal justice professionals, that is, the situation where there is concern by workers in one agency that a traditional area of service provision is being encroached upon by another agency (Edmunds et al., 1999). In a study of probation programmes for drug-using offenders, Rumgay and Cowan (1998: 130) recognised that 'the quality of relationships between partners appeared to be linked to the extent to which probation officers perceived substance misuse workers as enhancing or threatening their direct work with clients'. They noted that a frequent difficulty faced by drug workers in their study was that few or no referrals resulted where relationships with probation teams were poor. Thus the effectiveness of drug workers in a criminal justice context is highly dependent upon the efficacy of the partnership between them and criminal justice professionals. A major implication for drug workers is that to function effectively in this environment they need to allocate a significant proportion of their time to 'public relations' work and fostering positive working relationships with potential referrers (Rumgay and Cowan, 1998).

With the shift towards utilising the criminal justice service as a means of directing drug-using offenders to treatment services, it is vital that there is adequate service provision for this population, within both criminal justice and community settings, to enable drug workers to manage the associated increases in caseload. Many community drug treatment services are already operating at capacity or are oversubscribed, and pressure to accept more referrals from the criminal justice system may mean that drug workers are asked to prioritise criminal justice referrals at the expense of those referring themselves voluntarily. Clearly, the forced redistribution of existing resources would pose an ethical dilemma to drug workers. In their research, Edmunds et al. (1999) noted a tendency for referral workers to develop caseloads of clients with whom they were meeting regularly, due to a lack of appropriate drug services to refer clients on to. Without adequate service provision, the effect of the shift towards a criminal justice-led drug policy will be to place more burdens on drug workers, with consequences for the quality of service.

In addition, it is important that the services available to drug users are appropriate to their needs and not constrained by the criminal justice context of their commission and/or delivery. There is evidence to suggest that different types of treatment may vary in their effectiveness for different individuals (Hough, 1996). There is a need for the range of drug services available to offenders to be expanded, a process which will require more drug workers to work specifically within a criminal justice context. In addition, services provided by drug workers in community treatment agencies will need to be flexible enough to meet the requirements of referring criminal justice agencies. Finally, drug services across all settings need to be better integrated to ensure that appropriate treatment is available to clients moving in and out of the criminal justice system. As Hough (1996: 4) has noted: 'coercing a drug misuser into inappropriate treatment can arguably be regarded as a miscarriage of justice'.

Clearly there is a long way to go. CARAT teams operating in prisons have a specific throughcare function, but to date there is little evidence that this is being effectively put into practice. Although often optimistic about their intentions to stop using drugs, Edmunds et al. (1999) found that over half the prisoners in their study used drugs on the day of their release. With this statistic in mind, it is vital that effective links are forged between criminal justice drug workers and those working in community settings, to ensure that clients receive continuity of care. With the most recent research on DTTOs suggesting that high levels of positive drug tests, programme non-completion and reoffending are common (National Audit Office, 2004), the challenge of delivering high-quality and effective community services to drug users remains.

CONCLUSION

The increased experimentation, use and trafficking in a growing repertoire of illicit drugs in the UK in the last few years means that more social workers will be coming into contact with drug-involved clients and their families. Current drug policies envisage partnership between voluntary sector drug agencies and criminal justice agencies as an essential tool in achieving policy objectives which include the protection of communities from drug-related crime and access to appropriate treatment services for all problem drug users. However, the strategic shift from a primary focus on public health issues to a criminal justice-driven drug policy, at least at the national level, has had considerable implications for those working with drug users. This chapter has identified a number of potential obstacles to interagency and intersystem collaboration, in terms of differences in organisational values, objectives and practices. If recent policy developments are to be of value in tackling problematic drug use, it is vital that professionals within drug agencies and criminal justice agencies work together to address and overcome these barriers, to prevent the primary aim of partnerships from being obstructed. Perhaps a more fundamental issue, however, is whether key objectives of UK drug policy, such as the reduction of drug use and drug-related crime, are deliverable, or whether it is more important for policy to focus on meeting the needs of drug users, their families and the wider community, including drug-using offenders.

FURTHER READING

For an introductory overview of individual drugs for non-specialists in the field, the Sanctuary series is lively, informative and accessible, with six books in the current series published in 2002, specifically aimed at those with a general interest in drugs, including drug users: Nick Brownlee's *This is Alcohol*, Nick Constable's *This is Cocaine*, Karen Farrington's *This is Nicotine*, Gareth Thomas's *This is Ecstasy*, Nick Brownlee's *This is Cannabis*, and Robert Ashton's *This is Heroin*. Each book provides a historical and cultural overview of the individual drug, alongside health information and contemporary policy and treatment issues. The series is available from mainstream book shops.

Gossop, M. (2000) *Living with Drugs* (5th edn) (Aldershot: Ashgate). A classic introductory textbook for students of drugs.

South, N. (ed.) (1999) *Drugs: Cultures, Controls and Everyday Life* (London: Sage). For the social work researcher, this is an excellent collection of essays which has not yet been superseded. With articles by key researchers in the field, it provides a good overview of the research and debate surrounding drugs in the UK and includes chapters on gender, 'race', dance drugs, government policy and drugs in sport. This collection is complemented by the special editions on drugs of two journals: the *British Journal of Criminology* (Pearson, 1999), **39**(4) and *Probation Journal* (Measham, 2004) 'The decline of ecstasy, the rise of binge drinking and the persistence of pleasure', *Probation Journal,* Special edition, Rethinking drugs and crime, **51**(4) 309–26.

Peele, S. (1985) *The Meaning of Addiction: Compulsive Experience and its Interpretation* (Lexington: Lexington).

Orford, J. (2001) *Excessive Appetites: A Psychological View of Addictions* (2nd edn) (Chichester: Wiley).

Booth Davies, J. (1997) *The Myth of Addiction* (2nd edn) (Amsterdam: Harwood).

Three stimulating and quite different critiques of traditional disease models of 'addiction'. All three make robust challenges to classic, common-sense and medical models of addiction which social workers may come up against when working in the field. In addition, Prochaska and DiClemente's 'Cycle of Change' (Prochaska et al., 1994) promoted by Miller (1983), (see also Scott, 1989) is an approach that seeks to educate and empower the user by concentrating upon the identification of triggers, insight into high-risk situations, the development of relapse prevention strategies and positive self-talk. This approach emphasises client choice and client responsibility. Motivational interviewing techniques (Van Bilsen, 1986) have been widely used with much success in this area.

The latest official statistics and government-funded research on drugs, crime and the criminal justice system in England and Wales can be obtained free from the Home Office website. The two key sources on drugs are the official statistics on drug seizures and offenders, and the self-report survey of adult drug use administered as part of the annual British Crime Survey, both obtained directly from http://www.homeoffice.gov.uk. The Home Office website also contains research reports of a large number of government-funded studies of relevance to social work researchers and practitioners.

Pushing Ethical Boundaries for Children and Families: Confidentiality, Transparency and Transformation

Linda Briskman

Introduction

At different times and in different contexts social work is faced with new dilemmas and challenges and confronted with the need to interrogate and adapt its philosophies and practices. This is nowhere clearer than in the field of child and family welfare, where social workers have been compelled to move beyond their comfort zones to embrace 'new' approaches that appear in different guises. In many ways, social work has adapted well. In other ways the profession has lagged behind. This chapter explores some of the dilemmas facing the social work profession in clinging to traditional tenets in the wake of change. The chapter uses two examples from the Australian context: Indigenous people, asylum seekers and refugees. The term 'Indigenous' is the preferred term to describe Aboriginal and Torres Strait Islander people. The chapter explores the specific issue of whether concepts of confidentiality are oppositional to increasing pressures for transparency in policy and practice. This issue is one that challenges to the very core some of the fundamental values of social work, particularly as framed within codes of ethics, and exemplifies some of the contradictions inherent in the contemporary context of social work practice.

Changing conditions in which social work is managed and practised

In the policy context, social work is increasingly working within a managerialist framework, where corporate planning processes have been transplanted from the private sector into the human services (Hough and Briskman, 2003). No longer is social work practice based primarily on need, and effective practice is often conceptualised organisationally as meeting the demands of funding bodies where financial accountability and certainty evolve as key driving principles. This is happening at the same time that the profession is grappling to include human rights and social justice concepts in its everyday practice, concepts that do not sit easily in a managerialist climate. Managerialism creates a closed environment where the principles of privacy, containment, mainstreaming and competition thrive, constructs that are antithetical to social work's engagement with postmodern concepts of diversity and context. Managerialism pervades both the government and non-government sectors where child and family welfare are located.

Social work has also had to adjust to new family forms, with the increased acceptance of single-parent families, gay and lesbian families and newly arrived migrant families with varying cultural mores. The profession has had to discard Western views of family, acknowledging a range of child-rearing practices and adopting new forms of intervention. There has been pressure for social work to respond to media criticism of child protection practice, taking the privatised realm of the organisation into the public sphere. In addition, social work has had to adapt itself to interdisciplinary ways of working, accelerated by increasing deprofessionalisation and the claim by others that social work does not hold the keys to effective human services practice in its own right. In so doing it has to examine its conceptual frameworks as the private world of the caseworker/client has opened itself to new methodologies that combine advocacy and critical reflexiveness in its endeavours.

Despite continually emerging questions and contradictions, the social work profession largely resists major reforms. Although there are new theories, new styles and new pressures, social work traditionalism prevails, guided by competency-based practice and codes of ethics that are largely individualistic. These are vexed issues for a profession that is, at least in its rhetoric, endeavouring to reinvent itself.

The pervasiveness of notions of confidentiality reflects its importance in maintaining client interests, and there would be little justification for arguing for its abandonment. But maintaining confidentiality uncritically conflicts with notions of transparency, social change goals and advocacy, and has the potential to distance social workers from others working for social and political change. With increasing challenges to concepts of confidentiality, there is a revisiting of accusations of the social control function of social work and the view that social work, as it is still practised, emphasises power differentials.

Social work with children and families in the new era

Social work with children and families takes a number of forms, but in many Western nations, including Australia, the emphasis is on the 'protection' or 'hard' end of the scale, rather than prevention and support. To a degree, social workers have colluded with the media line that exposes child deaths and publishes photographs of damaged children. Public inquiries continue to reinforce the notion of protection in a narrow sense. In Australia, as elsewhere, child protection offers employment opportunities for social workers. Social work with children and families creates confusion and ideological conflicts for many. Social workers are confronted with a barrage of rules, procedural manuals and a lack of support structures. The turnover of social workers in these positions is high. Many do not have opportunities to question 'the system' and provide alternatives. In addition, they are usually restricted from speaking out or publicly challenging policies. The demands of the work to meet performance targets means that there is little time, energy or opportunity to work for social reform.

The centrality of confidentiality to child and family practice is often reinforced by privacy provisions, including in legislation, which provide penalties for those who breach them. In addition to constraints on freedom to speak, there may also be limits imposed on community engagement that are seen as a 'conflict of interest'. This contributes to the silencing of social workers and an inability to advocate for the interests of groups with whom they work.

There have been new challenges to confidentiality and privacy around the 'right to know' in spheres such as adoption, artificial insemination and IVF. The freedom of information provisions of governments in Australia have partially paved the way for an openness not previously contemplated. Social work also has to be mindful of debates and developments in other spheres. This includes the 'confessional' where Catholic priests are being challenged about maintaining secrecy in cases where the confession involves criminal offences including child sexual abuse. Social workers are aware that they may be commanded to appear in court to give testimony, or for their documentation to be compulsorily acquired for evidence.

The language of 'risk management' that has now entered the social work domain is a constraint to openness, flexibility and collaborative approaches for change (see Chapter 8 for further discussion of risk management). Although the intent is seemingly directed at reducing the potential for harm to the people with whom we work, much of the discourse is underpinned by fear of risk to governments or organisations. The fear of a backlash against harm to children results in increased regulation and procedurally driven practice. This has the effect of increasing organisational restrictiveness and creating a climate where there is little scope for responsiveness and transparency through open debate by social workers. Rather than exposing the irrationality of these practices, social work practice, enshrined within organisational settings that do not publicise their activities, colludes with repressive policies. Terms such as 'competencies', 'risk assessment' and 'case management' are now accepted in social work practice frameworks (Ward, 1998: 152).

Questions arise as to how social workers can identify the consequences of their actions when endeavouring to adhere to policy and practice directives. This naturally requires a great deal of reflexivity and analysis on the part of a social worker in determining a course of action, an approach that requires time and sometimes courage. Problems can particularly arise in settings where social work is not dominant.

The two examples from my own experience of child and family experience will hopefully resonate with others. Underlying the issues explored is a plea for social workers to move beyond the immediate pressures in their practice, in order to speak out, support alternative voices and join with activists. I argue for a changing accountability beyond the profession and the organisation to accountability based on relationships with the range of groups with whom social workers interact. To do so requires courage, reflexivity and a constant analysis of complex boundary questions that pervade social work practice.

The boundaries of confidentiality

The question of confidentiality raises ethical, legal, moral, organisational and professional issues. One of the ways forward in trying to apply tenets of confidentiality is to ask in whose interests social workers are operating. Certainly the answer should be the powerless and the most vulnerable and not the professions and the powerful.

There are some circumstances where confidentiality is clear, whether prescribed or not. But in their daily work social workers confront problems of many kinds, demonstrating that confidentiality is neither absolute nor sacred, but is contingent on a range of factors that need to be taken into account in specific situations. What does one do for example if a client's partner does not know they are HIV positive? What does a social worker do when a repeat child sex offender is living in a household with young children after serving a sentence? What is the right course of action when a young adolescent does not want his or her whereabouts disclosed to family members? What of the diversity of cultural understandings about confidentiality? And even though the primary responsibility is to the client, there are other competing responsibilities including to the wider community.

Government and community service organisations purport to have high degrees of confidentiality. Yet once a record and file-keeping system is established, the likelihood of total secrecy is diminished. With the advent of computerised records and the use of email, this is compounded. Over and beyond the technology, there has always been an informal sharing of client information between workers and between agencies, creating an artificial barrier between private information and public space. Social workers do not operate in a practice vacuum, are generally consultative and the 'social' in social work lends itself to practices that involve a large group of stakeholders. This collaboration is usually seen as meritorious, but it can also result in breaches of legal and policy standards and is justified 'in the interests of the client' and the 'duty of care'. In fact it becomes normative and is not questioned. Yet this can constitute a clear violation of the rights of the individual client. As clients begin to form themselves into 'consumer' organisations, these questions are likely to arise further.

The ethics of confidentiality

In my experience as a field educator, I found that when social work students and practitioners were asked what they knew of social work ethics most said they never used them. They were, however, able to refer to confidentiality as a key element of the code of ethics. Few students or their supervisors talked about influencing or even subverting policy. Many did not see the link between maintaining secrecy as a form of control and perpetuating a system that can act against the interests of families and communities.

A fundamental problem is that social work is still basically viewed as an individual rather than a collective activity. This is reinforced in codes of ethics and adherence to the concept of confidentiality per se reinforces this. Transparency, multiple accountabilities, critical and transformative practice remain elusive. The exploration of social work codes of ethics in a range of countries uncovered an emphasis on individual choice, minimising structural disadvantage and social dependency (Briskman and Noble, 1999).

Confidentiality is clearly enshrined in various social work codes of ethics throughout the world. For example the codes of the British (BASW, 2003), US (NASW, 1996) and Australian (AASW, 1999) social work associations all have clauses that refer to client confidentiality and/or privacy. However, it appears that the concept is under some challenge. A draft document on ethics, formally adopted by delegates to the 2004 AGM of the International Federation of Social Workers (IFSW) in Adelaide, states:

> Social workers should maintain confidentiality regarding information about people who use their services. Exceptions to this may only be justified on the basis of a greater ethical requirement (such as the preservation of life).

It is unclear what the full gamut of 'exception' might be, and to date there has been little exploration of issues of transparency, human rights, social justice and advocacy and how these might relate to confidentiality principles. This chapter is work in process in endeavouring to understand the limits to confidentiality and the ensuing boundary issues. The following examples highlight some key tensions.

Indigenous children

In a number of countries, including Australia, the USA and Canada, children were removed from their families in what was considered their 'best interests'. Although these policies and practices took different forms in each country and within each jurisdiction, children were often placed far from their families in institutions, or with foster care or adoptive families. This practice is no less than institutionalised and systemic abuse of children (Thorpe, 1986), and was usually assimilationist in intent. Assimilation in these contexts can be defined as endeavours to eliminate Indigenous peoples and cultures by ensuring that children, particularly those of 'mixed race', were absorbed into non-Indigenous lifeways and that their own cultures, languages and families were discarded. When the Human Rights and Equal Opportunity Commission (HREOC) in Australia (1997) brought out the findings of a national inquiry into what is now referred to as the 'stolen generations', there were many in the wider community who expressed astonishment and denied knowledge of the practices. The public disclosure was drawn from more than 500 oral testimonies from Indigenous people and the practices they describe have been referred to as 'evil' (Rintoul, 1996), 'an Australian holocaust' (Katona, 1996), 'genocide' (HREOC, 1997) and as attempts 'to take the Aboriginality out of Aboriginal children' (Dodson, 1997).

In 1997, I conducted research into the role of church agencies in the removal and placement of Aboriginal children in the state of Victoria. To their credit, the three participating churches – Anglican, Catholic and Uniting – saw this new openness as a form of reconciliation and apology to Aboriginal people for past wrongs. But their openness was restricted by a legacy of past practices, practices that remain hidden from public scrutiny. Examination of the records revealed that in the interests of assimilation, Aboriginal identity was not referred to on the files. It was sometimes only by racist comments contained within the documentation that Aboriginality was evident. It was even more disturbing to realise, as a researcher, that many of those who had been in the children's homes were probably unaware of their Aboriginal origins, the ultimate betrayal of confidentiality.

Part of the collusion in maintaining the secrecy has been a dominant discourse that privileges the views of professionals over those affected by the policies and practices. Since the time of European colonisation, policy-making has regrettably always been a 'white' activity in Australia. As historian Peter Read notes: 'white people have never been able to leave Aborigines alone' (1981: 20). This does not bode well for Indigenous groups who still struggle to have their voices heard on policy agendas. Despite the existence in legislation and policy throughout Australia of an Aboriginal Child Placement Principle that advocates for keeping Indigenous children with their families and communities, this has not been adhered to in practice (Briskman, 2003).

Powerful advocacy by Indigenous peoples in Australia and elsewhere ensures that alternative ways of changing hearts and minds are in the public arena. The confidentiality that shrouds the activities of social workers and others is in stark contrast to the songs, autobiographies and films that tell personal stories in order to paint a picture that touches hearts and minds in endeavours to expose the 'locked cupboard of history' (Hartley and McKee, 2001: 1) and prevent ongoing oppressive practices. Storytelling has the potential to be healing and influential. Indigenous groups have united in many ways to ensure that their experiences reach the public domain. In research undertaken by me (Briskman, 2003), Indigenous people told of how they 'had the same stories' throughout Australia, stories of the horror of child removal that were largely hidden from the public and only became exposed when they united to form national organisations to advocate for their causes (Briskman, 2003).

Indigenous organisations lobbied hard and long for an inquiry into the stolen generations to bring out the truth and determine how many children were taken away and how this occurred (Briskman, 2003). This was in part to counteract what Aboriginal writer and historian Jackie Huggins (1998: 120) describes as being 'fed on a diet of lies and invisibility about the true history of this country from a very young age'. This amounts to what was described by anthropologist Stanner as the 'great Australian silence' (cited in McGrath, 1995: 366).

Many of the practices involving the removal of Indigenous children from their families and communities were shrouded in the utmost secrecy. With many Indigenous children enslaved in missions, reserves and children's homes, the practices were hidden from public scrutiny. In some institutions the names of children were changed and their origins were not recognised (Minajalku, 1997).

Yet the extent of the success of the secrecy of these practices has been challenged. Newspapers reveal stories of public indignation at removal practices (Haebich, 1998), as well as evidence emerging of campaigns and public opinion against Aboriginal child removals (Paisley, 1997). Yet these endeavours did not reach the public sufficiently to bring about change.

CASE EXAMPLE

One high-profile story is that of James Savage, born Russell Moore, to a young Aboriginal mother in a rural town in Australia. James was taken from his biological mother soon after birth, adopted by a non-Aboriginal family and raised with no knowledge of his origins or identity. At the time of his adoption, records were kept secret and there is now evidence that young Aboriginal women, such as Russell's mother, were coerced into relinquishing their babies. When the secrecy shrouding adoption began to disappear following intensive advocacy by groups affected by adoption practices, his mother went on a search to find him. Tragically, he was on 'death row' in Florida following a conviction for rape and murder. The story reached the media as Aboriginal activists and others travelled to the USA to argue the case for life imprisonment, a quest that was ultimately successful. The story emerged of a young boy, an adolescent and an adult with no knowledge of his origins and severe identity confusion.

CASE EXAMPLE

The pervading myth of 'good intentions' and the view that governments are not responsible for the policies and practices of past times is exemplified by Warren Braedon's story. Warren Braedon, whose name was changed to Louis Johnson after adoption, was a young Aboriginal man, brutally murdered in Perth on 4 January 1992, his nineteenth birthday. In a submission to the Stolen Generations Inquiry, his adoptive father, Bill Johnson, told of being convinced by the authorities that the adoption meant doing the right thing by him (Haebich, 2000). Bill Johnson is among those who acted from these good intentions, and now feel duped by the misinformation provided.

There is now talk of a 'constructed silence' in Aboriginal affairs, not just based on mere ignorance of Australian history but an exercise in actively reconstructing known history to remove the crimes of white colonisation (Indigenous Social Justice Association, 2003: 1). Yet some social workers have refused to collude with the silence or cooperate with authorities. Bill Jordan (1990: 6) comments that social workers do participate in isolated acts of banditry, although there is limited engagement in a systematic manner to challenge systems that continue to oppress. One Indigenous activist, Mary Graham, told me of how in the early days of Indigenous people organising to control the future of their children, some social workers met with Indigenous organisations after hours and under cover, as they were not legally allowed to talk to them. She talked of car chases on the streets because the government department suspected that such meetings were occurring (Briskman, 2003).

Asylum seekers

There is a view that Indigenous child removal practices are of the past and based on 'good intentions', 'standards of the time' and a high level of community ignorance. There is no possibility for anyone to express such views about asylum-seeking children, in the light of information constantly before the general populace in a number of countries including Australia and England (Cemlyn and Briskman, 2003).

In Australia there is no clearer evidence of the systemic abuse of children than in the treatment of asylum seekers. The practices of immigration authorities are shrouded in secrecy, masked behind the political rhetoric of border protection, people-smuggling containment and controlled immigration. Through closed processes, the federal government has gone to great lengths to mask the abuses of children, even presenting false images of children being thrown overboard on their way to Australia, and refusing to acknowledge complicity in the tragic drowning of 353 asylum seekers, including children, on their way to Australia in 2001. Despite intense advocacy from many in the community, including legal challenges, children remain incarcerated in detention centres in Australia and Nauru, part of the so-called 'Pacific Solution', where a bankrupt nation shields Australian eyes from the injustices occurring and asylum seekers, including children, are denied basic rights such as legal advice.

There is a wall of silence in detention centres. Journalists are forbidden to visit and have contact. Nonetheless, one radio journalist encouraged children in detention to phone her and she recorded their stories that were later broadcast. The public heard such statements from the children as: 'We are not animals', 'Please we are human' and 'I lost everything. I forgot my learning' (Australian Broadcasting Commission, 2002). Journalists are not the only groups endeavouring to bring the injustices to the public domain. Church groups, actors, activist organisations and some professional bodies circulate information on individuals that the government hides in the name of confidentiality. Those inside detention centres have had some success in ensuring that their voices are heard and their stories disseminated.

In detaining children, Australia is flouting UN conventions, including the *UN Convention on the Rights of the Child*, which it has ratified. This has failed to outrage the social work profession as a whole, despite incorporation of human rights concepts in the Australian social work code of ethics (AASW, 1999). Notwithstanding increasing evidence of the impact of detention on children, the government continues to incarcerate minors in what are sometimes described as 'concentration camps'. I have personally observed children behind the razor wire and electric fences, and have heard stories of self-harm, despair and loss of hope. An inquiry conducted by the Human Rights and Equal Opportunity Commission in 2002 spoke of the effects of institutional living on parenting, the exposure of children to adult disturbances, the harsh and restrictive environments and the dehumanisation. The federal Human Rights Commissioner Sev Odowski says that treatment of refugees in detention centres is the harshest of the world, pointing out that by April 2003, 50 children had been detained for more than two years (Gallagher, 2003).

CASE EXAMPLE

Another high-profile case concerns two teenage boys who escaped from the Woomera Detention Centre and unsuccessfully sought asylum from British consular officials. These young boys were the subject of court challenges, whereby the Family Court of Australia intervened, resulting in the release of the boys into community settings. The federal government successfully appealed against their release and they were subsequently placed in alternative 'community' detention. The South Australian hospital where their mother gave birth to a daughter was designated a detention centre and she was under the control of guards during her hospitalisation. The baby will not be eligible for Australian citizenship. The father remains in detention.

The secrecy that veils detention has been described as an 'information lock-up'. This statement was coined by the *Business Review Weekly*, which revealed that the contents of a damning report on detention centres were kept secret (Washington, 2003: 18)). The newspaper gained access to the contents only after a long-running Freedom of Information request. Other groups have spoken out with information they have gleaned in various ways. This includes some former staff of detention centres who, despite having signed confidentiality clauses, have publicised the plight of children and other detainees through the media.

Social workers have little contact with detention centres. They do, however, have contact with many of those now in the community on much-criticised temporary visas. A combination of overwork and fear of losing funding prevents many social workers from speaking out about what they see and hear. Yet recent research revealed extensive barriers to services and found prolonged suffering and '"time torture" associated with temporary protection', with many refugees living in 'secondary detention' (Marston, 2003: 3).

A range of professional groups presented submissions to the national inquiry into children in detention. Submissions were received from former professional staff employed in detention centres, demonstrating the courage of some to speak out. Barbara Rogalla is a former nurse at the now-closed Woomera Detention Centre in South Australia. In a submission to the national inquiry into children in immigration detention she accused the Australian government of being culpable of the torture of children. She also commented that state child protection law is not sufficient to prevent the unlawful neglect that occurred inside (Rogalla, 2002).

The boundaries have in fact been tested by social work academics Chris Goddard and Max Liddell, who, in 2002, reported systemic abuse of all the children in the Woomera Detention Centre to the South Australian protection service. Yet the South Australian government relinquished its authority for investigating such reports to the federal immigration authorities (Cemlyn and Briskman, 2003: 175). Two social work academics in a newspaper article called for an inquiry into the stolen childhoods in detention centres so that those complicit in this 'organised and ritualised abuse' be held personally accountable (Goddard and Briskman, 2004: 17).

Other professionals who worked within the system spoke out to the human rights inquiry. A former teacher at the Port Hedland detention facility in Western Australia explained that students were too traumatised to concentrate and there was very little psychological help (Leaver, 2002). Among his comments, former Woomera psychologist Harold Bilboe (2002) told of how over time many people lost their ability to function effectively as parents and family relationships broke down.

As detention facilities are run by private prison operators, what are known as 'commercial-in-confidence' principles further diminish public knowledge on policies and practices. This was nowhere clearer than in a scenario I experienced within my own university, when, following fear of exposure, the university's public relations arm was forced to admit that a group of education faculty academics had participated in a tender with a private prison operator to provide education within Australia's detention centres. Together with another social work academic Heather Fraser and with the support of wide sections of the university including the staff and student union, some NGOs and detainees themselves, a newspaper article (Briskman and Fraser, 2002) was written to publicly outline the opposition, bringing some transparency into what had been a secretive process in the interests of commercial profit. In addition to the secrecy of the proposed venture there were a range of ethical issues that we identified, including the inappropriateness of financially profiting from people's misery, collusion in the government's propaganda war against asylum seekers and an implicit fatalism that mandatory detention was here to stay. The university withdrew the bid, established and resourced a refugee project to offer ethical and transparent assistance to asylum seekers and refugees, including the provision of free places to people on temporary protection visas. In taking our stance, as social workers, we saw our allegiance beyond the organisation in the interests of what we saw as a greater ethical good.

Interrogating accountability

One of the inherent contradictions in social work practice is that of competing accountabilities, some of which are vested in the scrutiny around professional practice. In delivering social work services to clients and families, social workers are confronted with contradictory expectations. Social work is very much an organisational activity (Jones and May, 1992), and there is strong pressure on social workers to work within the guidelines of their employing body, which usually has to comply with government funding agreements. Moreover, there is the accountability to the social work profession, with much of this framed by ethical codes.

Fred Powell (2001: 129) reminds us that a dual mandate defines the role and task of social work as promoting the interests both of the state and the service users whom they purport to help. By definition, this dual mandate makes social work a politicised activity. For some, this has involved a high degree of sensitisation to avoid the implications of the use of professional power. However, the majority of social workers avoid the implications of the dual mandate by adopting an individualised therapeutic approach that locates social work in the apolitical world of psychology and the personalisation of social problems (p. 129). As recently as 1997, the Human Rights and Equal Opportunity Commission maintained that welfare departments continued to pathologise and individualise the needs of Indigenous children (HREOC, 1997: 584). Bill Jordan talks of how many social workers have a stake in a style of work that is power-laden, formal and individualised (Jordan, 1997: 219).

In South Africa there has been some exploration around dual loyalty and human rights in the health sphere (Physicians for Human Rights, 2002), something from which the social work profession could learn. The Physicians for Human Rights note that dual loyalty becomes problematic when the professional acts to support the interests of the state or other entity instead of those of the individual, in a manner that violates the human rights of the individual. One example they raise is where under a repressive government, pervasive human rights abuses combined with restrictions on freedom of expression render it difficult to resist state demands and report abuses. They comment that closed institutions, and detention centres would come under this category, as they demand allegiance from health professionals even in the face of common human rights violations against those held there. The Physicians for Human Rights' analysis can extend further to asylum seekers and refugees in the community where they comment that violations of people's rights of access to services can arise from government-imposed policies, where professionals may be called on to withhold treatment from certain groups in discriminatory ways.

CONCLUSION

Opportunities for transformational social work

Social work is less able to hide behind the confidentiality mask as increasing attention is placed on human rights abuses, breaches of international obligations and practices that are antithetical to the values of social work. Although social workers are unlikely to be direct perpetrators of current abuses, their knowledge, skills and espoused human rights and social justices values should result in using their voices to join others in advocating for change, adopting what Malcolm Payne (1998: 127) refers to as the 'transformational potential of socialist-collectivist views'.

Jim Ife (2001: 1) points out that human rights is one of the most powerful concepts in contemporary social and political discourse. Yet, it is a framework rarely embraced by social work in a rigorous or applied manner. Although a somewhat contested concept, particularly because of legalistic underpinnings and Western-driven approaches, more relevant human rights discourses are increasingly finding their way into a range of forms of practice, including with Indigenous peoples and asylum seekers and refugees. This presents challenges to social work's focus on the micro-elements of practice, and provides opportunities for more transparent practice. It can help to move practice away from the narrower accountabilities and create a more rigorous engagement with the politics of social work.

If social workers are to be committed to social change, justice, inclusion, diversity and participation, they must develop theories and practices that place to the foreground social, political and economic power relations, as well as cultural relevance (Quinn, 2003). The profession needs to guard itself against cooption by a prevailing discourse that privileges individual rights and responsibilities (Briskman, 2001).

Jan Fook (2002) talks about what counts as legitimate knowledge and whose knowledge is privileged. This is one of the issues with confidentiality, drawn as it is on professional tenets and acted on in specific ways that maintain professional 'integrity'. Fook (2002) further tells us that dominant discourses are powerful often because they are unquestioned. She explains that by pointing out the contradictions there is scope to challenge and change dominant meaning systems (p. 89). Social work could rise to the challenge presented by Robert Adams (2002: 87) for the critical practitioner, whom he argues 'offers the prospect of transformation by not being bound by the status quo'. He sees the critical practitioner as bringing to bear on a situation, contextual, theoretical and conceptual understandings of social work, and incorporating political engagement for a broader good.

Instead of seeing alternative voices as irrelevant to social work, there are opportunities for the profession to advocate for their inclusion in policy and practice decision-making. For Jim Ife (1997: 181), social workers have a particular responsibility to allow the voices of the marginalised to be heard, by working alongside marginalised people and not taking it upon themselves to define the needs of the oppressed. Experience has shown that even those whose voices have been largely silenced through intentional government isolation, such as asylum seekers, are able to exercise their own agency to some extent and use other groups as vehicles to help in gaining access to the public domain.

A revisiting of social work codes of ethics is warranted, with less concern for professionalism and a greater articulation of social work's unique positioning for advocacy and social change. In so doing, social work codes need to shift from their more individualistic positioning to embracing collective issues, framed around a sense of justice and rights. As with other codes, the Australian social work code of ethics does not currently push for activism on the part of its members (De Maria, 1997), and hence is being left behind as other professions engage with collective action.

If social work is to be truly inclusive and contribute effectively as social change agents, it must reinvent its practice. The sphere of child and family welfare is a critical area for ongoing critique, analysis and engagement. A review of some of social work's basic tenets, including confidentiality, in the light of the ongoing challenges, is an urgent task for social work academics, professional organisations and practitioners.

=== **FURTHER READING** ===

Briskman, L. (2003) 'Indigenous Australians: Towards postcolonial social work', in Allan, J., Pease, B. and Briskman, L. (eds) *Critical Social Work: An Introduction to Theories and Practices* (Sydney: Allen & Unwin).

Briskman, L. and Noble, C. (1999) 'Social Work Ethics: Embracing Diversity?', in Pease, B. and Fook, J. (eds) *Transforming Social Work Practice: Postmodern Critical Perspectives* (St Leonards: Allen & Unwin).

Fook, J. (2002) *Social Work: Critical Theory and Practice* (London: Sage).

Hough, G. and Briskman, L. (2003) 'Responding to the Changing Socio-Political Context of Practice', in Allan, J., Pease, B. and Briskman, L. (eds) *Critical Social Work: An Introduction to Theories and Practices* (Sydney: Allen & Unwin).

Ife, J. (2001) *Human Rights and Social Work: Towards Rights-based Practice* (Cambridge: Cambridge University Press).

Social Work Research

Social Work Research: Contested Knowledge for Practice

Lena Dominelli

Introduction

Research has gained a new prominence in British social work. This development has been driven by: managers promoting evidence-based practice and evaluations of practitioners' performance and responses to new policy initiatives; practitioners undertaking their own or practitioner research; and academics being assessed on their research activities for funding purposes in ongoing research assessment exercises (RAEs). However, the concern to be a research-led discipline predates this particular emphasis. Research-based social work was endorsed by the 'founding mothers' of the profession who believed that its status would be enhanced if it included research and PhD students. Eileen Younghusband's reports on social work education in the UK and Hong Kong argued strongly for a research-led profession (Younghusband, 1959), as had Jane Addams (Elshtain, 2002) earlier in the USA. Extracting funding for their aspirations proved a major barrier to the realisation of their vision and until recently more effort was expended on education and training (Lyons, 2004).

In Britain, research was not given a high profile in the remit of the bodies responsible for social work education. Although there have been notable exceptions such as Whittaker and Archer's (1990) study on practice research, the Central Council for Education and Training in Social Work (CCETSW) and now the General Social Care Council (GSCC) in England and Wales and the Scottish Social Services Council (SSSC) in Scotland concentrate on training social workers rather than fostering research. This position may be altered somewhat by the Social Care Institute for Excellence (SCIE) which has been charged with improving practice and using research, especially that linked to 'what works' to do this. Aside from ignoring the distinction between social work and social care, its research has a narrow, evaluative focus which is unlikely to produce a substantive foundation for the theoretical and methodological innovations that social work needs (Dominelli, 2004).

This position has been exacerbated by the absence of social work as a named discipline in the Economic and Social Sciences Research Council (ESRC) funding forms and the Department of Health's support for applied research, particularly linked primarily to its concerns in child protection and welfare. The Department of Health's focus on applied research, that is, research concerned primarily with what happens on the ground, has been replicated in the research endeavours of other bodies with an interest in social work research, namely the Social Services Research Group (SSRG), the Association of Directors of Social Services (ADSS) and voluntary organisations undertaking research, for example, the National Society for the Prevention of Cruelty to Children (NSPCC), National Children's Homes (NCH) and Barnardo's. Whilst important, this applied focus neglects conceptual or basic research.

Basic research focuses on the fundamentals of knowledge – its conceptual building blocks rather than how knowledge is used, which is considered the province of applied research. Basic research enables us to ask fundamental questions about social work – what it is, how it works, how to gather data about it, how to make predictions about practice and how to test theories. Basic research aims to improve human well-being and ask questions that might otherwise be ignored. As basic research is led by experts in their field, it can be used to discredit the contributions to knowledge made by those holding what Foucault (1980) termed 'subjugated knowledges', for example knowledge that comes from the experience of being a service user. (It is difficult to find words that accurately describe people who access services. I use the terms 'service user', 'client' and 'consumer' interchangeably, while acknowledging that each is problematic and socially constructed.) The privileging of expert knowledge, particularly those forms that adopt the supremacy of natural science paradigms can carry intellectual arrogance as a byproduct. This approach holds sway in the social sciences and disinherits social work research with service users from a valued place in the academy. Basic research has also been critiqued by the Service User Research Enterprise (SURE) at King's College, London for being unable to deal helpfully with the messiness of issues explored in the social sciences (SURE, 2004).

Other social science disciplines, especially psychology, sociology and social policy, have appropriated much of the research agenda in social work and made research issues their own. In the process, social work research and what it had to say about itself as a research-based discipline and its input to other disciplines have been marginalised, a condition that is unlikely to shift easily in the current configuration of research. Social work managers, practitioners and educators have the responsibility of reclaiming these knowledge domains and taking an active role in (re)defining and (re)affirming their own contributions to general social sciences research.

rking under the aegis of the Joint Universities Council and the Social Work tion Committee (JUC-SWEC), British social work academics have recently attempted to claw back and/or identify this terrain by arguing for the distinctiveness of social work research. Ron Amann, head of the ESRC in the mid-1990s, challenged social work educators to make the intellectual case for recognition of social work as a discipline in its own right when replying to a letter I wrote to him asking for this in May 1996. The social work educator's response to his challenge ultimately yielded collaborative endeavours under the auspices of JUC-SWEC that led to the formation of the Theorising Social Work Research seminar series (TSWR), funded by the ESRC for three years. The TSWR produced publications that explored a range of important research issues (see http://www.elsc.org.uk/socialcareresource/tswr/tswrindex.htm).

The TSWR raised a number of issues for discussion and debate, resulting in the formulation of a code of ethics for social work research and a place for social work on the ESRC's Education Training Board. In my view, this last gain reaffirms an educational status for social work, but one that allows social work educators to have some impact on one element of the RAE – the provision of doctoral studies and studentships. Ian Diamond, the current head of the ESRC, proposes to consolidate this position by recognising social work as a named discipline with regards to doctoral studentships. Whilst I welcome this proposal because it will contribute to building capacity in social work research for the future, it does not address my overall concern about the lack of recognition for social work as a research-based discipline per se. Additionally, the social work academics on the ESRC Education and Training Board have worked to encourage practitioner involvement in research-based studies through the development of collaborative (CASE) studentships that involve partnerships between academic and practice-based institutions. But, as CASE funding involves a substantive contribution from an individual agency or employer, these are difficult to establish in significant numbers in a given locality. So the number of PhD students doing social work research remains low. Another reason for this is that some students doing social work research are registered in other disciplines, for example, sociology and social policy, and so the total figure remains unknown (Lyons, 1999).

After publication of the 2001 RAE results, the Higher Education Funding Council for England (HEFCE) agreed to fund a capability fund to improve social work's research base. The HEFCE has accepted the arguments that having a practitioner base disadvantaged social work research and provided extra funding to those getting 3 (national rating) in the RAE to raise their outputs to an international level (5 or 5*). The 2008 exercise will assess the impact of this particular approach to the issue. Commenting on the lack of research capability in social work in the USA, Gillespie and Glisson (1992) show that this is a concern elsewhere.

In this chapter, I argue that social work has to strengthen its research standing vis-à-vis other disciplines, whilst ensuring that more research is undertaken by social work academics, practitioners, service users and students. I also suggest that all those engaged in the profession should become more research-literate, that is, understand what research is, how it can be conducted as an ethical endeavour, what it has to offer practice and how social work educators, practitioners and service users can play a greater role in its development. Responding to this agenda requires social work managers, practitioners and academics to ask more searching questions about their contribution to social work research and problematise social work research in ways that enable it to engage meaningfully with the contested nature of knowledge and include service users more effectively in knowledge creation and validation.

What is social work research?

Research serves several purposes in social work. It can be used to:

- Enhance the status of the profession in both the field and the academy
- Improve services by finding out what service users think about those that have been delivered to them
- Evaluate the extent of their use and who utilises them
- Highlight issues
- Elucidate depth and complexities in practice
- Explore problems
- Raise additional questions
- Enhance critical reflection.

Responding to service user agendas and shifting the lack of high regard for social work research in academia highlight a need for research materials that can be used to (re)theorise social work practice and guide it in new directions. This can draw upon both applied and basic research.

Social work researchers, like Colin Barnes and his colleagues (Barnes and Mercer, 1997; Barnes et al., 1999), have challenged the idea that only experts can undertake research and argued that social work research can be undertaken by experts, practitioners and service users, or a combination of these. Experts in research are usually called 'researchers'. They hold a privileged status in knowledge creation by virtue of having specific skills in research methodologies and being paid for doing research by an organisation charged with the task of crafting knowledge. The expert approach to research tends to favour those who maintain a distance between the researcher and those upon whom they *do* research. By framing their efforts as 'doing' research, they establish power over relations in which the researcher is the subject who controls the process and the research respondents become objects of their expert ministrations. This sets up an unequal researcher–researched dynamic and a hierarchy of valuing what the researcher rather than the respondent says (Dominelli, 2005).

The research expert may be a consultant who claims a capacity to do research and undertakes a given piece of research through a specific contract. Many of these may be freelance operators rather than employees in a research-oriented organisation such as a university or research institute. Unless these experts in research also happen to have expertise in social work education and/or practice, they will not bring any specific understandings of social work to bear upon the studies they take, a point discussed at length by Beth Humphries in Chapter 20.

actitioner-researchers are likely to have been or remain involved in practice herefore bring a greater awareness of the needs of the field and research that carries significance or relevance for practice. These researchers might also find it easier to obtain access to service users for the purposes of doing research and have a strong motivation in forming research partnerships that include practitioners, academics and service users. This approach is not unproblematic. Examples of this way of working are discussed in all the chapters in this section. If practitioner-researchers remain committed to the field, they may find time for research squeezed against the demands of the vocational parts of the job and lack of immediate access to library facilities, computer-based technologies and statistical information. They may also risk their chances of promotion if their findings reveal material that is negatively perceived by their employers. These difficulties identify important dimensions in the 'politics of research', an issue covered extensively by Helen Brown in her contribution to this book (Chapter 18).

Service user researchers are a fairly recent phenomenon. But their demand for full participation in research has arisen from several insights. One is that some, for example those in the disability movement, have demanded this as their right and have introduced a new paradigm to convey their thoughts – 'emancipatory research' (Barnes and Mercer, 1997). As the experts on living in a disabling society, they argue that they have valid information to impart to others who are not. They see controlling what happens to them as their right as citizens, while creating knowledge and having it recognised as such is an entitlement they intend to have.

Service users who indicate an interest in research are ordinary members of the public who wish to be involved in a research process in which they are interested, for example to see an improvement in services, or they have been asked to partic-ipate in it by someone outside or within their own community. They may have to acquire formal research skills through training either before engaging in the research or alongside it. This will require the researcher working with them to demystify research processes and the expertise associated with these to shift the researcher–researched power dynamic in more egalitarian directions and embed the research in a holistic environment.

Stakeholders in the social work enterprise are doing research all the time. Research skills such as collecting information, evaluating it, theorising from it and acting upon it constitute activities that mimic research skills in daily work routines. However, much of this action is taken for granted and usually not considered research. This includes data collected in the course of everyday investigations into people's problems, including life histories and hidden social issues. This information is usually only seen by other practitioners, managers and magistrates who would not consider this research per se. Yet a systematic analysis of these documents could produce invaluable insights in retheorising social problems and finding new solutions, alongside showing how individual problems are rooted in social conditions.

What constitutes research is a contentious issue. Traditional empiricist approaches to research as propagated through positivist methodologies assume that knowledge is acquired through observation and experimentation. This way of proceeding has been termed the Enlightenment approach to knowledge creation (Crotty, 1998). It has been questioned by feminists (Stanley and Wise, 1997), postmodernists, poststructuralists and constructionists amongst others (Crotty, 1998). Their critiques emphasise the ways in which researchers examine the relationship between human thought and social existence when creating knowledge (Usher, 1997) and suggest that there is no 'truth' as such, but a description of things as we interpret them (Crotty, 1998). Thus, knowledge does not portray a universal truth, but is situational and context-specific (Gibbs, 2001a).

The controversial nature of research becomes even more evident in social work research because it has to straddle the academy's concerns for rigorous methodologies while simultaneously engaging effectively with the realities of practice and developing critical reflexive practitioners, difficult as this may be, as Sewpaul and Taniga demonstrate in Chapter 19. Social work researchers have to explore further important research issues. These include having to:

- Rethink what kind of research carries credibility and validity

- Question what counts as legitimate knowledge

- Deprivilege clinical knowledge and its claims to hold higher status because it defines itself as being more 'scientific' than other approaches

- Articulate alternative voices including those of service users and practitioners in discourses about research

- Reverse the undervaluing of the applied research undertaken in social work.

Hence, social work educators have to understand clearly what is meant by social work research, defend their distinctive stance to it and problematise dominant paradigms.

Sherman and Reid (1994: 1) define social work research by dividing it into *qualitative research* which is 'research that produces descriptive data, spoken or written words and observable behaviour' and *quantitative research* which is concerned primarily with 'numerically measuring the degree to which some feature is present'. This distinction is blurred by the achievement of qualitative researchers in developing systematic ways of picking up and enumerating or counting data. But the definitions are helpful in highlighting important differences in what can be achieved by either approach. Both have their different uses and validity. There is a richness in small-scale qualitative research that is absent from quantitative studies, but the latter can give indications of frequency that is absent from the former. I do not find the simple division of research endeavours into these two mutually exclusive categories constructive. There are areas of overlap between them, particularly in their search for authenticity and their attempt to clarify the nature of knowledge and 'truths' about the world we live in. In short, research is a complex undertaking that involves people forming research relationships that (re)configure knowledge and the status held by those who create it.

In the UK, the TSWR group considered the question 'What is social work research?' without reaching a conclusion except to say that social work research was not unique, in that it drew on the same methodologies as other disciplines in the social sciences. However, it was deemed distinctive in that it had to address the implications of research for practice rather than undertake research purely for its own sake.

As a member of the TSWR group, I agreed with these conclusions, but I also think that social work research, which I define as a field of investigation that examines human interactions around human well-being (or its lack), has to encompass more than a general concern with practice. I hold this view because social work research involves researchers and the subjects of research building relationships around a study *and* its outcomes, giving findings power over their lives and research the potential to become a site of exclusion. Thus, social work researchers should give thought to the consequences of their action (Dominelli, 2005). Power relations are at play within the dynamics of inclusion and exclusion. Not least amongst these is that of who forms part of the research community that decides what counts as research. So, research is an expression of power relations that have a direct bearing on the products of the research or knowledge-building enterprise. Social work research usually focuses on marginalised groups or people who hold limited social power. And it seeks to bring about social change that enhances human well-being. In other words, social work research enacts a moral and political standpoint rather than one that is indifferent to the purposes for which research is used.

The distinctiveness of social work research

Social work researchers determine whose story counts as worthy of being told and decide which group of people will be subjected to the research gaze. In deciding who to include in a research project, they should not limit their investigations to excluded groups and forego studies of power elites. In a traditional researcher–researched relationship this gaze favours the ruling elite who can find out what they want to know about subjugated peoples without exposing their own positions because there is no accountability back to the subjects of the research. This relation can be reversed through social work research that poses questions that are articulated by groups marginalised by dominant elites.

Research may also carry an emotional content that has to be taken into account. Social work researchers also have to address the emotional investment that each group of participants has in the research, giving it a holistic dimension often absent in research in other disciplines. Funders, researchers and the subjects of research will each have specific views about research and its end products. The commitment to enhancing well-being is a contentious position and not accepted by power holders who fear losing their privileges if the research gaze focuses on their comings, goings and doings. This problem is evidenced in Sewpaul and Raniga's chapter (Chapter 19) which shows how in controversial situations, regional and local authorities play safe by going along with dominant discourses and following central government research agendas rather than setting their own.

Social work research is also a creative process involving hard work and coordination of activities between researchers and the subjects of research. This means that they have to care for and about those with whom they are doing research. Power relations between the researcher and the subjects of research pose ethical considerations that have to be taken into account – permission to do the research (normally called obtaining informed consent) and making arrangements for the smooth conduct of the research. The research subject has to be respected and treated as a person with agency, that is, an active contributor to the research endeavour, not a passive object waiting for the researcher to ask questions and evaluate their answers. These issues raise important ethical points for social work research that, belatedly, are being explicitly and systematically considered in research conducted for student dissertations. Another source of difficulty in developing a distinctive approach to the holistic agenda of social work research is that a key funder of this research, the Department of Health, plans to apply the narrow, positivist models of NHS research and governance structures to social care, which in its view includes social work (see http://www.dh.gov.uk/policy andguidance/researchanddevelopmentAZ/researchgovernance/fs/en).

I would also argue that if social work researchers are to identify those features that distinguish them from others doing research in similar areas and perhaps using similar methodologies, they should also develop:

■ A change orientation

■ A more egalitarian relationship between themselves and those who are the subjects of their research

■ Accountability to 'clients'/service users for the products of their work

■ A holistic engagement with the different aspects of the problem(s) or people they are investigating.

In other words, social work research should engage with practice and transform it, alongside raising questions about what it is and what it can(not) do. It should also identify:

■ The arguments for change

■ The basis on which change is to be conducted

■ The opportunities for different actors to participate in change

■ How to evaluate existing endeavours

■ The potential for future developments.

Involving service users in research design, delivery and dissemination can be used to hold practitioners and academics accountable to those who are affected by their work and question the privileging of words that emanate from research. Engaging in more holistic forms of research is also more empowering as Helen Brown and Beth Humphries argue in Chapters 18 and 20 respectively.

There are other researchers for whom the first two requirements would apply. For example, feminist researchers examining domestic violence without a social work dimension would want to see change in the form of its elimination, create a relationship with the women they interview for the study and make arrangements to provide services for those who might be emotionally distressed by the research process (see Stanley and Wise, 1997). In this sense, they are involved in caring about others. However, they would not be held accountable for the changes in social workers' practice with the victim-survivors of domestic violence, nor would they have to confront the ethical challenge of reporting possible risks to others arising from the knowledge gained during the research.

Social work researchers have to consider not only what happens to the women victim-survivors and men perpetrating these assaults, but also to the children who live with them. This consideration becomes part of the 'holistic' dimension of social work research. Some of these concerns are explored by Vishanthie Sewpaul and Tanusha Raniga in their research on HIV/AIDS. In their chapter (Chapter 19), research has to meet the practice aspirations of an entire community and not just the agencies or individuals directly involved in the research.

Social work researchers are also distinctive in having to ensure that their research integrates theory with practice. But this is precisely where social work research is weak. As Gillespie and Glisson (1992) argue, social work research is inadequately theorised and has failed to spell out a research practice and methodology that it can call its own. This position is a contested one. Some argue that social work research draws on skills that are evident in practice. Sherman and Reid (1994) suggest that Mary Richmond's (1917) classic, *Social Diagnosis,* is a form of qualitative social work research that covers questions of judgement, choice, interpretation and situations that social workers investigate. Patton (1980) contends that a case study is a well-known form of in-depth social work research.

Gilgun (1994) argues that grounded theory, proposed by Glaser and Strauss (1967), is a social work research method because it replicates skills that social workers draw upon in practice. These include the concern to maintain confidentiality, interviewing and communication skills, analytical skills involved in the rigorous examination of the data collected and the dissemination of findings. She also claims that grounded theory gives voice to service users and enables what they say to provide the basis for theorising about their experiences (Glaser and Strauss, 1967). Those advocating these positions make important points. However, none of them considers the involvement of 'clients' in the actual research process.

Involving service users in research is not straightforward. The terms upon which they are integrated are important. Researchers' assumptions about knowledge and truth underpin the relationship between them (Usher, 1997). Unless researchers value their participation, the research will be conducted without their input except as objects of the research. In Dominelli (2005), I examine the weaknesses of grounded theory in this regard. The contractual conditions of research, the ownership of the findings, the institutional privileging of those labelled 'researchers' and the failure to benefit service users are not addressed in grounded theory approaches, and new forms of social exclusion are created in the process of involving service users and validating their knowledge (Dominelli, 2005). I also suggest that maintaining service user agency in research is a constant factor in the interaction between them. It is not a one-off event that can be forgotten once service users are included. Engaging service users as full partners in research is an essential aspect of every component of the social work research process, a point emphasised by those in the disability movement amongst others. But it remains an issue for further work. Sarah Banks and Di Barnes demonstrate in Chapter 17 how social work research involves an iterative process that engages the researcher and the subject of the research.

Beth Humphries' contribution to this book (Chapter 20) identifies the difficulty in using research to empower service users. Researchers have been employed to do research because they are skilled in this work. Training service users in these skills is done under tight scheduling and in conditions that limit the amount of knowledge and skills that can be passed on. It also assumes that existing research skills are those that 'clients' should adopt. But what about involving service users in developing new methodologies and techniques that are rooted in their ways of knowing about and experiencing the world? The wonder is that a number of researchers have claimed considerable success in sharing research skills in ways that do not devalue service users' involvement in the knowledge creation process, but they have not produced innovative research methodologies (SURE, 2004).

Empowering 'clients' in the research process involves a number of moves (Dominelli, 2005), including being clear about language and the power relations inherent within it. Talking about research 'interviewees' conveys a different meaning to one that refers to them as the 'subjects of research' or even its 'owners'. Differentiated power relations are also evident in getting research funders to pay for the time spent on training the subjects of research. Making a case requires considerable effort, but the request is not always agreed to. The argument about the 'value added' by this approach has to be made to convince a funder that this idea is worth putting money into. The culture of an organisation, particularly if it associates the label of researcher with someone from a university, also has to be changed to value the newly acquired research skills of the subjects of research.

At the same time, the issue arises of whether research questions should be asked differently to ensure that those who are not directly employed in research can engage effectively in the knowledge creation process. An example of this is not referring to 'evaluation', a term that can frighten people off if they think it is about an incomprehensible procedure, but asking a straightforward question that has the same effect. For instance, we can ask instead, 'How do you know what does or does not work?'

Becoming more research-literate and responding to controversies in social work research

In the past, British social work students and practitioners have given research a miss whenever given a choice and research methods courses were generally considered an optional extra. Students' eyes tended to glaze over when listening to lectures about research methods and practitioners were happy for someone else to engage in this activity. Even research-led teaching took a back seat on too many courses and requiring students to read social statistics engendered a fear that prompted most of them to avoid the subject if at all possible. As a result, the current social work labour force lacks the requisite research knowledge and skills and is poorly equipped either to undertake or use research in a critical reflexive manner. This reality constitutes a compelling reason for encouraging social work educators, practitioners and students to take an active role in promoting and engaging in social work research, and may change through the introduction of the three-year undergraduate degree in social work which provides space for research-mindedness to be given a high profile.

Why encourage those who have a direct interest in the profession to undertake social work research? Many changes in practice are making research important for practitioners. In Britain, the movement towards evidence-based practice (EBP) (Sheldon, 2000) and the government's determination to have practice that demonstrates its effectiveness – the penchant for 'what works' – have rekindled interest in social work research and require practitioners to become more research-aware. Becoming research-literate is critical in forming opinions about research, given the contested nature of what counts as research or evidence and who decides what or whose knowledge counts. Social work managers and practitioners will be commissioning research to improve practice. Many of the gaps in our knowledge about social work will begin to be filled, but not necessarily by those who best understand the profession if social work educators do not promote research and socialise the researchers who will do this work in the future into producing critical, reflexive research and practice.

Linking research accountability to 'what works' approaches to research is problematic. This is because questions are framed in terms of effectiveness and assume that there are fixed answers that are right or wrong. But we know that practice is full of uncertainties and ambiguities and there may be more than one way of responding to a given situation (Parton, 1998), none of which can guarantee a particular outcome. Moreover, practice tends to be messy and indeterminate (Parton, 2000). Grappling with these realities makes finding new ways of doing and theorising social work research an urgent matter. I am not convinced that an approach rooted in EBP as defined by Sheldon (2000) will provide the much-needed ways forward. This is because it focuses on a particularly narrow view of research, one that emphasises quantitative methods over qualitative ones and random controlled trials as *the* way of verifying research results. This formulation sets up an unnecessary division between the two methodologies which, as Sherman and Reid (1994) and Kirk and Reid (2002) argue, have much in common, including issues of judgement, choice and interpretation, activities involved in designing and executing both types of research. This construction of EBP foregoes the richer insights gained from qualitative methodologies and ignores the positivist's base in the systematic collection of anecdotal evidence (Dominelli, 2004).

EBP conceptualises data as unitary and knowable rather than disputed and disordered. The researchers' knowledge is privileged over that of the respondents', although the entire research enterprise rests on their contribution to the data collected. That is, the respondent is the data. Their interdependence can be ignored because respondents in these studies are treated as objects of the research and as such denied subjectivity. Consequently, the order that is imposed on the information collected by the researcher through the processes of analysing the material collected and finding meaning in or interpreting data is *presumed*, while that provided by the research *subject* or 'knower' is deemed irrelevant. Treating knowledge as fixed also encourages students and practitioners to look for a 'toolkit' that equips them with answers and a checklist that can be relied upon to provide them with the *correct* answer in a complex situation. This search for certainty ill-prepares practitioners to deal with uncertainties, ambiguities and the complications of practice (Parton, 1998). And, it permits social workers to ignore process issues and power relations involved in particular interactions including those evident within the research relationship.

Power and subjectivity in the processes of social work research

The neglect of process raises the issue of bypassing voice, that is, who is creating the statements and making sense of them to produce what counts as knowledge or is accepted as such. The processes involved in EBP research exclude people who are primarily positioned at the margins of society except to treat them as 'objects' of study able to give statements which are then ordered by an allegedly impartial and disinterested researcher in ways consistent with hegemonic expectations about knowledge (Belenky et al., 1997).

Feminists such as Harding (1991) have made this point in arguing that people's 'standpoint' or location in a society influences their views of what constitutes knowledge and understanding. EBP has a bias towards quantitative research and tends to privilege experts' assertions regarding what is valued. Moreover, it belongs to a tradition of research that privileges men's expertise and ways of knowing over those of women and marginalised others and divides the world into hierarchical, dichotomous and mutually exclusive categories (Harding, 1991; Belenky et al., 1997; Usher, 1997; Dominelli, 2004).

EBP has not made explicit either its ontological or epistemological underpinnings and is oblivious of the emphasis it gives to social science-based research that gives precedence to ways of working that are more consistent with the natural sciences' approach to knowledge, that is, treating research respondents as passive objects whose essence is there to be discovered by those doing the research. Social work research that emphasises its connections to people and acknowledges service users as key players along with the researchers in the knowledge creation process cannot get away with doing this. To gain a research literacy that takes on board these complexities, social work researchers have to treat research as an interaction that involves the researcher and the subjects of research as participants in a mutual knowledge-creating activity (Dominelli, 2005). Beth Humphries indicates the importance of this way of proceeding in Chapter 20. Those advocating a narrative-based approach to practice (Hall, 1997) make similar claims, in that both the practitioner and the 'client' are creating the intervention that makes sense in their jointly agreed version of events. They construct the story and each other in the process of articulating what occurred.

In order to intervene effectively in commissioning research, practitioners and managers will have to have sufficient knowledge for evaluating competing claims to the knowledge creation process and choose wisely from a vast array of research designs and methods. They will also have to acquire the skills that enable them to draw meaningful conclusions from the products of a particular piece of research. They will have to weigh up insights gained through an impressionistic study in which informed hunches are followed through to their logical end. What they are doing constitutes research. It creates data and draws upon that which is collected by listening carefully to anecdotal evidence and trying to make sense of what is being said. And it is as valid as that emanating from a sophisticated, systematic and well-tested approach to the problem that may have utilised quantitative or qualitative methodologies or triangulated them (Belenky et al., 1997). Managers and practitioners have to know what counts as evidence in research and who determines what counts and why, and be prepared for experimental forms of research, experiential expertise and more exploratory, unfocused studies that seek to break new frontiers. They may have to explain to sceptical others why scarce funds should be expended on research rather than much-needed services. In Henkel's (1995) words, they have to act as 'reflective participants in, rather than privileged observers of, particular phenomena and situations'.

Changes in contemporary practice are supplementing pressures from the academy that are simultaneously actively encouraging practitioners to do research as part of life-long learning and career progression, including at PhD level. Additionally, social work students are increasingly engaging with small pieces of research as part of their studies when writing their dissertations and more courses are offering research methods or research-mindedness courses in preparation for this. These developments have to be nurtured and the provision of sizeable student stipends to encourage those with various domestic responsibilities and commitments to participate is essential.

Involving service users more completely in research begs questions about the links between research and practice and these may have to be better understood than is currently the case. Their potential to contribute fully to the research design, implementation and dissemination processes remains underdeveloped and there is a long way to go before they are integrated as *equal and active subjects* in research. There are a number of barriers to their inclusion. Lacking skills in formal research methods is a key one. Funders are also reluctant to pay the additional costs associated with their involvement, although some like the Joseph Rowntree Foundation do pay small honoraria for the time that service users spend on research projects. Differential pay privileges researchers who receive an agreed salary and makes the statement that a researcher's time is more valuable than that of the research subjects (Dominelli, 2005).

Additionally, current funding schemes do not cover the initial stages of developing a proposal and so 'clients' are excluded at this point. This means that decisions about the research design, the methodologies to be used and the processes for delivering a project have been made before they become involved. And so, the role of service users in deciding the research question and how the research is to be conducted and who is to do it is diminished. Once funding is secured, it is usually easier to bring them on board and involve them more in the dissemination and ensure that findings influence policy and practice.

Given the critique of traditional or positivist approaches to research, there are three possibilities for future development in social work research. The first is to find ways of including service users more fully in the research process so that they can influence it from the beginning as well as engage in endeavours aimed at changing policy and practice at the end once the findings have been ascertained. The second involves creating the theories, knowledge and skills that will enable social work researchers to engage in research endeavours that link to practice and yet claim validity beyond the locality in which the research was conducted and address the question of generalisability. The third is that of ensuring that the personal elements in research are connected to their structural and contextual components. If it can achieve these, social work research will differ from psychological studies and sociological research as they have been traditionally conducted and will be forging new paths for researchers not just in social work, but in the social sciences more broadly.

<hr>
CONCLUSION
<hr>

Social work research has to meet new challenges and engage with those that bedevil research more generally. Crucial to this are:

- Emphasising the role of research subjects in the research process and ensuring that they are engaged as full participants in research

- Finding new methodologies that will meet the specific concerns of practice, namely discovering ways of dealing with uncertainty and ambiguities

- Inventing approaches that will enhance service user well-being

- Retheorising social work research

- Working out how practice-based research can involve practitioners without jeopardising their career prospects when they uncover material that portrays their employers in a negative light

- Involving service users as full partners in research.

Responding to these concerns may precipitate more controversies in social work research, but confronting these is an obligation that social work researchers cannot avoid if they are to articulate their distinctive approaches to their endeavours.

In the process, researchers who engage in fully participative research with service users and practitioners have to be prepared to deal with its pitfalls and take advantage of the opportunities offered by moving further in this direction. As they do so, social work researchers have better possibilities of responding to service user agendas while advancing and protecting the place of social work research in the academy. They can also work towards ensuring that social work becomes a social science discipline that does not use its authority to get caught up in replicating the models of research proffered by the natural sciences and treating people as objects of their ministrations. These paradigms do not meet the needs of people interacting in a research relationship. Consequently, social work researchers have to work together with service users, practitioners and managers to develop new and different methodologies and insights for social work research.

<hr>
FURTHER READING
<hr>

Ewalt, P.L., Freeman, E.M., Kirk, S.A. and Poole D.L. (eds) (1996) *Multicultural Issues in Social Work: Practice and Research* (Washington, DC: NASW).

Lovelock, R., Lyons, K. and Powell, J. (2004) *Reflecting on Social Work: Discipline and Profession* (Aldershot: Ashgate).

Royse, D.R. (2003) *Research Methods in Social Work* (4th edn) (Wadsworth).

Rutin, A. (2002) *Practice-Oriented Study Guide for Research Methods in Social Work* (Brooks/Cole).

Getting Started with a Piece of Research/Evaluation in Social Work

Sarah Banks and Di Barnes

Introduction

This chapter examines some of the processes and issues involved in setting out to do a piece of research as a practitioner. Specifically, it covers some of the tensions, dilemmas and ethical issues that may arise when working with service users, practitioners and agencies in the course of participatory research. Although this chapter is about 'getting started', it is important to anticipate and plan for as much of the research process as possible in advance, including consideration of how the research might end and the results be disseminated. This enables all the research participants to have a clear idea about what is expected and allows agreements to be made with various stakeholders that are both feasible and ethically sound.

In this chapter we assume that a research topic has been decided upon, therefore we cover matters relating to:

- Deciding on an approach to the research

- Confirming values and principles

- Clarifying roles and purpose with stakeholders

- Negotiating access and anticipating and agreeing issues relating to ownership of the research, privacy, consent and anonymity.

However, it is important to emphasise that the choice of topic in itself raises ethical and political issues. If research is funded or sponsored by an agency, government department or funding council, the boundaries of what counts as a researchable topic may already have been defined, and this severely limits the extent to which research can be initiated from the 'grassroots'. Frequently the topics for which funding is available are those that match with the latest government agenda or 'moral panic', with the result that much more research is undertaken on 'problematic' issues (such as young people's involvement in crime or drugs) than on the everyday routine matters, or positive aspects of people's lives.

The nature of research and evaluation

The title of this chapter refers to 'research/evaluation'. Although there is considerable overlap between what we commonly think of as 'research' and 'evaluation', it is important to distinguish between the two. *Research* is a broad term generally associated with a systematic investigation, involving a process of discovery or critical inquiry. According to Robson (2000: 9), it entails the activities of 'description, explanation and understanding'. An example of a piece of research might be a study of the levels and causes of youth crime on a particular housing estate.

Evaluation has a rather narrower meaning – literally 'an assessment of value'. In the field of public services, the importance of evaluation has grown rapidly alongside a growing concern with value for money and the targeting of services to meet the greatest needs. Evaluation involves making a judgement about the worth of a specific activity, project, programme or policy. An example of an evaluation might be a study of the effectiveness of a particular youth crime project in reducing reoffending on an estate. Insofar as evaluation should involve careful and systematic inquiry, then we would argue that it is a particular type of research. Sometimes the terms 'evaluation research' or 'evaluative research' are used (see, for example, Cheetham et al., 1992). It is in this sense that we are using the term 'evaluation' here.

Practitioner research

Often practitioners may find they are involved in research – whether as a researcher, commissioner, consultee, research user or a combination of these. In this chapter we are specifically concerned with the practitioner, or student practitioner, as researcher. This type of research has sometimes been termed *practitioner research* (Broad and Fletcher, 1993; Fuller and Petch, 1995). The term is used rather loosely, but tends to denote the fact that the person doing the research is a practising professional in the field they are researching. Therefore they may have insider knowledge and contacts, and a direct interest in both setting the research question and the results of the research. 'Practitioner-researchers' may undertake research in the setting or agency where they work. Alternatively, the research may be undertaken in different agencies/projects or using national data sources. Sometimes the 'practitioner-researcher' is distinguished from the 'academic researcher'. While this is rather a false distinction, it does highlight the fact that practitioner research is usually concerned with practical applications, whereas 'academic' research may be concerned more with understandings or theoretical insights.

Questions for the intending researcher to consider:

■ Do I think of myself as a practitioner-researcher? For example, am I a full-time practitioner researching in my own setting, a part-time student practitioner, a full-time student with practice experience or a full-time researcher with practice experience?

■ What are the advantages and disadvantages of this role?

Applied, action, participatory and emancipatory research

Categorisations such as 'applied research', 'action research', 'participatory research' and 'emancipatory research' are often used in the context of practitioner research. These types of research are not mutually exclusive. A piece of research or evaluation may fall into several categories, to varying degrees, depending on the purposes of the research and the principles by which the key stakeholders wish to operate. But the labels provide some useful headings for researchers to consider when placing themselves in relation to their research.

Applied research

The term 'applied' refers to the fact that the subject matter and findings of the research can be applied to matters of practice or policy relevance (Everitt et al., 1992). This is usually contrasted with 'pure research', where knowledge and understanding may be sought for its own sake. However, this distinction is not clear-cut, and is better thought of as a pure-applied continuum rather than mutually exclusive categories.

Questions for the intending researcher to consider:

■ To what extent is the research in which I will be involved expected to be relevant to policy or practice?

■ What does this mean about who should be involved/consulted in designing the questions and hearing the results?

Action research

This refers to research that has an explicit focus on bringing about change or improvement. This type of research is often undertaken by practitioners (see Hart and Bond, 1995), but not exclusively. A classic example of action research in the UK is the Home Office-sponsored community development projects set up in 12 neighbourhoods in the late 1960s, where teams of researchers from universities worked alongside community workers, feeding in the results of their research as the projects developed, with the aim of contributing both to government understanding of the causes and effective responses to poverty and the improvement of the practice of the projects (see Green, 1992).

Questions for the intending researcher to consider:

■ To what extent will the research focus on the aim of changing or improving policy/practice?

■ Will it inform practice as it proceeds on an ongoing basis?

■ How will this be achieved and what might be the barriers?

Participatory research

Participatory research involves those who might traditionally have been categorised as subjects of research (service users, young people or professional workers, for example) in carrying it out, usually alongside a principal researcher/evaluator (Feuerstein, 1986). The concept of 'stakeholders' is useful in this context, referring to all those who may have a stake in a piece of research, ranging from sponsors/funders to service users. Barr and colleagues (Barr and Hashagen, 2000; Barr, 2003) have developed an increasingly popular model for evaluating community development based on involving as many stakeholders as possible in designing the evaluation. Some people regard 'stakeholder' research/evaluation as a separate category (for example, Robson, 2000: 16–19), but for our purposes we see it as encompassed within 'participatory research', although stakeholders often play more of an advisory than an active participatory role. Participation in research can cover a broad spectrum of involvement, ranging from stakeholders (in particular service users) merely being consulted about design or findings through to them having full control over the whole research process.

Questions for the intending researcher to consider:

■ Who are the stakeholders in the research and to what extent will they be involved at each stage of the research?

■ Will some, all or none be advisors, designers, co-researchers, analysts, report writers?

Emancipatory research

Increasingly the term 'emancipatory' is being used in relation to research that is designed to focus largely on enhancing the power of service users (Zarb, 1992; Dullea and Mullender, 1999). Some of this is located at the radical end of the participatory research spectrum (for example Whitmore, 2001). However, some commentators imply it is a distinctive approach, involving research that clearly originates from and is conducted by service users (Evans and Fisher, 1999: 103). This focus on 'emancipatory research' has developed out of an increasing concern in social welfare work with the empowerment of service users and the promotion of anti-oppressive practice, along with developments in critical social research (Harvey, 1990) and feminist research (Roberts, 1981; Reinharz, 1992).

Critical research and evaluation has been put forward as a model that is particularly appropriate for social work (see Everitt and Hardiker, 1996). This is a form of participatory action research based on critical theory, which aims to work towards developing research participants' understanding of the political and policy context in which they are operating, with a view to bringing about radical change. The focus goes beyond simply developing the skills and confidence of service users by engaging them in the research process as participants, to a more radical educational process, akin to the approach promoted by Paulo Freire (1972), the Brazilian educator, where the aim is to challenge the existing power structures, with a stress on liberation and transformation. Feminist critiques of the traditional model of the researcher as a detached, objective collector of facts have also been influential in social work research and evaluation, with the emphasis on the researcher taking an explicit value position and engaging in reciprocal relationships with research participants (see Humphries, 1999).

Questions for the intending researcher to consider:

■ To what extent can or should the research be empowering in its process (participants gain respect, confidence and skills) and/or its outcomes (it results in changing power structures)?

■ Do all the stakeholders (including the commissioners of the research) share this aim?

■ How can these ideals be put into practice?

Issues of philosophy and values

Traditional social science textbooks and courses on research often start with philosophical questions about *ontology* – the nature of the social world – and *epistemology* – how we come to know the world. Whilst important, a more logical and accessible starting point might be consideration of issues of *ethics* – values and moral commitments about what makes for a good life or society and how we ought to behave towards other people.

Social work and related occupations rest clearly on a value base that entails respect for service users, promotion of their choices and rights and stresses the aim of working towards equality and social justice in society (Banks, 2001). So in taking on a piece of research as a practitioner, we would expect these values to be paramount. Indeed, in their codes of ethics for social work, most professional associations include a section applying to practitioners undertaking research and stress that the research process should be congruent with social work values (for example, BASW, 2002, section 6.3.4). Butler's (2002) code of ethics for social work and social care research states that social work/social care research should, where possible, 'seek to empower service users' and researchers should 'seek to promote emancipatory research'.

Butler's code of ethics for social work research, unlike most of the ethical statements for generic social research (for example British Sociological Association, 2003), seems to commit social work practitioners to a particular type of research endeavour – 'emancipatory research'. However, it is important to bear in mind that, like many codes of ethics, this code encourages the expression of statements of universal ideals that are both open to interpretation and may be impossible, or inappropriate, to achieve in particular contexts (see Banks, 2003). For example, we need to consider whether the research should aim to be emancipatory in its process and/or in its outcomes. We should also be wary of imposing our values on stakeholders who may not share them and hiding behind the illusion of equality in what is still an unequal relationship, as discussed in the previous chapter (see also Humphries, 1997; Shaw, 1999: 118–20 for a discussion of some of these points). There may be situations where improvement or reform is desired, rather than liberation.

Nevertheless, this code is useful in that it reminds us that we need to have the debate about what counts as 'emancipatory', whether 'emancipatory research' is what we can or should be doing, and if not, why not? It reminds us that it is important to offer an alternative to the traditional model, in a climate where much research and evaluation is commissioned and controlled by government bodies and senior agency managers, with the assumption that service users will feed into the process as passive respondents. The practitioner-researcher's own ideological and value position will inevitably make a difference to the type of research approach chosen. However, this does not preclude the use of traditional research methodologies in bringing about change, as in certain contexts it may be important that research results are regarded as credible in order to make an impact on policy makers.

In the light of this brief discussion, a crucial question for practitioners embarking on a piece of research might be: What are my personal, professional and political values and commitments? This might include considering questions such as:

- Who am I (for example what are my origins, job, gender, ethnicity)?

- Where do I stand on certain issues (such as religion, politics, feminism, ecology)?

- What values do I hold as an individual and a professional practitioner (for example honesty, integrity, equality)?

- Do others share my values?

- What does this mean for how I/we conduct this research?

This involves being clear about which value commitments one might be prepared to negotiate on and which are non-negotiable (see Everitt et al., 1992: 137–8 for a list of values for social work research). It also involves a process of reflexivity – identifying, acknowledging and questioning what we bring with us to the research process (see White, 2001 for a useful discussion of reflexivity in research). This process should continue throughout the process of a piece of research, as practitioner-researchers continually question their own role and interpretations, and stand back and see the people/policies being studied with fresh eyes in a broader social and economic context.

Although research that is participatory and empowering for service users fits well with the values of social work, this approach is fraught with challenges and can be more complex and time-consuming than more traditional models where the researcher has complete control. To illuminate our discussion about some of the practical and ethical issues to take into account in setting up a research project, we outline a research study with which one of the authors was involved.

CASE EXAMPLE

Two researchers from the University of Durham were commissioned to consult with disabled people in a borough in northeast England about a number of planned service developments and, more particularly, to find out how disabled people wished to be consulted in the future. The study was jointly funded by health and social services. The funders initially invited a local voluntary organisation to carry out the study, but as members of the organisation felt they lacked the necessary research expertise and experience to undertake such work, they sought help from the university. The researchers, on the other hand, were concerned that they had no direct experience of disability and would have preferred the work to have been carried out by disabled researchers. After some weeks of negotiations, it was agreed that the researchers would work in partnership with a small group of disabled volunteers from the local agency. They formed a 'research team' that worked together for the duration of the project, with advice from a multi-agency steering group made up of funders, service providers and practitioners.

Clarifying stakeholder expectations

In preparing the ground for a piece of research, there are three key areas worth discussing with the main stakeholders in advance and these are discussed below.

Clarifying purposes

If the research has been commissioned, or there is a process of negotiating with a host agency or group of service users, it is important to identify the various stakeholders in the research and discuss what they want to get out of it. Discussion with potential research participants and other stakeholders can also help to clarify the purpose of the research, highlight differences in expectations and stimulate the rethinking of a project.

If undertaking an evaluation, it is important to be clear whether the key stakeholders agree on its main focus. Robson (2000: 48–9) identifies four types of evaluation as follows:

1. *Evaluation of needs* – study of the extent to which the needs of an existing programme's target group are being met, or a needs analysis in preparation for planning a new programme

2. *Processes* – analysis of how the programme is working, who takes part, what happens on a day-to-day basis

3. *Outcomes* – analysis of the effect or impact of the programme on those taking part, or beyond

4. *Efficiency* – consideration of how the beneficial effects compare with the costs of running the programme.

An evaluation can also be *formative/developmental* – feeding in findings and ideas for improvement on an ongoing basis – or *summative* – making a judgement about the success of a project at the end. Action research projects may do both, but sometimes these roles fit together uneasily. Robson (2000: 52) distinguishes the different emphases in formative and summative evaluations. Formative evaluations tend to stress gathering information on processes, with the credibility of the evaluator depending on an understanding of the programme and rapport with the users/staff, whereas summative evaluations may focus more on outcomes, with credibility depending on technical competence and impartiality. Trying to do both, as inevitably happens in a two- or three-year ongoing evaluation, can be problematic for a researcher, who seeks acceptance as a semi-insider/critical friend, but also needs distance as an expert observer.

Clarifying principles

Having read a lot of literature on user empowerment, emancipatory research and research ethics, practitioner-researchers should have an idea about the values they want to underpin the research and how these translate into practice principles. However, these should be discussed and debated with stakeholders to develop a mutually agreed set of principles. Compromises may need to be made as we cannot assume that a researcher's high-minded ideals for maximum participation, power-sharing and radical action for change will be shared by any or all the various stakeholders.

In the case example, the researchers and volunteers in the research team worked together to explore the most appropriate way they could achieve the aims of the project. Each member of the team brought to the discussions their knowledge, experiences, values and beliefs. The volunteers had a strong influence in establishing some general principles, which the researchers had to ensure were met by the research methods they proposed. In this way, the principles formed an important framework within which the methodology had to operate (Barnes and Kendall, 2001). The principles adopted were:

- To work to a social model of disability, while respecting the important contribution that health services make to the lives of disabled people

- To work towards the inclusion of all disabled people aged between 18 and 65 who live in the borough, irrespective of whether they use health or social care services

▪ To ensure reciprocity by recognising that learning is a two-way process

▪ To aim for sustainability and continuation after the project

▪ To respect differences, giving participants a choice of ways in which to engage with the project

▪ To accept that the project provides a first stage towards empowerment

▪ To encourage better understanding of local service users' experiences and expectations of services through the use of qualitative research methods

▪ To value the knowledge, skills and expertise of all participants.

Clarifying roles and responsibilities

If the research design and process is to be a collaborative one, it is important to be as clear as possible at the outset what role the various stakeholders in the research will play. In the case example, five stakeholder groups were identified who wished to contribute to the study and therefore had to agree their roles and responsibilities, as described below:

1. *Commissioners* drew up a specification for the study and agreed to participate in an advisory group, which would meet for a fixed number of meetings to steer the project. They also made a commitment to taking action after the study had reported.

2. The *voluntary organisation* that had contracted the researchers agreed a substantial role in the project. The chief executive became a member of the advisory group. As the organisation and its staff were well known to disabled people in the town, they agreed to provide support for the volunteer researchers, administrative support and personal assistants for the focus groups and use of their database. For reasons of confidentiality, the research team could not have direct access to the database of names and addresses but the agency agreed to mail out a letter and questionnaire from researchers.

3. The *volunteer researchers* agreed to attend meetings to plan and manage the research. They only wished to have a small role in data collection because of limited energy and restricted mobility but they assisted in the focus groups and the survey administration. They also negotiated to attend the university to learn about data analysis and be involved in interpreting the findings. They did not wish to take responsibility for writing up the research but they agreed to read and comment on drafts. No powers of veto were discussed. However, recommendations were to be decided by the volunteers on discussion with the researchers and then presented locally by the volunteers. The volunteers also agreed to do what they could to ensure that the findings of the report were acted on.

4. The *researchers* agreed to take responsibility for seeing that the research was completed but their role was to be complementary to the volunteers. Expertise on disability issues and the locality would be provided by the volunteers, while research expertise would be provided by the researchers. In carrying out the research, the researchers would undertake the work that the volunteers did not wish or feel able to carry out.

5. *Service providers* gave the research team access to their services to meet with service users. Managers of key services agreed to introduce their service plans to focus groups which were held to discuss the proposals but to withdraw after their presentation if that was the wish of the group. Should conflicts arise in the research team, the chief executive of the voluntary agency agreed to provide support for the volunteers while the professional researchers would access supervision at the university.

Negotiating ethical issues

There is an increasing concern with ethical issues in research. The majority of recent textbooks on social research methods include a chapter on this theme (for example, Hammersley and Atkinson, 1995: 261–87; Bryman, 2001: 475–86; Bulmer, 2001) and there are several complete books on research ethics (Homan, 1991; Oliver, 2003). We cannot go into all the possible issues here, but will highlight several that are particularly important and may have added complexities in the context of participatory research with service users, to which many of the generic social research textbooks give little attention.

Rights of the sponsors/commissioners

If your research is being funded by an external body, certain conditions might be placed on the research, and if the research has actually been commissioned, then the controls imposed in the contract may be tighter still. Contract researchers may be left with little choice – acceptance of the contract as presented or rejection of the research commission. However, there may be room for negotiation, so it is worth thinking through in advance the implications of some of the implicit and explicit agreements with sponsors to ensure that they do not attempt to control the research process and findings in a way that may stifle justified criticism of policy, organisations or practice. In the case example, the research questions, timescale, costs and format of the final report were found to be non-negotiable, but the use of a participatory method was accepted, with all the uncertainties it brought about how the study might be conducted and the methodologies used.

The commissioner of a piece of research may ask to see a draft copy of your report and exercise the right to suggest or make amendments. While Oliver (2003) suggests that this is not desirable, as they may wish to change findings that are inconvenient to them, the risk is reduced in the kind of research/evaluation that we are looking at in this chapter. The commissioner of the research may be part of a stakeholder advisory group (as in the case example) and will share the role of feeding in views and amendments with other stakeholders. The issue to determine in advance is whether they have the right of veto, or are just regarded as part of a broader decision-making group. It is also important to plan in advance how any steering group will operate – seeking consensus, voting if necessary, giving the right of veto to certain parties.

Gaining permission/access

If you wish to undertake a piece of research that involves accessing records, staff and/or service users in a social work, health or related setting, you are likely to have to seek permission from more than one body or gatekeeper. For research in a health service setting (such as a hospital or clinic, which may sometimes be sites for social work research), a proposal outlining the full details of the research and methods to be used will have to be submitted to a research ethics committee if your research involves patients/service users.

Most universities also operate research ethics committees, and in some cases social work departments have their own committees that approve student disser-tation proposals. The purpose of such committees is to ensure that researchers do not engage in practices that exploit or harm service users, or collect information that does not contribute to answering the research questions. They also see that appropriate safeguards are in place for consent, confidentiality, anonymity and so on (as outlined below).

Gaining approval from a health service research ethics committee can be a lengthy process and may involve minor or substantial changes in your research proposal, or even its rejection. For pieces of social work research that are based on involving service users in research design and planning, the requirement to specify in advance details of the approach and methods can be restricting. Some research ethics committees may have little appreciation of the principles and methods of participatory action research, so it is important to justify the legiti-macy of such an approach.

Once past this hurdle, it may be important to gain permission from 'gatekeepers', such as hospital consultants, project managers, directors of social services departments or head teachers, in order to access the users of their services. It is then crucial to seek permission from the people you want to work with. Traditionally they have been the last people to be asked about participating in the research, if, indeed, they are asked at all.

Asking for consent

The principle of seeking the informed consent of research participants is now a standard requirement in all social research. Seeking informed consent is particu-larly important in a social work context, in that it is a mark of respect to research participants and offers them the right not to participate. It also gives some protection to researchers from later complaints or litigation. However, gaining informed consent is not a straightforward matter. Homan (1991: 71) offers a useful analysis of what might be meant by 'informed' and 'consent', as follows:

Informed

- That all pertinent aspects of what is to occur and what might occur are disclosed to the subject

- The subject should be able to understand this information.

Consent

- The subject is competent to make a rational and mature judgement

- The agreement to participate should be voluntary and free from coercion and undue influence.

This definition prompts the question of whether informed consent can ever really be given – often we do not know what might happen as a result of the research, especially in a social work context when it is participatory, with others taking part and steering its direction. And how do we judge the 'competence' of someone to understand the nature of research? All we can do is think carefully about what information a potential participant needs to know, and can understand.

There are particular issues in social work research, which may often be undertaken with people who are sick, young or vulnerable in other ways. It may be easy to manipulate or persuade people to agree to something they do not fully understand, especially if we already have a professional relationship with them. We have to decide when it is appropriate to seek 'proxy' consent from a guardian, parent or carer. On some occasions we may need to seek consent from both service users and family members/carers as the research may have an impact on both parties. With social work research that is user-led and/or participatory, it is important to consider whose responsibility it is to seek consent and whether and how to differentiate between researcher users and users who are respondents or interviewees.

There is also the question of whether it is ever ethical to undertake research into aspects of people's lives without informing them that you are doing so. This is an area of debate within the social research community – with some people arguing that *covert research* may be necessary to gain data that would not be otherwise available in order to further human knowledge, and others arguing that such research should never be done. There is an issue of what counts as 'covert research', how much 'deception' is involved and whether it is acceptable in public places. For example, it might be regarded as acceptable for a researcher to undertake observations of teacher–children interactions in a classroom without informing the participants that she is looking for differences in the way boys and girls are treated (because the teachers may change their behaviour accordingly). However, it might be regarded as highly questionable for a researcher to disguise his or her identity and take on the role of look out (or 'watch queen') in a men's public lavatory in order to gain information on 'impersonal sexual relations', as Humphreys did in his highly controversial study in 1975. In participatory and practitioner research in social work, the issue of hiding the researcher's identity is rarely feasible and would generally be regarded as unethical.

Maintaining privacy

The commitment on the part of researchers to respect the right to privacy of the research participants is particularly important in practitioner research in a social work context. According to Bok (1984: 10–11), 'privacy is the condition of being protected from unwanted access by others – either physical access, personal information, or attention'.

If the research involves interviewing or observing people, it is important to be clear with participants, at the time their consent is sought, to what extent confidentiality and anonymity will be preserved. Confidentiality involves maintaining secrecy in relation to private information gained in the course of the research relationship that, if revealed, might be damaging to the person concerned. Obviously the main reason for interviewing people is to find out information that can be used in the research and reported in any findings. So to make a blanket promise of confidentiality would be rather counterproductive. Usually what can be offered is anonymity, that is, removing identifying features so that the source of the information cannot be identified.

Particular thought may need to be given to issues around privacy in relation to participatory research in social work where service users may be interviewing other service users and may come to know sensitive information. When writing up the research, it may be hard to ensure anonymity, as members of the project, service or tightly knit community may easily recognise the turn of phrase used by people they know, or a description may only fit one person (for example chair of the management committee). As Woodman et al. (1995: 61) point out in relation to researching the lesbian community: 'even with the careful elimination of names in the write-up, it may be possible to identify participants through demographic data published in the results'.

CONCLUSION

When embarking upon a piece of research/evaluation, particularly if the evaluation is intended to be participative, there are a number of preparatory questions that should be considered before detailed plans for the methodology can be drawn up. It is helpful to try to predict some of the potential difficulties in advance. This requires you to be flexible in your planning and allow plenty of time. Some of the issues for consideration include:

- Clarifying the purpose of the research, as this will guide the broad approach to be taken and the role you might play in the work

- Identifying who the stakeholders will be, the roles they might play and their lines of responsibility and accountability

- Negotiating the principles by which the research will be pursued with the stakeholders (such as reciprocity, open communication, respect for difference), including reference to codes of practice/conduct (for example BASW, BSA)

- Negotiating acceptable constraints with funders or commissioners to ensure that the research can be conducted and reported as the participants would wish

■ Identifying who might be the gatekeepers to the individuals and data required

■ Considering what can/should be promised with respect to anonymity and privacy and how you will reach people not normally reached (for example deaf people).

Some of these considerations may have to be revisited when the research methodology has been agreed. Thinking about research is a constant process and research design is not a linear activity, but rather an iterative process in which issues are discussed and renegotiated until the best possible approach can be found. Inevitably, in participatory research, with a number of stakeholders to satisfy, the set-up phase can be challenging, but good preparation can help all participants to understand the research and therefore contribute to it and own its results.

FURTHER READING

Bryman, A. (2001) *Social Research Methods* (Oxford: Oxford University Press). A comprehensive overview of research methods designed for students, including chapters on research designs, ethics and conducting a small-scale project.

Evans, C. and Fisher, M. (1999) 'Collaborative Evaluation with Service Users', in Shaw, I. and Lishman, J. (eds) *Evaluation and Social Work Practice*. (London: Sage) pp. 101–17. Thoughtful practical discussion of the issues surrounding user-led and user-controlled research.

Fuller, R. and Petch, A. (eds) (1995) *Practitioner Research. The Reflective Social Worker* (Buckingham: Open University Press). Good overview of the nature of practitioner research, with chapters covering examples of research by practitioners.

Hart, E. and Bond, M. (1995) *Action Research for Health and Social Care: A Guide to Practice* (Milton Keynes: Open University Press). Useful coverage of action research, with chapters on examples from the authors' own practice.

Oliver, P. (2003) *The Student's Guide to Research Ethics* (Maidenhead: Open University Press/McGraw-Hill Education). Accessible text with exercises covering practical aspects of research ethics from a rather traditional perspective.

Carrying Out Research in Social Work

Helen Brown

Introduction

Research, like social work, is primarily a practical activity and, like most practical activities, to be conducted in a capable fashion requires relevant and applicable knowledge to achieve desirable outcomes. Like social work, research is a messy social and political activity, fraught with contested ideas, ideological debates and ethical and moral considerations. Both are primarily about 'trying to find out', investigation, assessment, analysis, and synthesis. They are also, it can be argued, about trying to obtain better outcomes.

This chapter will draw on two examples of very different types of research to apply themes related to the 'practice' of research in social work. These themes will be explored via the vehicles of the research examples. The only commonality of these two research examples is that they are both small scale and qualitative in nature. The two pieces of research are, firstly, work that Buchanan (1999) would describe as 'practice experience' and secondly, a time-limited commissioned piece of action research. The first is my own work on the development of social work practice with lesbians and gay men. The second is research evaluation that I managed, in its early years of life, on the integration of care management and the Care Programme Approach (CPA) for people with severe mental health problems in one local authority. Although these two pieces of research are quite different, the following themes emerge from them to differing degrees. These are:

- The endeavour of trying to obtain better outcomes for service users through knowledge generation

- Service user involvement in research

- The role of the practitioner-researcher and their visibility within knowledge production

- Research findings and their application to practice.

Trying to obtain better outcomes for service users through knowledge generation

I have assumed, within the introduction to this chapter, that social work research has at the core of its purpose the improvement of social work practice and service provision. As a consequence of the application of social work findings, it follows that the lot of the users of social work and its services will be improved. It would be a cynical author who would argue otherwise. However, the practice of research does not happen within a vacuum but rather in a space that is fraught with political, economic and social constraints and the research output might be used in ways that are not totally controlled by the researcher.

Funding

Research, like many other practical activities, has to be financially resourced in order to take place. Interestingly, very little is written about the relationship between money and social work knowledge generation, despite the acquisition of money absorbing considerable amounts of time and energy on the part of social work researchers. Research funding and the generation of research knowledge are of course intricately linked and the values and motivations of the funders may impact on the research process and consequently on the resulting research outcome.

Sheldon (2001: 807), writing about the research related to cognitive-behavioural intervention outcomes, says that:

> the reason for the appearance of cognitive-behavioural references in CEBSS' [The Centre for Evidence-Based Social Services] work on childcare, mental health, learning disability and the rehabilitation of frail elderly people, is that the most rigorous (that is, the most bias-reducing) studies in these fields and many related ones, show that nothing ever does better.

Although he may be right, he omits to say that research looking at cognitive-behavioural interventions, particularly that conducted in clinical settings, is more likely to be funded than many other approaches, not least because it is relatively straightforward to create a credible research design around such interventions. Moreover, such interventions have been proven to have positive short-term outcomes and are therefore considered worthy of further evaluative research funding. This tendency for certain types of interventions to have evidence-based research to underpin them might have more to do with the politics of funding certain types of interventions, research designs and approaches, than the interventions themselves being more effective. Other theoretically oriented interventions may be underresearched because the evaluation of their effectiveness might be less attractive to funders.

The funding of research has also become of central concern to universities, the sites in which much research activity takes place. It is not just a question of researchers being able to secure funding for their research but for universities to secure research as an income generation activity for themselves. Research is crucial for many universities' finances both in relation to securing research assessment exercise (RAE) monies from the Higher Education Funding Council for England (HEFCE) but also by successfully bidding for research tenders. This can mean that researchers are focusing considerable energies in relation to income generation activities for their higher education institutions rather than generating knowledge to enhance the capability and effectiveness of social work practitioners for the benefit of service users.

Any piece of research has a number of interested stakeholders: service users, carers, agencies, the research institution, social work practitioners and managers. The funder of the research is also an interested party. However, in social work research reports and publications this is rarely made explicit. Indeed the funding of the research is often not mentioned at all. One of the advantages of government department-funded research is that the funding is at least explicit. This explicitness about the funding of research is a necessary part of the 'visibility' of the research process. It is an essential part of the information necessary for a practitioner, policy maker or member of the public to be able to assess the reliability and validity of the research findings in relation to potential bias. This lack of visibility would be considered sloppy, indeed unethical, in other subject areas. For example, we would find it extraordinary if a research report evaluating the efficacy of a drug, funded by a pharmaceutical company, did not make explicit the funding arrangements. The funding of research by partial stakeholders does not necessarily undermine the rigour or reliability of the research process or the findings but it is necessary for this to be explicit.

Politics with a small 'p'

As stated earlier, research does not happen within a vacuum but rather in a political, economic and social space fraught with constraints that impact throughout the entire research process. The politics of social work research changes according to the social and political context of the moment. However, some of the current debates have been articulated for decades, for example the question of social work's effectiveness (Sheldon, 1978). These debates have been articulated in different ways over time, with the use of such terms as 'effectiveness', 'what works' and 'evidence-based practice' (EBP). Newman and McNeish (2002: 55), arguing the case for evidence-based practice, write:

> While a degree of controversy surrounds the applicability of evidence based practice to social work, with some concerns that this will over value technocratic

solutions to human problems, the empowering potential for users and practitioners in having interventions based on sound evidence is substantial.

They go on to say in relation to childcare:

> we suggest that evidence-based childcare practice may be defined as a process of systematically locating, critically reviewing and using research findings as the basis for decisions in child care practice.

Their aspirations are indeed laudable and it might be difficult to imagine why this might generate 'controversy'; probably best articulated by the debate between Sheldon and Webb in two articles published in 2001 (Sheldon, 2001; Webb, 2001). The essential component of Newman and McNeish's definition is 'critically reviewing' the research findings. This is also articulated by Sellick and Thoburn (1996: 26), in relation to childcare, when they write:

> when it comes to using research to throw light on specific decisions to be made about specific children, there is no alternative to a careful scrutiny of the studies which seem most relevant. An appraisal must then be made as to the validity of their conclusions in the context of the specific case.

If this is lost, the uncritical application of research findings to individual cases can, in my experience, be as damaging to service users as research ignorance. The difficulty of 'ideological camps' developing in relation to EBP is that inevitably there is a hardening of views and a simplification of the other's argument, which militates against this 'critical analysis' and this 'careful scrutiny'. We need both if we are to endeavour to improve outcomes for service users.

Research examples

Both research examples in this chapter had the improvement of practice as their key purpose. The work relating to social work with lesbians and gay men was inductive, meaning that the ideas that were developed arose out of the consideration of practice. The writing was the culmination of ten years in social work practice as a social worker and a team leader of a generic team in an inner London social services department during the 1980s. The writing was a synthesis of my reflections on practice experience and literature reviews, the culmination of which were a number of publications (Brown, 1991, 1992, 1998a, b, c). These publications fall within what Fuller and Petch (1995) refer to as 'practitioner research' and Buchanan (1999) refers to as 'practice experience' – they could not be described as 'evidence-based'.

The publications were a record of my practice experience, reflections, contribution to and learning from practice. Why the subject area? My experience in social services entailed a lot of work with lesbian service users, because of demographic peculiarities in relation to the geographical location of the social services department. My experience exposed me to the degree of anxiety that homosexuality in combination with social work provoked in social workers, social and health-related professionals and agencies, as well as the degree of fear and ignorance it aroused, to the detriment of outcomes for clients. As a lesbian with my own children and a then trade union activist in relation to lesbian and gay men's rights, I was confronted by what I considered the problematic nature of many of the approaches towards working with lesbians and gay men. However, it was also my experience that it was possible to offer effective social work interventions and services to lesbians and gay men, when the anxiety was contained. The 'practice experience' writings were what I described as 'one contribution to the knowledge base on which social workers may discriminatingly draw' (Brown, 1998a: 7), with the hope that 'when we engage with or intervene in the lives of lesbians and gay men, our interventions and the services we provide are competent' (1998a: 137).

The mental health action research – implementing and evaluating the outcome of the integration of assessment and care management and the CPA – was also about improving service users' experiences. The aim of the research project was to examine in detail how an integrated model of care management and the CPA could be developed, implemented and evaluated within one local authority. A mental health trust, a local authority, a health authority and a university jointly funded the research. The research started in 1998 and the final research report is imminent. The funding arrangements were explicit and the management of the research, although located within the university, was also shared with a research project management group, which was separate from the research steering group. The political context was directly related to the mental health initiatives developed by the government during the 1990s (Department of Health, 1990, 1996). This action research was intended to lead to an integrated approach to the care of people with serious mental ill-health. The integration related to professional groups working together as well as the integration of care management and CPA. The intention of the integration of both was to improve the quality of experience for mental health service users.

How do we really know whether or not both research endeavours realised their intentions of trying to better outcomes for service users? This is an often unanswered question in relation to the impact of research and remains unanswered here as well.

Service user involvement in research

Within the mental health research example, service users' involvement in every area of the research was intended. However, in the research example related to social work with lesbians and gay men, the lack of empirical research, other than a small piece drawn on in one publication (Brown, 1998a), meant two things in relation to the work. Firstly, there was no opportunity to 'test' deductively (the testing of existing ideas through research) ideas developed within the publications and, secondly, the inclusion of empirical research could have given a voice to service users and social workers. The voices of both these groups were aired through my interpretations but never directly and that was a major limitation.

Beresford (2000), discussing service users' involvement in research, argues that funders increasingly expect researchers to include service users. The mental health research example included service users at an organisational level (a mental health service user group was one of the stakeholders), as researchers and as interviewers. The involvement of mental health service users had to be sufficiently flexible and resourceful to manage periods when individuals were too unwell to participate fully. These periods of unwellness, for a minority of service user participants, did impact on the timetable of the project and the degree of user participation at different times. For this research project this was manageable, as the stakeholders were sufficiently flexible and realistic in relation to the overall management of the process. However in different circumstances, with a tighter timetable and limited funding, the outcome might have been different.

Beresford, writing about service users' generation of knowledge, writes:

> to set in train an inclusive process of theory development means working towards equality between service users and other actors in discussion and action in three main ways. These are equality of respect; equality of validity of contributions and equality of ownership and control of the debate and of knowledge.
>
> (2000: 500)

In the mental health research example, although at the start of the project there was, I would argue, equality of respect, during the project's life there was a change in relation to Beresford's last point; 'equality of ownership and control of the debate and knowledge'. At the start of the project the management group controlled the generation and ownership of the knowledge. However, towards the end of the project, there had been greater involvement of mental health service users in the generation and ownership of knowledge. In the final stage of the research project, after the stakeholders had implemented the integration of assessment, care management and the CPA, the research management group negotiated with a service users' organisation, working in partnership to recruit and train service users to conduct user-focused monitoring interviews with service users subject to CPA about its effectiveness. Both the research management group and the mental health service user organisation were responsible for the support of the service user interviewers, who were paid for their attendance at training as well as their interviewing work.

The training was run by a researcher and a service user consultant and included the definition of user-focused monitoring, care management and CPA, the purpose of the interviews and the draft interview schedule, confidentiality, 'tricky situations' and practice interviews.

The involvement of service users as research interviewers led to an improvement of the interview tools. For example, the interviewers suggested the development of an information pack, including a fact sheet explaining care management and CPA, notes involving practical tips for interviewers and a sheet on confidentiality, including a description of how and when confidentiality might be broken. Pilot interviews were conducted and the interview schedule was altered in accordance with the feedback. Thirty-three interviews were conducted. Hansen (2003: 3) writes: 'the interviewers were very interested and motivated to carry out the project … interviewers participated in the meetings and showed their commitment by making many positive and imaginative suggestions for the project'. Some aspects of the research findings have still to be presented and Hansen writes in relation to service users involvement in this aspect of the project:

> it is hoped that the service user interviewers will be involved in both the planning of the presentation as well as in the actual presentation. It is also hoped that the service users who have been trained and who now are quite experienced interviewers will continue to play a role in auditing and monitoring mental health services.
>
> (Hansen, 2003: 4)

The level of participation of service users and collaboration between the research project and service users developed considerably over a four-year period, moving from service user representation on the steering group and the management group to full participation, being joint generators of service user and mental health knowledge. Evans and Fisher (1999: 104) define user-controlled research in the following terms:

> It must bring service users greater power to define their needs and the outcomes that matter to them. Service users must select the issues for research and acquire control over the funds to conduct it. We think that service users should wherever possible become researchers, so that their influence pervades the research; this includes responsibility for data analysis and for dissemination.

The above research example falls short of their definition and to be fair it was never intended to be user-controlled research. However, during the project's development, service user involvement did move from a position of representation to collaboration. This collaboration undoubtedly increased the validity of the research findings, their legitimacy and their usefulness in relation to their application to practice.

The role of the practitioner researcher and their visibility within knowledge production

In the mental health research example, the lead researcher was a mental health practitioner of many years standing, however she was not conducting the research in her own work setting. Whereas in the research example which looked at the development of social work with lesbians and gay men, I drew on my experiences and data collection over a fifteen-year period. This material was interpreted through my eyes and mind alone, whereas the mental health research example findings were analysed and processed through many individuals' eyes and minds, therefore drawing on a variety of experiences, views and intellects.

If it is legitimate to use 'practice experience' as one type of knowledge to inform social work practice, a position I am advocating, we need to be careful about what this 'practice experience' is and how it is used. Macdonald and Macdonald (1999), when discussing ethical issues in social work, give an excellent example of the misuse of 'practice experience' in relation to child sexual abuse:

in the constant search for 'tools' which aid the therapeutic process with abused children and adults, we have found a new medium which seems in many ways ideal for post-disclosure therapy. This medium is ice. It can be very cheaply made in large amounts, and sustains a child's interest.

(Zelickman and Martin, 1991, quoted in Macdonald and Macdonald, 1999: 48)

Quite how ice, in this context, is 'therapeutic' is at the very least debatable. For other practitioners to draw on this 'practitioner experience' intervention which is neither proven nor tested might legitimately be argued as being less than ethical. It might well be pleasurable to play with ice but that is quite different from arguing that it is a 'therapeutic tool'.

My 'research' on social work practice with lesbians and gay men is, as I said in the introduction, what Buchanan (1999) refers to as 'practice experience', and as such falls within what Fuller and Petch (1995) describe as 'practitioner research'. However, the related publications were not just a record of experience. The experience was processed through reflection and my own subjective interpretation and understanding of my biography which inevitably affected that reflection.

There are arguments against the use of practitioner experience and examples of its misuse (like the ice example above) which question the validity and usefulness of such contributions to knowledge. If we are to use practice experience, we need to make sure it meets certain criteria and is not purely anecdotal description. I am arguing that the knowledge base of social work should be and indeed has to be more than the collection of 'research evidence' and needs also to include 'practice experience'. The role of ideas and records of practice are also valid contributions to knowledge.

Reflection is an activity embedded at the heart of research, which takes place throughout the entire research process. What is 'reflection'? It is a concept used both in practice and in research, often referred to as 'reflection' in practice and 'reflexivity' in research (although in reality the processes are very similar). A major exponent of the practice reflection model was Schön (1983) who referred to 'thinking-in-action'. Through this inductive process the practitioner developed perceptions and ideas. Schön (1983: 61) argued that reflection also happened in retrospect: 'they may do this in a mood of idle speculation, or in a deliberate effort to prepare themselves for future cases'. Alsop and Ryan (1996: 184) also recognised the retrospective nature of reflection. They suggested that the reflective practitioner 'must arrest a particular moment in time, ponder over it, go back through it and only then will you gain insights into different aspects of the situation'. My publications fell within this retrospective reflective approach and as such were inductive, in that my ideas developed as a result of reflection upon the preceding practice, designed to enable myself and others to prepare for future practice.

McCarthy (1999) identified reflexivity within research as one of the key components of feminist research methodology. Reflexivity was a key element of my research process. As part of feminism's contribution to reflexive research, it located the subjective researcher visibly within the research process, as well as developing critical self-awareness of the research endeavour. 'Reflection means interpreting one's own interpretations, looking at one's perspectives from others' perspectives, and turning a self-critical eye onto one's own authority as interpreter and author' (Alvesson and Skoldberg, 2000: vii). The same authors argued that as well as having an inward-looking eye in relation to the research process, there was also the need for an outward-looking eye:

> Reflection means thinking about the conditions for what one is doing, investigating the way in which the theoretical, cultural and political context of individual and intellectual involvement affects interaction with whatever is being researched, often in ways difficult to become conscious of.
>
> (Alvesson and Skoldberg, 2000: 245)

Feminist researchers pioneered the concern with the reflexivity of the researcher and his/her awareness of self at a time when there was, within academia, less acceptance of this approach. In 1983 Stanley and Wise argued:

> We feel that it is inevitable that the researcher's own experiences and consciousness will be involved in the research process as much as they are in life, and we shall argue that all research must be concerned with the experiences and consciousness of the researcher as an integral part of the research process.
>
> (1983: 48)

Social work as a profession had accepted this position as part of the psychodynamic social casework tradition long before 1983, whereas mainstream positivist research was still resistant to these ideas. Wise, both a social worker and an academic, used her reflective approach as a social worker and her reflexivity as a researcher to good effect in an important contribution to the feminist social work literature in a monograph, where she reflected upon her work as a local authority social worker (Wise, 1985).

Another way of articulating the above is to emphasise the need to make the subjective experience and consciousness of the researcher explicit. Crowley and Himmelweit (1992: 7) defined subjectivity as 'that combination of conscious and unconscious thoughts and emotions that make up our sense of ourselves, our relations to the world and our ability to act in that world'. One of the differences between the psychodynamic tradition in social work and what Stanley and Wise argue in relation to research is the role of the unconscious, in the former tradition. Holloway and Jefferson (2000) brought these two areas together in what they described as 'defended subjectivity'. They argued that it is not easy to 'know' our subjective selves as researchers because we are defended against 'knowing' as part of the normal mechanisms of 'defences against anxiety'. Whether or not we agree with their psychoanalytic approach, I would agree that 'knowing' your own thought processes, both conscious and unconscious, is a complex business and we only partially 'know' ourselves as the researcher. There will be areas of our unconscious that may influence our research approaches of which we remain unaware. So to be a visible researcher is only ever to be partially visible, but the commitment to work towards achieving that visibility will improve the rigour of the research process and enhance the ethical dimension.

My own flawed contribution to knowledge generation relating to the development of social work with lesbians and gay men involved a number of related activities, based on a critical review of the literature, particularly analysis and synthesis. In the preparations for writing the publications I reviewed the literature using content analysis, although somewhat loosely. I drew on the widest literature I could as I was exploring areas about which little had been written. I used electronic databases to gather relevant texts and extensively used Gays the Word bookshop in London, which had a wealth of information and its finger on the pulse in relation to relevant publications in the UK, America and Australia. I only used secondary sources written in English and written predominately from the 1960s onwards.

My subjective approach, which also tried to be rigorous, fell in line with Hart's (1998: 13) definition of a literature review:

> The selection of available documents (both published and unpublished) on the topic, which contain information from a particular standpoint to fulfil certain aims or expose certain views on the nature of the topic and how it is to be investigated, and the effective evaluation of these documents in relation to the research.

I had available to me a range of primary sources, because of my own biography, which I utilised within the publications. These included:

- Five years of supervision notes from when I was a team leader in a social services department

- Trade union material from the 1980s and 90s including NALGO, UNISON, NAPO, AUT, and NATFHE

- My own High Court expert advice notes

- Notes from relevant conferences from 1982

- Fostering panel minutes

- My own training materials used in consultancy and training events that I had run

- Documents made available to me from the New South Wales Anti-discriminatory Board.

These primary sources were crucial in that they were part of a three-pronged approach in relation to checking the validity of my subjective reflections. They were part of a process of triangulation in checking my reflections against the secondary sources of the time as well as my own primary sources. What became evident was that sometimes my memory of events was different from the records evidenced in the primary sources.

I used a 'loose' form of content analysis for analysing my primary sources as I had with the reading of the literature. This method of analysis has been associated primarily with the analysis of documents (Denscombe, 1998). However, it has also been used to analyse such 'documents' as interview transcripts. For my purposes, drawing on original documents as well as the existing literature content analysis proved to be a useful tool. However, this did not mean that I adopted the process to the letter and methodically on all occasions over a ten-year period.

To illustrate this, I will discuss child protection issues in lesbian families, an area considered in two of the publications (Brown, 1992, 1998a). The 'primary sources' drawn on were five years of supervision notes and a research report I wrote for a local authority in relation to lesbian and gay issues in childcare. The supervision notes were carefully read and the content in relation to lesbian households identified. A subcategory from the 'lesbian households' category was 'child protection issues', which were duly identified. Another category identified from the supervisory notes was 'child protection' (in relation to the whole service user population) and a subcategory identified from that was 'professional fear'. These two subcategories; 'professional fear' and 'child protection in lesbian households' were then compared. This comparison revealed that lesbian and gay social workers working with child protection cases often manifested fear in relation to being inappropriately 'outed', as opposed to being physically harmed, which was the fear of the heterosexual workers (Brown, 1992: 16, 1998a: 81). I was key to this process because I defined the categories and decided what and how the content was analysed, so inevitably it was a subjective and biased process.

The publications were the product of my reflection upon practice and my reflexivity as a researcher, synthesised with both the secondary and primary data. The analysis occurred as part of the reflection on practice as well as the reading of the literature; the synthesis was the bringing together of both processes. I am arguing that practice experience, if we are to use it as one aspect of knowledge, needs to include these processes and not remain purely at the level of anecdotal description, as with the 'ice' example above.

Hart (1998) describes analysis and synthesis simply as follows: 'analysis is the job of systematically breaking down something into its component parts and describing how they relate to each other – it is not random dissection but a methodological examination'. Synthesis is: 'the act of making connections between the parts identified in analysis. It is not simply a matter of reassembling the parts into the original order, but looking for a new order' (1998: 110). I am not arguing that we have to 'create a new order' in its wider meaning, but that for practice experience to have legitimacy, as one component of social work knowledge, we need to analyse both a significant amount of practice and literature which are then synthesised into new material.

CONCLUSION

The two examples of small-scale social work research cited in this chapter highlight four main points for both researchers and practitioners using research to bear in mind:

1. The involvement of service users in all aspects of the research process doesn't just add to the legitimacy of the creation of knowledge but is also likely to improve the quality of the research output.

2. If we are going to use 'practice experience' as part of social work knowledge, we need to develop further guidance about the processes by which this 'knowledge' is generated to ensure that such 'knowledge' has sufficient legitimacy.

3. We must remember that 'evidence' is always contested and that 'knowledge', within our lifetimes, will only ever be partial.

4. The application of research findings to practice is not a precise science and needs to be approached with humility and caution.

Research is about the general and social work is about the specific and the particular. General research 'findings' have to be treated with great caution when applying them to individual cases. 'Research literacy' should involve understanding research but also, in the social work context, assessing its relevance to the unique and specific individuals and circumstances being worked with. It is helpful as guidance but it does not provide certainty. Both research examples within this chapter were practitioner research contributions to that 'guidance' and will hopefully be used alongside other research which will be various in its nature and should include a breadth of different 'types' of research from 'practice experience' through to random controlled trials. Both research examples, although very different and with their own limitations, offer qualitative material to add to the detail and depth of social work knowledge.

The debates regarding EBP have as a central theme the legitimate concern of reliability and validity about research findings and their application to practice. The application of research findings to practice is a serious matter as it impacts on people's lives and possibly on their life chances. Webb (2001) and Frost (2002) both discuss the problematic nature of 'evidence' in this context. In the world of lawyers, 'evidence' is always contested and is presented, by definition, in support of a particular argument, it is not assumed to be fact or indeed the truth.

The current preoccupation in some quarters of social work academia, research and policy with EBP can be argued to be as much to do with an inability to stay with the anxiety and ambiguity of 'not knowing', as it is about improving outcomes for service users. Uncertainty and individual assessment are integral to and difficult aspects of critical social work practice. My concern relates to the notion that research about human experience can ever be seen as conclusive and that social workers might apply research 'evidence' in a mechanistic, procedural fashion, irrespective of the detail of specific individuals and circumstances. This is as dangerous as research ignorance. Also this positivist paradigm of research gives only certain types of information, it does not reveal the detail, ambiguity and complexity of lived experience which, I believe, can only be revealed through qualitative research approaches. In other words, it has its place in helping to throw light on specific problems and interventions, but not to the exclusion of other methods of research. Macdonald and Macdonald (1995: 46) write tellingly of their view of research: 'research might be viewed as the continual battle against the bewitchment of our senses by immediate experience'. In contrast to this position, I would see research as the analysis of the bewitchment and a recording of that experience and the Macdonald approach as a defence against the anxiety that both provoke.

Acknowledgement

I would like to acknowledge the work of Grethe Hansen in the writing of this chapter.

FURTHER READING

Evans, C. and Fisher, M. (1999) 'Collaborative Evaluation with Service Users: Moving Towards User-controlled Research', in Shaw, I. and Lishman, J. (eds) *Evaluation and Social Work Practice* (London: Sage) pp. 101–17. This chapter sets out the desirability of service user involvement in research and some of the issues involved.

Frost, N. (2002) 'A Problematic Relationship? Evidence and Practice in the Workplace', *Social Work and Social Sciences Review* 10(1): 38–50. This article expands on some of the complexities of applying research findings to practice and the debates about EBP.

Macdonald, G. and Macdonald, K. (1995) 'Ethical Issues in Social Work Research', in Hugman, R. and Smith, D. (eds) *Ethical Issues in Social Work* (London: Routledge) pp. 46–64. Exponents of EBP, the authors expand on a number of ethical issues in relation to social work research and practice in an accessible fashion.

Newman, T. and McNeish, D. (2002) 'Promoting evidence based practice in a child care charity: the Barnardo's experience', *Social Work and Social Science Review* 10(1): 55–62. Advocates of EBP, the authors persuasively argue the benefits of such an approach in relation to childcare.

Spencer, L., Ritchie, J. and Dillon, L. (2003) *Quality in Qualitative Evaluation: A Framework for Assessing Research Evidence* (London: Cabinet Office). The authors offer a useful framework for assessing the quality of qualitative research.

Producing Results: Researching Social Work Interventions on HIV/AIDS in the Context of the School

Vishanthie Sewpaul and Tanusha Raniga

Introduction

Social work research has been applied in various contexts and specialised fields. One of these has been the response to calls to tackle the rising incidence of HIV/AIDS in South Africa (Department of Welfare and Population Development, 1997; Department of Education, 1999; Van Dyk, 2001). Such calls have recommended holistic approaches in preventing and managing the HIV/AIDS crisis and found that successful strategies involve government departments playing key roles in policy-making and implementation (Van Rensburg et al., 2002). We have no problem with the recommended changes.

Although we touch on strategies that arose from a particular collaborative initiative, a key concern of this chapter is to identify the action research processes that produce results in solving crucial social problems. In it, we examine who defined the issue to be addressed, who constituted the research team, how we accessed research subjects, how the research was conducted, the sensitivities of participants, what findings were produced and how these were used to promote preventive work with young people vulnerable to HIV/AIDS. Producing results in this context means pulling together a research team that crossed departmental, sectoral and professional boundaries, as well as coming up with a strategy that meets the government's objective of reducing the incidence of HIV/AIDS amongst school children. Producing outcomes that enhance people's well-being is the end point of a successful research project in social work.

Using social work research to solve a social problem – HIV/AIDS

The National HIV/AIDS School Policy in South Africa calls for each school to have an HIV/AIDS implementation plan and set up a Health Advisory Committee. To stem the loss of South African youth, the ex-Minister of Education, Kader Asmal, released a national policy that called for comprehensive HIV/AIDS intervention programmes in schools, based on the principles of non-discrimination, inclusivity and universal precaution. A problem of implementation is that the development of HIV/AIDS policies at provincial level follows initiatives set by central government rather than starting their own (Van Rensburg et al., 2002). The gap between policy formulation at central government level and awareness and implementation of policy proposals at provincial and district level was investigated in this research. Our study had a number of objectives. A primary one was to ascertain the extent to which educators were aware of the National HIV/AIDS School Policy (Department of Education, 1999) and its provisions, and how far the policy was being implemented in schools in Durban. Our research investigated whether schools in the Durban area were aware of, and were implementing this policy and assessed the institutional capacities for its realisation. A pilot project conducted with teachers in one school comprised the action component of the study; the other component consisted of an audit of schools. The pilot was designed to implement and evaluate a particular HIV/AIDS education programme and comment on how this policy could be more effectively implemented nationally.

As is widely known, HIV/AIDS is a critical issue for South Africa. The government has prioritised policies and programmes that focus on young people at school, because studies show that young people are prone to risk-taking behaviour in the teenage years when they engage in greater sexual activity as they negotiate and explore sexual identities (Newman and Newman, 1995; Hyde and DeLamater, 2000; Zastrow and Kirst-Ashman, 2001; Morrell et al., 2002). Moreover, the proportion of teenagers having sexual intercourse has been increasing recently, with the age of first intercourse becoming younger (Hyde and DeLamater, 2000; Van Dyk, 2001). Van Dyk's (2001) survey of six provinces in South Africa revealed that 10 per cent of respondents had sex by the age of 11 or younger. In the province of KwaZulu Natal, about which the authors write in this chapter, 76 per cent of girls and 90 per cent of boys claimed to be sexually active by 16. This translates into high HIV/AIDS prevalence rates (UNAIDS, 2000). For various sociostructural, cultural and biological reasons, South African girls aged 15–19 are more vulnerable to HIV infection than boys: 15.64 per cent and 2.58 per cent respectively in KwaZulu Natal (Morrell et al., 2001).

The proportion of young people who will die of AIDS in sub-Saharan Africa is extremely high – about 35 per cent of those now aged 15 (UNAIDS, 2000).

The HIV/AIDS crisis has serious implications for the contribution that education makes to the country's development (Badcock-Walters, 2002: 95). In areas where HIV rates are high, HIV-related illness is taking its toll on the education system by:

■ Decreasing the numbers of educators in schools, thus increasing class sizes

- Adding to the pool of children who are growing up without the support of their parents, which eventually diminishes their ability to stay in school

- Adversely affecting family budgets, thereby reducing monies available for school fees and increasing the pressure on children to drop out of school to enter the workforce or take to the streets.

Parental ill-health affects the quality of children's education and the broader socioeconomic climate of South Africa, where an estimated 1 million children will be orphaned by 2005. So, making the school a site for social work intervention to encourage safe behaviour requires urgent attention to curb infection rates (UNAIDS, 2000: 44). Giving children and young people the information, education and skills to deal with HIV empowers them to reduce the risk of infection. 'Schools are a high-risk environment, but also a key strategic ground on which the battle to mitigate its impact will be won or lost' (Badcock-Walters, 2002: 95). Ensuring success in a particular school was a key feature of this research.

Gaining a successful outcome meant helping service providers including educators to face the severe challenges in confronting values and attitudes towards sexuality and entrenched patriarchal sexual scripts that say that sex is something that we do not talk about, and where women have little or no say in sexual decision-making and sex role stereotyping. When issues of love, intimacy, companionship, and at times economic survival are at stake (or associated with issues of mistrust when condoms are introduced into the relationship), safer sex practices can become less of a priority (Sewpaul and Rollins, 1999). Abdool Karim et al. (1992) pointed out that numerous surveys demonstrate that while adolescents have knowledge of HIV and other sexually transmitted infections, many continue to engage in risky behaviour, thus reflecting the complex interplay of factors that influence sexual decision-making and sexual behaviour. Bridging this gap is essential in achieving results. Our information about safer sex had to go beyond a condom slogan, such as 'be wise, condomise' that has become popularised in the South African media.

These complexities might account for the discrepancy between knowledge and awareness of HIV/AIDS and sexual practices. We tried to build on understanding sexuality and the need for intimacy as central to total personality functioning rather than sexuality being seen as something outside the realm of day-to-day functioning and as distinct from other aspects of our lives to allow for the adoption of realistic approaches to HIV/AIDS education. HIV/AIDS education, within the context of human sexuality, should ideally be done within small groups adopting experiential strategies that allow for fuller assimilation of HIV/AIDS information (Sewpaul and Rollins, 1999), the development of self-exploration and self-awareness, and acquisition of skills in negotiation, assertiveness and problem-solving. As Van Dyk (2001) stated, for HIV/AIDS education programmes to be successful, they should incorporate a balance between knowledge, life skills, values and attitudes.

Building a research team

The devastatingly high rate of new infections among young people in South Africa has demanded a multiprofessional interplay of knowledge, resources and skills to reduce HIV transmission. Our research team involved collaboration between HIV-positive persons, health personnel, educators and NGO workers providing specialist HIV/AIDS services in Edu-Aids and the National Association for People Living with HIV/AIDS (NAPWA), and the Centre for Social Work at the University of Natal (Sewpaul and Mahlalela, 1998; Sewpaul and Rollins, 1999).

The research involved the end users, namely a group of HIV-positive women who were trained to participate in the schools-based project described below. The inclusion of HIV-positive people in researching the impact of services such as HIV/AIDS counselling and outreach programmes delivered to them has several merits (Sewpaul and Rollins, 1999), and accords with the Greater Involvement of People Living with HIV/AIDS (GIPA) initiative suggested by UNAIDS (2000). The two social workers involved were not in full-time practice, one was a social work professor and the other a Masters student. This limited their availability and the extent of research and outreach that could be provided.

Educators have a vital role in the socialisation of learners, but they often do not have the knowledge and skills necessary to deal with the non-academic aspects of learners' lives. This is especially so when dealing with sensitive issues such as love, intimacy, sex, HIV/AIDS and death and dying. The devastating effects of HIV/AIDS amongst educators and young people in South Africa and its national development imperatives for HIV/AIDS prevention and management programmes in schools make interagency collaboration amongst social workers, other professionals and end users a necessity.

Including educators within the research team was important in reducing infection rates among school educators and young people. The pilot project engaged educators in a training programme to produce attitudinal and behavioural changes amongst them and the young people they work with and ease the implementation of national policy. It did so by enabling teachers to gain appropriate HIV/AIDS-related knowledge and skills, involving them in discussions on the national development imperatives regarding HIV/AIDS contained in the National HIV/AIDS School Policy (Department of Education, 1999), contributing to capacity-building for teachers, and setting up a Health Advisory Committee that would make services more sustainable in the long run. We used this alternative approach to assess whether the limitations of the cascading model of HIV/AIDS intervention in schools discussed later in this chapter could be overcome.

Social workers' ability to work at the interface where people's coping skills interact with patterns in the environment is useful in understanding practitioners' roles in the prevention and management of problems in schools (Constable and Flynn, 1982). Hancock (1982) contends that social workers in the school context have the training and skills that educators and principals do not necessarily have. In this study the social workers were enablers in the HIV/AIDS empowerment and educational process. Their primary aim was to prepare educators with the relevant knowledge and skills for operationalising the National HIV/AIDS School Policy. This research was a means of evaluating their success in achieving this goal.

Social workers are often in a position to develop a school's networks of services and resources. As this study involved the extensive collaborative network described earlier, social workers used these interresource linkages to facilitate collaboration and create a service network that dealt with HIV/AIDS within the school in a holistic manner. Constable and Flynn (1982: 25) maintained that, 'school social workers are in the middle of a system, within an organisational structure, in an environment of social and environmental networks'. Social workers': (McKendrick, 2001: 108)

> well-developed skills in developmental group work, their community work expertise, their proven ability to advocate, their programme design and evaluation skills, their strength-based perspective, their traditional emphasis on the empowerment of others, their notable capacity to not only work in teams but to facilitate the effective teamwork that intersectoral activity requires ...

were harnessed for this project to emphasise working *with*, rather than *for* people. Social workers were central to building an effective research team and ensuring the success of the action research project.

Accessing research subjects and dealing with their vulnerabilities

Research into HIV/AIDS is problematic as it exposes institutional vulnerability in not following policy guidelines and government requirements and resource deficiencies. Also, people could run the risk of disclosure around unacceptable values, attitudes and behaviours. Thus, researchers had to be mindful of a number of sensitivities if they were to have a successful conclusion to the study and its planned interventions. The educators indicated that this was the first time they had focused on HIV/AIDS as a serious issue. Their responses to the school's admission policy and disclosure of one's HIV-positive status were generally consistent with the constitutional rights of HIV-positive persons. These reflected acceptance, non-discrimination, the right to confidentiality and access to school and employment. We encouraged their positive attitudes to the project and were 'there' for them, as reflected in regular visits to the school, their inclusion in discussions, listening to their concerns and suggestions, and attempting to jointly find answers to their questions. Positive attitudes contributed to the successful outcome of the project, in that they began HIV/AIDS programmes in the school and established a Heath Advisory Committee. By working with people at their own pace and with sensitivity, this research produced an outcome that was consistent with national policy.

Designing and conducting action research

Social workers became involved in the study to ensure that policies reached the targeted beneficiaries by translating intentions and objectives into action (Sewpaul, 2001a: 319) and moving beyond a reflective understanding of people and society to meet national policy imperatives. The following section describes the research design and details the various phases of the research.

Action research is associated with hands-on, small-scale studies that involve practical and real-world problems and issues. It is directed at producing change as it seeks 'action consequences rather than the reflective truths of research' (Bhana, 1999: 228). Action researchers accept that research is pragmatic and contextual. They do not seek value-free knowledge but direct their endeavours at investigating the most serious social, economic, political and environmental problems facing a group of people (Reardon and Shields, 1997). It also accepts that for growth and change to occur or achieve results, researchers need the support and wisdom of others.

Action research emphasises empowerment of the most marginalised and oppressed groups in society, with the aim of uncovering truths with people, rather than about people. It involves the participation of people in the research process, with encouragement of equal relationships between researchers and participants, and is cyclical in nature (Bhana, 1999). The research involves a feedback loop in which initial findings generate possibilities for change. These are then implemented and evaluated as a prelude to further investigation within a developmental approach. The success of the research depends on the full participation and engagement of people in the research process. This chapter describes action research as a practitioner-researcher approach, where practice and research occur simultaneously as a set of integrated activities. The different phases of the research are described below.

We aimed to empower young people in schools by involving them in the study and designed the project as action research to encourage this. We hoped that doing so would 'produce results' by raising awareness of the national prevention strategy and lowering the incidence of HIV/AIDS in the school. A multiphase intervention research design (research that includes intervention conducted in different phases) incorporating qualitative research was utilised in the study. These phases of the research included:

1. Training HIV-positive women in the Bambanani support group

2. An audit of schools on HIV/AIDS schools-based policy

3. A pilot project of action in a school

4. Follow-up evaluation.

Phase one: training women in the Bambanani support group

Achieving results involves the careful and extensive preparation of participants in research. In this case, there was a lengthy phase that entailed the training of HIV-positive women who were part of a support group initiated by Vishanthie Sewpaul and Dr Nigel Rollins at the King Edward VIII Hospital, Durban in 1996 (see Sewpaul and Rollins, 1999). The women in the support group had training in HIV/AIDS counselling and education and had been conducting peer counselling and awareness programmes primarily within hospitals and clinics. Outreach – the need to reach out and provide HIV/AIDS prevention programmes in schools – emerged as one of the developmental objectives of the work with the women in the hospital. They recognised the need to educate people in the community and reach out to South African youth who are at risk. The women spoke about their ethical responsibility in raising awareness about HIV/AIDS and curbing its spread.

To enhance their skills in doing outreach education at public schools, the women received further advanced training in participatory approaches to human sexuality and HIV/AIDS education, and facilitation skills in conducting workshops. The counselling and outreach experiences of the women informed the content of the training programme. While the training sessions were being conducted, the women were simultaneously involved in peer counselling and HIV/AIDS education outreach initiatives. This provided for the feed-back loop required in action research and the use of praxis or reflection-in-action strategies, as the women used the training sessions to report and reflect on their peer counselling and outreach experiences.

A life skills HIV/AIDS training programme of ten sessions of three hours each was implemented with a group of 13 women. Those who successfully completed were awarded certificates from the Centre for Social Work, University of Natal, Durban which proved useful in their search for paid work. The programme used experiential strategies that allowed for self-exploration and the development of self-awareness; the fuller assimilation of HIV/AIDS information; and opportunities to acquire skills in coping with stress, assertiveness, negotiation, problem-solving, communication, empathy and counselling. We also explored attitudes towards HIV/AIDS and ethical concerns around HIV testing, management and prevention, including culture-specific values and orientations regarding sexuality, HIV and AIDS. The workshops on the National HIV/AIDS School Policy were run with the women employing their skills as AIDS educators to do outreach education in public schools. Their endeavours contributed to the supportive environment that is crucial in achieving success in complex interventions.

Producing results draws upon carefully trained participants and evaluation that provides lessons that will sustain action in the long term. To these ends, formative evaluation strategies were utilised in the training programme and, after each session, the women completed written evaluations. A summative evaluation was conducted in the last training session. The researchers observed the women directly as they conducted their outreach sessions in the hospital. This revealed that women who were willing to disclose their status during the outreach sessions were more successful in gaining the interest and participation of others. This observation confirmed the value of involving HIV-positive persons who make far more credible educators and counsellors (Sewpaul and Rollins, 1999) and so achieve better results. An earlier evaluation of their HIV/AIDS outreach programmes in the hospital (Dano, 1998) had also elicited praise from participants.

Training in research methods can also improve the employability of those involved, a point that highlights how research can contribute to achieving personal objectives. In this project, the training programme increased women's knowledge about HIV/AIDS, enhanced their coping skills and self-confidence as AIDS educators and outreach workers and got the majority of them actively involved in their own communities implementing awareness programmes. Two women started support groups in their communities while others networked with NGOs such as the National Association for People Living with HIV/AIDS (NAPWA), the Treatment Action Campaign (TAC) and Edu-Aids to do further outreach work.

That some women were formally employed by the Department of Health as HIV/AIDS counsellors attests to the successful outcome of this training. Thus, the project achieved one of the primary goals of developmental social welfare – facilitating self-reliance, economic self-sufficiency and independence in people (Department of Welfare and Population Development, 1997). This is particularly important in South Africa where social security benefits are limited and employment opportunities poor (Terreblanche, 2002). The 13 women were collectively able to reach thousands of people, which would have been impossible for social workers to do alone. Networks that reach large numbers of people can be effective in disseminating policy discourses and research findings and sustaining action over the long term.

Phase two: audit among schools regarding the HIV/AIDS schools-based policy

As the project focused on enabling educators to implement HIV/AIDS programmes in schools rather than doing direct work with young people, we had to investigate how the HIV/AIDS policy and programmes were already working to meet that goal. We applied to the University of Natal Research Fund to do an audit of at least 50 schools in the Durban Metropolitan Region. This was to be followed by action research in four schools. We secured limited funding and so conducted interviews with the principals of 18 secondary schools in a designated part of Durban. The key questions explored were:

- Are you and your staff aware of the National HIV/AIDS School Policy for learners and educators as per the government Gazette, Notice 1926 of 1999?

- Has your school been involved in HIV/AIDS awareness programmes?

- If yes, provide some details of these.

- Do you experience problems implementing such programmes at your school?

The principals unanimously indicated that they had little awareness of the policy and there was limited implementation of HIV/AIDS awareness programmes in schools. This supported our assumption that policy initiated at national level is slow to be implemented at provincial and district levels. The principals also commented that they did not have the time, staff and expertise required to implement these HIV/AIDS awareness programmes. The findings also exposed the lack of institutional capacity in terms of time and finance to deal with

HIV/AIDS and follow the recommendations of the National HIV/AIDS School Policy. Thus, the research identified problem points in the implementation of national policy.

Phase three: action research as the school pilot programme

This phase entailed the implementation of a pilot HIV/AIDS programme with educators in a secondary school in Phoenix. The initial audit of schools assisted in its selection. Moreover, we responded to a principal who requested assistance in implementing HIV/AIDS programmes, and understanding and implementing the guidelines of the National HIV/AIDS School Policy. As a gatekeeper to the school system, this principle facilitated entry for the researchers. At the time of the study in March 2001, the school had 43 teachers and 1450 students. Seventy per cent of students attending the school were from the nearby township of Inanda, which has high rates of poverty, unemployment and HIV/AIDS. Interventions to reduce these forms of social exclusion were central concerns of government.

The primary facilitator, a social worker, and the co-facilitator, an HIV-positive woman, had two initial interviews with the principal and the deputy principal of the school. Both supported the project and provided access. This contact was used to establish rapport with the school's management, discuss the objectives of the action research and give them a copy of the Policy for review. Together, we planned the preliminary content of the five training workshops to be conducted with the educators. Gaining the support and approval of senior personnel are key to the success of action research in any organisation. Participation in the programme was voluntary and 27 of the 43 teachers attended. Ideally, we would have liked to involve the entire staff group but this was not feasible, given time constraints and the educators' teaching commitments, so those with prior commitments and extracurricula school activities did not attend.

The workshop sessions began with relationship-building. The educators clarified their expectations and amended the preliminary programme to meet their needs. The preliminary programme was discussed and planned together with management members at the school. The content of this programme mainly focused on the knowledge component of HIV/AIDS and the National HIV/AIDS School Policy. So besides gaining the approval of senior staff, we ensured that the educators played an active role in shaping the workshop programme and taking ownership of its content and the research process.

The workshop sessions were experiential in nature and included both small group and plenary sessions. Specialists from a hospital and NGOs were included in discussions and information dissemination in two sessions. The themes covered during the workshops contributed to the overall goal of reducing risk and included:

1. *Knowledge component of HIV/AIDS* – including modes of transmission, the course of infection, understanding the significance of the 'window period' and methods of reducing risks of HIV infection.

2. *Living with HIV/AIDS* – the personal testimony of a healthy looking, smart,

articulate HIV-positive woman who had experienced the losses of her partner and baby to AIDS helped to make HIV/AIDS real by confronting, demystifying and eliminating the myths and stereotypes associated with HIV/AIDS.

3. *HIV/AIDS within the context of human sexuality* – here, we tackled the discrepancy between people's knowledge of HIV/AIDS and their failure to translate it into behavioural change as it remains one of the biggest challenges in South Africa. To do so, we had to confront the difficult question of helping adults and young people to understand the powerful forces of love and sex while being mindful of making life or death decisions. As it deals with some of the most profound mysteries of human existence, people do not generally want to enter this terrain. How we dealt with the issues to maintain interest was also important; we eschewed didactic teaching for small experiential groups that facilitate their safe and secure exploration. Understanding the centrality of sex to one's life and not labelling those who contracted HIV through sex as 'guilty', while deeming as 'innocent victims' those contracting it through other modes of transmission, brought the discussion to support for and acceptance of HIV-positive persons. Educators questioned what they thought to be a paradox in the Policy: how could they support colleagues and children who might be HIV-positive, if disclosure were voluntary? They expressed the view that it was not possible to provide support and assistance to a person who is HIV-positive, if they did not know the HIV-positive status of the person.

4. *Voluntary testing* – linked to the discussion on disclosure, some educators thought that testing should be compulsory; others that this would be a violation of human rights. The pros and cons of voluntary testing and counselling were considered in relation to people's constitutional rights and current policy that rejects compulsory testing in South Africa.

5. *The National HIV/AIDS School Policy* – given the focus of this research, the policy was given specific in-depth attention. This comprised a three-hour experiential workshop with the educators deliberating the content of the Policy.

6. *Integration of life skills, sexuality and HIV/AIDS into the school curriculum* – the introduction of outcomes-based education in 1997 made this learning area part of the Department of Education's life orientation programme. A majority of educators expressed concerns about the challenges they faced in implementing this programme. The main one was feeling ill-equipped to deal with the sensitive area of sexuality and HIV/AIDS. They also believed that the cultural values held by parents in the Phoenix community were conservative and many were 'displeased with the use of condoms and sex being discussed in the classroom'. One educator said: 'the Indian community are in denial that such a problem exists'.

7. *Infection control and universal precaution in the school context* – as recommended in Section 7 of the National HIV/AIDS School Policy – and mechanisms for the establishment of the Health Advisory Committee were given particular attention. The first part of this session comprised a presenta-

tion by a nurse from the local hospital on infection control and universal precautions to ensure safety in the school context. The second part of the session was an experiential workshop with the educators about the establishment of the Health Advisory Committee in school.

The obstacles to successfully implementing HIV/AIDS programmes in the school that educators identified were:

■ Lack of funding, material resources and time

■ Low morale of educators

■ Lack of training and expertise to deal with sexuality and HIV/AIDS

■ Little or no support for sexuality education amongst parents

■ Ignorance in the wider community about the seriousness and extent of the problem

■ Lack of planning and coordination of an implementation plan at school.

They also indicated that they lacked expertise in counselling to respond to children or fellow educators who might be HIV-positive. Their comments revealed that teachers who attended the provincial Department of Education's training workshops had not shared their learning with the rest of the staff, highlighting a key limitation of the cascading model of HIV/AIDS intervention in schools favoured by government. Addressing these issues and getting the content across are crucial in securing success for this policy nationally.

Analysing findings and determining their generalisability are crucial to understanding how far small-scale action research can solve social problems. Students attending school were seen as a high-risk group for contracting HIV by 26 of the 27 educators. Their reasons for this view were:

■ Large enrolment numbers at school

■ Sexually active learners

■ Learners coming from areas with large numbers of HIV-infected people

■ Learners being parents already

■ Learners' impoverished and economically poor backgrounds, making them more vulnerable to infection

■ The lack of HIV/AIDS programmes in schools

■ Teenagers being at a stage of development that involves sexual experimentation

■ A high rate of rape in the community

■ High levels of drug taking.

Each of these factors has to be addressed to reduce infection rates.

Seventeen of the 27 educators thought that teachers were also at risk of contracting HIV/AIDS. Research conducted by the Health Economics and HIV/AIDS Research Division (HEARD) at the University of Natal revealed that over 680 educators in KwaZulu Natal died in service in 2000, with an average age of 36 (Cullinan, 2003). Badcock-Walters (2002: 105) suggests that these figures may be an underestimate.

While educators acknowledged the high risk of HIV infection amongst students and teachers, when the study began they had not implemented any of the provisions of the National HIV/AIDS School Policy (most were not aware of the policy recommendations) and had no HIV/AIDS programmes in place. That they had done so at its conclusion was a mark of success.

Phase four: follow-up evaluation

A post-evaluation follow-up after 16 months was conducted with the school to assess whether or not educators had been implementing the programmes with learners. The deputy principal involved in the earlier training sessions indicated that the school had developed an HIV/AIDS implementation plan. He said, 'we are now aware of the contents of the Policy and are taking HIV/AIDS more seriously'. A representative Health Advisory Committee had been established and included parents and learners in its work. He indicated that other NGOs and the Department of Health supported their endeavours. He maintained that 'the training sessions (attended by educators) were most informative and have impacted positively in the school with regard to dealing with HIV/AIDS'. His statement confirms that close cooperation amongst all stakeholders within the school and wider community is essential to the development of a cohesive and comprehensive HIV/AIDS implementation plan.

The other schools involved at the inception of this study were also contacted during this period to compare results and assess the extent to which schools not covered by the training programme had initiated HIV/AIDS awareness programmes. The same initial key questions were posed again. This time 16 of the 18 schools were aware of the policy, a marked difference from the initial responses where almost all were unaware. The researcher's initial interviews with the principals may have raised awareness, but a more probable cause was that the national policy had filtered down to the local school level. Although aware of the provisions and requirements of the national policy, 16 of the 18 principals had had problems in implementing it. A key recommendation of the National HIV/AIDS School Policy is that each school should have a Health Advisory Committee in place to coordinate and plan for HIV/AIDS intervention in the school. The only school that had one in place was the pilot site for this study. One other school had established a student health committee. As this did not include parents and educators, it had not been established according to policy recommendations. The importance of the Health Advisory Committee was highlighted by the principal of the pilot site during the follow-up evaluation. He said:

This study has really helped the educators and management members of the school with skills to put the policy into practice. The Health Advisory Committee has helped us to put an implementation plan into place for the school which we never had before.

Seven of the principals interviewed revealed that they had made some attempt to implement HIV/AIDS awareness programmes at their respective schools. They were able to do this by networking with the local child welfare organisation, the city health department and church organisations where speakers were invited to address students. In addition, HIV/AIDS education was incorporated in the national curriculum 2005 as one of the eight learning areas called *life orientation*.

All the principals indicated that one of their teachers had attended HIV/AIDS training workshops facilitated by the provincial Department of Education. These adopt a cascading model whereby key trainers are responsible for training two teachers per secondary school on child abuse, life skills and HIV/AIDS education. These two teachers are expected to continue training within the school. However, the principals did not perceive the cascading model used by the Department of Education as helpful. Scott (cited in Sewpaul, 2001b) identified the following problems with the cascading model:

- Training can lose impact every time the next cascade takes place

- It takes a long time for the process to reach all staff members

- The process is dependent on the commitment of trainers and principals

- Young, inexperienced teachers may be unable to convince principals, teachers and governing bodies about the need for such programmes

- Teachers may lack the confidence to train others

- Teachers may lack facilitation skills.

Despite the limitations of the cascading model and its failure to produce results, as reflected in the Gauteng Department of Education's experience (Sewpaul, 2001b), it has been retained by the KwaZulu Natal Department of Education. The model used in our study produced more beneficial results than the cascading model, because it included all educators in the training programme and was assisted in the implementation process by the successful establishment of the Health Advisory Committee in the school.

One principal, arguing for specific training for all, stated that 'they are trained as teachers and employed to teach, HIV/AIDS education is beyond their capacity'. More importantly, he said: 'sexuality is something that they [educators] do not feel comfortable talking about even among themselves so to deal with it with learners poses a major challenge'. His comments highlight the importance of addressing people's fears in order to produce results. Many of the principals recommended that specialist persons, for example, counsellors or social workers, be employed by the Department of Education in each school to make operationalising the National HIV/AIDS School Policy truly effective.

Using research to reduce the incidence of HIV/AIDS and enhance well-being

Research that evaluates interventions and formulates recommendations based on a systematic consideration of experiences can enhance success in outcomes. Each workshop session was separately evaluated. Educators indicated both in writing and verbally that these training sessions were extremely helpful. Some specific benefits they cited included:

- Increased knowledge and understanding of the National HIV/AIDS School Policy and the Health Advisory Committee

- Clarification of the roles and functions of schools in dealing with HIV/AIDS

- Strengthening their support for HIV-positive learners

- Heightening awareness of universal precautions

- Dispelling misconceptions about HIV/AIDS.

Having benefited from the workshops, educators made some specific recommendations to enhance success in the implementation of the national policy. These included having a specialist in the school to deal with HIV/AIDS, to put implementation plans in place and support educators in implementing sexuality and HIV/AIDS programmes in the curriculum. Of particular salience was the need for the Department of Education to provide the specialised equipment necessary for implementing HIV/AIDS programmes, especially that of universal precaution in schools.

CONCLUSION

Policy documents cannot be translated into action strategies when key players are unaware of them. The pilot project demonstrated that social work intervention in schools can get policy proposals down to the people who are directly affected by them and involve them in their operationalisation. Action research that adopts a practitioner-researcher approach engages HIV-positive people as participants and can produce results in line with national policy by planning and implementing HIV/AIDS programmes in the school. Project facilitators – social workers collaborating with health practitioners, HIV-positive persons, and several NGOs – cooperated in a long-term developmental process to engender change in the school and mobilise educators to take constructive action to address one of the most challenging issues confronting South African educators and learners.

School social work is not an established feature of South African schools but this study reflected the dire need for it. Social work, with its small group facilitation skills, understanding of human and cultural diversity, ability to connect micro- and macro-levels of assessment and intervention, emphasis on values, knowledge and skills and training in the areas of human sexuality and HIV/AIDS, is a suitable discipline for implementing HIV/AIDS prevention and management programmes in schools. Currently social workers form part of the Psychological Guidance and Special Educational Services of the Department of Education, with three social workers for 370 secondary schools in the Durban region. Increasing their numbers and locating them within the schools directly could improve this situation. Consistent with following through on action research, the finding concerning the necessity of establishing school social work with social workers dedicated to specific schools was communicated to the chief educational specialist and a social worker in the Psychological and Special Educational Services Department. They have been advocating broadening the scope of social work intervention in schools.

This study supports the view that the Department of Education must employ social workers and include them in multidisciplinary teams in schools. The national and provincial education departments have to play a far more active role in ensuring clear mechanisms of communication to filter relevant information down to schools. Both participants in the pilot site and principals in the other schools acknowledged that educators have neither the knowledge nor skills to deal with HIV/AIDS, an issue that must be addressed. While the results of this study reflect successful outcomes with tangible results, given the problems elucidated by school principals and educators, it is uncertain whether or not the gains produced can be sustained.

Finally, this research contributed to the development of a larger study involving 74 schools in KwaZulu Natal. Currently in progress, it utilises a triangulated methodology, including both quantitative and qualitative research methods and various sources of data including school principals, learners, parents and the provincial and district coordinators of the Department of Education who are responsible for the training of educators in the area of HIV/AIDS and life skills. If the results of the larger study support the findings of the preliminary one, it will be used to advocate further for the inclusion of social workers as core team members in schools. In this way, producing results in the implementation of national policy on HIV/AIDS could be strengthened appreciably and a small-scale study will have proved useful in its implementation.

FURTHER READING

Fuller, R. and Petch, A. (eds) (1995) *Practitioner Research: The Reflexive Social Worker* (Buckingham: Open University Press).

Gow, J. and Desmond, C. (eds) (2002) *The HIV/AIDS Epidemic and the Children of South Africa* (Pietermaritzburg: University of Natal Press).

Jackson, H. (2002) *AIDS AFRICA: Continent in Crisis* (Harare: SafAIDS).

Strachan, K. and Clarke, E. (2000) *Everybody's Business: The Enlightening Truth About AIDS* (Cape Town: Metropolitan Group).

From Margin to Centre: Shifting the Emphasis of Social Work Research

Beth Humphries

Introduction

Neither social work nor social research is a neutral activity. Like other social practices they are both subject to external and internal forces that influence them towards being instruments of 'empowerment' or otherwise. That they are unambiguously a 'good' cannot be taken for granted. The contested nature of social work is made clear by, on the one hand, statements made by the International Association of Schools of Social Work and the International Federation of Social Workers that social work 'addresses the barriers, inequalities and injustices that exist in society', and, on the other hand, by the former UK Minister for Health, Jacqui Smith, that social work 'is a very practical job ... not about being able to give a ... theoretical explanation of why [people] got into difficulties in the first place' (both quoted in Horner, 2003: 2–3). The meaning and purpose of social work is contested and contradictory, and its history is illustrative of struggles for dominance of different versions at different moments. As generations of practitioners know only too well, many aspects of their practice lead into activities, the ethical and political implications of which need to be questioned.

Similarly, social work research reflects contemporary views of what constitutes social problems, whose interests are met by these definitions and what are seen as desirable outcomes of intervention. Arguments have raged about the merits or superiority of various research paradigms or methods but, however it is viewed, social research is not an impersonal activity. It is imbued with the values of researchers, institutions and governments, and both its processes and findings reflect those values. Social research can have profoundly conservative consequences (for example in confirming and reinforcing diagnoses of schizophrenia in young black men), or it can have radical potential (for example in opening to the public gaze the extent of sexual harassment at work, the widespread nature of domestic violence and abuse of children in the home). All research is political, imbued with power and engaged in a moral struggle about what is 'normal', what is 'truth', what is legitimate 'knowledge' and who can be validated as a 'knower'.

It is naive not to recognise that, as with all social practices, social work research needs to be interrogated concerning its origins, its purposes and the ends for which it is intended. In considering social work futures, we need to recognise the struggles for meaning that are involved, and that the outcomes of these struggles can profoundly affect the nature of social work and its impact on service users. This chapter is openly concerned with the radical potential of research in social work, starting from an assumption that a major aim of social work is social justice and anti-oppression. Practitioners should be informed and alerted to all research as value-loaded and able to pursue models that do not perpetuate the disadvantage experienced by poor and relatively powerless people. In that case, the profession is obliged to strive for a research practice that takes account of its moral purpose to engage with oppressive structures and political and social action to change them. Here I am concerned to explore the extent to which this might be achieved by ongoing research in social work.

There is currently an unprecedented interest in 'research-based practice' and both central and local government, as well as social care agencies of all sorts, have an energetic concern to carry out research that will influence practice and demonstrate the influence of research studies on their work. Such studies are not to be regarded as 'helpful' per se, in the sense that they inevitably contribute to anti-oppressive practice. Because they represent particular interests, they are as much a site of conflict as other social activities and are therefore to be entered into with an attitude of critical, reflexive caution. In doing so we can be informed by Butler's words of warning when he notes that 'accommodations' among the New Labour government, local authorities and those delivering social care services may operate to the detriment of service users, but also to the 'disputed and often dangerous activity' of social work as a form of welfare practice (Butler, 2003: 20).

An orthodoxy has developed within social work research that focuses on outcomes, and a 'what works' pragmatism characterises many contemporary studies (Humphries, 2003). This orthodoxy is based on the scientific (and political) assumption that 'a formal rationality of practice based on scientific methods can produce a more effective and economically accountable means of delivering social services' (Webb, 2001: 60). A research approach that is able to demonstrate its utility, practicality and reliability in providing clear solutions to 'real' problems is a particularly attractive prospect for governments and a way of achieving prestige and credibility for the profession. This positivist orientation – that the world is predictable, knowable and measurable, behaviour can be explained in causal, deterministic ways and knowledge arises out of experiments and observations using quantitative methods – has driven social work research towards an agenda that focuses on practical means to change behaviour in order to achieve social control. Indeed, the manipulation and control of human behaviour is an explicit aim of such research and outcomes are measured in terms of changes in behaviour. The evidence-based practice movement that has emerged from this philosophy is popular with governments and researchers because it offers definitive answers to social problems, it claims to discover 'what works'. There are, however, fundamental problems concerning 'objectivity', being 'value-free' and 'neutral', to say nothing about the processes of inference that lead from evidence to explanation, which the evidence-based movement has still to confront.

This narrow perspective tends to ignore the context in which particular behaviours take place, to the detriment of any reflection on, for example, how the behaviour has come to be constructed as a problem, what norms (that is, the standard considered acceptable) the behaviour is measured against and their legitimacy, what contextual factors contribute to it and what are its meanings to the people targeted for change? These questions have been marginalised in a climate where the emphasis is on the technical, 'checking evidence' approach and a preoccupation with cause and effect or cost-effectiveness. In this 'politics of enforcement' (Parton, 2000: 461) of a model of research obsessed with measurement, outcomes and targets, the question for social work becomes, is there a place for research that takes account of moral considerations, takes sides, makes anti-oppressive ideals a fundamental aspect of the conception and design of studies in social work, and shifts these concerns from margin to centre?

Social research as a moral and political activity

Such questions identify social research as an explicitly moral and political activity. One of the consequences of the drive for an evidence base has been a distancing of research practice (and social work practice) from a critique of policy. Beresford and Evans (1999) have pointed out that social research in the latter half of the twentieth century shifted from a role in initiating policy developments to one of evaluating, monitoring and legitimating them. It now occupies a reactive position, with an emphasis on exploring the 'effectiveness, efficiency and economy of policy ... reflected in its increasing preoccupation with managerially and professionally defined outcomes and outcome measurement' (Beresford and Evans, 1999: 672). Any role examining policies themselves has been removed (see Humphries, 2004a for a more detailed discussion of this). This move betrays a moral and political conservatism in the profession and holds a risk that social work is robbed of its radical and transformatory potential. The questions that affect research can never be only with 'what works?' Ethical research is concerned also with the conditions that lead to or hinder the self-realisation of individuals and social groups, and is based on an examination of the ways in which power regulates both material and ideological realities. Is there any merit in researchers being impartial to human suffering and injustice? Surely, one of the basic aims of research is to bring to public notice realities that were previously hidden and new perspectives on worlds that have been taken for granted.

What is being advocated here is research that is contentious, in that it does not separate itself from a critique of social policies or from struggles for social transformation, but assumes a praxis – a unity of thought and action – that has at its heart changes in the lives of oppressed peoples and in the way they are treated within the social care system (see Hayes and Humphries, 1999). Butler (2003: 27) argues for the recognition and embracing of social work research as a 'value based, politically aware and engaged form of endeavour'. This may bring it into conflict with conventional expectations of the roles of social work and social research, but then the battle for social justice has to be what Butler calls 'unbiddable' (p. 28).

With such an approach comes a clear 'positioning' of the researcher in terms of taking sides and reframing questions about knowledge and truth. In 'taking sides', I am not advocating an undiscriminating approach that supports individuals, groups or communities whether right or wrong, even if they are oppressed. We all have partial knowledge that, although crucial to our survival, is sometimes oblivious to or excludes other people's truths (for example we may recognise disablism and be antagonistic to anti-racism, or be anti-racist and at the same time homophobic). These truths need to be taken as 'valid' but never without response, or left unproblematised. Taking sides involves a commitment not to factions, but to a particular set of values:

> In social work these values include an opposition to injustices and a commitment to alleviating and even preventing suffering. Research that is concerned to expose and challenge inequalities is entirely compatible with these values. Research that attempts solely to measure the impact of interventions regardless of their relationship to the social context is not value free. Rather it has taken the side of whatever values have inspired the interventions it uncritically evaluates.
>
> (Humphries, 2004a: 114)

This process depends on social work researchers taking a position of conscious partiality, a notion suggested by Mies (1993) that recognises our limited understanding of the experiences of the oppression of others, but requires us to take sides in the realities of vulnerability and marginalisation. This positioning involves a creative and imaginative leap beyond common-sense assumptions and taken-for-granted beliefs, to ask different questions and seek different answers, unsettle established practices and surprise ourselves and others with the discovery that there *are* alternatives after all.

Critical social research

Any approach that addresses the aims described above needs to have a number of features that characterise it as critical. I do not use 'critical' in the strictly academic sense of approaching all knowledge with a questioning attitude, but in the sense described by Harvey (1990: 2):

> At the heart of critical social research is the idea that knowledge is structured by existing sets of social relations. The aim of a critical methodology is to provide knowledge which engages the prevailing social structures. These social structures are seen by critical researchers, in one way or another, as oppressive structures.

The features of critical social research are broadly that:

- It regards social structures as oppressive, maintained through political and economic power, and supported by a range of legitimating strategies

- It seeks to make these legitimations visible for examination and identify the oppressive and exploitative practices they underpin

- By focusing on specific social phenomena, it aims to get beyond common-sense and taken-for-granted understandings, to how they relate to wider social and historical structures

- A legitimate target for analysis is the concepts that frame and define an area of inquiry

- It goes beyond simply identifying oppressive structures towards seeking ways to combat, resist and change them.

- The critical researcher should be flexible enough to engage with these power dynamics in specific situations.

Critical research may be based on a range (or a combination) of epistemologies, such as those suggested by, for example, Marxisms, feminisms, theories of anti-racism, some poststructuralist approaches, disability, age-related and sexuality studies. Methods might include both qualitative and quantitative approaches. The key criterion is that they demonstrate the above features. Writers such as Leonard (1997) and Soper (1993) have offered useful frameworks drawn from a combination of theoretical perspectives. Leonard drew together Marxist and feminist critiques as well as postmodern deconstruction in his book on reconstructing welfare. Soper attempted a similar project in her efforts to construct a principled position from which to evaluate social theory.

From margin to centre

Audre Lorde (1984) created a framework for analysing class, 'race', gender, sexuality, age and disability. As commented by the editors of her book, her writing is an impulse towards wholeness, theorising out of her experiences as a black woman, lesbian, feminist, mother, daughter of immigrants, educator, cancer survivor, activist. This does not mean that authentic knowledge is the property only of those who have had similar experiences. Others may achieve partial identification with oppressed peoples, as I have discussed above. Lorde asserts that 'the master's tools will never dismantle the master's house' (p. 112), by which she means that those who are concerned to bring genuine changes to the lives of poor and exploited groups need to find new methods and new ways of thinking about social problems. If they allow themselves to be occupied by concerns constructed out of dominant interests, their energies will be diverted and they will continue to operate in a framework defined for them by others. Within social work – statutory, voluntary or private – it is impossible to avoid 'the master's interests', but even there it is possible perhaps to bring different tools to bear to define and examine them.

Some of these issues are also addressed by bell hooks (1984) through her analysis of the condition of black women and men in relation to their exploitation, position in social structures and, in the case of black women, their relationship to white feminism. She used the metaphor of 'margin and centre' to analyse these features through an attempt to displace issues regarded as important by dominant groups and bring into focus the concerns of those relegated to the margins. Her approach has been taken up by other groups and can be adopted more generally. I use it here to consider how social work research, driven by a moral and political agenda, might challenge the normative concerns of dominant research approaches by asking different questions and centring the interests and experiences of those most affected by social work, rather than the interests of practitioners, researchers, government or organisations. In this way, by turning the research questions on their head, I hope that practitioner-researchers might practise 'making the invisible visible', revealing an oppositional world-view that will raise different questions and provide different answers.

Much feminist theory, argued hooks (1984), emerges from privileged women who live at the centre and whose perspectives on reality rarely include knowledge and awareness of the lives of women and men who live on the margin. As a consequence, she said, such theory lacks wholeness, the broad analysis that could encompass a variety of human experiences. At its most visionary, an encompassing theory will emerge from individuals who have knowledge of both margin and centre. Marginalised people may have knowledge of the 'centre' through close observation of the actions of powerful groups. They may also have this knowledge through their multiple positioning at both margin and centre. Others may gain such knowledge out of the effort to listen to and empathise with those at the margin. It is this insight that is key to a perspective that challenges top-down interpretations and seeks to bring to light other understandings.

Subjugated knowledges

One of the basic differences between traditional research and alternative perspectives revolves around who can be a knower and the status of different kinds of knowledge. Traditionally the 'knower' is the researcher who brings scientific objectivity to his/her work, gathers information from 'informants', analyses and interprets such data and writes about it in a way that addresses the questions she/he had set out to answer. Phenomenological approaches have not particularly challenged this notion of the 'knower', but did begin to recognise the knowledge of marginalised groups and are interested in the subjective elements of human experience, that is, the *meanings* attributed to events and behaviour by particular social actors, and make this knowledge available. Other approaches to research, notably feminist and participatory, explicitly set out to bring to light what hooks called 'subjugated knowledges'. In other words, there is more than one kind of knower and there is a range of kinds of knowledges. Moreover, subjugated knowledges are legitimate forms of knowing. Dominant groups may arbitrate on the authenticity of such knowledges, but the aim of critical research is to assert their legitimacy and insist that they be heard and recognised.

The importance of this is illustrated by Anne Fadiman's remarkable book *The Spirit Catches You and You Fall Down* (1997), about a Hmong child, her

American doctors, the doctors' dismissal of the cultural knowledge of the child's family and community and their faith in the Western medicine tradition. The book is a single case study, meticulously reported and deeply revealing. It is an ethnographic study of the medical problems of a little girl, three months old when she and her parents arrived as refugees from Laos and came into contact with the American medical system. The problems hinged on the fact that the Hmong see illness and healing as spiritual matters linked to virtually everything in the universe, while the medical community marks a division between body and soul and concerns itself exclusively with the former. Lia Lee was diagnosed as an epileptic, caused by the 'misfiring of her cerebral neurons'. Her parents called her illness *quag dab peg* – 'the spirit catches you and you fall down'.

The ideas within the two cultures about diagnosis, care and treatment could hardly have been more different, and the medical community tended to dismiss Hmong knowledge as superstitious and harmful. For its part, the Hmong community was fearful and suspicious of medical approaches that refused to recognise a holistic world-view. After years of confusion, anger and misunder-standings, tragically Lia Lee died while still in her childhood. The stakes in how subjugated knowledges are valued are often high, sometimes with life and death consequences. Fadiman's treatment of the case study captured both the dominant medical view and that of the minority culture, and she was not unsympathetic to either perspective, although she had direct experience of neither. Of relevance to social work is, on the one hand, her capturing of the frustration expressed by caring doctors about what they saw as uncooperative, obstructive parents who were not concerned about the dangers to their child and, on the other, the cushion of love and concern emanating from the Hmong community and the child's family.

The lesson for practice is that social workers often experience such frustration with service users, resulting in pathological perceptions of them (in this case they might have instituted child protection proceedings). For once, however, the social worker is a hero, in that she managed to empathise with and gain the trust of the family and understood and valued their perspective. The time and effort needed to understand these cultural differences is a fundamental condition for negotiating the appropriate help. On this point, Fadiman's ethnographic research took place over a number of years and she immersed herself in both the cultures studied. Many social work practitioners may see this as an unrealistic task, and in any case the approach is alien to a culture of research that emphasises efficiency, effectiveness and definitive answers, as discussed earlier in this chapter. On the contrary, it seems entirely appropriate research for a practitioner to conduct as part of her practice over time, and as a way of resisting dominant, and often oppressive, approaches.

Another point to be made about Fadiman's study is that although it involved a single case study approach, the researcher was able to theorise from this to analyse cultural difference and dominance and the workings of institutional racism. She was also able to explore the connections between this and the colonial history of the USA and Laos. Starting from a single moment, she wove a tapestry that encompassed global political patterns. Her work demonstrated a critical approach that was grounded in but did not end with the experiences of an individual family, their community and the particular practitioners engaged with them. The situation under examination was used to construct a number of layers of analysis and provided lessons for how practice, organisational structures and indeed wider social institutions and even international activity need to change if they are to have an evidence base that is in the interests of service users.

Talking back

A way of ensuring that research practice shifts the margin to the centre is providing the opportunity for marginalised groups to 'come to voice', and particularly to 'talk back'. As bell hooks (1989: 14) said: 'those who understand the power of voice as gesture of rebellion and resistance urge the exploited, the oppressed to speak'. When people speak of their oppression it is a painful thing, calling for courage and daring. It is a dangerous thing, because what the voice has to say may not be heard, may be rejected, may be seen as threatening or irrational or may be appropriated and exploited. It is an unsettling thing, because it disrupts polite social relationships and it risks a loss of approval from friends, colleagues and acquaintances. Yet often the struggle out of silence is an essential one towards healing and wholeness.

Andrew Durham (2003) carried out a practitioner research study of young men living through and with child sexual abuse. In doing so he brought their voices into focus, allowing them to talk back to those who had abused them and a society that had neglected them. He interviewed seven young men using a methodology influenced by ethnographic (particularly life story approach), feminist, anti-oppressive and social work practitioner research. Durham (2003: 310) developed an analytic framework that sought to 'draw on the tensions between the potential fragmentation of post-structuralism and the overdetermination of structural theory'. I understand this to mean an attempt to reconcile competing theories that, on the one hand, tend to dismiss the structural determinants of oppression in favour of localised explanations and, on the other, reduce all oppressions to economic causes. He argued that such a framework allows a socially contextualised analysis of the young men's experiences, which emphasises the importance of narrative and discourse, centralises issues of power, gender and sexuality and allows for an examination of the ongoing impact of widespread social oppression. Durham's article includes a potentially useful analytic framework expressed in a diagram that attempts to encompass power relationships at different interrelated levels of social interaction in the context of oppression and political influences. This allows not only for a description of the vividness and horror of individual experiences of child sexual abuse, but also for linking these to discourses of power and sexuality and prescribed gender roles. Such a framework has obvious potential for use in wider social work practice. In these ways, the emphasis is shifted from entirely individualistic explanations of social problems to take account of factors that have been relegated to the margin.

Durham's (2003) report of the study has strengths and weaknesses. By centring the voices of the young men interviewed, he conveys the damage, confusion, contradictory feelings and ongoing injury experienced by them into adulthood. The reader is left in no doubt as to the long-term consequences of such abuse, and the urgency of understanding and developing strategies to help people to overcome the resulting trauma. Although Durham does not go on to explore how social work might respond to people such as those in the study, the article offers insights into thoughts and feelings not often made public, and is therefore of use to practitioners. It is a tribute both to the methods chosen and the skills of the practitioner-researcher that he was able to access and make available survivors' constructions of the events described (presumably as a practitioner engaged in therapeutic relationships, he was using case material from his own practice. We also assume that the young men gave their consent to the material being used in this way, although this is not declared).

Nevertheless, the article might have gone further in making the links with wider discourses and taking readers beyond widespread beliefs that child sexual abuse arises from individual pathology. This promised to be one of the most valuable elements of the piece. The opportunity was presented to explore how feminism and poststructuralism might offer theoretical insights into the sexual abuse of boys by men (and thus pursue their potential for contributing to wider social theory), yet these critiques are only marginally and superficially used in the analysis. Furthermore, Durham's argument that 'no single aspect of social oppression is seen as an absolute determinant of social power' (p. 311) held out a possibility of progress from the reductionist, compartmentalised and hierarchical view of oppression still pervasive in social work. The analysis did not, however, achieve fluency among class, age, 'race' and ability. Indeed these are virtually ignored in the discussion, the main focus of which was sexuality, with gender not directly addressed. Indeed, although there is a connection made between the anxieties of the young men about the implications of the abuse for their masculinity and 'compulsory heterosexuality', the argument does not offer any critique of compulsory heterosexuality. Such a critique would identify compulsory heterosexuality as a normative practice in society, embodied in the assumption that the ideal identity is a heterosexual one, with clearly defined behaviours allocated to women and men. In the case of young men, this entails performing the behaviours associated with the prevailing view of masculinity, reinforced by celebrity role models and ridicule and punishment for non-conformity. This failure to decentre heterosexuality results in the young men's anxieties, that they might be or be seen to be 'queer', not being politicised, leaving the normative notion of heterosexuality unchallenged and therefore being queer as pathological. In other words, social structures that hold heterosexuality as the implicit point of reference remain intact, are not displaced from centre to margin and the opportunity for a creative challenge to structures of power is lost.

These criticisms may appear to some readers to be unnecessarily pedantic and nit-picking. I would argue first that in order to make them I am using the terms of reference of the author himself, in that Durham is claiming to demonstrate these elements in his article. It is not sufficient that the young men's voices are heard. They must be analysed in the light of insights about the nature of oppression. It is with a sense of disappointment that one finds the opportunity for theoretical, methodological and political developments have been missed. Also, where research claims to be anti-oppressive, not to carefully unpack normative assumptions around 'compulsory heterosexuality', for example, is a serious omission.

Reframing knowledge

Part of the project of critical research is to identify the ways in which knowledge is produced. In social work there has been a growth in faith in 'scientific' knowledge over what Usher and Edwards (1994: 158) call 'narrative' knowledge. They quote Sarup (1993: 136) to show that 'the main difference is that scientific knowledge requires that one language game, denotation, be retained and all others excluded'. In social work, the dominance of rational-technical approaches to practice privileges scientific knowledge, rendering other kinds of knowledges illegitimate and creating an imperialist culture of research and practice that is concerned with criteria of efficiency and inefficiency, rather than being governed by some vision of a just society.

Some of this is illustrated by research conducted by Gwen Robinson (2003) to test the hypothesis that an increase in 'technicality' (scientific knowledge) in probation practice results in a decrease in professionalism (narrative knowledge). In taking research in probation as an example, I recognise that comparisons between probation and social work have limitations, since probation is excluded from social work in England and Wales. However, they have both been subjected to the same modernisation agenda in the shift to instrumentalism and managerialism. This has raised concerns within both professions of a deskilling process, a reduction in the scope for judgement and interpretation of regulations and a move towards work that is mechanical and administrative (Jordan, 2000).

To this extent Robinson's (2003) research has relevance for social work, in that she addresses one of the central preoccupations in contemporary practice, the perceived assault on professional identity by managerialist and technicist models of practice and research. This trend has been associated with negative professional consequences and a process of 'technical proletarianisation', with practitioners constrained, controlled and deskilled. In the absence of research on the actual implementation and impact of 'technical' initiatives, Robinson wanted to know whether frontline staff are really being robbed of the 'last remnants of discretion' (Nellis, 1995: 28), how they understand relationships between concepts of technicality, indeterminacy and professionalism, and whether practitioners are able to find ways to avoid or subvert attempts to dictate the shape of practice.

Robinson's study examined in detail the implementation and deployment of a risk/needs assessment instrument to establish how far it contributed to the erosion of indeterminacy or discretion, and examine the relationship between the instrument's implementation and perceptions of 'professionalism'. The instrument was the Level of Service Inventory – Revised (LSI-R), a highly structured risk assessment instrument. Scores allocated to a number of risk factors are said to predict possibilities of reconviction. This in turn informs decisions about the type or 'level of service' appropriate to individual offenders.

Robinson used two area probation services where the instrument had been in use for some time, to develop a case study approach. She adopted a 'stakeholder' model, so that the experiences and perceptions of the full range of personnel within the two organisations could be taken into account. She conducted 29 in-depth interviews, with personnel ranging from administrative staff to senior managers, and analysed the data by quantitative methods. She also carried out an analysis of organisational documents to augment the data. She examined correlations across the data and concluded that both the technical properties of the instrument and the policies established in the two area services regarding the use of LSI-R indicated a high level of technicality or prescription, in respect of the assessment process per se and the post-assessment resource allocation decisions. However, Robinson's work questioned the easy assumption of a significant erosion of indeterminacy. She discovered a more complex process at work.

First, the way the LSI-R was sold to practitioners by managers emphasised not only the technical skill needed to use the instrument, but also the professional skills necessary – 'it doesn't and never was *intended* to take completely away from professional judgement' (a manager quoted by Robinson, 2003: 598). Furthermore, a number of practitioners themselves saw the instrument as a reflection of or a *supplement* to their own assessment, rather than an alternative to it. And importantly, Robinson's examination of practice revealed that the LSI-R scores were far from pivotal in respect of allocations decisions, and professional judgement and negotiation still had an important part to play. The most significant barrier to a purely actuarial approach ('government-by-numbers', p. 599) was in fact the *offender population*. This meant that many of those offenders deemed suitable for intensive probation programmes by virtue of high LSI-R scores were not good candidates in view of issues such as mental health, drug use or a history of failure to complete programmes. In addition, magistrates were resistant to the instrument, as they perceived it as a threat to their discretion in sentencing. Robinson concluded that claims for the 'technical' profile of contemporary probation and social work practice may have been exaggerated, the experience of technical innovations may be shaped to a significant extent by context, or perceptions of purpose and the experience of deprofessionalisation may depend on the maintenance of an acceptable degree of indeterminancy.

One of the lessons from this research points to the limitations of methods led by apparently scientific knowledge which do not take account of narrative knowledge – the meanings attributed by social actors to behaviour and tasks undertaken. Had Robinson's study counted the number of times the instrument had been used, and measured its routine technical application and the outcomes of scores and their influence on decisions about the level of service, she might have produced knowledge that concluded that indeed the probation task is now dominated by technicality. She might also have concluded that the LSI-R 'works'. However, she found that the *perceptions* of those administering it did not suggest that they viewed it as a threat to their professional skills. Rather they saw it as an aid that supplemented a professional clinical assessment. All this suggests that they were able to resist and *subvert* the technical process by insisting on the role of professional judgement and ensuring that factors other than solely auditing techniques influenced the process.

The study is also evocative of decades of debates about the 'scientific method' versus interpretive approaches to social research. One of the key epistemological issues this debate addresses is whether it is appropriate to apply similar principles to the study of people to those applied in the physical sciences about the nature of reality and the rules that govern it. The implicit hypothesis that the application of a particular instrument will measure suitability for and identify appropriate treatment could not take account of the context of offenders' lives. In dealing with human beings, it is not possible to control variables as in a laboratory experiment, because of the unpredictability and contingency of lived experience and factors such as (in this case) illness and drug use, which are not conducive to measurement. Robinson (2003) rightly identified the offender population as the most significant barrier to a purely actuarial approach. This rather undermines the aim of the experiment, since 'offenders' or 'service users' are the *raison d'être* of the professions involved and cannot easily be dispensed with as inconvenient intrusions.

Robinson's tentative conclusion, that a professional future lies in a 'balance' between technicality and indeterminancy, may be that of a cautious researcher who perhaps realistically cannot envisage a future free of increasingly technical applications to social problems. At the same time, her agreement with a senior manager that the ultimate guardians of indeterminancy are not likely to be practitioners or their managers, but rather the clients with whom professionals work, is somehow a reassuring confirmation of the need for a research approach that does not take anything for granted and opens up spaces for contesting and relocating definitions of power and the purposes of social work.

Nevertheless, unanswered questions concern the legitimacy of the knowledge constructed out of Robinson's research. Will the belief amongst practitioners that their clinical judgement and professional discretion are not fundamentally threatened by galloping technicality make any difference at the end of the day? Or is it convenient for managers and politicians to patronise them by asserting no threat to their professionalism, whilst nevertheless pursuing the technical route and thus rendering practitioners' views inauthentic and irrelevant? Do subjective meanings make a difference, beyond being an interesting 'finding'? What are the advantages and drawbacks of 'professional judgement' in any case? Are clients benefited or disadvantaged by them?

Robinson (2003: 608) believes that the complexity described in her research may confound attempts to render probation practice and social work a wholly technical enterprise. If so, this is to be welcomed in order to recapture notions of uncertainty and ambiguity in professional practice, as urged by Parton (1998). Nevertheless, a critical research perspective would go beyond identifying oppressive structures and the activities that sustain them, to take action to combat and challenge them. Robinson's uncommitted positioning on the issue does not contribute to this aspect.

Analysed within the framework I have suggested for critical research, there are a number of other points to be made. The first is to do with the *positioning* of the researcher. Robinson's study is unreflexive, in that she does not say anything about her own standpoint and attempts to maintain the illusion of the 'neutral' researcher. We are not told what her beliefs are about the topic under examination and how these might have influenced the aims and methods of the study. She does not share her views about notions of professionalism and its relation to the modernisation plans of New Labour. She does not concern herself with the impact the changes might have on probationers themselves.

Some clues are discernable in what she omitted to address in the study. Robinson did not set out to concern herself with the experiences or the 'bringing to voice' of people convicted of crimes, but with the professional power of probation officers. This is not a criticism of the study as such, since clear and manageable parameters have to be set for any research undertaken and Robinson's focus is a relevant and legitimate one. It is simply to make the point that the basic concern was not with the 'empowerment' of probationers. In this respect her article did not address ethical questions about, for example, whether informed consent was sought and gained from probationers to take part in the LSI-R experiment or whether it was assumed this was not necessary (in any case, the issue of whether genuine consent could be gained where people are subject to legal authority is a moot point).

Moreover, even within its own terms of reference, the study might have addressed the wider structures that impact on the work of professionals, as for example in the increasing surveillance of and disciplining of the self as an essential part of governmentality, a crucial aspect of the regulatory practices of a range of modern institutions, as described by Usher and Edwards (1994). Robinson's suggestion of a 'balance' between technicality and indeterminancy evades the issue of the hegemony of managerialism and technicism as disciplinary practices. From this perspective, what *appears* to be resistance from professionals can be viewed as no more than an accommodation to a regime where 'power is hidden from the awareness of those through whom it circulates' (Usher and Edwards, 1994: 97). The study does not transgress, disrupt, challenge and change the material and ideological realities.

CONCLUSION

The degree in social work places emphasis on three characteristics of professionalism: theory, practice and research. What I have been arguing for here offers the potential to trace a seamless connection among these elements, by identifying a moral and political position to critique theory and inform practice, whether it is defined as 'research' or not. It is a perspective that centres the experiences of those who are oppressed by social institutions, facilitates a description of the processes by which this happens and provides the language to argue for an ultimate research focus on the working of the institutions of power in order to construct a holistic understanding of the forces that impact on service users' lives.

Research and practice that isolates individual behaviour and experience from the wider social and political context and focuses narrowly on outcomes and effectiveness (as in the 'what works?' agenda) is blinkered and limited. In that model, 'objectivity' (ironically valued highly in constructing research designs) is sacrificed in a climate where 'outcomes' hold the dominant value and questions are not asked about origins, aims, motives, ideology and context. A critical approach does not mean necessarily that service users should themselves always be the objects of research. The workings of power can just as well be examined by a focus on elites, or on the mediators of power, as in Robinson's study of probation officers.

This is not to ignore the fact that oppressed groups can themselves be oppressors, or romanticise the working class, women, black people or whoever. It is to reveal the links between their exploitation and social structures, and influence research practice towards more informed and effective ways of confronting their problems. My choice of studies to examine in this chapter does not privilege any particular methodology, and I would argue that there are few methods that do not lend themselves to a critical approach. It is the attitude of mind, the desire to make the invisible visible, the urge to centre issues of justice, equality and empowerment that constitute the radical potential of social work research. In this way, the focus is not only on how 'deviant' individual behaviour can be changed, but also on policies and institutional practices and their impact on the poor and the marginalised. It is on how such policies and practices are or can be challenged by those affected by them. I end with a plea and a hope that the futures of social work will include an attitude to research that sets its critical sights on policies, institutions and structures as targets for change, rather than a meek acceptance that these are irrelevant to an individualistic and often demeaning practice. The motivation for such a shift in research focus – and a legitimate role for social work – is *social* transformation.

FURTHER READING

D'Cruz, H. and Jones, M. (2004) *Social Work Research: A Political and Ethical Practice?* (London: Sage). An introductory research text for students on the degree in social work. It regards research as another social work method and is informed by social work's 'emancipatory' goals and objectives. At the same time it is a useful practical guide to the design, methods and processes of carrying out a research project. It is structured around exercises to reinforce learning.

Fook, J. (2002) *Social Work: Critical Theory and Practice* (London: Sage). Fook explores a theoretical framework that attempts to integrate classic critical and postmodernist perspectives to produce a framework for social work. The book also advocates an approach to social work theory, practice and research as a seamless whole. It is clear, accessible and grounded in examples and exercises easily recognisable from everyday practice.

Truman, C. (2004) *Transforming Social Research* (London: Routledge). Truman's book is written for experienced researchers and those on professional courses who are concerned to pursue research with marginalised groups in society. It bridges the gap between texts that are solely about 'methods' and those that tackle epistemological and ethical issues. In particular it acknowledges differences across marginalised groups and how these can be taken account of in research practice. It uses both quantitative and qualitative research studies to illustrate how this approach can be used within a framework of evidence-based policy and practice.

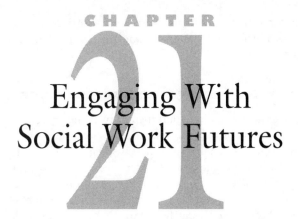

CHAPTER 21

Engaging With
Social Work Futures

Robert Adams, Lena Dominelli and Malcolm Payne

Introduction

Transformation has been a central theme of this book. In it, we have demonstrated some of the major ways in which our reflective and critical practice may be transformational. We set the scene for social work as a continuing transformational activity in the diversity of settings for future practice. We recognise that the task of transforming practice is an unfinished and unending project, exciting but risky. The changes affecting social work and the uncertainties about its future throw up potential pitfalls but also offer opportunities for dynamic and innovative activity. It is helpful to remind ourselves of the ambiguities inherent in social work. It may be exciting and stimulating to be practising amid the ferment of constant change, but it is also likely to be stressful and anxiety-provoking.

We are in a position now to review some of the main themes which have emerged during this book. Some, like boundaries and complexity, were in the foreground when we started out. Others, like connectedness, have become more important as we have proceeded. No single book can cover the entire range of practice and we have chosen chapters that concentrate on some key areas of practice. In whatever area of practice, it is necessary for you, the reader, to evaluate your own practice critically and self-critically to sustain your professional and personal development and update your knowledge and skills in future. Bearing in mind that the emphasis you give is a matter of your own personal judgement, this chapter presents our view of the three major themes providing opportunities for transforming practice: the context of future changes and uncertainties; a transformed understanding of practice; and the handling of complexity in practice.

Context of future changes and uncertainties

Social work is governed by laws and bureaucratic rules and procedures, which confer powers on practitioners but may also restrict professional autonomy. Social workers experience multiple accountabilities: to the law, their employers, their professional ethics and standards, colleagues, service users and carers. To some extent, these organisational settings and working conditions make for uncertainty. Social workers have to work in complex environments, in multidisciplinary, multi-agency teams.

The impossibility of predicting how future changes affect the context and shape social work adds to the inevitable uncertainties of service users' lives, which are inherent in practice. Social workers practise in conditions of great uncertainty. The problems and difficulties of people with whom they work are evident and all too often permit no ready or obvious solutions. In families, for instance, one person's interests may be ranged against another's. Every possible decision may benefit some family members and disadvantage others. Let us reframe these uncertainties as opportunities for change. Change is embedded in all aspects of practice and has the potential to transform lives. Transformation reality may involve changing how we represent it. There are two elements to representation. In one, representation means showing the nature of someone or something. In the other, it means acting on someone's behalf to speak up for them. For example, in representing a person, we speak up for them. In doing so, we represent them in a new way. Also, in performing a set of transformations, we change ourselves, our practice and the setting as well as the lives of the people we work with. In listening, we change them again, because we understand the representation differently. Therefore, practice involves us interacting with colleagues, service users and carers, as well as (re)interpreting meaning by trying to understand, reflect on and (re)evaluate our practice as we seek change.

Our transformed understanding of practice

The three major parts of this book have tackled social work processes, aspects of practice and the aspiration of developing ourselves as research-capable practitioners. In Part I, we have gone beyond the study of things and outcomes in order to understand processes. We realise how, as practitioners, we examine our practice as a current and ongoing activity and on looking back, encounter freshness in what we have simply glanced at earlier or may even have taken for granted. This is a constant process of discovery and rediscovery, connecting then and now, in which we recognise that we are probably missing things now.

In Part II, we have highlighted how, in crossing boundaries, it is the connections that are important. The methods of doing this and how these are perceived are crucial, as important as the destination. Through the complexities of practice, we see how social work encounters paradoxical themes and, although these are not dissolved, practitioners grapple creatively with them. Chapter 7 examined boundaries from the viewpoint of perpetual change and uncertainty. The way forward is not to find a way back to an assumed, but mythical, golden age but to transform practice.

We view the development of practice research in Part III, not in the narrow sense of a search for essential results and truth, but as an opportunity to interpret and reinterpret realities. The common outcome of this journey is that we find no final, essential, absolute truth on which to base a transformational practice, but we achieve transformed understandings. This provides a realistic basis from which to regard the diversity of our world.

Our handling of complexity in practice

We have encountered complexities throughout the book. Complexities lie at the heart of social work. Often, complexity, tensions and dilemmas go hand in hand and we have confirmed how important it is to manage and move beyond these. We can instance four particular areas where this is important: managing the relationship between theory and practice; handling boundaries and connections; dealing with globalisation and fragmentation; and bureaucratisation and creative practice.

Managing the relationship between theory and practice

In this book we have engaged with theory and practice and the idea that theory is embedded in practice. Theory and practice may seem to have separate boundaries, but are also interdependent. There is a need to manage this interdependence and separation and constantly keep it under review.

Handling boundaries and connections

We have seen in Chapter 7 how the notion of boundary is ambiguous, in the sense that we can regard boundaries as barriers inhibiting progress or as a usual way of demarcating territory and defining areas of work. We can see these ambiguities in analogies. In Chapter 7, we witnessed the residential staff member working with young people describing the function of the symbolic bars, representing the rules round the boundary of the residential setting. The young person can lean on the bars when wanting support. Sometimes, they represent authority and may be gripped and shaken, in frustration. In these ways, boundaries perform markedly contrasting roles, which on occasions may contradict each other.

In different games and sports, boundaries fulfil a range of positive and negative functions. In football, when the ball crosses the boundary, it is out of play. In rugby, players kick the ball over a boundary in order to make time to regroup themselves for the next advance. In the game of cricket, the boundary offers the potential for high scoring because when the ball crosses the boundary, the team gains. We have sought a richer and more complex view of boundaries than this. They emerge as spanning the continuum between what we desire and what we shun. We have seen the need to reconceptualise our boundaries around practice as permeable and porous, at the same time as restating them. The problem is how to restate the boundaries without them becoming associated with what is negative, defensive and static, and account for social work as a profession in flux.

The ideas of connections and connectedness have emerged as important themes in this book. Connections are the flip side of boundaries as demarcation points. The more boundaries are emphasised, the more important it is to make and maintain links, or bring out the connectedness they also encompass. A transforming practice is based on making good connections and making the most of them. It also involves managing tensions, even contradictions, maintaining as well as working across boundaries.

Dealing with globalisation and fragmentation

We have examined global boundaries. Globalisation is a reality in most aspects of our lives and work. In the past, globalisation may have seemed to offer the promise of greater equality. This has not happened. While wealth has increased, inequality due to poverty has also increased both within and between countries and the mass migration of people as a result of natural disasters, conflict and the desire to improve their well-being have created new problems for social workers to address alongside complicating specific responses in any given nation state (Dominelli, 2004). Additionally, localism is as strong, if not stronger than previously. Thus, practitioners engage with a globalising world, which is fragmenting to give prominence to locality and regionalism, greatly increasing the range of diversities that social workers address.

In several chapters, we have crossed geographical boundaries and examined diversities in different countries. In Australia (Chapter 15), for instance, practice is more creative because it is not as dominated by state bureaucracies as it is in Britain. In the UK, creative and innovative practice, although by no means monopolised by the voluntary sector, is found in some voluntary agencies such as those working in childcare and palliative care. It is possible to find exciting and stimulating practice 'hidden' in statutory agencies.

In other countries, particularly those in Eastern Europe, the not-for-profit sector has enabled NGOs to flourish. The vitality of organisations such as the Red Cross and Oxfam enables us to scrutinise critically arguments about the assumed 'end of politics'. These organisations, like the forceful campaigns associated with War on Want which challenged the Thatcher government's lack of commitment to anti-poverty strategies twenty years ago, have risked their UK charitable status to engage in politics aimed at promoting people's well-being. Yet the growing influence of such bodies raises questions about their accountability. Whilst smaller voluntary and not-for-profit groups may be accountable to local people, the accountability of larger organisations which operate across national borders and continents is more difficult to realise (Duffield, 2001).

Sustaining creative practice in highly regulated settings

A further area of complexity and tension exists between the trends towards greater bureaucratic and managerialist control over practice and opportunities for creative practice. Bureaucracy and regulation, in the UK at any rate, go hand in hand, with practice being skewed by politicians who intervene to change its professional orientation, organisation and commitment to social change. Often their response is to control its creative dimensions by restructuring and organising it along more bureaucratic, managerialist lines.

We have touched on regulation and managerialism. These trends contribute towards increasing bureaucratisation, inspection, regulation and surveillance. But are these developments inevitably the enemies of good practice? In Britain, the state tends to bureaucratise and regulate as an inevitable consequence of providing social work services through the public sector. In a world of exclusively private provision, markets would self-regulate. In British social work, the imposition of standards has acquired additional momentum partly because of widespread public concern about specific failures and shortcomings of practice that sometimes result in adults and children being harmed or killed through abuse or neglect. This does not imply that residential childcare, for instance, is inherently harmful. However, welfare services do not ensure people's betterment automatically. So there must be protection for the client, the consumer, the user of services to ensure that he or she does not become the victim of professional malpractice, but survives and prospers. Given these complexities, the demands for higher standards and quality assurance and the implementation of regional, national and supernational policies and laws, it is unrealistic in today's world to relegate the state to a merely enabling role.

In general, we have acknowledged the importance of regulations and standards, but have chosen to emphasise the need for children, adults, residents, people receiving social work services to have more choices, more rights, more power. More broadly perhaps, practitioners and those employing them need to seek ways of changing how politicians and the public at large perceive social workers.

Managing tensions between frailty and strength in critical practice

The paradox of a strong critical practice is its frailty, through its aspiration to be stringently self-aware and searingly self-critical. We have written previously of the need for critical practitioners to remain open and self-critical (Payne et al., 2002). Self-criticism has the advantage of promoting more secure and adequate future practice. Self-criticism is not a negative trait but it exposes the practitioner to critical scrutiny by others and is open about personal weaknesses and failings. Self-critical practitioners are required to state where they are coming from – in terms of their gender, 'race', power and other relevant aspects – when working with another person. Over and above this, is the expectation that they will identify their own personal and professional shortcomings. Admitting one's failings may be construed wrongly as evidence of failure; openness may be regarded as a sign of weakness. In a real sense, becoming more critical and self-critical invites others to criticise. The more open we are in this process, the more we acknowledge the weaknesses of our practice. This frailty is, paradoxically, the strength of good practice. In contrast, the reality is that the open practitioner is more likely to be able to take on board critical comments by service users, evaluate previous practice self-critically, adapt to changing circumstances and modify future practice accordingly.

We should be aware of the strengths of a self-aware, frail practice. The frailty of social work also lies beyond its commitment to self-critical and critical practice and is embedded in the nature of its organisational contexts and the working conditions to which we referred above. In Britain, the fragility of social work is skewed further by politics and bureaucracies. In particular, social workers in larger, statutory settings lack the freedom to develop professional practice in the ways experienced by colleagues in countries where organisational controls are weak or non-existent. There are contrasts also in Britain between social work in local authority settings and voluntary agencies.

CONCLUSION

The complex, uncertain and unfinished nature of most social work and the pace of change shape this conclusion by ensuring that nothing is finally concluded. However, we can be certain that the future will involve practitioners in tackling situations of greater complexity, working increasingly across many different boundaries and engaging in more collaborative work with others. At the same time, we can anticipate the additional stresses created by such work. Practitioners will need to develop inner resources to deal with uncertainties and disappointments. They will be subjected to changes and responsible for empowering others. But they may have neither the resources nor the power to effect the changes they would like to bring about. They will need to manage their own anger, frustration and hope, whilst engaging in transformational practice and seeking alliances with others to achieve alternative ends.

Acting as professional social workers touches upon our personal values and makes it crucial that we examine these whilst in training and in our chosen career afterwards. We have to understand our beliefs and taken-for-granted assumptions and make them explicit. We have to be prepared to question them self-critically and have them challenged by others. As we develop as critical practitioners, we have to adopt this self-critical, self-questioning approach as a way of work. This forms part of our commitment to engaging in continuing professional development. Post-qualifying study is a necessary part of lifelong learning. Because our own values interact with our work, we have to accept that critical practice in social work isn't only a way of work; it's a way of life.

It is crucial for practitioners to feed their criticality and self-critical awareness by keeping up to date with other people's research and also engage in their own evaluation of their practice. Evaluation should be *with* service users, not practised in isolation from them. The practitioner-researcher should be confident in using research evidence judiciously in practice and remorselessly critical of narrow and rigid approaches to evidence-based practice. In particular, the research-aware and capable practitioner should be confident in making connections between the work done with service users and issues in the wider community.

Because critical practice in social work crosses boundaries between our work and the rest of our lives, our personal and our professional activities, our future practice requires us to engage in continuous personal and professional development. These two aspects need to develop side by side. Our minds, our emotions and our actions are affected. It is important, therefore, to recognise the contribution of all our being to practice development and not restrict critical practice just to work, but see it as a way of life. Jan Fook reminds us that the integration of theory with practice does not happen when knowledge is applied mechanistically to practice, any more than research evidence can be lifted off the shelf and applied mechanistically to 'solve' people's problems. Critical reflection is a process, 'a way in which we engage with our contexts in order to deconstruct and critically reconstruct' (Fook, 1999: 207). Fook also emphasises the importance of not handing down a critically reflective approach to practice from academics and theorists to practitioners and enjoins us all to have the humility to learn from the experiences of practitioners and people receiving services. Chapter 7 uses the term 'sceptical' to describe the questioning and self-questioning of the critical practitioner. A healthy scepticism does not imply a lack of commitment, but rather a dedication to constant critical self-scrutiny and study of every aspect of practice.

Whether we prefer the term 'sceptical' or 'critical', we can and should retain our optimism about our present and future practice. Our continuing learning, like the future development of our practice, is lifelong and carries enormous potential to open new avenues for further development. Criticality is transformational, in that it extends social work into a variety of forms of future practice and the choices, conflicts, tensions and uncertainties which accompany these. In order to retain our vitality as practitioners, we need constantly to regenerate our questioning, renew our criticality and continue to transform our thinking and practice.

Bibliography

AASW (Australian Association of Social Workers) (1999) *Code of Ethics* (Canberra: AASW).

Abdool Karim, S.S., Abdool Karim, Q., Preston-Whyte, E. and Sankar, N. (1992) 'Reasons for Lack of Condom Use among High School Students in Natal, South Africa', *South African Medical Journal* (82).

Abramson, R.J. (2003) 'The Unity of Mind, Body, and Spirit: A Five-element View of Cancer', *Advances in Mind-Body Medicine* **19**(2): 20–1.

Acheson, Sir D. (1998) Independent Inquiry into Inequalities in Health Report (London: Stationery Office).

Adams, J. (1995) *Risk* (London: UCL Press).

Adams, R. (1981) 'Outsiders Inside Penal Establishments: Servants or Reformers?', *AMBOV* (2): 6–9.

Adams, R. (1998) in Adams, R., Dominelli, L. and Payne, M. (1998) (eds) *Social Work Themes, Issues and Critical Debates* (Basingstoke, Macmillan – now Palgrave Macmillan) Chp. 21, pp. 253–72.

Adams, R. (2002) 'Developing Critical Practice in Social Work', in Adams, R., Dominelli, L. and Payne, M. (eds) *Critical Practice in Social Work* (Basingstoke: Palgrave – now Palgrave Macmillan).

Adams, R., Dominelli, L. and Payne, M. (eds) (2002a) S*ocial Work: Themes, Issues and Critical Debates* (2nd edn) (Basingstoke: Palgrave Macmillan).

Adams, R., Dominelli, L. and Payne, M. (2002b) *Critical Practice in Social Work* (Basingstoke: Palgrave Macmillan).

Ader, F., Felten, D.L. and Cohen, N. (1991) *Psychoneuroimmunology* (San Diego: Academic Press).

Alaszewski, A. and Walsh, M. (1995) 'Typologies of Welfare Organisations: A Literature Review', *British Journal of Social Work* **25**: 805–15.

Aldridge, J., Parker, H. and Measham, F. (1999) 'Drug Trying and Drug Use across Adolescence: A Longitudinal Study of Young People's Drug Taking in Two Regions of Northern England', DPAS Paper No.1 (London: Home Office).

Alexander, L.A. and Link, B.G. (2003) 'The Impact of Contact on Stigmatising Attitudes towards People with Mental Illness', *Journal of Mental Health* 12(3): 271–90.

Alsop, A. and Ryan, S. (1996) *Making the Most of Fieldwork Education: A Practical Approach* (London: Chapman & Hall).

Alston, M. and Bowles, W. (1998) *Research for Social Workers: An Introduction to Methods* (London: Allen & Unwin).

Alvesson, M. and Skoldberg, K. (2000) *Reflexive Methodology: New Vistas for Qualitative Research* (London: Sage).

Appleby, G.A. and Anastas, J.W. (1998) *Not Just a Passing Phase: Social Work with Gay, Lesbian, and Bisexual People* (New York: Columbia University Press).

Argyris, C. and Schön, D.A. (1974) *Theory in Practice: Increasing Professional Effectiveness* (San Francisco: Jossey-Bass).

Audit Commission (1994) *Seen but not Heard* (London: HMSO).

Australian Broadcasting Commission (2002) *Street Stories: Children in Detention* (Sydney: Radio National).

Badcock-Walters, P. (2002) 'Impacts: Education', in Gow, J. and Desmond, C. (eds) *Impacts and Interventions: The HIV/AIDS Epidemic and the Children of South Africa* (Pietermaritzburg: University of Natal Press).

Baer, R.A. (2003) 'Mindfulness Training as a Clinical Intervention: A Conceptual and Empirical Review', *Clinical Psychology: Science and Practice* 10(2): 125–43.

Bailar, J.C. and Bailer, A.J. (1999) 'Risk Assessment – the Mother of All Uncertainties: Disciplinary Perspectives on Uncertainty in Risk Assessment', in *Annals of New York Academy of Sciences* 895: 273–85.

Balding, J. (2001) *Young People in 2000* (Exeter: Schools Health Education Unit).

Baldwin, N. (ed.) (2000) *Protecting Children and Promoting their Rights* (London: Whiting & Birch).

Baldwin, N. and Spencer, N. (2000) 'Strategic Planning to Prevent Harm to Children', in Baldwin, N. (ed.) *Protecting Children, Promoting their Rights* (London: Whiting & Birch).

Bandalli, S. (1998) 'Abolition of the Presumption of Doli Incapax and the Criminalisation of Children', *Howard Journal of Criminal Justice* 37(2): 114–23.

Banks, S. (2001) *Ethics and Values in Social Work* (2nd edn) (Basingstoke: Palgrave – now Palgrave Macmillan).

Banks, S. (2003) 'From Oaths to Rulebooks: a Critical Examination of Codes of Ethics for the Social Professions', *European Journal of Social Work* 6(2): 133–44.

Barnes, C. (1991) *Disabled People in Britain and Discrimination: A Case for Anti-discrimination Legislation* (London: Hurst & Co).

Barnes, C. and Mercer, G. (eds) (1997) *Doing Disability Research* (Leeds: The Disability Press).

Barnes, C., Mercer, G. and Shakespeare, T. (1999) *Exploring Disability* (Cambridge: Polity Press).

Barnes, D. and Kendall, M. (2001) 'Working with Disabled People in Consultation and Research', *Research Policy and Planning* 19(1): 17–24.

Barr, A. (2003) 'Participative Planning and Evaluation Skills', in Banks, S., Butcher, H., Henderson, P. and Robertson, J. (eds) *Managing Community Practice: Principles, Policies and Programmes* (Bristol: Policy Press) pp. 57–82.

Barr, A. and Hashagen, S. (2000) *ABCD Handbook: A Framework for Evaluating Community Development* (London: Community Development Foundation).

Bauld, L., Chesterman, J. and Judge, K. (2000) 'Measuring Satisfaction with Social Care amongst Older Service Users: Issues from the Literature', *Health and Social Care in the Community* **8**(5): 316–24.

Bayley, J. (1999) *Iris and the Friends* (London: Abacus).

Beck, U. (1992) *Risk Society: Towards a New Modernity* (London: Sage).

Beck, U. (1999) *World Risk Society* (Cambridge: Polity Press).

Beckett, C. (2003) *Child Protection* (London: Sage).

Belenky, M.F., Clinchy, M.B., Goldberger, N.R. and Tarule, M.J. (1997) *Women's Ways of Knowing: The Development of Self, Voice and Mind* (New York: Basic Books).

Belsky, J. (1980) 'Child Maltreatment: an Ecological Integration', *American Psychologist* **35**: 320–35.

Ben-Ari, A.T. (2001) 'Homosexuality and heterosexism: Views from Academics in the Helping Professions', *British Journal of Social Work* **31**: 119–31.

Beresford, P. (2000) 'Users' Knowledges and Social Work Theory', *British Journal of Social Work* **30**(4): 489–503.

Beresford, P. and Evans, C. (1999) 'Research Note: Research and Empowerment', *British Journal of Social Work* **29**(5): 671–7.

Berridge, V. (1999[1981]) *Opium and the People: Opiate Use and Drug Control Policy in Nineteenth and Early Twentieth Century England* (London: Free Association Books).

Bhana, A. (1999) 'Participatory Action Research: A Practical Guide for Realistic Radicals', in Terre Blanche, M. and Durrheim, K. (eds) *Research in Practice: Applied Methods for the Social Sciences* (Cape Town: University of Cape Town Press).

Bilboe, H. (2002) *Submission to National Inquiry into Children in Immigration Detention* (Sydney: Human Rights and Equal Opportunity Commission) http://www.humanrights.gov.au/human_rights/ children_detention/statements/bilboe.html.

Black, D. (2001) 'The Limitations of Evidence', in Heller, T., Muston, R., Sidell, M. and Lloyd, C. (eds) *Working for Health* (London: Open University/Sage).

Blears, H. (2003) 'Freedom for the prisoners of fear', *Policy Review* Winter: 8–9.

Blom-Cooper, Sir L. QC. (1993) 'Public Inquiries', in Freeman, M. and Hepple, B. (eds) *Current Legal Problems* (Oxford: Oxford University Press).

Bok, S. (1984) *Secrets: Concealment and Revelation* (Oxford: Oxford University Press).

Bottoms, A.E. (1977) 'Reflections on the Renaissance of Dangerousness', *Howard Journal of Criminal Justice* **16**(2): 70–96.

Bottoms, A.E. (1995) 'The Philosophy and Politics of Punishment and Sentencing', in Clark, C. and Morgan, R. (eds) *The Politics of Sentencing Reform* (Clarendon Press: Oxford).

Brah, A. (1996) *Cartographies of Diaspora* (London: Routledge).

Brigham, L. (2000) 'Understanding Segregation from the Nineteenth to the Twentieth Century: Re-drawing Boundaries and the Problems of "Pollution"', in Brigham, L., Atkinson, D., Jackson, M., Rolph, S. and Walmsley, J. (eds) *Crossing Boundaries: Change and Continuity in the History of Learning Disability* (Kidderminster: British Institute of Learning Disabilities (BILD)).

Briskman, L. (2001) 'A Moral Crisis for Social Work', *Critical Social Work* **2**(1): 34–8, http://www.criticalsocialwork.com/CSW_2001_1.html.

Briskman, L. (2003) *The Black Grapevine: Aboriginal Activism and the Stolen Generations* (Sydney: Federation Press).

Briskman, L. and Fraser, H. (2002) 'Freedom First, then Education', *The Age* Melbourne, 7 August.

Briskman, L. and Noble, C. (1999) 'Social Work Ethics: Embracing Diversity?', in Pease, B. and Fook, J. (eds) *Transforming Social Work Practice: Postmodern Critical Perspectives* (St Leonards: Allen & Unwin).

British Association of Social Work (2002) *Code of Ethics for Social Work* (Birmingham: BASW).

British Association of Social Work (2003) *Code of Ethics for Social Work* (Birmingham: BASW).

British Sociological Association (2003) 'Statement of Ethical Practice', http://www. britsoc.org.uk/about/ethic.htm, accessed 31.07.03.

Broad, B. and Fletcher, C. (eds) (1993) *Practitioner Social Work Research In Action* (London: Whiting & Birch).

Bronfenbrenner, U. (1977) 'Toward an Experiential Ecology of Human Development', *American Psychologist* **32**: 513–31.

Brookfield, S. (1987) *Developing Critical Thinkers* (Buckingham: Open University Press).

Brown, C. (2004) 'Social Work Intervention: the Deconstruction of Individuals as a Means of Remaining in the UK', in Hayes, D. and Humphries, B. (eds) *Social Work, Immigration and Asylum* (London: Jessica Kingsley).

Brown, H.C. (1991) 'Competent Child-Focused Practice: Working with Lesbians and Gay Carers', *Adoption and Fostering* **15**(2): 11–17.

Brown, H.C. (1992) 'Lesbians, the State and Social Work Practice', in Langan, M. and Day, L. (eds) *Women, Oppression and Social Work: Issues in Anti-discriminatory Practice* (London: Routledge) pp. 201–19.

Brown, H.C. (1996) 'The Knowledge Base of Social Work', in Vass, A. (ed.) *Social Work Competences* (London: Sage).

Brown, H.C. (1998a) *Social Work and Sexuality: Working with Lesbians and Gay Men* (Basingstoke: Macmillan – now Palgrave Macmillan).

Brown, H.C. (1998b) 'Working with Lesbians and Gay Men: Sexuality and Practice Teaching', in Lawson, H. (ed.) *Working with Lesbians and Gay Men: Sexuality and Practice Teaching* (London: Jessica Kingsley) pp. 49–65.

Brown, H.C. (1998c) 'Lesbians and Gay Men: Social Work and Discrimination', in Lesnik, B. (ed.) *Countering Discrimination in Social Work: International Perspectives in Social Work* (Aldershot: Arena) pp. 89–110.

Bryman, A. (2001) *Social Research Methods* (Oxford: Oxford University Press).

Buchanan, A. (1999) *What Works for Troubled Children: Family Support for Children with Emotional and Behavioural Problems* (Ilford: Barnardo's).

Bulmer, M. (2001) 'The Ethics of Social Research', in Gilbert, N. (ed.) *Researching Social Life* (2nd edn) (London: Sage) pp. 45–57.

Burnett, A. and Fassil, Y. (2002) *Meeting the Health Needs of Refugees and Asylum Seekers in the UK* (London: NHS Publications).

Burney, E. (1999) *Crime and Banishment: Nuisance and Exclusion in Social Housing* (Winchester: Waterside Press).

Burney, E. (2002) 'Talking Tough, Acting Coy: Whatever happened to the Anti-Social Behaviour Order', *Howard Journal of Criminal Justice* **41**(5): 469–84.

Burton, M. and Kellaway, M. (1998) *Developing and Managing High Quality Services for People with Learning Disabilities* (Aldershot: Ashgate).

Butler, I. (2002) 'A Code of Ethics for Social Work and Social Care Research', *British Journal of Social Work* **32**: 239–48.

Butler, I. (2003) 'Doing Good Research and Doing it Well: Ethical Awareness and the Production of Social Work Research', *Social Work Education* **22**(1): 19–30.

Butler, I. and Drakeford, M. (2003) *Social Policy, Social Welfare and Scandal. How British Public Policy is Made* (Basingstoke: Palgrave Macmillan).

Butler-Sloss, E. (2003) *Are we Failing the Family? Human Rights, Children and the Meaning of Family in the 21st Century*, http://www.led.gov.uk/judicial/speeches/dbs030403.htm.

Butrym, Z.T. (1976) *The Nature of Social Work* (London: Macmillan – now Palgrave Macmillan).

Cable, S. (2002) 'The Context – Why the Current Interest?', in Glen, S. and Leiba, T. (eds) *Multi-Professional Learning for Nurses: Breaking the Boundaries* (Basingstoke: Palgrave Macmillan).

Caddick, B. and Watson, D. (1999) 'Rehabilitation and the Distribution of Risk', in Parsloe, P. (ed.) *Risk Assessment in Social Care and Social Work* (London: Jessica Kingsley) pp. 53–68.

Calder, M. (2003) 'The Assessment Framework: A Critique and Reformulation', in Calder, M.C. and Hackett, S. (2003) *Assessment in Child Care: Using and Developing Frameworks for Practice* (Lyme Regis: Russell House).

Calder, M.C. with Peake, A. and Rose, K. (2001) *Mothers of Sexually Abused Children: A Framework for Assessment, Understanding and Support* (Lyme Regis: Russell House).

Cameron, L. and Freeman, I. (1996) 'Care Management: Meeting Different Needs', in Clark, C. and Lapsley, I. (eds) *Planning and Costing Community Care* (London: Jessica Kingsley).

Campbell, J. and Oliver, M. (1996) *Disability Politics: Understanding our Past, Changing our Future* (London: Routledge).

Carpenter, V. (1988) 'Amnesia and antagonism: Anti-lesbianism in the Youth Service', in Cant, B. and Hemmings, S. (eds) *Radical Records: Thirty Years of Lesbian & Gay History, 1957–1987* (London: Routledge) pp. 169–80.

Carson, D. (1994) 'Dangerous People: Through a Broader Concept of Risk and Danger to Better Decisions', *Expert Evidence* 3(2): 21–69.

Cemlyn, S. and Briskman, L. (2003) 'Asylum, Children's Rights and Social Work', *Child and Family Social Work* 8(3): 163–78.

Chambon, A.S. and Irving, A. (1999) 'Introduction', in Chambon, A.S., Irving, A. and Epstein, L. (eds) *Reading Foucault for Social Work* (New York: Columbia University Press) pp. xiii–xxx.

Chan, C.L.W. (2001) *An Eastern Body-Mind-Spirit Approach – A Training Manual with One-second Techniques* (Hong Kong: Department of Social Work and Social Administration, University of Hong Kong).

Chan, C.L.W., Chan, Y. and Lou, V.W.Q. (2001a) Evaluating an Empowerment Group for Divorced Chinese Women in Hong Kong, *Research on Social Work Practice* 12: 558–69.

Chan, C.L.W., Ho, P.S.Y. and Chow, E. (2001b) 'A Body-Mind-Spirit Model in Health: an Eastern Approach', *Social Work in Health Care* 34(3/4): 261–82.

Chan, C.L.W., Law, M.Y.Y. and Yeung, P.P.Y. (2000) 'An Empowerment Group for Chinese Cancer Patients in Hong Kong', in Chan, C.L.W. and Fielding, R. (eds) *Psychosocial Oncology & Palliative Care in Hong Kong: The First Decade* (Hong Kong: Hong Kong University Press).

Chan, H.Y., Chan, C.L.W., Ho, R.T.H., Ng, S.M., Ho, S.M.Y., Sham, J.S.T. et al. (2004) 'Tallying the Pains and Gains: Development of a Spiritual Outlook Inventory for Cancer Survivors.' Manuscript submitted for publication.

Charing, G., Deswardt, P., Henry, M., Launder, M., McDermott, A. and Pollard, N. (eds) (1975) *Case Con – Gay Issue*, (18).

Cheek, J. (2000) *Postmodern and Poststructural Approaches to Nursing Research* (Thousand Oak, CA: Sage).

Cheetham, J., Fuller, R., McIvor, G. and Petch, A. (1992) *Evaluating Social Work Effectiveness* (Buckingham: Open University Press).

Cheng, W.K. and Macfarlane, D.J. (2001) 'Effects of a Modified Tai Chi Programme on the Physical and Psychological Wellbeing of Elderly Chinese.' Paper presented at the 2nd International Symposium on Chinese Elderly, Shanghai.

Clarke, A. (1999) *Evaluation Research: An Introduction to Principles, Methods and Practice* (London: Sage).

Cleaver, H. and Department of Health (2000) *Assessment Recording Forms* (London: Stationery Office).

Cohen, S. (2001) *Immigration Controls, the Family and the Welfare State* (London: Jessica Kingsley).

Cohen, S. (2003) *No-one is Illegal: Asylum and Immigration Control, Past and Present* (London: Trentham Books).

Cohen, S. and Hayes, D. (1998) *They Make you Sick: Essays in Immigration Control and Health* (Manchester: Greater Manchester Immigration Aid Unit/Manchester Metropolitan University).

Cohen, S., Humphries, B. and Mynott, E. (eds) (2002) *From Immigration Controls to Welfare Controls* (London: Routledge).

Community Care (2002a) 'Council Loses Fight over Cancer Sufferer', *Community Care* (1445): 6.

Community Care (2002b) 'Seeking Education', *Community Care* (1440): 14.

Community Care (2003a) 'Blunkett: "Use New Powers or Face Sack"', *Community Care* (1463): 9.

Community Care (2003b) 'Discharged Asylum Seekers not Getting Support', *Community Care* (1464): 34–5.

Compton, B.R. and Galloway, B. (1999) *Social Work Processes* (6th edn) (Pacific Grove, CA: Brooks/Cole).

Condon, J. and Smith, N. (2003) *Prevalence of Drug Use: Key Finding from the 2002/2003 British Crime Survey*, Research Findings 229 (London: Home Office Research, Development and Statistics Directorate).

Constable, R.T. and Flynn, J.P. (1982) *School Social Work: Practice and Research Perspectives*. (Illinios: Dorsey Press).

Coombes, R. (2003) 'Adolescents who Sexually Abuse', in Matravers, A. (ed.) *Sex Offenders in the Community: Managing and Reducing the Risks* (Cullompton: Willan Publishing).

Cooper, B. (2000) 'The Measure of a Competent Childcare Social Worker?', *Journal of Social Work Practice* 14(2): 113–24.

Corden, J. and Preston-Shoot, M. (1987) *Contracts in Social Work* (Aldershot: Gower).

Corkery, J. (2002) *Drug Seizure and Offender Statistics*, Home Office Statistical Bulletin 4/02 (London: Home Office).

Corrigan, P.W. and Penn, D.L. (1999) 'Lessons from Social Psychology on Discrediting Psychiatric Stigma', *American Psychologist* 54(9): 765–76.

Corrigan, P.W., Edwards, A.B., Green, A., Diwan, S.L. and Penn, D.L. (2001) 'Prejudice, social distance and familiarity with mental illness', *Schizophrenia Bulletin* 27(2): 219–25.

Coulshed, V. and Orme, J. (1998) *Social Work Practice: An Introduction* (Basingstoke: Macmillan – now Palgrave Macmillan).

Couture, S.M. and Penn, D.L. (2003) 'Interpersonal Contact and the Stigma of Mental Illness: a Review of the Literature', *Journal of Mental Health* 12(3): 291–306.

Cowen, H. (1999) *Community Care, Ideology and Social Policy* (London: Prentice Hall).

Cree, V.E. (2000) *Sociology for Social Workers and Probation Officers* (London: Routledge).

Cresswell, J. (1994) *Research Design: Qualitative and Quantitative Approaches* (London: Sage).

Crotty, M. (1998) *The Foundations of Social Research: Meaning and Perspective in the Research Process* (London: Sage).

Crowley, H. and Himmelweit, S. (eds) (1992) *Knowing Women: Feminism and Knowledge* (Cambridge: Polity Press).

Culliford, L. (2002) 'Spirituality and Clinical Care', *British Medical Journal* **325**: 1434–5.

Cullinan, K. (2003) 'Over 55 KZN teachers died every month'. http://www.hivan.org.za.

Dano, U.B. (1998) 'An Evaluation of the Effectiveness of Peer-mediated AIDS Workshops at King Edward VIII Hospital: A Participatory Research Approach', unpublished honours dissertation (Durban: University of Natal).

Davies, C.G., Nolen-Hoeksema, S. and Larson, J. (1998) 'Making Sense of Loss and Benefiting from the Experience: Two Construals of Meaning', *Journal of Personality and Social Psychology* **75**(2): 561–74.

Davis, A. (1996) 'Risk Work and Mental Health', in Kemshall, H. and Pritchard, J. (eds) *Good Practice in Risk Assessment and Risk Management* (London: Jessica Kingsley).

De Maria, W. (1997) 'Flapping on Clipped Wings: Social Work Ethics in the Age of Activism', *Australian Social Work* **50**(4): 3–19.

Deacon, A. (2002) *Perspectives on Welfare* (London: Open University Press).

Decrescenzo, T.S. (1984) 'Homophobia: a Study of the Attitudes of Mental Health Professionals toward Homosexuality', in Schoenberg, R., Goldberg, R.S. and Shore, D.A. (eds) *Homosexuality and Social Work* (New York: Haworth Press) pp. 39–52.

Deegan, P.E. (1994) 'Recovery: the Lived Experience of Rehabilitation', in Spaniol, L. and Koehler, M. (eds) *The Experience of Recovery* (Boston: Center for Psychiatric Rehabilitation).

Denscombe, M. (1998) *The Good Research Guide: For Small-scale Research Projects* (Buckingham: Open University Press).

Department for Work and Pensions (2001) *Recruiting Benefit Claimants: Qualitative Research with Employers in ONE Pilot Areas*, Research Series Paper No 150, prepared by Bunt, K., Shury, J. and Vivian, D. (London: Department for Work and Pensions).

Department of Education (Notice 1926 of 1999) *National Policy on HIV/AIDS, for Learners and Educators in Public Schools and Students and Educators in Further Education and Training Institutions* (Pretoria: Department of Education).

Department of Health (1990) *The Care Programme Approach for People with a Mental Illness Referred to the Specialist Psychiatric Services*, HC (90)23 LASSL(90) 11 (London: Department of Health).

Department of Health (1991a) *The Children Act Guidance and Regulations*, Vol. 2 *Family Support, Day Care and Educational Provision for Young Children* (London: HMSO).

Department of Health (1991b) *The Children Act Guidance and Regulations*, Vol. 3 *Family Placements* (London: HMSO).

Department of Health (1991c) *Working Together under the Children Act 1989. A Guide to Inter-agency Cooperation for the Protection of Children from Abuse* (London: HMSO).

Department of Health (1991d) *The Children Act 1989. Guidance and Regulations*, Vol. 4, *Residential Care* (London: HMSO).

Department of Health (1994) *Implementing Caring for People. Community Care Packages for Older People* (London: HMSO).

Department of Health (1995) *Child Protection: Messages from Research* (London: HMSO).

Department of Health (1996) *Building Bridges: A Guide to Arrangements for Inter-Agency Working for the Care and Protection of Severely Mentally Ill People* (London: HMSO).

Department of Health (1998) *Modernising Social Services*, Cm 4169 (London: Stationery Office).

Department of Health (1999a) *Adoption Now: Messages from Research* (Chichester: John Wiley).

Department of Health (1999b): *National Service Framework for Mental Health* (London: NHS).

Department of Health (1999c) *The Government's Objectives for Children's Social Services* (London: Stationery Office).

Department of Health (1999d) *Working Together to Safeguard Children. A Guide to Interagency Working to Safeguard and Promote the Welfare of Children* (London: Stationery Office).

Department of Health (2000a) *Framework for the Assessment of Children in Need and Their Families* (London: HMSO).

Department of Health (2000b) *The Children Act 1989: Messages from Research* (London: HMSO).

Department of Health (2001a) *The National Service Framework for Mental Health* (London: Stationery Office).

Department of Health (2001b) *The National Service Framework for Older People* (London: Stationery Office).

Department of Health (2002a) *Mental Health and Employment in the NHS* (London: Department of Health).

Department of Health (2002b) *PSS Performance Assessment Framework* (London: Department of Health).

Department of Health (2002c) *Requirements for Social Work Training* (London: Stationery Office).

Department of Health (2004) *The National Service Framework for Children, Young People and Maternity Services* (London: Stationery Office).

Department of Health and Social Security (1988) *Community Care: Agenda for Action* (Griffiths Report) (London: HMSO).

Department of Health, Home Office, and the Department for Education and Employment (1999) *Working Together to Safeguard Children: A Guide to Inter-agency Working to Safeguard and Promote the Welfare of Children* (London: Stationery Office).

Department of Health/Social Services Inspectorate (1991) *Care Management and Assessment Practice Guidance* (London: HMSO).

Department of Health/Social Services Inspectorate (1995) *Planning for Life: Developing Community Services for People with Complex Multiple Disabilities*, No 3 *Good Practice in the Independent Sector* (London: HMSO).

Department of Health/Social Services Inspectorate (1996) *Planning for Life: Developing Community Services for People with Complex Multiple Disabilities*, No. 2 *Good Practice in Manchester* (London: HMSO).

Department of Welfare and Population Development (1997) *White Paper for Social Welfare* 386 (18166) Notice 1108 of 1997 (Pretoria: Government Gazette).

Desforges, D.M., Lord, C.G., Ramsay, S.L., Mason, J.A., Van Leeuwen, M.D., West, S.C. and Lepper, M.R. (1991) 'Effects of Structured Co-operative Contact on Changing Negative Attitudes towards Stigmatised Groups', *Journal of Personality and Social Psychology* **60**(4): 531–44.

Dixon, N. (1999) *The Organisational Learning Cycle: How We can Learn Collectively* (Aldershot: Gower).

Dodson, M. (1997) *Bringing Them Home* (video) (Sydney: Human Rights and Equal Opportunity Commission (HREOC)).

Dominelli, L. (1996) 'Deprofessionalising Social Work: Anti-oppressive Practice, Competencies and Post-modernism', *British Journal of Social Work* **26**: 153–7.

Dominelli, L. (2002) *Anti-Oppressive Social Work Theory and Practice* (Basingstoke: Palgrave Macmillan).

Dominelli, L. (2004) *Social Work: Theory and Practice for a Changing Profession* (Cambridge: Polity Press).

Dominelli, L. (2005) 'Social Inclusion in Research: Reflections upon a Project Involving Young Mothers', *International Journal of Social Welfare* **14**(1) 13–22.

Dorn, N. and Lee, M. (1999) 'Drugs and Policing in Europe: From Low Streets to High Places', in South, N. (ed.) *Drugs: Cultures, Controls and Everyday Life* (London: Sage).

Dorn, N., Murji, K. and South, N. (1992) *Traffickers: Drug Markets and Law Enforcement* (London: Routledge).

Douglas, M. (1966) *Purity and Danger: An Analysis of the Concepts of Pollution and Taboo* (London: Routledge).

DRC (Disability Rights Commission) (2002a) *Response to Draft Mental Health Bill, England and Wales* (London: Disability Rights Commission).

DRC (Disability Rights Commission) (2002b) *Public Attitudes Survey*, conducted by BMRB (London: Disability Rights Commission).

DRC (Disability Rights Commission) (2003) *Disability Equality: Making it Happen. A Review of the Disability Discrimination Act 1995* (London: Disability Rights Commission).

DRC (Disability Rights Commission) (2004) *Strategic Plan 2004–7* (London: Disability Rights Commission).

DRC (Disability Rights Commission) and HSE (2003) *Review of UK Case Law on the Use of Health and Safety Requirements as a False Excuse for Not Employing Sick or Disabled Persons* (London: Disability Rights Commission and Health and Safety Executive).

Driver, S. and Martell, L. (2002) *Blair's Britain* (Cambridge: Polity Press).

Duffield, M. (2001) 'Governing the Borderlands: Decoding the Power of Aid', in *Disasters* **25**(4): 216–29.

Dulaney, D.D. and Kelly, J. (1982) 'Improving Services to Gay and Lesbian Clients', *Social Work* **27**(2): 178–83.

Dullea, K. and Mullender, A. (1999) 'Evaluation and Empowerment', in Shaw, I. and Lishman, J. (eds) *Evaluation and Social Work Practice* (London: Sage) pp. 81–100.

Durham, A. (2003) 'Young Men Living through and with Child Abuse: A Practitioner Research Study', *British Journal of Social Work* **33**(3): 309–23.

Earle, R., Crawford, A. and Newburn, T. (2003) 'Referral Orders: Some Reflections on Policy Transfer and "What Works"', *Youth Justice* **2**(3): 141–50.

Edmunds, M., Hough, M., Turnbull, P.J. and May, T. (1999) *Doing Justice to Treatment: Referring Offenders to Drug Services*, DPAS Paper No.2 (London: Home Office).

Edmunds, M., May, T., Hearden, I. and Hough, M. (1998) *Arrest Referral: Emerging Lessons from Research*, Drugs Prevention Initiative Paper 23 (London: Home Office Central Drugs Prevention Unit).

Ellison, M.L., Russinova, Z., MacDonald-Wilson, K.L. and Lyass, A. (2003) 'Patterns and Correlates of Workplace Disclosure among Professionals and Managers with Psychiatric Conditions', *Journal of Vocational Rehabilitation* 18(1): 3–14.

Elshtain, J.B. (ed.) (2002) *Jane Addams: A Reader* (New York: Basic Books).

Employers Forum on Disability (1998) *Practical Guide to Employment Adjustments for People with Mental Health Problems* (London: Employers Forum on Disability).

Englander, D. (1994) *A Documentary History of Jewish Immigrants in Britain 1840–1920* (Leicester: Leicester University Press).

Epstein, S. (1998[1987]) 'Gay Politics, Ethnic Identity: The Limits of Social Constructionism', in Nardi, P.M. and Schneider, B.E. (eds) *Social Perspectives in Lesbian and Gay Studies: A Reader* (London: Routledge) pp. 134–59.

Evans, C. and Fisher, M. (1999) 'Collaborative Evaluation with Service Users', in Shaw, I. and Lishman, J. (eds) *Evaluation and Social Work Practice* (London: Sage) pp. 101–17.

Evans, D. and Kearney, J. (1996) *Working in Social Care: A Systemic Approach* (Aldershot: Arena).

Evans, R. and Puech, K. (2001) 'Reprimands and Warnings: Populist Punitiveness or Restorative Justice', *Criminal Law Review* October: 794–805.

Everitt, A. and Hardiker, P. (1996) *Evaluating for Good Practice* (Basingstoke: BASW/ Macmillan – now Palgrave Macmillan).

Everitt, A., Hardicker, P., Littlewood, J. and Mullender, A. (1992) *Applied Research for Better Practice* (Basingstoke: Macmillan – now Palgrave Macmillan).

Fadiman, A. (1997) *The Spirit Catches You and You Fall Down* (New York: Farrar, Strauss & Giroux).

Farrall, S. (2002) *Rethinking What Works With Offenders* (Cullompton: Willan Publishing).

Farrington, D.P. and Tarling, R. (1985) *Prediction in Criminology* (Albany, NY: Albany State University Press).

Fell, P. (2004) And Now it has Started to Rain: Support and Advocacy with Adult Asylum Seekers in the Voluntary Sector', in Hayes, D. and Humphries, B. (eds) *Social Work, Immigration and Asylum* (London: Jessica Kingsley).

Ferard, M.L. and Hunnybun, N.K. (1962) *The Caseworker's Use of Relationships* (London: Tavistock).

Ferris, D. (1977) *Homosexuality and the Social Services: The Report of an NCCL Survey of Local Authority Social Services Committees* (London: National Council for Civil Liberties).

Feuerstein, M.T. (1986) *Partners in Evaluation: Evaluating Development and Community Programmes with Participants* (London: Macmillan – now Palgrave Macmillan).

Fife, B.L. (1994) 'The Conceptualization of Meaning in Illness', *Social Science & Medicine* 38(2): 309–16.

Follett, M.P. (1918) 'The New State' (New York: Longmans, Green), reprinted in Pumphrey, R.E. and Pumphrey, M.W. (eds) (1961) *The Heritage of American Social Work* (New York: Columbia University Press) p. 363.

Fook, J. (1999) 'Critical Reflectivity in Education and Practice', in Pease, B. and Fook, J. (eds) *Transforming Social Work Practice: Postmodern Critical Perspectives* (St Leonards: Allen & Unwin).

Fook, J. (2000) 'Theorising from Frontline Practice: Towards an Inclusive Approach for Social Work Research', in the Researching the Social Work Process Seminars, SCIE eLEC.

Fook, J. (2002) *Social Work: Critical Theory and Practice* (London: Sage).

Foucault, M. (1978[1976]) *The History of Sexuality*, Volume 1: *An Introduction* (New York: Random House).

Foucault, M. (1980) *Power/Knowledge: Selected Interviews and Other Writings, 1972–1977*, edited by C. Gordon (Brighton: Harvester Press).

Foucault, M. (1988) 'Technologies of the Self', in Martin, L., Gutman, H. and Hutton, P. (eds) *Technologies of the Self: A Seminar with Michel Foucault* (London: Tavistock) pp. 16–49.

Foucault, M. (2000) 'Foucault' in J.D. Faubion (ed.) *Essential Works of Michel Foucault 1954–1984*, Volume 2: *Aesthetics, Method, and Epistemology* (London: Penguin) pp. 459–63.

Freire, P. (1972) *The Pedagogy of the Oppressed* (Harmondsworth: Penguin).

Frost, N. (2002) 'A Problematic Relationship? Evidence and Practice in the Workplace', *Social Work and Social Sciences Review* 10(1): 38–50.

Fuller, R. and Petch, A. (eds) (1995) *Practitioner Research: The Reflective Social Worker* (Buckingham: Open University Press).

Gallagher, G. (2003) 'Refugee Treatment the World's Harshest: Ozdowski', *The Age*, 10 October.

Garbarino, J. (1992) *Children and Families in the Social Environment* (New York: Aldine).

Garland, D. (2001) *The Culture of Control: Crime and Social Order in Contemporary Society* (Oxford: Clarendon Press).

Gathorne-Hardy, F. (1995) *Devising and Resourcing Personal Care Packages* (London: Disablement Income Group).

Gibbons, A. (1999) *A Fight to Belong* (London: Save the Children).

Gibbs, A. (2001a) 'The Changing Nature and Context of Social Work Research', British *Journal of Social Work* 31: 689–701.

Gibbs, A. (2001b) 'Partnerships between the Probation Service and Voluntary Sector Organizations', *British Journal of Criminology* 31(1): 15–18.

Gibbs, L. and Gambrill, E. (2002) 'Evidence-based Practice: Counterarguments to Objectives', *Research in Social Work Practice* 12(3): 452–76.

Gilgun, J. (1994) 'Hand into Glove: The Grounded Theory Approach and Social Work Practice Research', in Sherman, E. and Reid, W.J. (eds) *Qualitative Research in Social Work* (New York: Columbia University Press).

Gillespie, D. and Glisson, C. (eds) (1992) *Quantitative Methods in Social Work: The State of the Art* (Binghampton, NY: Haworth Press).

Gilman, M. (2000) 'Social Exclusion and Drug Using Parents', in Harbin, F. and Murphy, M. (eds) *Substance Misuse and Child Care: How to Understand, Assist and Intervene When Drugs Affect Parenting* (Lyme Regis: Russell House).

Ginsberg, N. (1989) 'Institutional Racism and Local Authority Housing', *Critical Social Policy* 8(3): 4–19.

Glaser, B. and Strauss, A. (1967) *The Discovery of Grounded Theory* (Chicago: Aldine).

GLC Women's Committee (1986) *Tackling Heterosexism: A Handbook of Lesbian Rights* (London: GLC).

Goddard, C. and Briskman, L. (2004) 'By any Measure, It's Official Child Abuse', *Herald Sun* 19 February, p. 17.

Goffman, E. (1961) *Asylums: Essays on the Social Situation of Mental Patients and Other Inmates* (Harmondsworth: Penguin).

Goffman, E. (1963) *Stigma: Notes on the Management of Spoiled Identity* (Harmondsworth: Penguin).

Golan, N. (1978) *Treatment in Crisis Situations* (New York: Free Press).

Goldson, B. and Jamieson, J. (2002) 'Youth Crime, the "Parenting Deficit" and State Intervention: a Contextual Critique', *Youth Justice* 2(2): 82–99.

Goldstein, E. (1995) *Ego Psychology and Social Work Practice* (2nd edn) (New York: Free Press).

Golombok, S. (2000) *Parenting: What Really Counts?* (London: Routledge).

Gordon, P. and Newnham, A. (1985) *Passport to Benefits: Racism in Social Security* (London: CPAG/Runnymede Trust).

Gorman, H. (2000a) 'Collaboration in Community Care and Primary Care', in Davies, M. (ed.) *The Blackwell Encyclopaedia of Social Work* pp. 67–9 (Oxford: Blackwell).

Gorman, H. (2000b) 'Winning Hearts and Minds? Emotional Labour and Learning for Care Management Work', *Journal of Social Work Practice* 14(2): 149–58.

Gorman, H. (2003) 'Which Skills do Care Managers Need? A Research Project on Skills, Competency and Continuing Professional Development', *Social Work Education* 22(3): 245–61.

Gorman, H. and Postle, K. (2003) *Transforming Community Care: A Distorted Vision?* (Birmingham: Venture Press).

Goulbourne, H. (2002) *The Caribbean Transnational Experience* (London: Pluto Press).

Grady, P. (2004) 'Social Work Responses to Accompanied Asylum Seeking Children', in Hayes, D. and Humphries, B. (eds) *Social Work, Immigration and Asylum* (London: Jessica Kingsley).

Graham, J. (1998) *Fast-Tracking of Persistent Young Offenders*, Research Findings No. 74 (London: Home Office Research and Statistics Directorate).

Gramick, J. (1983) 'Homophobia: a New Challenge', *Social Work* 28(2): 137–41.

Gray, P. (2002) 'Disability Discrimination in Education'. A review undertaken on behalf of the Disability Rights Commission. London.

Green, J. (1992) 'The Community Development Project Revisited', in Carter, P., Jeffs, T. and Smith, M. (eds) *Changing Social Work and Welfare* (Buckingham: Open University Press).

Grier, A. and Thomas, T. (2003) 'Out of Order', *Young People Now* 16–22 July.

GSCC (General Social Care Council) (2002) *Codes of Practice for Social Service Workers and Employers* (London: GSCC).

Guardian, the (2001) 'Welcome to Britain', compilation of articles originally published 20–3 May 2001, London, *Guardian* newspaper.

Hadorn, D.D., Baker, D., Hodges, J.S. and Hicks, N. (1996) 'Rating the Quality of Evidence for Clinical Practice Guidelines', *Journal of Clinical Epidemiology* 49: 749–54.

Haebich, A. (1998) 'Grim Facts We've Known', *The Adelaide Review* 173: 8–9.

Haebich, A. (2000) *Broken Circles: Fragmenting Indigenous Families 1800–2000* (Fremantle: Fremantle Arts Centre Press).

Hagell, A. and Newburn, T. (1994) *Persistent Young Offenders* (London: Policy Studies Institute).

Hales, L. (2002) 'Do Drug Testing and Treatment Orders Really Work?', *Criminal Justice Matters* 47: 18–19.

Hall, C. (1997) *Social Work as Narratives: Storytelling and Persuasion in Professional Texts* (Aldershot: Ashgate).

Hall, M.R.P., Maclennan W.J. and Lye M.D.W. (1993) *Medical Care of the Elderly* (Chichester: John Wiley).

Hallett, C. (1995) *Inter-agency Co-ordination in Child Protection* (London: HMSO).

Hallett, C. and Birchall, E. (1992) *Co-ordination and Child Protection: A Review of the Literature* (Edinburgh: Stationery Office).

Hamer, S. (2002) 'It Takes Two to Tango', *Criminal Justice Matters* 47: 14–15.

Hamer, S. and Collinson, G. (eds) (1999) *Achieving Evidence-based Practice – A Handbook for Practitioners* (London: Bailliere Tindall).

Hamilton, G. (1951) *Theory and Practice of Social Case Work* (2nd edn) (New York: Columbia University Press).

Hammersley, M. and Atkinson, P. (1995) *Ethnography: Principles in Practice* (London: Routledge).

Hancock, B.L. (1982) *School Social Work* (New Jersey: Prentice Hall).

Hansen, G. (1998) *Integration of Assessment and Care Management and the Care Programme Approach: An Implementation and Outcome Study in a London Borough* (Hatfield: University of Hertfordshire).

Hansen, G. (2003) *Integration of Assessment and Care Management and the Care Programme Approach: An Implementation and Outcome Study in a London Borough. Update Report: Background to Service User Involvement* (Hatfield: University of Hertfordshire).

Harbin, F. and Murphy, M. (2000) *Substance Misuse and Child Care: How to Understand, Assist and Intervene When Drugs Affect Parenting* (Lyme Regis: Russell House).

Harding, J. (2000) *The Uninvited: Refugees at the Rich Man's Gate* (London: Profile Books).

Harding, S. (1991) *Whose Science? Whose Knowledge: Thinking from Women's Lives* (Milton Keynes: Open University Press).

Hardman, Karen L.J. (1997) 'Social Workers' Attitudes to Lesbian Clients', *British Journal of Social Work* 27(4): 545–63.

Harman, K. and Paylor, I. (2002) 'A Shift in Strategy', *Criminal Justice Matters* 47: 8–9.

Harris, D.J. (1995) *Law of the European Convention on Human Rights* (London: Butterworth).

Harris, J. and Roberts, K. (2002) *Disabled People in Refugee and Asylum Seeking Communities* (Bristol: Policy Press/Joseph Rowntree Foundation)

Harris, M. (1999) *Risk Assessments in Pre-Sentence Reports: Their Impact on the Sentencing Process*, http:// www.crim.ac.uk/research/cropwood/1999MarkHarris.

Hart, C. (1998) *Doing a Literature Review: Releasing the Social Science Research Imagination* (London: Sage).

Hart, E. and Bond, M. (1995) *Action Research for Health and Social Care: A Guide to Practice* (Buckingham: Open University Press).

Hartley, J. and McKee, A. (2001) *The Indigenous Public Sphere: The Reporting and Recognition of Indigenous Issues in the Australian Media, 1994–1997* (Oxford University Press: New York).

Harvey, L. (1990) *Critical Social Research* (London: Unwin Hyman).

Hayes, D. (2002) 'From Aliens to Asylum Seekers: A History of Immigration Controls and Welfare in Britain', in Cohen, S., Humphries, B. and Mynott, E. (eds) *From Immigration Controls to Welfare Controls* (London: Routledge) pp. 30–46.

Hayes, D. and Humphries, B. (1999) 'Negotiating Contentious Research Topics', in *The Politics of Social Work Research and Evaluation* (Birmingham: Venture Press) pp. 19–30.

Hayes, D. and Humphries, B. (2004) *Social Work, Immigration and Asylum: Debates, Dilemmas and Ethical Issues for Social Work and Social Care Practice* (London: Jessica Kingsley).

Hayter, T. (2000) *Open Borders: The Case Against Immigration Controls* (London: Pluto Press).

Healey, K. (2000) *Social Work Practices: Contemporary Perspectives on Change* (London: Sage).

Heath, S. (1982) *The Sexual Fix* (London: Macmillan – now Palgrave Macmillan).

Heath, T., Jeffries, R. and Purcell, J. (2003) 'Asylum Statistics UK, 2003 (2nd edn) accessed via website 24/8/04, www.homeoffice.gov.uk/rds.

Heather, N. and Robertson, I. (2003) *Problem Drinking* (3rd edn) (Oxford: Oxford University Press).

Henkel, M. (1995) 'Conceptions of Knowledge in Social Work Education', in Yellolly, M. and Henkel, M. (eds) *Learning and Teaching in Social Work: Towards Reflective Practice* (London: Jessica Kingsley).

Hepworth, M. (2000) *Stories of Ageing* (Buckingham: Open University Press).

Heron, J. (1996) *Cooperative Inquiry: Research into the Human Condition* (London: Sage).

Hewstone, M. (2003) 'Intergroup contact: panacea for prejudice?', *The Psychologist* 16(7): 352–5.

Hicks, S. (1996) 'The "Last Resort"?: Lesbian and Gay Experiences of the Social Work Assessment Process in Fostering and Adoption', *Practice* 8(2): 15–24.

Hicks, S. (1997) 'Taking the Risk? Assessing Lesbian and Gay Carers', in Kemshall, H. and Pritchard, J. (eds) *Good Practice in Risk Assessment and Risk Management 2: Protection, Rights and Responsibilities* (London: Jessica Kingsley) pp. 27–39.

Hicks, S. (2000) '"Good Lesbian, Bad Lesbian ...": Regulating Heterosexuality in Fostering and Adoption Assessments', *Child & Family Social Work* 5(2): 157–68.

Hicks, S. (2003) 'The Christian Right and Homophobic Discourse: A Response to "Evidence" that Lesbian and Gay Parenting Damages Children', *Sociological Research Online* 8(4), www.socresonline.org.uk/8/4/hicks.html.

Hicks, S. and McDermott, J. (eds) (1999) *Lesbian and Gay Fostering and Adoption: Extraordinary Yet Ordinary* (London: Jessica Kingsley).

Hicks, S. and Watson, K. (2003) 'Desire Lines: "Queering" Health and Social Welfare', *Sociological Research Online* 8(1), www.socresonline.org.uk/8/1/hicks.html.

Hidalgo, H., Peterson, T.L. and Woodman, N.J. (eds) (1985) *Lesbian and Gay Issues: A Resource Manual for Social Workers* (Silver Springs, MD: National Association of Social Workers).

Hillin, A. (1985) 'When You Stop Hiding Your Sexuality ...', *Social Work Today* 4: 18–19.

Hirschman, A.O. (1998) *Crossing Boundaries: Selected Writings* (New York: Zone Books).

HM Prison Service (1998) *Tackling Drugs in Prison: The Prison Service Drugs Strategy* (London: HM Prison Service).

Ho, R.T.H., and Chan, C.L.W. (2002) 'The Effect of Eastern Psychosocial Intervention Support Group in Breast Cancer Patients in Hong Kong: A Pilot Study on Salivary Cortisol, GHQ12 and HADS'. Paper presented at the 6th Psycho-oncology Conference, Hong Kong.

Hofstein, S. (1964) 'The Nature of Process: its Implications For Social Work', *Journal of the Social Work Process* 14: 13–53.

Hollis, F. (1964) *Casework: A Psychosocial Therapy* (New York: Random House).

Holloway, W. and Jefferson, T. (2000) 'Biography, Anxiety and the Experience of Locality', in Chamberlayne, P., Bornat, J. and Wengraf, T. (eds) *The Turn to Biographical Methods in Social Science: Comparative Issues and Examples* (London: Routledge) pp. 167–80.

Holwerda, O. (2002) 'Love and Sex: Homosexuality', in Gruber, C. and Stefanov, H. (eds) *Gender in Social Work: Promoting Equality* (Lyme Regis: Russell House) pp. 54–9.

Homan, R. (1991) *The Ethics of Social Research* (London: Longman).

Home Office (1996) *Exchange of Information with the IND of the Home Office*, ref. IMG/96 1176/1193/23, circular to local authorities.

Home Office (1999) 'Home Secretary Urges Councils to Use New Powers to Protect the Vulnerable' (press release) 15 October.

Home Office (2001) 'Hard-hitting New Programme to Tackle Persistent Young Offenders goes Live' (press release) 17 July.

Home Office (2002a) 'Blunkett: new powers to tackle youth crime' (press release) 13 September.

Home Office (2002b) 'Protecting the Public: Strengthening Protection against Sex Offenders and Reforming the Law on Sexual Offences', Cm.5668 (Norwich: Trading Standard Office).

Home Office (2002c) 'Secure Remands Extended Nationally' (press release) 13 September.

Home Office (2002d) *Secure Borders Safe Haven: Integration with Diversity 2002* (London: HMSO).

Home Office, Department of Health, DES and Welsh Office (1991) *Working Together: A Guide to Arrangements for Inter-agency Cooperation for the Protection of Children from Abuse* (London: HMSO).

Home Office/Scottish Executive (2001) *Consultation Paper on the Review of Part I of the Sex Offenders Act 1997* (London: HMSO).

Home Office/Youth Justice Board (2002) *Final Warning Scheme: Guidance for the Police and Youth Offending Teams* (London: Home Office).

hooks, b. (1984) *Feminist Theory from Margin to Center* (Boston: South End Press).

hooks, b. (1989) *Talking Back* (Boston: Sheba).

Horder, W. (2002) 'Care Management', in Davies, M. (ed.) *Companion to Social Work* (Oxford: Blackwell).

Horner, N. (2003) *What is Social Work?* (Exeter: Learning Matters).

Hough, G. and Briskman, L. (2003) 'Responding to the Changing Socio-Political Context of Practice', in Allan, J., Pease, B. and Briskman, L. (eds) *Critical Social Work: An Introduction to Theories and Practices* (Sydney: Allen & Unwin).

Hough, M. (1996) *Drug Misuse and the Criminal Justice System: A Review of the Literature*, Drugs Prevention Initiative Paper No.15 (London: Home Office Central Drugs Prevention Unit).

House of Commons (1993) Juvenile Offenders, Home Affairs Committee, Session 1992–3.

Howe, D. (1987) *An Introduction to Social Work Theory* (Aldershot: Gower).

Hudson, B., Young, R., Hardy, B. and Glendinning, C. (2001) *National Evaluation of Notifications for Use of the Section 3 Partnership Flexibilities of the Health Act 1999*, Second Interim Report (Leeds and Manchester: Nuffield Institute of Health/ Primary Care Research and Development Centre).

Huggins, J. (1998) *Sister Girl: The Writings of an Aboriginal Activist and Historian*, (Brisbane, University of Queensland Press) p. 120.

Hughes, B. (1995) *Older People and Community Care: Critical Theory and Practice* (Buckingham: Open University Press).

Hughes, K., Bellis, M.A. and Kilfoyle-Carrington, M. (2001) *Alcohol, Tobacco and Drugs in the North West of England: Identifying a Shared Agenda* (Liverpool: Liverpool John Moores University).

Hughes, M., McNeish, D., Newman, T., Roberts, H. and Sachdev, D. (2000) *What Works? Making Connections: Linking Research and Practice* (Ilford: Barnardo's).

Human Rights and Equal Opportunity Commission (1997) *Bringing Them Home: Report of the National Inquiry into the Separation of Aboriginal and Islander Children from their Families* (Sydney: HREOC).

Humphreys, L. (1975) *Tearoom Trade: Impersonal Sex in Public Places* (Chicago: Aldine).

Humphries, B. (1997) 'From Critical Thought to Emancipatory Action: Contradictory Research Goals', *Sociological Research Online* 2(1): http://www.socresonline.org.uk/socresonline/2/1/3.html.

Humphries, B. (1999) 'Feminist Evaluation', in Shaw, I. and Lishman, J. (eds) *Evaluation and Social Work Practice* (Buckingham: Open University Press) pp. 118–32.

Humphries, B. (2003) 'What *Else* Counts as Evidence in Evidence-based Social Work?' *Social Work Education* 22(1): 81–91.

Humphries, B. (2004a) 'Taking Sides: Social Work Research as a Moral and Political Activity', in Lovelock, R., Lyons, K. and Powell J. (eds) *Reflecting on Social Work – Discipline and Profession* (Aldershot: Ashgate) pp. 113–29.

Humphries, B. (2004b) 'The Construction and Reconstruction of Social Work', in Hayes, D. and Humphries, B. (eds) *Social Work, Immigration and Asylum* (London: Jessica Kingsley) pp. 113–29.

Hunt, B. (2003) *The Timid Corporation. Why Business is Terrified of Taking Risk* (Chichester: John Wiley).

Hunter, N.D. and Polikoff, N.D. (1976) 'Custody Rights of Lesbian Mothers: Legal Theory and Litigation Strategy', *Buffalo Law Review* 25: 691–733.

Hunter, S., Shannon, C., Knox, J. and Martin, J.I. (1998) *Lesbian, Gay, and Bisexual Youths and Adults: Knowledge for Human Services Practice* (Thousand Oak, CA: Sage).

Hyde, J.S. and DeLamater, J.D. (2000) *Understanding Human Sexuality* (Boston: McGraw-Hill).

Ife, J. (1997) *Rethinking Social Work: Towards Critical Practice* (Melbourne: Addison Wesley Longman).

Ife, J. (2001) *Human Rights and Social Work: Towards Rights-Based Practice* (Cambridge: Cambridge University Press).

Indigenous Social Justice Association (2003) 'Deaths in Custody – An Aboriginal Inquisition', *Djadi – Dugarang* 5(1): 1–32.

Inquest (2003) Call for a Public Inquiry into the Death of 16-year-old Joseph Scholes (press release) 11 November.

International Federation of Social Workers (IFSW) (2003) *Second Draft Document: Ethics in Social Work Statement of Principles*, http://www.ifsw.org/GM-2004/GM-Ethics-2draft.html.

Irvine, E.E. (1966) 'A New Look at Casework', in Younghusband, E. (ed.) *New Developments in Casework* (London: Allen & Unwin) pp. 38–46.

Isaac, B.C., Minty, E.B. and Morrison, R.M. (1986) 'Children in Care: The Association with Mental Disorder in Patients', *British Journal of Social Work* 16(3): 325–39.

Jack, C. and Gill, O. (2003) *The Missing Side of the Triangle: Assessing the Importance of Family and Environmental Factors in the Lives of Children* (Ilford: Barnardo's).

Jackson, S. and Scott, S. (eds) (1996) *Feminism & Sexuality: A Reader* (Edinburgh: Edinburgh University Press).

Janoff-Bulman, R. and Berg, M. (1998) 'Disillusionment and the Creation of Values', in Harvey, H. (ed.) *Perspectives on Loss* (New York: Brunner/Mazel).

Jasper, M. (2003) *Beginning Reflective Practice* (Cheltenham: Nelson Thornes).

Jerrom, C. (2003) 'Anti-social Behaviour: Blunkett's Plans Leave Social Workers in Quandary over "Enforcement" Role', *Community Care* 20–26 March: 18–19.

Johnson, P., Wistow, G., Schulz, R. and Hardy, B. (2003) 'Interagency and Interprofessional Collaboration in Community Care: The Interdependence of Structures and Values', *Journal of Interprofessional Care* 17(1): 69–85.

Johnstone, G. (2002) *Restorative Justice: Ideas, Values, Debates* (Cullompton: Willan Publishing).

Jones, A. and May, J. (1992) *Working in Human Service Organisations* (Melbourne: Longman).

Jordan, B. (1990) *Social Work in an Unjust Society* (Hemel Hamstead: Harvester Wheatsheaf).

Jordan, B. (1997) 'Partnership with Service Users in Child Protection and Family Support', in Parton, N. (ed.) *Child Protection and Family Support: Tensions, Contradictions and Possibilities* (London: Routledge).

Jordan, B. with Jordan, C. (2000) *Social Work and the Third Way: Tough Love as Social Policy* (London: Sage).

Kabat-Zinn, J. (2003) 'Mindfulness-based Intervention in Context: Past, Present, and Future', *Clinical Psychology: Science and Practice* 10(2): 144–56.

Katona, J. (1996) cited in McLean, L. 'Forced Removal of Children: An Australian Holocaust', *The Age* 28 May, p. 4.

Keene, J. (1997) 'Drug Misuse in Prison: Views from Inside: A Qualitative Study of Prison Staff and Inmates', *The Howard Journal* 36(1): 28–41.

Kemshall, H. (1997) *Reviewing Risk: A Review of Research on the Assessment and Management of Risk and Dangerousness: Implications for Policy and Practice in the Probation Service* (London: Home Office).

Kemshall, H. (2002a) *Risk, Social Policy and Welfare* (Buckingham: Open University Press).

Kemshall, H. (2002b) *Risk Assessment and Management of Serious Violent and Sexual Offenders: A Review of Current Issues* (Edinburgh: Scottish Executive Social Research).

Kemshall, H. and Maguire, M. (2001) 'Public Protection, Partnership and Risk Penalty', *Punishment and Society* 3(2): 237–64.

Kemshall, H. and Pritchard, J. (eds) (1997) *Good Practice in Risk Assessment and Risk Management* Vol 2 (London: Jessica Kingsley).

Kirk, S.A. and Reid, W.J. (eds) (2002) *Science and Social Work: A Critical Appraisal* (New York: Columbia University Press).

Kirkwood, T. (1998) *Dementia Reconsidered: The Person Comes First* (Buckingham: Open University Press).

Knight, J., Heaven, C. and Christie, I. (2002) *Inclusive Citizenship: The Leonard Cheshire Social Exclusion Report* (London: Leonard Cheshire).

Laing, R.D. (1969) *Intervention in Social Situations* (London: Association of Family Caseworkers/Philadelphia Association Ltd).

Laming, Lord (2003) *The Victoria Climbié Inquiry* (London: Stationery Office).

Langan, M. (1998) 'The Contested Concept of Need', in Langan, M. (ed.) *Welfare: Needs Rights and Risks* (London: Routledge).

Langan, M. and Lee, P. (eds) (1989) *Radical Social Work Today* (London: Unwin Hyman).

Langley, J. (2001) 'Developing Anti-Oppressive Empowering Social Work Practice with Older Lesbian Women and Gay Men', *British Journal of Social Work* 31: 917–32.

Lart, R. (1997) *Crossing Boundaries: Accessing Community Mental Health Services for Prisoners on Release* (Bristol: Policy Press).

Lawson, J. (1996) 'Framework of Risk Assessment and Management for Older People', in Kemshall, H. and Pritchard, J. (eds) *Good Practice in Risk Assessment and Risk Management* (London: Jessica Kingsley).

Layder, D. (1993) *New Strategies in Social Research* (Cambridge: Polity Press).

Lazarus, R.S. and Folkman, S. (1984) *Stress, Appraisal, and Coping* (New York: Springer).

Leathard, A. (1994) *Going Interprofessional, Working Together for Health and Welfare* (London: Routledge).

Leathard, A. (2003) *Interprofessional Collaboration: From Policy to Practice in Health and Social Care* (Hove: Brunner-Routledge).

Leaver, E. (2002) *Submission to National Inquiry into Children in Immigration Detention* (Sydney: Human Rights and Equal Opportunity Commission), http://www.humanrights.gov.au/human_rights/children_detention/statements/leaver.html.

Lee, J.A.B. (2001) *The Empowerment Approach to Social Work Practice: Building the Beloved Community* (2nd edn) (New York: Columbia University Press).

Leete, E. (1989) 'How I perceive and manage my illness', *Schizophrenia Bulletin* **15**(2): 197–200.

Leff, J., Trieman, N. and Gooch, C. (1996) 'Teams Assessment of Psychiatric Services (TAPS) Project 33: Prospective Follow-up Study of Long-stay Patients Discharged from Two Psychiatric Hospitals', *American Journal of Psychiatry* **153**(10): 1318–24.

Leonard, P. (1997) *Postmodern Welfare: Reconstructing an Emancipatory Project* (London: Sage).

Lewis, L.A. (1984) 'The Coming-Out Process for Lesbians: Integrating a Stable Identity', *Social Work* **29**(5): 464–9.

Link, B.G. and Phelan, J.C. (2001) 'On the Nature and Consequences of Stigma', *Annual Review of Sociology* **27**: 363–85.

Link, B.G., Struening, E.L., Rahav, M., Phelan, J.C. and Nuttnrock, L. (1997) 'On Stigma and its Consequences: Evidence from a Longitudinal Study of Men with Dual Diagnoses of Mental Illness and Substance Abuse', *Journal of Health and Social Behavior* **38**: 177–90.

Link, B.G., Phelan, J.C., Bresnahan, M., Stuene, A. and Pescosolido, B.A. (1999) 'Public Conceptions of Mental Illness: Labels, Causes, Dangerousness and Social Distance', *American Journal of Public Health* **89**: 1328–33.

Little, M. (1997) 'The Refocusing of Children's Services: the Contribution of Research' in Parton, N. (ed.) *Child Protection and Family Support: Tensions, Contradictions and Possibilities* (London: Routledge).

Logan, J. (2001) 'Sexuality, Child Care and Social Work Education', *Social Work Education* **20**(5): 563–75.

Logan, J., Kershaw, S., Karban, K., Mills, S., Trotter, J. and Sinclair, M. (1996) *Confronting Prejudice: Lesbian and Gay Issues in Social Work Education* (Aldershot: Arena).

Lonergan, P. (2000) 'James: Moving On to Independent Living', in Martyn, H. (ed.) *Developing Reflective Practice* (Bristol: The Policy Press).

Lord Chancellor's Department (1997) 'Handling Persistent Offenders in the Youth Court' (press release) 22 May.

Lorde, A. (1984) *Sister Outsider: Essays & Speeches* (Freedom, CA: Crossing Press).

Lyons, K (1999) 'Social Work: What Kinds of Knowledge? The Place of Research in Social Work Education' (Belfast: Paper for TSWR seminar).

Lyons, K. (2004) 'Dame Eileen Younghusband', *Social Work and Society:* The *International On-Line-Only Journal*, http://www.socwork.de accessed 04/06/04.

McBeath, G. and Webb, S.A. (2002) 'Virtue Ethics and Social Work: Being Lucky, Realistic, and Not Doing One's Duty', *British Journal of Social Work* **32**: 1015–36.

McCarrick, C., Over, A. and Wood, P. (2000) 'Towards User Friendly Assessment' and 'A Framework for Assessment in Child Protection' in Baldwin, N. (ed.) *Protecting Children: Promoting their Rights* (London: Sage).

McCarthy, M. (1999) *Sexuality and Women with Learning Disabilities* (London: Jessica Kingsley).

McCluskey, J. (2000) *NCH: Action for Children Factfile 2000* (London: NCH Action for Children).

Macdonald, G. (2000) 'Social Care: Rhetoric or Reality?', in Davies, H.T.O., Nutley, S.M. and Smith, P.C. (eds) (2000) *What Works? Evidence-based Policy and Practice in Public Services* (Bristol: Policy Press).

Macdonald, G. and Macdonald, K. (1995) 'Ethical Issues in Social Work Research', in Hugman, R. and Smith, D. (eds) *Ethical Issues in Social Work* (London: Routledge) pp. 46–64.

Macdonald, G. with Winkley, A. (1999) *What Works in Child Protection?* (Ilford: Barnardo's).

Macdonald, K.I. and Macdonald, G.M. (1999) 'Perceptions of Risk', in Parsloe, P. (ed.) (1999) *Risk Assessment in Social Care and Social Work* (London: Jessica Kingsley) pp. 17–52.

McDonald, T. and Marks, T. (1991) 'A Review of Risk Factors Assessed in Child Protective Services', *Social Services Review*, March: 112–32.

McGrail, S. (2003) 'It's Raining Plans', *Druglink* 18(4): 6–7.

McGrath, A. (1995) *Contested Ground: Australian Aborigines Under the British Crown* (Sydney: Allen & Unwin).

McGuire, J. (1995) *What Works: Reducing Reoffending* (Chichester: John Wiley).

McKendrick, B.W. (2001) 'The Promise of Social Work: Directions for the Future', *Social Work/Maatskaplike Werk* 37(2): 105–11.

McMillan, S. (1989) 'Lesbians and Gay Men Need Services Too', *Social Work Today*, 4th July: 31.

Maddock, J.W. and Larson, N. (1995) *Incestuous Families: An Ecological Approach to Understanding the Treatment* (New York: WW Norton).

Mair, G. (2002) Arrest Referral Schemes: First Port of Call for Drug Users in the Criminal Justice System, *Criminal Justice Matters* 47: 16–17.

Malin, N., Manthorpe, J., Race, D. and Wilmot, S. (1999) *Community Care for Nurses and the Caring Professions* (Buckingham: Open University Press).

Mallon, G.P. (1999) *Let's Get This Straight: A Gay- and Lesbian-Affirming Approach to Child Welfare* (New York: Columbia University Press).

Manocha, R., Marks, G.B., Kenchington, P., Peters, D. and Salome, C.M. (2002) 'Sahaja Yoga in the Management of Moderate to Severe Asthma: A Randomized Controlled Trial', *Thorax* 57(2): 110–15.

Manthorpe, J. (2003) 'Nearest and Dearest? The Neglect of Lesbians in Caring Relationships', *British Journal of Social Work* 33: 753–68.

Marks, L. (1991) *Home and Hospital Care: Redrawing the Boundaries* (London: King's Fund Institute).

Marlow, J. (1996) 'Helpers, helplessness and self-help', in Gopfert, M., Webster, J. and Seeman, M. (eds) *Parental Psychiatric Disorder – Distressed Parents and their Children* (Cambridge: Cambridge University Press) pp. 101–5.

Marsh, P. and Crow, G. (1998) *Family Group Conferences in Child Welfare* (Oxford: Blackwell).

Marston, G. (2003) *Temporary Protection Permanent Uncertainty: The Experience of Refugees Living on Temporary Protection Visas* (Melbourne: Centre for Applied Social Research, RMIT University).

Martinson, R.L. (1974) 'What Works? – Question and Answers About Prison Reform', *The Public Interest* **35**: 22–54.

Maslow, A.H. (1954) *Motivation and Personality* (New York: Harper).

Maye-Banbury, A. and Walley, E. (2003) 'As Easy as ABC', *Housing*, April.

Measham, F. (2002) '"Doing Gender" – "Doing Drugs": Conceptualising the Gendering of Drugs Cultures', *Contemporary Drug Problems* **29**(2): 335–73.

Measham, F. (2004) 'The Decline of Ecstasy, the Rise of "Binge" Drinking and the Persistence of Pleasure', *Probation Journal*, Special edition: Rethinking drugs and crime **51**(4): 309–26.

Measham, F., Parker, H. and Aldridge, J. (1998) *Starting, Switching, Slowing and Stopping: Report for the Drugs Prevention Initiative Integrated Programme*, Drugs Prevention Initiative Paper No. 21 (London: Home Office).

Mies, M. (1993) 'Feminist Research: Science, Violence and Responsibility', in Mies, M. and Shiva, V. (eds) *Ecofeminism* (London: Zed Books) pp. 36–54.

Miller, W. (1983) Motivational Interviewing with Problem Drinkers, *Behavioural Psychology* (11).

Milligan, D. (1975) 'Homosexuality: Sexual Needs and Social Problems', in Bailey, R. and Brake, M. (eds) *Radical Social Work* (London: Edward Arnold) pp. 96–111.

Mills, S. (1997) *Discourse* (London: Routledge).

Milner, J. and O'Byrne, P. (1998) *Assessment in Social Work* (Basingstoke: Macmillan – now Palgrave Macmillan).

Minajalku Aboriginal Corporation (1997) *Home Still Waiting* (Melbourne: Minajalku).

Mitchell, J.T. and Everly, G.S. (2000) 'Critical Incident Stress Management and Critical Incident Stress Debriefings: Evolutions, Effects and Outcomes', in Raphael, B. and Wilson, J.P. (eds) *Psychological Debriefing – Theory, Practice and Evidence* (Cambridge: Cambridge University Press) pp. 71–90.

Morgan, G. (1986) *Images of Organization* (London: Sage).

Morrell, R., Unterhalter, E., Moletsane, R. and Epstein, D. (2001) 'HIV/AIDs Policies, Schools and Gender Identities', *Moniter SA* **18**:2.

Morrell, R., Moletsane, R., Abdool-Karim, Q., Epstein, D. and Unterhalter, E. (2002) 'The School Setting: Opportunities for Integrating Gender Equality and HIV Risk Reduction Interventions', *Agenda* **53**: 11–21.

Morrison, T. (2001) *Staff Supervision in Social Care: Making a Real Difference for Staff and Service Users* (Brighton: Pavilion).

Mullender, A. and Ward, D. (1991) *Self-Directed Groupwork: Users Take Action for Empowerment* (London: Whiting & Birch).

Munro, E. (1999) 'Common Errors of Reasoning in Child Protection Work', *Abuse and Neglect*, **23**(8): 745–58.

Munro, E. (2002) *Effective Child Protection* (London: Sage).

Myers, S. (2001) 'The Registration of Children and Young People under the Sex Offenders Act 1997: Time for a Change?', *Youth Justice* **1**(2).

Mynott, E. (2002) 'Nationalism, Racism and Immigration Control: from Anti-racism to Anti-capitalism', in Cohen, S., Humphries, B. and Mynott, E. (eds) *From Immigration Controls to Welfare Controls* (London: Routledge) pp. 11–29.

NAPO (National Association of Probation Officers) (1998) *Briefing on the Crime and Disorder Bill*, February (London: NAPO).

NASW (National Association of Social Workers) (1996) *Code of Ethics* (Washington: NASW).

National Audit Office (2004) *The Drug Treatment and Testing Order: Early Lessons* (London: Stationery Office). Also available online.

National Schizophrenia Fellowship (1992) *How to Involve Users and Carers: Guidelines on Involvement in Planning, Running and Monitoring Care Services* (Kingston Upon Thames: National Schizophrenia Fellowship).

NCH (National Children's Homes) (1992) *Report of the Committee of Inquiry into Children and Young People Who Sexually Abuse Other Children* (London: NCH).

Neimeyer, R.A. (2000) 'Searching for the Meaning of Meaning: Grief Therapy and the Process of Reconstruction', *Death Studies* 24(6): 541–59.

Neimeyer, R.A. (2002) 'Mourning and meaning', *American Behavioral Scientist* 46: 235–51.

Nellis, M. (1995) 'Probation Values for the 1990s', *The Howard Journal* 34(99): 19–44.

New Zealand Ministry of Health (2003) *Like Minds, Like Mine*. National Plan 2003–2005 (Wellington: Ministry of Health).

Newburn, T. (1999) 'Drug Prevention and Youth Justice', *The British Journal of Criminology* 39(4): 609–24.

Newman, B.M. and Newman, P.R. (1995) *Development through Life: A Psychosocial Approach* (California: Brooks/Cole).

Newman, B.S. (1989) 'Including Curriculum Content on Lesbian and Gay Issues', *Journal of Social Work Education* 25: 202–11.

Newman, T. and McNeish, D. (2002) 'Promoting Evidence Based Practice in a Child Care Charity: the Barnardo's Experience', *Social Work and Social Science Review* 10(1): 55–62.

NHS Centre for Reviews and Dissemination (1997) 'Brief Intervention and Alcohol Use', *Effective Health Care* 3 (London: Department of Health).

NSPCC (National Society for the Prevention of Cruelty to Children) (1997) 'NSPCC Concerned re Inclusion of Juvenile Offenders on Sex Offenders Register', (press release) 24 October.

O'Brien, S. (2003) *Report of the Caleb Ness Inquiry* (Edinburgh: Edinburgh and the Lothians Child Protection Committee).

O'Hagan, K. (1986) *Crisis Intervention in Social Services* (London: Macmillan – now Palgrave Macmillan).

O'Neill, O. (2002) *A Question of Trust. The BBC Reith Lectures 2002* (Cambridge: Cambridge University Press).

Oakley, A. and Roberts, H. (eds) (1996) *What Works? Effective Social Interventions in Child Welfare* (Ilford: Barnardo's).

Oliver, C., Owen, C., Statham, J. and Moss, P. (2001) *Figures and Facts: Local Authority Variance on Indicators Concerning Child Protection and Children Looked After* (London: Institute of Education).

Oliver, P. (2003) *The Student's Guide to Research Ethics* (Maidenhead: Open University Press/McGraw-Hill Education).

Ovretveit, J. (1993) *Coordinating Community Care, Multidisciplinary Teams and Care Management* (Buckingham: Open University Press).

Paisley, F. (1997) 'Assimilation: A Protest as Old as the Policy', *The Australian*, 5 June.

Panjwani, U., Selvamurthy, W., Singh, S.H., Gupta, H.L., Mukhopadhyay, S. and Thakur, L. (2000) 'Effects of Sahaja Yoga Meditation on Auditory Evoked Potentials (AEP) and Visual Contrast Sensitivity (VCS) in Epileptics', *Applied Psychophysiology and Biofeedback* 25(1): 1–12.

Parker, H. (2001) 'Unenforceable? How Young Britons Obtain their Drugs', in Parker, H., Aldridge, J. and Egginton, R. (eds) *UK Drugs Unlimited: New Research and Policy Lessons on Illicit Drug Use* (Basingstoke: Palgrave – now Palgrave Macmillan) pp. 14–30.

Parker, H., Aldridge, J. and Measham, F. (1998) *Illegal Leisure: The Normalization of Adolescent Recreational Drug Use* (London: Routledge).

Parker, J. and Bradley, G. (2003) *Social Work Practice: Assessment, Planning, Intervention and Review* (Exeter: Learning Matters).

Parton, N. (1998) 'Risk, Advanced Liberalism and Child Welfare: The Need to Rediscover Ambiguity and Uncertainty', *British Journal of Social Work* 28(1): 5–27.

Parton, N. (2000) 'Some Thoughts on the Relationship between Theory and Practice in and for Social Work', *British Journal of Social Work* 30(4): 449–63.

Patton, M.Q. (1980) *Qualitative Evaluation Research* (Newbury Park, CA: Sage).

Payne, M. (1995) *Social Work and Community Care* (London: Macmillan – now Palgrave Macmillan).

Payne, M. (1998) 'Social Work Theories and Reflective Practice', in Adams, R., Dominelli, L. and Payne, M. (eds) *Social Work: Themes, Issues and Critical Debates* (Basingstoke: Macmillan – now Palgrave Macmillan).

Payne, M. (2000) *Teamwork in Multiprofessional Care* (London: Routledge).

Payne, M. (2002) 'Social Work Theories and Reflective Practice', in Adams, R., Dominelli, L. and Payne, M. (eds) *Social Work: Themes, Issues and Critical Debates* (2nd edn) (Basingstoke: Palgrave Macmillan) pp. 123–38.

Payne, M., Adams, R. and Dominelli, L. (2002) 'On Being Critical in Social Work', in Adams, R., Dominelli, L. and Payne, M. (eds) *Critical Practice in Social Work* (Basingstoke: Palgrave Macmillan) pp. 1–12.

Pearce, J. and Smith, R. (2003) 'Rebels Without a Clause', *Community Care*, 12th June, 34–5.

Pearson, G. (1983) *Hooligan: A History of Respectable Fears.* (London: Macmillan – now Palgrave Macmillan).

Pearson, G. (1999) 'Drugs at the End of the Century', *The British Journal of Criminology* 39(4): 477–87.

Pearson, G. and Hobbs, D. (2001) *Middle Market Drug Distribution,* Home Office Research Study No. 227 (London: Home Office Research, Development and Statistics Directorate). Also available online.

Peay, J. (1996) *Inquiries after Homicide* (London: Duckworth).

Penn, D.L., Komman, S., Mansfield, M. and Link, B.G. (1999) 'Dispelling the Stigma of Schizophrenia II. The Impact of Information on Dangerousness', *Schizophrenia Bulletin* 25(3): 437–46.

Perlman, H.H. (1957) *Social Casework: A Problem-Solving Process* (Chicago: Chicago University Press).

Petch, A. (2002) 'Work with Adult Service Users', in Davies, M. (ed.) *Companion to Social Work* (Oxford: Blackwell).

Physicians for Human Rights and School of Public Health and Primary Health Care (2002) *Dual Loyalty and Human Rights in Health Professional Practice: Proposed Guidelines and Institutional Mechanisms* (Capetown: University of Capetown).

Pincus, A. and Minahan, A. (1973) *Social Work Practice: Model and Method* (Itasca, IL: F.E. Peacock).

Pitts, J. (2003) 'Changing Youth Justice', *Youth Justice* 3(1): 3–18.

Police Foundation (1999) *Drugs and the Law: Report of the Independent Inquiry into the Misuse of Drugs Act 1971* (the Runciman Report) (London: The Police Foundation) Also available at http://www.druglibrary.org/schaffer/Library/studies/runciman/default.htm.

Pollard, C. (2003) 'Keeping Kids on the Straight and Narrow', *Policy Review,* Winter: 11–12.

Powell, F. (2001) *The Politics of Social Work* (London: Sage).

Prins, H. (1988) 'Dangerous Client: Further Observations on the Limitations of Mayhem', *British Journal of Social Work* **18**: 593–609.

Prins, H. (1999) *Will They Do It Again? Risk Assessment and Management in Criminal Justice and Psychiatry* (London: Routledge).

Prochaska, J.O., Diclemente, C.C. and Norcross, J.C. (1994) *Changing For Good* (New York: Avon Books).

QAA (Quality Assurance Agency for Higher Education) (2000) *Subject Benchmark Statement: Academic Standards – Social Work* (London: QAA).

Quinn, M. (2003) 'Immigrants and Refugees: Towards Anti-racist and Culturally Affirming Practices', in Allan, J., Pease, B. and Briskman, L. (eds) *Critical Social Work: An Introduction to Theories and Practices* (Sydney: Allen & Unwin).

Ramsay, M., Baker, P., Goulden, C., Sharp, C. and Sondhi, A. (2001) *Drug Misuse Declared in 2000: Results from the British Crime Survey,* Home Office Research Study No. 224 (London: Home Office Research, Development and Statistics Directorate).

Read, J. and Harre, N. (2001) 'The Role of Biological and Genetic Causal Beliefs in the Stigmatisation of "Mental Patients"', *Journal of Mental Health* **10**(2): 223–35.

Read, J. and Law, A. (1999) 'The Relationships of Causal Beliefs and Contact with Users of Mental Health Services to Attitudes to the "Mentally Ill"', *International Journal of Social Psychiatry* **45**(3): 216–29.

Read, P. (1981) *The Stolen Generations: The Removal of Aboriginal People in NSW 1883 to 1969,* Occasional paper no. 1 (Sydney: NSW Ministry of Aboriginal Affairs).

Reardon, K. and Shields, T. (1997) 'Promoting Sustainable Community/University Partnerships through Participatory Action Research', *National Society for Experiential Education Quarterly* **23**:1.

Reder, P. and Duncan, S. (2002) 'Predicting Fatal Child Abuse and Neglect', in Browne, K.D., Hanks, H., Stratton, P. and Hamilton, C. (eds) *Early Prediction and Prevention of Child Abuse* (Chichester: John Wiley).

Reder, P., Duncan, S. and Gray, M. (1993) *Beyond Blame: Child Abuse Tragedies Revisited* (London: Routledge).

Refugee Council (2002) *The Nationality, Immigration and Asylum Act 2002: Changes to the Asylum System in the UK,* briefing paper (London: Refugee Council).

Reid, W. (1988) 'Service Effectiveness and the Social Agency', in Patti, R., Pocrtner, J. and Rapp, C. (eds) *Managing for Effectiveness in Social Welfare Organisations* (New York: Haworth Press).

Reid, W.J. and Epstein, L. (1972) *Task-Centered Casework* (New York: Columbia University Press).

Reinharz, S. (1992) *Feminist Methods in Social Research* (Oxford: Oxford University Press).

Repper, J., Sayce, L., Strong, S., Wilmot, J. and Haines, M. (1997) *Tall Stories from the Back Yard. A Survey of Nimby Opposition to Community Mental Health Facilities Experienced by Key Service Providers in England and Wales* (London: Mind).

Repper, J.M. and Perkins, R.E. (2003) *Social Inclusion, Recovery and Mental Health Practice* (London: Balliere Tindall).

Rescher, N. (2002) 'Process Philosophy', in Zalta, E.N. (ed.) *The Stanford Encyclopedia of Philosophy,* http://plato.stanford.edu/archives/sum2002/entries/process-philosophy/.

Rhead, A. (1994) 'Age of Innocence', *Community Care* 11–17 August (1029): 18.

Rich, A. (1980) 'Compulsory Heterosexuality and Lesbian Existence', *Signs* **5**: 631–60.

Richmond, M. (1917) *Social Diagnosis* (New York: Russell Sage Foundation).

Rinaldi, M. and Hill, R. (2000) *Insufficient Concern* (London: Merton Mind).

Rintoul, S. (1996) cited in K. Garrett, 'Missing', *Background Briefing*, Radio National Transcript, 11 Feb, p. 3.

Roberts, H. (ed.) (1981) *Doing Feminist Research* (London: Routledge & Kegan Paul).

Robinson, G. (2003) 'Technicality and Indeterminacy in Probation Practice: A Case Study', *British Journal of Social Work* **33**(5): 593–610.

Robson, C. (2000) *Small-Scale Evaluation: Principles and Practice* (London: Sage).

Rogalla, B. (2002) *Submission to National Inquiry into Children in Immigration Detention* (Sydney: Human Rights and Equal Opportunity Commission, http://www.humanrights.gov.au/human_rights/children_detention/submissions/rogalla. html 31 May 2003).

Rogers, C.R. (1967) *On Becoming a Person: A Therapist's View of Psychotherapy* (London: Constable).

Rose, N. (1998) 'Governing Risky Individuals: The Role of Psychiatry in New Regimes of Control', *Psychiatry, Psychology and Law* **5**(2): 177–95.

Rumgay, J. (2000) *The Addicted Offender: Developments in British Policy and Practice* (Basingstoke: Palgrave – now Palgrave Macmillan).

Rumgay, J. (2003) 'Partnerships in the Probation Service', in Hong Chui, W. and Nellis, M. (eds) *Moving Probation Forward* (Harlow: Pearson Longman).

Rumgay, J. and Cowan, S. (1998) 'Pitfalls and Prospects in Partnership: Probation Programmes for Substance Misusing Offenders', *The Howard Journal* **37**(2): 124–36.

Sales, R. and Hek, R. (2004) 'Dilemmas of Care and Control: The Work of an Asylum Team in a London Borough', in Hayes, D. and Humphries, B. (eds) *Social Work, Immigration and Asylum* (London: Jessica Kingsley).

Samra-Tibbets, C. and Raynes, B. (1999) 'Assessment and Planning', in Calder, M.C. and Horwath, J. (eds) *Working for Children on the Child Protection Register: An Inter-agency Practice Guide* (Aldershot: Arena) pp. 81–117.

Sarason, S.B. and Lorentz, E.M. (1998) *Crossing Boundaries: Collaboration, Coordination, and the Redefinition of Resources* (San Francisco: Jossey-Bass).

Sarup, M. (1993) *An Introductory Guide to Poststructuralism and Postmodernism* (London: Harvester Wheatsheaf).

Sayce, L. (1995) 'Response to Violence: A Framework for Fair Treatment', in Crighton, J. (ed.) *Psychiatric Patient Violence* (London: Duckworth).

Sayce, L. (1999) 'Parenting as a Civil Right: Supporting Users Who Choose to Have Children', in Weir, A. and Douglas, A. (eds) *Child Protection and Mental Health: Conflict of Interest?* (Oxford: Butterworth Heinemman).

Sayce, L. (2000) *From Psychiatric Patient to Citizen: Overcoming Discrimination and Social Exclusion* (Basingstoke: Macmillan – now Palgrave Macmillan).

Sayce, L. (2003) 'Beyond Good Intentions: Making Anti-discrimination Strategies Work', *Disability and Society* **18**(5): 625–42.

Sayce, L. (2004) 'Tackling Social Exclusion Across Europe', in Knapp, M., McDaid D., Mossialos, E. and Thornicroft, G. (eds) (2005) *Mental Health Policy and Practice Across Europe* (Buckingham: Open University).

Sayce, L. and Boardman, A.P. (2003) 'The Disability Discrimination Act 1995: Implications for Psychiatrists', *Advances in Psychiatric Treatment* **9**: 397–404.

Sayce, L. and Wilmot, J. (1997) *Gaining Respect. A Guide to Preventing and Tackling Community Opposition to Mental Health Services* (London: Mind).

Schoenberg, R., Goldberg, R.S. and Shore, D.A. (eds) (1984) *Homosexuality and Social Work* (New York: Haworth Press).

Schön, D.A. (1971) *Beyond the Stable State* (London: Temple Smith).

Schön, D.A. (1983) *The Reflective Practitioner: How Professionals Think in Action* (New York: Basic Books).

Schön, D.A. (1987) *Educating the Reflective Practitioner* (San Francisco: Jossey-Bass).

Scott, M. (1989) *A Cognitive Behavioural Approach to Clients' Problems* (London: Routledge).

Scottish Executive (2000) *Community Care: A Joint Future*. Report by the Joint Future Group (Edinburgh: Scottish Executive).

Scottish Executive (2001) *Guidance on Single Shared Assessment of Community Care Needs* (Edinburgh: Scottish Executive).

Scottish Executive (2002) *The Framework for Social Work Education* (Edinburgh: Scottish Executive).

Scottish Executive (2003) *The Framework for Social Work Education in Scotland* (Edinburgh: Stationery Office).

Scottish Social Services Council (2002) *Codes of Practice for Social Service Workers and Employers* (Dundee: SSSC).

Seddon, D. (ed.) (2002) *Immigration, Nationality and Refugee Law Handbook* (London: Joint Council for the Welfare of Immigrants).

Sellick, C. and Thoburn, J. (1996) *What Works in Family Placement?* (Barkingside: Barnardo's).

Sewpaul, V. (2001a) 'Economic Globalisation and Social Policy Reform: Social Work Curricula in the South African Context', *Social Work/Maatskaplike Werk* 37(4): 309–23.

Sewpaul, V. (2001b) 'Models of Intervention for Children in Difficult Circumstances in South Africa', *Child Welfare* 80(5): 571–86.

Sewpaul, V. and Mahlalela, T.V. (1998) 'The Power of the Small Group: From Fear to Disclosure, *Agenda* 39: 34–43.

Sewpaul, V. and Rollins, N. (1999) 'Operationalising Developmental Social Work: The Implementation of an HIV/AIDS Project', *Social Work/Maatskaplike Werk* 35(3): 250–63.

Shaw, I. (1996) *Evaluating Practice* (Aldershot: Arena).

Shaw, I. (1999) 'Seeing the Trees for the Wood: The Politics of Evaluating in Practice', in Broad, B. (ed.) *The Politics of Social Research and Evaluation* (Birmingham: Venture Press) pp. 109–26.

Sheldon, B. (1978) 'Theory and Practice in Social Work: A Re-examination of a Tenuous Relationship', *British Journal of Social Work* 8(1): 1–22.

Sheldon, B. (2000) *Evidence-Based Practice* (Lyme Regis: Russell House Publishing).

Sheldon, B. (2001) 'The Validity of Evidenced-Based Practice in Social Work: A Reply to Stephen Webb', *British Journal of Social Work* 31(5): 801–9.

Sheldon, B. and Chivers, R. (2000) *Evidence-based Social Care* (Lyme Regis: Russell House).

Sheppard, M. and Ryan, K. (2003) 'Practitioners as Rule-using Analysts: a Further Development of Process Knowledge in Social Work', *British Journal of Social Work* 33(2): 157–76.

Sheppard, M., Newstead, S., Di Caccavo, A. and Ryan, K. (2000) 'Reflexivity and the Development of Process Knowledge in Social Work: a Classification and Empirical Study', *British Journal of Social Work* 30(4): 465–88.

Sherman, E. and Reid, W.J. (eds) (1994) *Qualitative Research in Social Work* (New York: Columbia University Press).

Shiner, M. (2003) 'Out of Harm's Way? Illicit Drug Use, Medicalization and the Law', *British Journal of Criminology* 43(4): 772–96.

Silver, E. and Miller, L.L. (2002) 'A Cautionary Note on the Use of Actuarial Tools in Social Control', *Crime and Delinquency* 48(1): 138–61.

Simey, M. (2000) 'How and Where I Found Independence', in Simmons, M. (ed.) *Getting a Life, Older People Talking* (London: Peter Owen/Help the Aged) pp. 133–8.

Skeates, J. and Jabri, D. (eds) (1988) *Fostering and Adoption by Lesbians and Gay Men* (London: London Strategic Policy Unit).

Smale, G. and Tuson, G. with Biehal, N. and Marsh, P. (1993) *Empowerment, Assessment, Care Management and the Skilled Worker* (London: NISW).

Smalley, R. (1967) *Theory for Social Work Practice* (New York: Columbia University Press).

Smalley, R.E. (1970) 'The Functional Approach to Casework Practice', in Roberts, R.W. and Nee, R.H. (eds) *Theories of Social Casework* (Chicago: Chicago University Press) pp. 77–128.

Smith, C. (1982) *Social Work with the Dying and Bereaved* (Basingstoke: Macmillan – now Palgrave Macmillan).

Smith, D. and Vanstone, M. (2002) 'Probation and Social Justice', *British Journal of Social Work* 32: 815–30.

Smith, P. (ed.) (1996) *Measuring Outcome in the Public Sector* (London: Taylor & Francis).

Smythe, J. (1991) *Teachers as Collaborative Learners: Challenging Dominant Forms of Supervision* (Milton Keynes: Open University Press).

Social Research Association 'Ethical Guidelines', http://www.the-sra.org.uk, accessed 04.08.03.

Sondhi, A., O'Shea, J. and Williams, T. (2002) *DPAS Briefing Paper 18: Arrest Referral: Emerging Findings from the National Monitoring and Evaluation Programme* (London: Home Office).

Social Work Services Inspectorate (2003) *National Standards for the Care and Protection of Children* (Edinburgh: Scottish Executive) (also available from http://www.scotland.gov.uk/about/ED/CnF/ 00017834/page496855780.doc).

Solomon, B.B. (1976) *Black Empowerment: Social Work in Oppressed Communities* (New York: Columbia University Press).

Soothill, K. (1997) 'Rapists Under 14 in the News', *Howard Journal of Criminal Justice* 36(4): 367–77.

Soper, K. (1993) 'Postmodernism, Subjectivity and the Question of Value', in Squires, J. (ed.) *Principled Positions* (London: Lawrence & Wishart) pp. 17–30.

South, N. (ed.) (1999) *Drugs: Cultures, Controls and Everyday Life* (London: Sage).

Spratt, T. (2001) 'The Influence of Child Protection Orientation on Child Welfare Practice', *British Journal of Social Work* 31: 933–54.

SSI (Social Services Inspectorate) (1992) *Social Services for Hospital Patients 1: Working at the Interface* (London: Department of Health).

SSI (Social Services Inspectorate) (2002) *Delivering Quality Children's Services* (London: HMSO).

SSI/SWSG (1991) *Care Management and Assessment: Practitioners' Guide* (London: Department of Health).

Stanley, K. (2001) *Cold Comfort, Young Separated Refugees in England* (London: Save the Children).

Stanley, L. and Wise, S. (1983) *Breaking Out: Feminist Consciousness and Feminist Research* (London: Routledge & Kegan Paul).

Stanley, L. and Wise, S. (1997) *Breaking Out: Feminist Consciousness and Feminist Research* (2nd edn) (London: Routledge & Kegan Paul).

Stanley, N. and Penhale, B. (1999) 'The Mental Health Problems of Mothers Experiencing the Child Protection System: Identifying Needs and Appropriate Responses', *Child Abuse Review* 8(1): 34–46.

SURE (2004) Service User Research Enterprise (SURE). Details available from http://www.iop.kcl.ac.uk/iopweb/departments accessed 08/06/04.

Taylor, P. and Gunn, J. (1999) 'Homicides by People with Mental Illness: Myth and Reality', *British Journal of Psychiatry* 174: 9–14.

Taylor, S. (1983) 'Adjustment to threatening events: a cognitive theory of adaptation', *American Psychologist* 38: 1161–73.

Terreblanche, S. (2002) *A History of Inequality in South Africa 1652–2002* (University of Natal Press (Scottsville)/KMM Review (Sandton)).

Terry, J. (1999) *An American Obsession: Science, Medicine, and Homosexuality* (Chicago: University of Chicago Press.)

Thane, P. (1996) *Foundations of the Welfare State* (London: Longman).

Thomas, T. (1994) 'Police Truancy Patrols', *New Law Journal* 15 July: 966–7.

Thomas, T. (2003) 'The Sex Offender Register: The Registration of Young People', *Childright* (194): 10–11.

Thompson, M. (1998) *The Problem of Mental Deficiency, Eugenics, Democracy and Social Policy in Britain c. 1870-1959* (Oxford: Clarendon Press).

Thompson, N. (1993) *Anti-Discriminatory Practice* (Basingstoke: Macmillan – now Palgrave Macmillan).

Thompson, N. (1995) *Age and Dignity, Working with Older People* (Aldershot: Arena).

Thompson, S. and Kahn, J.H. (1970) *The Group Process as a Helping Technique* (Oxford: Pergamon).

Thorpe, M. (1986) 'Child Abuse and Neglect from an Aboriginal Perspective'. Paper presented at the Sixth International Congress on Child Abuse and Neglect, Sydney.

Thyer, B.A. and Kazi, M.A.F. (eds) (2004) *International Perspectives on Evidence-Based Practice in Social Work* (Birmingham: Venture).

Tievsky, D.L. (1988) 'Homosexual Clients and Homophobic Social Workers', *Journal of Independent Social Work* 2: 51–62.

Timmins, N. (1996) *The Five Giants: A Biography of the Welfare State* (London: Fontana).

Titterton, M. (1999) 'Training Professionals in Risk Assessment and Risk Management: What Does the Research Tell Us?', in Parsloe, P. (ed.) *Risk Assessment in Social Care and Social Work* (London: Jessica Kingsley).

TOPSS (Training Organisation for the Personal Social Services) (2002) *The National Occupational Standards for Social Work* (London: TOPSS).

Trotter, C. (1999) *Working With Involuntary Clients* (London: Sage).

Tulloch, J. and Lupton, D. (2003) *Risk and Everyday Life* (London: Sage).

Turnbull, P.J., McSweeney, T., Webster, R., Edmunds, M. and Hough, M. (2000) *Drug Treatment and Testing Orders: Final Evaluation Report*, Home Office Research Study 212 (London: Home Office).

Turner, W.B. (2000) *A Genealogy of Queer Theory* (Philadelphia: Temple University Press).

UN (1950) *European Convention for the Protection of Human Rights and Fundamental Freedoms* (Geneva: United Nations).

UN (1989) *UN Convention on the Rights of the Child* (Geneva: United Nations).

UN (2002) *Concluding Observations of the UN Committee on the Rights of the Child*, United Kingdom (Geneva: Office of the UN Commissioner for Human Rights).

UNAIDS (2000) *Report on the Global HIV/AIDS Epidemic* (Geneva: UNAIDS).

Usher, P. (1997) 'Challenging the Power of Rationality', in McKenzie, G., Powell, J. and Usher, R. (eds) *Understanding Social Research: Perspectives on Methodology and Practice* (Brighton: Falmer Press).

Usher, R. and Edwards, R. (1994) *Postmodernism and Education* (London: Routledge).

Vaid, U. (1995) *Virtual Equality: The Mainstreaming of Gay and Lesbian Liberation* (New York: Anchor Books).

Van Bilsen, H.P.J.G. (1986) 'Heroin Addiction: Morals Revisited', *Journal of Substance Abuse* 3(4): 279–84.

van Brussel, G.H.A. (1998) 'Services – the Amsterdam Model', in Robertson, R. (ed.) *Management of Drug Users in the Community* (London: Arnold).

Van Dyk, A. (2001) *HIV/AIDS Care and Counselling: A Multidisciplinary Approach* (2nd edn) (Cape Town: Pearson Education).

Van Rensburg, D., Friedman, I., Ngwena, C., Pelser, A., Steyn, F., Booysen, F. and Adendorff, E. (2002) *Strengthening Local Government and Civic Responses to the HIV/AIDS Epidemic in South Africa* (Bloemfontein: Centre for Health Systems Research and Development).

Victor, C. (1991) *Health and Healthcare in Later Life* (Buckingham: Open University Press).

Vincent, J. (1999) *Politics, Power and Old Age* (Buckingham: Open University Press).

Walden, J. and Mountfield, H. (1998) *Blackstone's Guide to the Human Rights Act* (London: Blackstones).

Wallace, S. (2000) 'Responding to the Human Rights Act', *Probation Journal* 47(1): 53–6.

Walsh, M. (2000) *Nursing Frontiers: Accountability and the Boundaries of Care* (Oxford: Butterworth Heinemann).

Ward, D. (1998) 'Groupwork', in Adams, R., Dominelli, L. and Payne, M. (eds) *Social Work: Themes, Issues and Critical Debates* (Basingstoke: Macmillan – now Palgrave Macmillan).

Warner, J. (2003) 'An Initial Assessment of the Extent to Which Risk Factors, Frequently Identified in Research, are Taken into Account When Asssessing Risk to Children in Child Protection Cases', *Journal of Social Work* 3(3): 339–63.

Warner, R. (1985) *Recovery from Schizophrenia. Psychiatry and Political Economy* (London: Routledge).

Washington, S. (2003) 'Ruddock's Secret Report', *Business Review Weekly* 9–15 October, p. 18.

Webb, S. (2001) 'Some Considerations on the Validity of Evidence-based Practice in Social Work', *British Journal of Social Work* 31(1): 57–79.

Weeks, J. (1985) *Sexuality and its Discontents: Meanings, Myths and Modern Sexualities* (London: Routledge & Kegan Paul).

Weeks, J. (2003) *Sexuality* (2nd edn) (London: Routledge).

Weinberg, G. (1972) *Society and the Healthy Homosexual* (Garden City, NY: Doubleday Anchor).

Weinstein, J., Wittington, C. and Leiba, T. (2003) *Collaboration in Social Work Practice* (London: Jessica Kingsley).

White, S. (2001) 'Auto-Ethnography as Reflexive Inquiry: The Research Act as Self-Surveillance', in Shaw, I. and Gould, N. (eds) *Qualitative Research in Social Work* (London: Sage) pp. 100–15.

Whitmore, E. (2001) '"People Listened to What We Had to Say": Reflections on an Emancipatory Qualitative Evaluation', in Shaw, I. and Gould, N. (eds) *Qualitative Research in Social Work* (London: Sage) pp. 83–99.

Whittaker, D.S. and Archer L.L. (1990) 'Using Practice Research for Change', *Social Work and Social Sciences Review* 2(1): 29–37.

WHO (1973) *Continuing Education for Physicians*, Technical Report Series No. 534 (Geneva: WHO).

WHO (1979) *Primary Health Care in Europe,* Euro Report No. 14 (Geneva: WHO).

WHO (1988) Steering Group on Multi-professional Education, *Learning Together to Work Together for Health. The Team Approach* (Geneva: WHO).

Williams, F., Popay, J. and Oakley, A. (1999) *Welfare Research: A Critical Review* (London: University College London Press).

Wilson, G. (ed.) (1995) *Community Care, Asking the Users* (London: Chapman & Hall).

Wilson, V. and Pirrie, A. (2000) 'Multi-disciplinary Team-working: Beyond the Barriers? A Review of the Issues', SCRE research paper 96 (Glasgow: Glasgow University Press).

Wise, I. (2003) 'The Children Act and Young Prisoners', *Howard League Magazine* 21(2): 15.

Wise, S. (1985) 'Series of Occasional Papers on Becoming a Feminist Social Worker', *Studies in Sexual Politics* 6. (Manchester: University of Manchester).

Wisniewski, J.J. and Toomey, B.G. (1987) 'Are Social Workers Homophobic?', *Social Work* 32(5): 454–5.

Wolfensberger, W. (1994) 'A Personal Interpretation of the Mental Retardation Scene in the Light of the "Signs of the Times"', *Mental Retardation* 32(1): 19–33.

Wong, B., and Mckeen, J. (1998) *The New Manual for Life* (British Columbia: PD Publishing).

Woodman, N., Tully, C. and Barranti, C. (1995) 'Research in Lesbian Communities: Ethical Dilemmas', *Journal of Gay and Lesbian Studies* 3(1): 57–66.

Wright, D.J. and Easthorne, V. (2003) 'Supporting adults with disabilities', *Nursing Standard* 18(11): 37–42.

YJB (Youth Justice Board) (2003) 'Hazel Blears Praises Youth Justice Reforms and Announces National ISSP' (press release).

Young, A. (1992[1972]) 'Out of the Closets, Into the Streets', in Jay, K. and Young, A. (eds) *Out of the Closets: Voices of Gay Liberation* (London: The Gay Men's Press) pp. 6–31.

Younghusband, E. (1959) *Social Workers in Local Authority Health and Social Services* (London: Ministry of Health).

Zarb, G. (1992) 'On the Road to Damascus: First Steps towards Changing the Relations of Disability Research Production', *Disability, Handicap and Society* 7(2): 125–39.

Zastrow, C. and Kirst-Ashman, K.K. (2001) *Understanding Human Behaviour and the Social Environment* (Belmont: Brookes/Cole).

Zelickman, I. and Martin, J. (1991) 'Feeling the Way Forward', *Community Care* 16 May: 16–17.

Author Index

Subject Index